Statistical games and human affairs

Statistical games and human affairs

The view from within

ROGER J. BOWDEN
University of New South Wales

The right of the
University of Cambridge
to print and sell
all manner of books
was granted by
Henry VIII in 1534.
The University has printed
and published continuously
since 1584.

CAMBRIDGE UNIVERSITY PRESS

Cambridge
New York   New Rochelle   Melbourne   Sydney

Published by the Press Syndicate of the University of Cambridge
The Pitt Building, Trumpington Street, Cambridge CB2 1RP
32 East 57th Street, New York, NY 10022, USA
10 Stamford Road, Oakleigh, Melbourne 3166, Australia

First published 1989

Printed in the United States of America

Library of Congress Cataloging-in-Publication Data
Bowden, Roger J. (Roger John), 1943–
Statistical games and human affairs : the view from within / Roger
J. Bowden.
p. cm.
Includes index.
ISBN 0-521-36178-8
1. Social sciences – Statistical methods. 2. Game theory.
I. Title.
HA29.B7565 1988
300′.1′5195 – dc19   88–6527

British Library Cataloguing in Publication Data
Bowden, Roger J. (Roger John), 1943–
Statistical games and human affairs :
the view from within
1. Social sciences. Statistical methods
I. Title
300′.28

ISBN 0 521 36178 8

Contents

Contents

Preface

Some of the fringe benefits of experience are memory and the opportunity to indulge that faculty in writing the preface to a book of this nature. A few decades ago the hope was that social scientists would, by their mastery of statistical methodology, succeed in laying bare the facts and forces that drive social systems. The economists set the pace, for these were the years of the great macroeconometric models – in the later years of their evolution, gargantuan structures with hundreds of equations tended by a small army of priests and acolytes. We had high ambitions in those days, even if reality all too often had to be uncomfortably bought off. Thus the aim was to produce an explanation (in, e.g., a regression context) in which all systematic influences were to be accounted for and the residual to be unstructured white noise; but if the latter were not immediately available, one simply transformed the equation to get it, invoking ritual incantations of habit formation, partial adjustment mechanisms, and the like. Later it was held to be unrealistic to attempt to capture every possible systematic influence. Perhaps serial correlation or heteroscedasticity in our residuals might after all be allowable if one recognized it, hopefully could justify it, and certainly could design one's regression methodology to cope with it. The last aspect proved to be a kiss of life to an otherwise semi-moribund technical priesthood, for there arose new developmental possibilities: the integration of regression theory with time series analysis, the handling of heteroscedasticity, and very probably the incorporation of special error distributions (exhibiting leptokurtosis perhaps) in the years to come. I have no doubt that similar technical attempts to cope with a frustrating reality have characterized other topics and other disciplines in the social sciences. Certainly, the most casual perusal of current menus for standard statistical packages would lead to the conclusion that we have come a long way in the range and technical power of our methodology, an impression reinforced by the proliferating journals in the various areas of socioeconomic statistics.

Yet it seems to me that our high-powered statistical methodology has done little to fulfill the explanatory ambitions that I can recall from 20 or so years back; and with regard to empirical economics in particular, it cannot be claimed that morale in the profession is particularly high.

Although the technical work continues to fill an expanding number of journals, one is left to wonder who reads it apart from the incestuous few who produce the material and their Ph.D. students. The problem is not so much that the material is difficult but that too much of it is boring and ineffectual; that in the face of the poor explanatory power of econometrics (as the leading methodological discipline of the social sciences), such technical refinements amount to fiddling while Rome burns. It is indeed galling that methods such as chartism, widely despised by the academic fraternity as necromancy, can consistently outperform the predictive capabilities of econometric models based on fundamentals. Moreover, a different line of attack comes from the rational expectationists, who in many instances deny the usefulness of forecasting from anything more complicated than a simple random walk or first-order Markov scheme, none of which requires anyone to pore over the pages of learned journals of methodology.

Perhaps the study of statistics in the social sciences has reached the kind of middle age where one realizes that the limit is regrettably much closer than the sky. But it would indeed be a pity to discard our ambitions as to explanation and prediction, for it is also true that the areas in which one perceives a deficiency also happen by and large to be those of greatest intrinsic or policy interest. It seems that we need to do two things: first to decide on exactly what sort of facts one can hope to learn from socioeconomic data and, second, to design methods that yield a greater prospect for success in this endeavor, whether they are concerned with experimental design, the type of data to be gathered, inferential techniques, or an appropriate methodology for prediction problems. Socioeconomic data often – depending upon the precise context – incorporate a crucial distinction from the observations of the natural sciences in the existence of mutual interactions between statistician, however such a figure is to be interpreted, and subjects. The data is generated as the outcome of a process that should itself be modeled either explicitly or implicitly. It is a thesis of the book that such interactions can be illuminated with the language, if not the modus operandi, of game theory. It is a benefit of these insights that we can understand why classical statistical methodology might sometimes fail and what we might possibly do to fix things.

Reviewers of the manuscript and one or two of the papers from which it evolved have tended to identify the subject material with an adaptation, at least, of rational-expectations theory. At the outset, I should like to disclaim any such tag, both personally and with respect to the book. It is, on reflection, rather remarkable that rational expectations has gained so much credence as a theory of how people behave. I had not fully realized this until a short time ago when a graduate student here on interview from an American university declared, with that lack of doubt so characteristic of his peers and their midwestern professors, that it was necessary to accept rational expectations as a behavioral supposition unless one could put up a special story to the contrary. Times have evidently changed: This author (and I have no doubt others) had papers rejected on the controllability of systems under rational expectations and on consumption behavior because the expectational hypothesis was judged, in the very early seventies, to be too extreme in terms of the informational capabilities of the subjects. I conceded at that time some justice to such objections and I still do. Part of the problem lies precisely in what is meant by the rational-expectations hypothesis. If it means of a financial market that no possibilities for arbitrage can exist as derived from publicly available past information, then I should have no quarrel with it – presumably the technocratic yuppies of the securities industry are clever enough to run Box–Jenkins models and so forth. If, on the other hand, it means that the economy in question runs itself as an invariant stochastic process and that well-defined probability distributions for future values always exist on the strength of which mathematical expectations can be formed, then I have serious doubts. Game-theoretic spectacles enable one to recognize that such states of the world can indeed exist in certain special cases as equilibrium regimes, but to claim their wide applicability to the phenomena of interest is surely a mistake. The stationary stochastic process and its conditional distributions are a convenient story for textbook expositions, but I am much less certain whether they are empirically useful. So what – in reply to our graduate student – should we put in place of the rational-expectations hypothesis interpreted in the sense just described? I must confess that I do not know. The virtue of the game-theoretic interpretation is that our ignorance becomes standardized since it can be related to similar areas of indeterminism in behavior under imperfect information, disequilibrium regimes, or the outcomes with few participants or of repeated games. If we cannot accept the elegant determinism of rational expectations, then at least we can refine our ignorance a little.

Somewhat paradoxically, I should also like to discourage the view that this is a book about game theory. It is actually a book about statistics. The game theory is used to organize discussion and to focus reflection, but apart from this, it is rather incidental. Partly this is a matter of my own lack of expertise in game theory. In the long run, I do however believe that social statistics will come to be regarded in the light of an inferential game, by which is meant the acquisition of information by one group about another, or as a predictive game, where one or both parties try to predict the outcome of an event itself dependent upon their prognostications and known by both parties to be so. As a matter of game theory, I do not believe that the theorists have recognized the importance of such games, and I can only hope that the ideas contained in this book will tempt the full-time game theorists to go one better.

The book is very much about the political economy of inference and prediction. We all know – or we should – that hypothesis testing in classical statistics has a foundation in decision theory in terms of minimal expected loss under various informational assumptions as to the weighting functions involved. Nonetheless, social statisticians may look askance at the intrusion of political economy into such areas as response, selection bias, nontruthful revelation, and the like. But after all, we have economic theories of democracy, of slavery, of political polling, and even of extramarital affairs. Economics is getting dreadfully intrusive these days, and we should not expect so important a topic as information gathering to be exempt. This said, however, we have a clear duty to the kind of reader we hope to attract and so abstain from rigorous economics, even though the temptation was there at one or two points.

So much for claimers and disclaimers. Now for the credits. Parts of the book draw on published and unpublished papers, and I should like to thank the referees of these papers, where applicable, for their time and their comments. I should mention in particular that Chapter 4 draws heavily on an article in *Journal of the American Statistical Association* (Bowden, 1987a) and discussion by P. C. Ordeshook. In many ways this chapter represented a golden opportunity, denied to most journal authors, to rewrite and extend the original treatment with the advantage of time and hindsight, but in so doing I have nevertheless chosen to preserve a fair bit of the original discussion. I am grateful to the editor and the American Statistical Association for their generous policy with respect to reproducing this material. Thanks go also to anonymous readers of Cambridge University Press. Colin Day, at the Press, deserves much credit for his long-standing interest in the project and his patience at times when he must have wondered just what it was all about. Under difficult circumstances, Marie Green typed the manuscript using the T3 package with her invariant perfection. This book is the swan song for our long and harmonious collaboration. If a good typist is a rare and precious jewel, Marie is a champagne diamond.

CHAPTER 1

The reactive sample space

1.1 Ephphatha

If we were better at forecasting human affairs than we are, world fairs would never go bankrupt, political pollsters would never get egg on their faces, and the perennial snake-oil merchants of economic and financial forecasting would become only a curiosum of economic history. Although the consequences may be less dramatic than failures in prediction, inference in the economic sciences has been dogged by the disquieting shadow of indefiniteness and more recently by dispiriting claims of outright failure: After half a century of intensive effort we have learned from economic data less than what we might have expected and far less than what we should have liked. With respect to another discipline Whyte (1969) remarks that the eminent sociologist Louis Wirth "used to terrify Ph.D candidates by requiring them to name *one* proposition that has been reasonably well supported by research data," a state of affairs that according to Phillips (1973) has not changed much in more recent times. In this book, we shall be concentrating on just one of a multitude of possible reasons why things have gone wrong. From the methodological point of view, however, we think that it is important. It may be summarized thus: In our adaptations of statistical methods from the natural or engineering sciences, we have tended to forget an important difference, namely, that our sample space is cognitive and that as statisticians we are cognate participants. Knowledge of human affairs is neither established nor disseminated in a vacuum. This book is an exploration of the consequences of the reactive sample space.

To those of us who were actively engaged in the brave new world of empirical economics only two decades ago, the representational possibilities seemed boundless and their empirical implementation a matter only of better data, more powerful algorithms, more precise specifications, and better guidance from what seemed an equally brave new world of economic theory. Underlying this work was an implied assumption of a system of equations invariant over time; a structural constancy from which, given enough data, the important characteristics of the system – and certainly those of relevance for policy control – could be empirically identified. When it became apparent that the predictive performance of the large- (sometimes *very* large-) scale econometric models hardly warranted all the effort and expense, the pendulum of fashion swung around to the more minimal approach of time series analysis. The most extreme proponents of the latter approach denied any particular role for underlying economic theory. In the terms of one eminent practitioner, prior specification from economic theory would reflect and constitute only the "prejudices" of the researcher. Any finitely generated data has a minimal canonical representation, the identification of which can in principle be reduced to a mechanical procedure based upon input–output data – such a "system-theoretic critique will eventually force a total revision of econometrics as a viable field of research" (Kalman, 1980).

Nevertheless, underlying the time series approach as well as the eclectic theory-derived methodology lies a common conception of an underlying structure that is stationary, or else nonstationary in a relatively trivial way (time-varying coefficients, dichotomous variables, etc.), and that moreover has an existence independently of the observer. All that was needed to uncover the model was a suitably insightful modeler, or in the case of the time series approach a suitable algorithm backed by appropriate computer hardware, plus the right amount of data, preferably copious, the perceived inadequacies of which became a sort of econometrician's lament. Researchers in sociology and social psychology had to face up much earlier than economists to the existence of interactional problems between researcher and subject (the idea, e.g., that interviewer characteristics could exert a profound effect upon the quality of the information extracted from the subject). But a common methodological hope emerged: that inferences about human characteristics could be unambiguously derived from data or experiments that are concrete, preferably under public access, and verifiable by other workers in the field; that once again, such traits had an existence independent of the observer.

One outcome of these invariance concepts was a misplaced perception of precision in the outcome of statistical investigations in the social sciences. A frequent manifestation of this misplaced concreteness appears in the quotation of confidence intervals of a narrowness that suggests to the reader that any residual or inherent uncertainty is merely a technical matter of the variation in a stable disturbance process of apparently minor proportions. One result is that published confidence limits for socioeconomic events and variables are wildly dissonant with the ultimately realized prediction error, with a frequency that suggests misspecification problems of the most fundamental kind rather than the chance appearance of large outliers.

The search for invariance is very proper: It is indeed difficult to conceive of any science of human affairs that is founded upon any other presumption. Much of the loss of morale in the empirical social sciences has been the realization that deciding what forms these invariants are to take, let alone the process of looking for them, is evidently much harder than we originally thought. Even worse, it may involve time devoted to thinking about methodology as distinct from technique, something that few researchers, including the present author, would ever willingly become involved in. Two aspects are of interest in this respect. The first, a matter we shall explicitly consider in this book, is that in order to search for invariance, we have to study not only interrelationships among elements of the sample space but also their relationship to those who are attempting to study that sample space: A nexus links the statistician and the subjects, one with the other. The most determinate way of studying such interactions that has yet been devised is the theory of games, and we shall be drawing extensively on ideas derived from this discipline. In the terms of this theory, the various notions of invariance are associated in particular with the equilibria of the resulting games and the characteristics of the various parties – the researcher as well as the subjects and also their institutional setting – that affect those equilibria. We should not wish to limit the scope of invariance concepts to equilibrium states. Nevertheless, by recognizing that games are involved, we shall at least know what to look for in the way of invariance.

A second aspect refers to the manner in which we shall approach the problem of identifying the structural invariants. We lay no great claim to originality in rejecting the input–output, or black-box approach, of the unreconstituted time series analyst. One of the implications of the rational-expectations "revolution" in economics is that naive positivism can be extremely dangerous where questions of policy, let alone understanding, are concerned. To label introspection and other forms of theoretical insight as "prejudices" is, in this author's view, absurdly limiting as to the scope of evidence and runs quite counter to the widely accepted methodological philosophy of Karl Popper and his school (e.g., Popper, 1965) as to the nature of scientific progress. Without wishing at all to enter into a full-scale debate on the philosophy of method, any socioeconomic researcher who limits consideration to a black-box analysis of the given data is unconsciously excluding the data of experience plus any prior knowledge of the structure acquired on a deductive basis. Likewise, following Phillips (1971), we are quite happy about utilizing the insights of introspection. For it cannot necessarily be claimed that the data resulting from an organized experiment (e.g., sample surveys) is categorically different from the data of experience: Indeed one of the themes of the present study is that data from surveys reflect implicit theorizing on the part of both the researcher and the subjects. In summary, we shall reject a strict inductionist approach. Statistical inference in the social sciences cannot be pursued in isolation from explicit recognition of the social context in which data is to be gathered and the results of the study disseminated.

Finally, we should not overstate our claims. Not all data in economics or social sciences is contentious or generated from a cognate and reactive sample space, and not all predictions are reflexive. Very many situations have no need of a game-theoretic resolution to the problems of empirical identification or prediction. Our point is simply that many do, and those that are of this kind frequently happen to cover situations of substantial economic or political importance. Where the stakes are high, the participants are liable to start playing games.

1.2   Games against nature and games against people

It has long been recognized that problems of statistical estimation and hypothesis testing, as aspects of decision theory, can be placed into correspondence with two-person noncooperative game theory, with "nature" playing the role of the second player. The need to do this arises from the fact that the state of nature actually holding is an unknown quantity and that to guard against the worst outcomes, the statistician might as well pretend that nature is actively antagonistic and budget for the worst. The result is the minimax strategy of statistical decision theory. Thus let $R(\theta, \delta)$ denote the expected loss from action δ when the true state of nature is θ. The minimax criterion is then to choose δ to $\min_\delta \max_\theta R(\theta, \delta)$. A rather more structured procedure is to introduce a class of possible Bayesian priors, or weighting functions, with respect to the unknown parameter θ. For any given distribution $\tau(\theta)$ from this class, one minimizes the risk $r(\tau, \delta)$ defined by

$$r(\tau, \delta) = \int_\theta R(\theta, \delta)\, \tau(\theta)\, d\theta,$$

assuming that the density and integral exist. In general, however, the problem remains of choosing the prior $\tau(\theta)$, and one approach is again to assume that nature is hostile and budget for the worst with respect to this prior. What results is again a minimax rule, this time with respect to the distribution τ. Indeed, under suitable conditions (Ferguson, 1967, especially ch. 2) an equilibrium will exist in the implied game against nature. This is defined as a pair τ^*, δ^* that satisfy the equality

$$\max_\tau \min_\delta r(\tau, \delta) = \min_\delta \max_\tau r(\tau, \delta).$$

The right side sets a lower bound (we assume actually attained) on the statistician's expected losses no matter what nature can do. The left side gives the upper bound on nature's winnings from the use of the least favorable distribution (from the statistician's point of view). Given a suitable topological structure on the set $\{\delta\}$ of (possibly randomized) decision rules, a minimax strategy will exist. Moreover, if τ^* is the corresponding state of nature prior, then the strategy δ^* will be a Bayes rule, that is, will minimize the risk $r(\tau, \delta)$ with respect to the prior density $\tau = \tau^*$.

In principle, therefore, the statistical decision theory of estimation or hypothesis testing is perfectly capable of handling an active rather than impassive or invariant sample space. All that is required in terms of the preceding exposition is to regard the choice of state of nature as being informed by an actual game rather than a notional one. Thus it can hardly be claimed that the profession has not been alive to the theoretical possibility that nature, however specified or interpreted, may be an active protagonist in problems of statistical decision theory.

This does not mean, on the other hand, that in practice the games are quite as simple as the game on the kernel $r(\tau, \delta)$ that we have just considered. Indeed, the emphasis is rather differently placed, even if only at one remove. Consider, for instance, the structure of a typical inferential game of the types considered in the early chapters of the book. Given a distribution $\phi(i)$ of possible values of some variable, the objective is to estimate some parameter or characteristic whose true value is I_0. Thus given a random sample $i_1, i_2, \ldots, i_n$ from an impassive population, one might estimate I_0 as $\hat{I}_0 = I(i_1, i_2, \ldots, i_n)$, some sufficient statistic for I_0. But suppose that people do not necessarily respond as in the preceding. Instead they have available a set $\{s\}$ of possible strategies such as: do not respond to the survey; respond but lie (by how much); or respond truthfully. The statistician, realizing this, also has a set $\{\sigma\}$ of possible strategies: to make response compulsory; to offer specific inducements to respond; to invoke devices to encourage truth telling; or simply to take no special action. The individual responses may be represented as

$$i_j^m = m_j(\sigma, s_j, i_j, I_0), \quad j = 1, 2, \ldots, n,$$

where the manifested responses i_j^m are somewhat schematically represented to allow for simple acts of nonresponse in addition to functional relationships of a more conventional kind. Then the estimate prepared on the basis of the manifested responses is of the form

$$\hat{I}_m = I^m(i_1^m, i_2^m, \ldots, i_n^m),$$

some function on the realized responses (and nonresponses, if applicable). The payoff structure is then of the form of a set of welfare functions

$$\{W, \mathbf{w}\} = \{W_s(\hat{I}^m, I_0); w_1(\hat{I}^m, i_1), w_2(\hat{I}^m, i_2), \ldots, w_n(\hat{I}^m, i_n)\}.$$

The payoff W_s to the statistician is of the classical loss function type. The individual payoffs w_j to members of the sample reflect the importance to them of the outcome of the measurement process and are conditioned by their specific i values. Such payoffs are not necessarily of the classical loss function type.

Without entering at this stage into detailed discussion of this or similar inferential games, several points can be made with respect to the preceding game. It is clear that it maintains a generic similarity with the classical decision-theoretic game in that the underlying parameter or characteristic I_0 is unknown and the statistician may well have to budget for the worst in this respect, that is, seek strategies that are ultimately minimax with respect to I_0 or its prior distribution $\tau(I_0)$. Nevertheless the game-theoretic structure is appreciably more complex than the simple kernel game $r(\tau, \delta)$ considered earlier. As set up, the game $\{W, \mathbf{w}\}$ is basically a noncooperative game since no collusion is envisaged between members of the sample. (It may be of interest to note that the classical idea of independent random sampling would presumably be incompatible with cooperative behavior on the part of the sample members, which connotes a lack of independence in the manifested values.) It is overlain also with a dominant-player aspect, which may involve an informational asymmetry between the statistician and the subjects. Thus the statistician announces a strategy σ, a matter of importance to the subjects. Depending upon the problem and the nature of the various strategy sets, the statistician may announce σ either in the certain knowledge of which strategy set $\{s_j\}$ will follow or else with no precise knowledge of the reactions of the subjects. The information asymmetry arises because the subjects are able to make up their minds with full foreknowledge of the statistician's strategy σ.

In general, the combination of the explicit strategic behavior just described together with the original indeterminacy with respect to I_0 or its prior distribution adds up to a game of considerable complexity. The saving grace, so far as inferential games are concerned, is that the strategy sets $\{\sigma\}, \{s\}$ are often of very limited diversity and the dominant-player reactions reasonably predictable with the aid of a little understanding of human behavior. We have not so far mentioned predictive games, but rather similar comments apply: Although the full problem may exhibit several degrees of complexity with elements from more than one category of game involved, one can often achieve a fair degree of understanding and predictive power by abstracting in terms of quite simple models of gamelike behavior.

Disequilibria and nonstationary equilibria

The pursuit of equilibria in general game theory results in a determinateness that is pleasing both mathematically and aesthetically. But if we are to study gamelike behavior in the field, as it were, then we have to reckon with the possibility that the parties may for one reason or another not be able to achieve an equilibrium by actual play, and their observed behavior may be more characteristic of disequilibrium states. A positivist approach therefore requires some sort of hypothesis about modeling disequilibrium behavior or ways to account for it in a nonparametric framework. The statistician must also bear in mind that such disequilibria can be created by the very act of observation and publication and again must be accounted for in some way. Now in view of the comparative lack of success (although there certainly are exceptions) among game theorists in showing how even simple solutions can arise from initial disequilibrium states, a description of disequilibrium behavior in the present context might seem an ambitious, if not hazardous, undertaking. Nevertheless it turns out to be possible to devise simple disequilibrium rules that do have appeal either as normative prescriptions or as plausible descriptions of actual behavior. For instance, we show that methods of stochastic approximation may be turned into predictive algorithms for at least two classes of statistical games.

Even where the essential features of a statistical problem can be described in terms of a game-theoretic equilibrium of some kind, it should be remembered that the cognitive behavior that collectively established that equilibrium is also capable of modifying the equilibrium over time through learning. For instance, people may learn what happens when they respond to a certain kind of survey (or in many cases that nothing happens!) and modify their response behavior over time. For example, we refer in Chapter 2 to secularly declining response rates to questionnaire surveys. In the case of agents involved in predictive games, an incentive exists to update their forecasting methodology, perhaps by utilizing the very results of the statistician who has studied their behavior. As we have already remarked, a tendency exists for social statisticians to view individual or collective behavior as temporally invariant, and the systems embodying such behavior as stationary over time. It is worth reiterating that as socioeconomic commentators we are part of the system that we seek to study, and the consequences of this are not only that the immediate equilibrium reflects our influence but also that the sequence of equilibria may evolve secularly as society absorbs the information about itself presented by its social commentators. The existence of nonstationarities occasioned by such influences will concern us at various points throughout the book.

Applications: an example

At this stage we shall not embark on a catalog of prospective applications, preferring to develop these on a topic-by-topic basis throughout

Table 1.1. *Forecasting post mortem, 1986-7 America's Cup*

| | October 1986 | | | November 1986 | | |
| | Forecast | | | Forecast | | |
	May 1985	April 1986	Actual	May 1985	April 1986	Actual
Interstate						
A. Baseline	27.8	–	–	22.5	–	–
B. Non-America's Cup	39.6	50.0	–	22.7	24.0	–
C. America's Cup	70.8	64.2	–	33.5	17.6	–
D. Total (B+C)	110.4	114.2	**53.7**	56.2	41.6	**46.4**
	(±10.3)	(±13.6)		(±5.3)	(±5.0)	
Overseas						
E. Non-America's Cup	13.8	–	–	15.5	–	–
F. America's Cup	10.4	–	–	5.8	–	–
G. Total (E+F)	24.2	–	**34.0**	21.3	–	**31.3**

Notes: All figures are in thousands. Numbers in parentheses are "confidence limits"; see text. April 1986 forecasts incorporate slightly higher probability weights with respect to intentions (see text) than do the May 1985 forecasts. A second set of forecasts was also prepared with original weights, with marginally more conservative results.

the book. However it may be useful to preview things by means of an actual example in which we may comment on aspects that prima facie have a game-theoretic aspect. The example is a forecasting problem, but as for most such exercises, it contains an inferential element.

The first defense of the America's Cup held outside the United States attracted widespread interest and activity from the participants, the media, and the social "glitterati." Less predictable was the effect on visitor numbers: The city of Perth had experienced a steadily growing but still rather small growth in the tourist trade, and a major influx of visitors from the country areas, interstate, and abroad would place severe strain on the supply of accommodation, transport, and other services and entertainment facilities. With the need for such planning in mind (and naturally also the desire to capitalize on the event in other respects), the state and federal governments jointly commissioned a major forecasting exercise from the Centre for Applied and Business Research (CABR), a consulting organization affiliated with the University of Western Australia. The scope of the present study will permit only a limited commentary on the methodology of the study: For details and for related studies of so-called hallmark events we refer the reader to CABR (1985, 1986); a subsequent paper by the authors of the CABR study (McLeod and Soutar, 1986); and authors in the travel research literature such as Louviére and Hensher (1983), Ritchie (1984), and Uysal and Crompton (1985).

| December 1986 | | | January 1987 | | | February 1987 | | |
| Forecast | | | Forecast | | | Forecast | | |
May 1985	April 1986	Actual	May 1985	April 1986	Actual	May 1985	April 1986	Actual
20.5	–	–	35.8	–	–	12.8	–	–
22.6	27.6	–	17.3	17.0	–	12.3	15.0	–
47.5	48.6	–	96.8	68.3	–	114.4	–	–
70.1	76.2	**73.4**	114.0	85.3	**85.7**	126.7	120.7	**52.4**
(±6.6)	(±9.1)		(±10.7)	(±10.2)		(±11.8)	(±14.8)	
19.6	–	–	13.3	–	–	13.8	–	–
12.7	–	–	20.5	–	–	21.1	–	–
32.3	–	**34.1**	33.8	–	**40.0**	34.9	–	**30.1**

Table 1.1 is a postmortem of the two forecasts and the actual, ex post numbers with respect to interstate and overseas visitors over the period of the Challenge series from the first trials in October 1986 to the finals in February 1987. With respect to the interstate visitors, the major informational device was a telephone survey administered in the four principal mainland states by a national firm of market research consultants. The survey was administered in May 1985 and repeated in April 1986, resulting in the two forecasts shown. These forecasts were prepared under two headings, namely, visitors whose intentions were not affected by the cup (row B) and those who would have been less likely to visit in the absence of the America's Cup series and related festivities (row C). Row A of the table refers to a benchmark forecast based upon statistical trend fitting from previous years: This was prepared by CABR as a validational check on the survey results, but we have included it since it shows the underlying normal seasonal pattern. In bold type (row D) are the official estimates of actual interstate visitor numbers derived from air, rail, and Eyre highway (road access) statistics. In the case of international visitors only one forecast was prepared (rows E–G) based upon a variety of sources such as surveys of travel agents and airlines, friends and relatives in Perth, the competing syndicates and their yacht clubs, and the media. The actual numbers from abroad are shown in bold type in row G.

The ex post performance of the monthly forecasts may be summarized as good for one month (December), mixed to good for two months (November and January), and spectacularly wide of the mark for the beginning month, October, and the month of the finals, February. Note that the "confidence levels" bear little relation to the ex post results; indeed, this is an illustration of our earlier observation of the extent to which things can go wrong in the forecasting of socioeconomic events. It is noticeable that the worst results are obtained by those forecasts, namely, interstate, which (a) rely most heavily upon a survey of intentions and (b) are subject to more informational feedback – information about the cup preparations and indeed the forecasted visitor numbers would be relayed more frequently and in more detail to the eastern states than to points overseas.

The survey in question was administered to four urban areas and four country areas of the four populous mainland states, namely, New South Wales, Victoria, Queensland, and South Australia. The survey itself appears to have been competently conducted and unexceptionally worded, although in view of the small numbers replying affirmatively, it might perhaps have been preferable to concentrate resources on fewer, urban areas with a corresponding limitation on the population base from which inferences were to be drawn. However, two more tangential aspects of the forecasting procedure will be of relevance for our current concerns.

The first is that heavy reliance was placed upon stated intentions from respondents. To begin with, it could reasonably be hypothesized that those who did not respond – the overall nonresponse rate was 28 percent – would be less interested in the event. More particularly, however, those who did respond were asked to indicate their probability of coming as one of four categories: "definitely," "very likely," "just likely," and "not likely," and in order to convert these intentions to expected visitor numbers, probabilities of attendance were arbitrarily assigned to each category as 0.9–1.0, 0.65–0.75, 0.15–0.25, and zero, respectively. Treating these ranges as uniform prior distributions results in a probability density for expected visitor numbers, and it is from the mean and variance of this density that the expected visitor numbers and associated "confidence limits" of Table 1.1 were computed. One could comment further on this procedure and on the apparent neglect of sampling error in the computation of confidence limits, but the point that we wish to underscore here is the lack of corroborating or validating evidence used in the assignment of probabilities to the stated intentions. For one might expect people to overstate their intentions for attendance from motives that ultimately derive from an apprehension of the uses to which the survey is to be put (see Chapter 4). In the present instance a certain amount of potentially corroborating information (membership of a yacht club, income, etc.) was asked for elsewhere in the survey questionnaire and was indeed made the subject of a formal discriminant analysis; yet the results were not incorporated in any manner into the estimated probabilities of attendance. More generally, one might perceive a problem with respect to surveyed intentions as to the encouragement of accurate or truthful responses and testing procedures for nontruthful reporting.

A second aspect refers to the informational feedback from the survey. It was certainly true that the published forecasts achieved wide circulation in Australia. The implications of predicted visitor numbers over the Challenge period of 500,000 against the normal 100,000 would not have been lost on potential visitors, and a discouragement effect from fears of overcrowding, expensive accommodation, and so on, during the month of the finals, in particular, may well have accounted for some of the shortfall in that month. Of course, it is important to remember that the forecast–outcome process takes place in real time, and any forecast is of a conditional nature against the possibility of interim events. Thus it could very well be that by the end of January the public had been thoroughly overexposed to 12 m sailing and the associated media hype or, on the other hand, quite habituated to armchair viewing from excellent television coverage. Nevertheless, a type of informational game exists in such situations in which the forecaster must bear in mind the effect of his (or her) published forecasts upon the behavior that he is attempting to forecast, for the information that he provides modifies the private information sets that condition the behavior that he is attempting to predict.

In summary, at least two types of game-theoretic influence are embedded in this example. In the inferential phase, strategic behavior on the part of the sample space arises from the public's view of the purposes of the questioner and the likely effects of his ultimate prediction. In the predictive phase, the published forecasts induce behavioral reactions the forecaster may or may not choose to anticipate.

1.3   Outline: a taxonomy of statistical games

Information and inference

The early chapters of the book are concerned with what might be called pure information games in which the objective of the statistician is simply to draw inferences about the population he or she is dealing with or to discover something about the structural system that describes their collective behavior. Of course, the adjective *pure* is really a misnomer – one usually collects information with some sort of objective in mind, and often it is the reaction to these objectives, correctly perceived or not, that generates the game. Nevertheless, the label of informational games will have to suffice for present purposes.

In many ways, one can think of the statistician as a dominant player having to "defeat" his or her subjects in order to gain the information desired. Thus the statistician may be concerned with encouraging response to a survey and in particular with discouraging the kind of nonresponse behavior that could give rise to selective bias from nonresponse. In doing so, he or she will be aware that the option of not responding constitutes a strategy as to the provision of information on the part of the subjects, a strategy that may be predicated on their perception of the statistician's purpose in conducting the survey. Chapter 2 is concerned with such questions of response and nonresponse, as is the first part of Chapter 3. The division of material is organized according to the type of motivation involved on the part of the subject population. Simple costs of response will constitute a possible motivation in Chapter 2: Individuals, in choosing whether to respond, will balance the benefits of response versus the costs, pecuniary or otherwise, of responding. However, the matter is not the simple profit-and-loss calculation that this description suggests: One has to consider the problem of free riding in which individuals may elect not to respond and nevertheless benefit from the outcome of the survey. Thus the outcomes of opinion polls and elections (as an opinion poll with executive consequences) are of the character of public goods in the terminology of economics, and the question of nonresponse may be tackled in terms of the language of cooperative games and coalitions. What is at issue is whether such phenomena hinder or can help the statistician avoid bias from selective nonresponses.

Chapter 3 takes a somewhat different tack. It is concerned with cases where the strategic behavior on the part of respondents is directed not so much at taking advantage of other respondents (as in the public good categorization) but at anticipating the purposes of the statistician. Not to respond in this context is again a strategy, and one that may on occasion be more appealing than alternatives such as responding, but doing so untruthfully. Social statisticians have long been aware of the problem of encouraging truthful response (although we are of the opinion that as a problem its pervasiveness and importance have never been adequately recognized). Its formal study may be said to have begun with Warner's technique of randomized responses, which represents a way for subjects to submerge their personal identification, even in a face-to-face situation, in an anonymous sample space. On the game-theoretic level, this may be regarded as an encouragement to make truth telling on sensitive issues a more palatable personal strategy. In Chapter 3 we review the entire problem, starting with the biasing effects of nonresponse as an antagonistic strategy and proceeding to the problem of testing a given set of responses for truthful revelation and devices that might encourage truth telling. The chapter concludes with a comparison of the biasing effects of the two alternative types of antagonistic strategy, namely, nonresponse and untruthful response, with conclusions relevant to the design of the national census.

We have referred so far to the noncooperative or antagonistic elements of informational games, the idea that the statistician has to struggle – metaphorically speaking – with the sample space. However, it is also possible to conceive of a more cooperative nexus in which the statistician may in fact take advantage of the cognate and reactive nature of the sample space. In Chapter 2 we look at procedures whereby the statistician is able to augment inferential procedures of a conventional kind with community or social information as to the object of interest. If the published results of the statistician are widely perceived to be wrong or incomplete, this may lead to a homeostatic (self-correcting) response behavior in a second survey so that the option of repeated surveys together with publication becomes a strategic device.

Publication

More generally, this is our first point of contact with the important informational implications of publication. When a statistician's results are published – and if he or she is regarded as credible or authoritative – this becomes an additional input into whatever information sets the subjects are using to guide their expectations, intentions, or actions. So we now have an informational feedback: Not only are the subjects providing information to the statistician but vice-versa, the statistician is returning information to them via publication. This information is concerned with the attitudes of others, and although social information of this kind may not be altogether unknown to the subjects, the statistician's results can be expected to alter the degree of confidence or centering with which such notions are held. In Bayesian terms, the individuals of the sample space are turning their prior beliefs as to the attitudes of others into publication-induced posteriors. Few of us are unaffected by the attitudes of others, and the range of affectations encompasses not only possible alterations in our own attitudes, but even where these remain invariant, response decisions with respect to second-round surveys. Moreover, publication may carry with it a perceived promise, suspicion, or threat of forthcoming policy action. Because of the statistician's central position as a purveyor of information, he or she acquires a dominant-player aspect. This is the way that we approach the question of publication in the early part of the book, although echoes of the central notion – that wherever external observers exist, they acquire through publication a perturbational influence – linger in the later chapters. Thus at various points in Chapters 5 and 6, which tend otherwise to be concerned with decentralized noncooperative predictive games, we observe that such structures may have to be overlain by dominant-player elements when they are studied by a social scientist or become the subject of influential but independent published predictions or when a policymaker steps in with the object of economic control. The games that result from such overlays do not always fall neatly within any of the established categories of game theory.

In any such context, the problems of invariance assume center stage, for here we have the problem that the structure may not remain independent of the observer. This kind of methodological problem is quite familiar from the physics of quantum theory as one implication of the Heisenberg uncertainty principle. Such analogies are interesting but will not be pursued: Methodological history is strewn with the rusty relics of attempts to homologize economics and the social sciences with key insights of the physical sciences, and we have no desire to add to this methodological litter.

Predictive games

As we saw in the America's Cup example, predictions are often based on a prior informational phase so it is difficult to conceive of a statistical game as being purely predictive in character. However, it is useful to isolate the predictive phase simply because the potential for reactivity is so obvious and its implications so far reaching for the success of a prediction. If the predictions of one party affect the realizations of another, then their various predictions should be mutually consistent for predictive success. This mutual-consistency property appears, in one of its manifestations, as the rational-expectations property familiar to economists. This is in fact an equilibrium state for an implied game; in the classic formulation, the game is a noncooperative one with many individually insignificant agents, and rational expectations corresponds to a Nash equilibrium. An equilibrium in which expectations are unbiased extends, however, to a variety of other predictive games, both of the dominant-player variety and the cooperative variety. Although we hesitate to use the term *rational expectations* for such equilibria, they do share the unbiased-expectations property; and they also illustrate that the property of structural linearity is not necessary for the achievement of rational-expectations equilibria if we interpret the latter term in a very broad way.

Whether or not rational expectations can exist out of equilibrium is problematical. In dominant-player games, it is less important for any kind of expectations to be formed since the rules for feedback are reasonably clear. A difficulty with other kinds of games is that out of equilibrium, probabilities to serve as inputs into the required mathematical expectations may not even be defined or definable, and one may be forced into a kind of disequilibrium behavior that proceeds by simple mechanical rules that may in turn be vulnerable to gamelike behavior.

Our discussion of predictive games is organized as follows. Chapter 4 considers in detail a dominant-player game in which the public reacts to the statistician's announcement either of the current state of the system or of the statistician's forecast with respect to the event of interest. For example, if the ultimate object is to predict visitor numbers to a forthcoming major event, the state of the system would correspond to current-visitor intentions as just surveyed, and people could react either to these numbers or else to the statistician's forecast, which may utilize information from previous surveys, or from some other source, in addition to the current survey. Once published, the public reacts to the new information (state or forecast), giving rise to the dominant-player aspect. Equilibrium states and disequilibrium behavior are considered, and algorithms are proposed to enable forecasts of the equilibrium state resulting from repeated surveys. We point out, however, that in practice, such games may themselves be overlain by strategic informational games. Thus incentives may exist for both the forecaster and the public to dissimulate, fudge, or lie outright in their revelation of crucial information. Moreover, questions can legitimately be raised about whether an equilibrium state is in itself desirable either to the forecaster or to the public.

From here we turn to more decentralized predictive games. As already mentioned, the extensive literature on rational expectations is in the main concerned with the equilibria of noncooperative competitive games. Chapter 5 is an introductory survey of the various properties and types of rational-expectations equilibrium in structural systems, at this point laying relatively little stress on the game-theoretic provenance of such equilibria. It discusses such phenomena as the introduction of extraneous expectational solutions and what happens when information among the agents is heterogeneous in quality. The latter contingency makes the equilibria subject to perturbational influences from an otherwise external observer so that the decentralized noncooperative framework may be disturbed by dominant-player influences. The chapter concludes with a short survey on problems of empirically testing for the existence of classic rational-expectations equilibria.

Chapter 6 burrows a bit deeper into problems concerned with the applicability and logical possibility of rational-expectations predictive equilibria. On the applicability aspect, we commence by reviewing the literature on the problem of policy in the presence of the kind of anticipative behavior characteristic of a rational-expectations equilibrium. The general problem of optimal control as a formal representation of economic or social policy has much in common with the problem of successful prediction: To control a system means to push a (successful) prediction in the desired direction. Now if the expectations of agents are rational, several problems arise for control theory. In the first place, the conventional approach of designing policy from a knowledge of the system derived from empirical regularities prior to the policy imposition will break down. That in itself does not invalidate control theory, which must be recast in terms of the true structural invariants of the system, which poses fresh problems for estimation techniques. A more damaging objection has come to be known as policy inconsistency. In the presence of rational expectations and a dominant player (the government or policymaker), optimal control regimes do not obey Bellman's dynamic programming principle, leading to a temptation for later revisions to a previously announced policy. Equilibrium can be reestablished but is no longer of the classic rational-expectations variety, being characterized rather better as an equilibrium to a cooperative or noncooperative game with individually significant parties. If different kinds of equilibrium can arise or if one predominant kind is interspersed with periods of disequilibrium, then problems arise for the statistical identification of behavioral relationships. In the remaining part of Chapter 6, we return to the classic noncooperative competitive game, picking up in a more detailed way some of the parallels with classic multiperson noncooperative games. An implied task on the part of each agent is to predict the expectation of others in a kind of solution by fictitious play. A discussion of whether, even in principle, agents are able to do this throws some light on the attainability of the Nash equilibrium to decentralized predictive games.

It may be said of any form of game as a positive description of human affairs that the possibility of equilibrium depends upon disequilibrium behavior: We could not claim that equilibrium occurs empirically or is even a terribly useful concept unless we are confident that some method or mechanism exists other than pure chance by which the system can attain such a state starting from initial disequilibrium. Chapter 7 is a detailed investigation of the convergence problem for decentralized, noncooperative predictive games. If agents adopt simple estimation schemes based upon stochastic approximation, convergence *may* occur in certain circumstances, generally those associated with what we call parameter-mediated learning in the presence of simple dynamic structures. Consideration of what might be required for convergence throws considerable light on the possibility that mutually consistent forecasting equilibria can exist for multiperson noncooperative predictive games.

The preceding discussion – whether of informational or predictive games; many or few players; dominant, cooperative, or noncooperative; and equilibrium or disequilibrium – is in the last analysis directed toward a more sophisticated understanding of just what we can hope to learn from socioeconomic data and what kind of actual or conceptual experiments will help us to derive good and useful data. Chapter 8 reviews what we can learn from such considerations and adds some general remarks about the stationarity and invariance of socioeconomic structures in the presence of anticipative and strategic behavior.

A final word concerns the nature and scope of the game theory. Throughout the book we employ at least some of the language of game theory, and at times one can recognize that more or less standard classifications and notions of game theory are applicable. Frequently, however, one finds that standard typologies break down or that one particular type, having been established, is distorted or contaminated by the process of observation. At times, therefore, we are forced to abandon the clear distinctions and mathematical elegance of classical game theory. This book should not therefore be regarded as a treatise on applied game theory. Our intentions in this respect are more modest: to utilize game theory as a frame of reference in the pursuit of insights into the application of statistics to human affairs.

CHAPTER 2

Response and social information

2.1 Introduction

The getting of information begins with an act of response, and for good reasons, statisticians have long been concerned about problems of response to surveys and polls. The most elementary source of concern is simply that people may refuse to respond or may neglect to do so. In the early years of social research and political polling, the novelty and even gratification at being asked an opinion on some issue may well have been sufficient to induce participation. Such times are passing. Many authors (e.g., Hawkins, 1977; Brooks and Bailar, 1978; Martin, 1983) have noted the secular decline in the response rate to surveys. Hawkins notes that nonresponse rates, largely due to refusals, have increased secularly at annual rates approaching 1 percent. The most immediately recognizable consequence of a low response rate is a corresponding loss of precision with increased sampling variability of estimators and loss of degrees of freedom in hypothesis testing. We have already remarked on a further problem associated with a low response rate as such. Even if the sample size is nevertheless formally sufficient to accept or reject the appropriate null hypothesis at apparently reasonable levels of significance, the statistician may experience considerable difficulties in getting the conclusions accepted by his or her readership. The precise difficulty may vary according to the survey subject and the readership. It may arise in connection with perceived problems of nonneutrality of a kind to be considered shortly. It may be that the sample is considered too small to be "representative" by a statistically unsophisticated readership, a judgment based either upon the target sample size or upon the effective sample size, taking into account nonresponse. Or it may be raised as a criticism simply because if n is evidently considered by the statistician to be a minimally acceptable sample size, then 33.3 percent of n is clearly unacceptable if only a third of the target sample respond.

A second general source of concern is with the idea of neutrality in response. The primary worry here is actually with the character of response rather than its magnitude; however, the low response rate can be a signal that problems of nonneutrality may be attendant. The notion of representativeness takes on in this context a more precise meaning: We are concerned with the kind of selection or self-selection phenomena that may cause those who respond to come from a different population, statistically speaking, from those who do not; in other words, we worry about whether respondents are truly representative of the population as a whole. Such problems are not necessarily curable by taking expensive action to increase the effective sample size, say, by adding callback procedures. Moreover, the problems may arise even when the statistician has access to the entire population, a facility that has in the past existed at intermittent intervals (such as a national census) but may become a more regular occurrence given the continuing development of communications technology. In other words, the problem of nonneutrality is not primarily a problem of sampling theory as such.

Whether our primary concern is with sample size or with the verification of neutrality, a study of the response decision on the part of individuals is called for. Over the years, the statistical profession has developed a remarkable body of knowledge on the theory and practice of sampling. Nevertheless, a flaw exists in the application of this theory to human populations, namely, that only a rather rudimentary theory exists as to the nature and determinants of response. It is as though these questions have been relegated to the domain of social psychology and are as such only of marginal relevance for the practicing statistician. Yet the most sophisticated inferential analysis cannot change the statistical swine's ear into a silk purse. Part of the problem is the very complexity of the whole question of response. One may be considering response to individual questions or items or response to the entire questionnaire, and different considerations may apply to each. The nature of response is heavily conditioned by the subject material of the survey, by the way in which it is administered, and by the choice of interviewer. A literature exists of greater or lesser sophistication on each of the preceding aspects; for detail that we cannot hope to include here we refer the reader to Rossi, Wright, and Anderson (1983) and other surveys. Our own plan is to pursue insights through strategic simplification, setting aside the complications of topic, administration, and other contextual determinants of response, to concentrate on a conceptual single-item survey or poll in which the decision to respond is taken with the individual's self-interest in mind. The latter is to be construed as broadly as possible; it may, for instance, contain reference to the interests of the social or political group to which the individual belongs. In other words, we shall treat the response decision as an economic one based on an assessment of benefits together with costs, the latter again being considered as broadly as possible and guided also by the information available to the individual. What results could be regarded as an economic theory of sampling response. In some respects it is very possibly still rudimentary so that we shall not have escaped entirely from our own criticism as to the state of response theory. Nevertheless, the response models that result are in principle statistically verifiable and provide a fair means of insight as to what can go wrong and what remedial methods are available.

As in most other problems of economic optimization, the response decision may very well be guided by information that one can reasonably assume to be available to the individual. In what follows we shall be arguing that this type of decision often has a social referral in that the response decision of any individual is conditioned by perceptions of the attitudes of others. The reasons for this conditioning will be enlarged upon but may include an assessment of the possibility of changes in custom, rules, or legislation that may result from the survey. Thus the individual information sets may well incorporate assessments about the attitudes of others, about the likely findings of the survey, and about the various outcomes that might result from its publication. Social information, described as any or all of these bits of knowledge, is therefore an important input in individual response decisions.

Moreover, the social context of a response decision introduces a game-theoretic aspect. The outcome from the survey entails – directly or indirectly, perhaps probabilistically – a payoff to every member of the surveyed population. In such circumstances, the individuals in the community can be regarded as players in a cooperative game. One might think that the optimal strategies for such a game are clear-cut: If it is worthwhile to incur the cost of a response, the individual will respond and respond truthfully. Two groups would emerge, those in favor and those against the item in question, with appropriate categorizations for multiple choices. The existence of such post hoc groupings cannot be called coalitions, to invoke the language of cooperative game theory. Suppose, however, that an individual knows that his or her preferred position or choice is shared by others in the community and perhaps also that a significant body of opinion to the contrary exists. This social information introduces the possibility of true gamelike behavior, that is, the formation of tacit but nonetheless existent coalitions. The implications of this for the theory of response are developed at length in the present chapter. It could also be remarked that incentives exist for replies to be nontruthful, or strategic. This latter contingency (and a further possibility that the very act of response could be strategic) is discussed in the next chapter. The present chapter limits consideration to response alone: Individuals who respond are assumed to do so truthfully.

The scheme of the chapter is as follows. Our primary concern will be with nonneutrality in sampling response and with explaining or predicting ways in which such selective effects will arise. Statistically speaking, the expression of these effects is via the general phenomenon of selection bias. Accordingly, Section 2.2 constitutes a brief survey of the theory of selection and self-selection bias, covering in particular its relationship with the response–nonresponse dichotomy. We consider models of measurement and models of covariation. In Section 2.3 we turn to the origins of self-selection bias. A detailed discussion of the social reference in the response decision draws on diverse material from the social sciences literature. This is followed by a discussion of a game-theoretic framework for the provision of information to the statistician. The notion of free riding in sampling response follows from the public good character of the information provided and may be viewed as a statistical tendency to depart from the full cooperative solution. Section 2.4 works out the detailed implications of the public good theory of sampling response in the context of a model of simple measurement. We consider also the possibility of a cycle of sampling and publication or even a real-time survey process that may entail significant homeostatic, or error-correcting, tendencies with respect to self-selection bias. This material is briefly extended to models of covariation in Section 2.5, which contains also a short evaluative discussion.

2.2   Selection and nonneutrality

The act of response to a poll or survey is an act of self-selection. To be sure, where the survey is a national census or an income tax return, the facultative connotation of self-selection is not entirely apparent; yet the obligatory case is only a special instance where the costs of nonresponse overwhelmingly direct the individual to respond. Now the question of whether the kind of selection or self-selection (to emphasize its volitional aspect) that is involved in an act of response is neutral can be answered in terms of an argument based on a well-known selection theorem of Lawley (1943): Suppose that our dependent variables of interest (the "score") have a structural relationship with certain observable variables (the explanatory variables), and suppose that observations fall into categories according to the values of selection variables that may or may not be observable. Then the structural disturbances, that is, the unsystematic part of the dependent variables, must be independent of the selection variables. The essence of the condition is that all selection information must be passed to the dependent variables via the observable explanatory variables. Then key parameters from mean- or covariance-based statistical techniques will remain invariant to the restriction of the sample observations to those selected or self-selected. In what follows we shall illustrate this principle with some generic examples.

Measurement

Perhaps the most familiar and most intuitive instance of selection bias arises in the estimation of simple means or proportions when the sample, although randomly selected, is nevertheless subject to differential response rates. Suppose that the tendency of individuals to respond is correlated with their score; for example, in a random sample of incomes, people of higher income usually tend to a lower probability of response. Then the sample (of size n) is restricted to $n_R < n$ respondents and moreover the measured score statistic $(\bar{x}, \hat{p}, \ldots)$ will clearly exhibit bias. The requirement for neutrality can be put thus: Could the n_R respondents be regarded as constituting a random sample of the population with respect to the score? In terms of the Lawley selection condition, selection information is certainly being passed to the score but in a way that is outside the control of the statistician; that is, it is not being explicitly modeled.

We can use this particular context to construct the beginnings of a model of sampling response, one that will be elaborated sequentially as subsequent discussion proceeds. Suppose that the object is to estimate a population mean μ. Actual scores y_i differ by a zero-mean term ζ_i representing the random variation

$$y_i = \mu + \zeta_i. \tag{1}$$

Suppose that the decision to respond is mediated in terms of another zero-mean random variable ϵ_i. Thus let us assume that an individual i will respond if and only if

$$\delta_i = \beta_0 + \epsilon_i > 0. \tag{2}$$

The variable δ_i may be interpreted as a random threshold for response, with the parameter β_0 containing its mean or systematic part. Note that we may normalize the variance of the unsystematic part ϵ_i to be unity with no loss of generality. Evidently, individuals characterized by a negative ϵ_i are less likely to respond. The probability of a response from an individual selected at random is $1 - F_\epsilon(-\beta_0)$, where F_ϵ is the distribution function of ϵ_i. If $F_\epsilon(\cdot)$ is symmetric about zero, then

$$1 - F_\epsilon(-\beta_0) = F_\epsilon(\beta_0).$$

Given the binomial character of the sampling experiment, $1 - F_\epsilon(-\beta_0)$ is the expected response rate, which we may adjust by means of the parameter β_0.

Our specific interest is with the conditions under which the restriction of the sample to the respondents entails no bias in the estimation of μ. Let the joint density of δ_i and ϵ_i be $p(\delta_i, \epsilon_i)$. Denote the event $\{i \in R\}$, or for brevity simply R, as a response from individual i. Then

$$E(\zeta_i/R) = E\zeta_i/\{\epsilon_i > -\beta_0\} \tag{3}$$

gives the expectation of the disturbance term ζ_i given that the individual is a respondent. The conditional density of ζ_i given $i \in R$ is

$$p(\zeta_i/R) = \frac{\text{prob}(\zeta_i \cap \{\epsilon_i > -\beta_0\})}{\text{prob}\{\epsilon_i > -\beta_0\}}$$

$$= \int_{\epsilon > -\beta_0} \frac{p(\zeta_i, \epsilon) \, d\epsilon_i}{1 - F_\epsilon(-\beta_0)}.$$

Hence the conditional expectation is given by

$$E(\zeta_i/R) = \int_\zeta \int_{\epsilon > -\beta_0} \frac{\zeta p(\zeta, \epsilon) \, d\epsilon \, d\zeta}{1 - F_\epsilon(-\beta_0)} \tag{4}$$

Now the joint density $p(\zeta_i, \epsilon_i)$ may be factored into the conditional times the marginal:

$$p(\zeta_i, \epsilon_i) = p(\epsilon_i/\zeta_i) \, p(\zeta_i).$$

Hence reversing also the order of integration in (4), we find

$$E(\zeta_i/R) = \int_{\epsilon > -\beta_0} \frac{[\int_\zeta \zeta p(\zeta/\epsilon) \, d\zeta] \, p(\epsilon) \, d\epsilon}{1 - F_\epsilon(-\beta_0)}$$

$$= \int_{\epsilon > -\beta_0} \frac{e(\epsilon) \, p(\epsilon) \, d\epsilon}{1 - F_\epsilon(-\beta_0)}, \tag{5}$$

where $e(\epsilon_i) = E(\zeta_i/\epsilon_i)$ is the conditional expectation of ζ_i given ϵ_i.

The neutrality requirement is essentially that

$$\int_{\epsilon > -\beta_0} e(\epsilon) \, p(\epsilon) \, d\epsilon = 0. \tag{6}$$

If this is the case, then $E y_i/R = \mu$, the desired value. Note that even if (6) is correct, this does not imply that the conditional variance $\text{Var}(y_i/R)$ is the same among respondents as for the population at large. Writing $v(\epsilon_i) = \text{Var}(\zeta_i/\epsilon_i)$, the conditional variance of ζ_i given ϵ_i and supposing first-order neutrality [i.e., equation (6)] gives

$$E(\zeta_i^2/R) = \int_{\epsilon > -\beta_0} \frac{v(\epsilon)\,p(\epsilon)\,d\epsilon}{1 - F_\epsilon(-\beta_0)}$$

$$\neq \text{Var } \zeta_i, \tag{7}$$

the unconditional variance, at least in general. Thus even though the mean, or first-order, properties are invariant to selection, it does not necessarily follow that the second-order, or covariance, properties are likewise invariant.

Provided the neutrality condition (6) holds and provided also that the usual regularity conditions hold with respect to the conditional density $p(y_i/R)$, the sample of n_R respondents may be viewed as a random sample from this density, and the usual large-number and central-limit laws apply. Thus the mean estimate

$$\bar{y}_R = \sum_{i=1}^{n_R} y_i$$

will be an unbiased and consistent estimator of μ, asymptotically normal with asymptotic variance given by equation (7).

From equation (6), the mean estimator will be neutral with regard to sample selection if $e(\epsilon_i) = 0$: The structural disturbance ζ_i is expectationally independent of the selection disturbance ϵ_i. The leading case is where the two disturbances are statistically independent, neither containing information about the other. This will be recognized as a statement of the Lawley selection conditions.

For future reference, we note the special case where the joint density $p(\zeta_i, \epsilon_i)$ is normal with covariance matrix

$$\begin{bmatrix} \sigma_\zeta^2 & \sigma_{\zeta\epsilon} \\ \sigma_{\epsilon\zeta} & 1 \end{bmatrix}.$$

In this case the conditional density of ζ_i given ϵ_i is normal with mean $\sigma_{\zeta\epsilon}\epsilon_i$ and variance $\sigma_\zeta^2(1-r^2)$, where $r = \sigma_{\zeta\epsilon}/\sigma_\zeta$ is the correlation coefficient between ζ_i and ϵ_i. This is the *theoretical regression* of ζ_i on ϵ_i (e.g., Cramér, 1961, ch. 23). Let us adopt the general notation $\Phi(x; \mu, \sigma^2)$ to indicate the normal distribution function with mean μ and variance σ^2 with $\phi(x; \mu, \sigma^2)$ the corresponding density. Also, denote $\Phi(x)$ – without parametric qualification – as the unit normal distribution function $\Phi(x) = \Phi(x; 0, 1)$, with a similar meaning for the density $\phi(x)$. Then under the normality assumption

$$1 - F_\epsilon(-\beta_0) = \Phi(\beta_0)$$

and

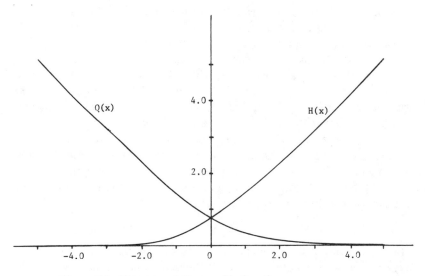

Figure 2.1. Hazard and Quenouille functions.

$$E(y_i/R) = \mu + \sigma_{\zeta\epsilon} \int_{\epsilon > -\beta_0} \frac{\epsilon\phi(\epsilon)\,d\epsilon}{\Phi(\beta_0)}$$

$$= \mu + \sigma_{\zeta\epsilon} \frac{\phi(\beta_0)}{\Phi(\beta_0)}. \tag{8}$$

To derive the integral (8), we have used result A4 of Appendix 1, which is a list of integral properties of the normal distribution.

The function $Q(x) = \phi(x)/\Phi(x)$ (the *Quenouille function*) is a mirror image about the vertical axis of the normal hazard function $H(x) = \phi(x)/[1 - \Phi(x)]$ of statistical reliability theory. It is a convex, monotonically declining function of its argument, sketched in Figure 2.1. We observe that for the normal model, the biasing factor is related to the expected response rate $\theta = \Phi(\beta_0)$:

$$\text{Bias} = \sigma_{\zeta\epsilon} \frac{d \log \theta}{d\beta_0}.$$

The bias is large for low response rates since this is the region in which the elasticity of the response rate is largest as β_0 increases. The direction of the bias depends upon the sign of the covariance $\sigma_{\zeta\epsilon}$. As we have set up the response decision, $\sigma_{\zeta\epsilon} > 0$ means that a higher score is associated with readier response. Hence, as we should expect, the observed sample estimate $\bar{y}_R$ is an overestimate in such circumstances.

At least two broad avenues have been pursued in the rectification of self-selection bias in problems of more or less simple measurement. The first is based on a resampling of those who did not respond, for example, the formal use of callbacks for respondents not at home. In the well-known method of Hansen and Hurwitz (1946) (see also Cochran, 1977, p. 371), a further random subsample is taken of the $n - n_R$ persons who were not reached on the initial sample of n and intensive efforts made to secure the participation of this subsample. Suppose n_2 are drawn from the $n - n_R$ initial nonrespondents. Then the two samples available are treated as having come from two independent strata (stratum 1, those who would reply on the initial call; stratum 2, those who would respond only to the second call). Assuming that all those designated for the second subsample do reply, the unbiased estimate is

$$\hat{\mu} = w_1 \bar{y}_R + w_2 \bar{y}_2$$

where $\bar{y}_2$ is the observed mean from the subsample. The weights $w_1 = n_R/n$ and $w_2 = 1 - w_1$ are estimates of the population proportions W_1, W_2 in the two strata. The drawbacks to the implicit theorizing about response in terms of the "strata" should be apparent: If not all of the persons sampled on the second occasion respond, then another callback will be necessary, with a corresponding third stratum, and so on, in a potentially infinite regression.

A second general class of rectification procedures is to change the conditions of response in such a way as to restore the representativeness of the sample by removing as far as possible the influences that would otherwise induce a selective response. This may be as straightforward as shortening or simplifying the questionnaire or arranging for the right kind of interviewer. Where selective response arises from concerns with confidentiality or the sensitive nature of the survey, the technique of randomized responses due originally to Warner (1965) is potentially applicable. By means of a randomization device with known probabilities, some of the participants answer an innocuous question whereas others answer the question of substantive interest. Since participants are aware that the questioner remains in ignorance of which of the two questions has been posed, embarrassment or personal confidentiality are in theory less of a barrier to response. The investigator is able to deduce statistically, but not individually, the behavior of the respondents with respect to the matter in hand. The technique has been applied to topics such as attitudes or experience with abortions, drugs, unreported income, and so on, with some measure of success. For a further account we refer the reader to Greenberg et al. (1969) and Horwitz, Greenberg, and Abernethy (1975).

Finally, it may be of interest to remark that nonneutral selection is sometimes unwittingly created in the pursuit of a higher rate of response. A good example is a recent survey received by the author seeking data relating to insurance needs. As an inducement to respond, the market research firm offered a chance for a free weekend in one of the local luxury hotels. Whereas this could indeed be expected to increase the overall response rate, it is plainly not neutral in relation to different socioeconomic groups in the sample, an aspect of interest to the marketing of insurance products.

Selection and covariation

Although the effects of self-selection on simple measurement are often fairly predictable, at least as to the existence and sign of bias, the various contingencies are far less clear when studies of covariation are involved. At first sight, a low response rate may appear to impact less when the object of the study is correlational, since both variables – or the dependent and independent variables in the case of regression – are apparently equally affected. Provided that enough variation is left in each, the nature of the covariation should continue to be detectable. Such a view may or may not be correct, depending again on the conditions of the Lawley selection criterion.

Let us start with such covariance-based techniques as regression and the analysis of variance (ANOVA). The following model is general enough to encompass both. Given r categories, define categorical dummy variables as

$$d_{ki} = \begin{cases} 1 & \text{if } i \in k, \\ 0 & \text{otherwise,} \end{cases} \quad k = 1, 2, \ldots, r.$$

Our object is to explain a dependent score y_i in terms of these categories plus a vector $\mathbf{x}_i$ of concomitant variables. In terms of the example considered in Bowden (1986), the score y_i could relate to the performance of a sample of schoolgirls of a certain level in mathematics. The object is to test whether a categorization of their fathers in terms of conservative, center, or liberal attitudes toward the role of women in society is influential in determining the mathematical achievement of their daughters. The concomitant variables $\mathbf{x}_i$ might include information on the girl's age in months, sibling position, and family variables such as income or indexes of socioeconomic status.

Thus let us write

$$y_i = \boldsymbol{\gamma}'\mathbf{x}_i + \sum_{k=1}^{r} \alpha_k d_{ki} + \zeta_i, \quad i = 1, \ldots, n, \tag{9}$$

where ζ_i is a disturbance independently and identically distributed (i.i.d.) over i with mean 0 and variance σ^2. The primary object is to examine the categorical parameters α_k and test for equality with suitably nested significance tests. Where a regression is contemplated, we assume some suitable identifiability restriction on the categorical variables or parameters, such as $\sum_k \alpha_k = 0$ or else the inclusion of only $r-1$ dummy variables d_k. Note that if $\gamma = 0$, the score is explained entirely in terms of the categorical dummies. A regression in these circumstances can be made to correspond to classic ANOVA testing for categorical differences. Thus model (9) can subsume both regression and standard ANOVA or covariance techniques.

Now for a regression or ANOVA to be based correctly upon equation (9), a necessary condition is that

$$E(y_i/R) = \gamma' \mathbf{x}_i + \sum_k \alpha_k d_{ki}. \tag{10}$$

Following the analysis of equations (1)–(5), let us imagine that the response decision is modeled after equation (2). Then we have in fact

$$E(y_i/R) = \gamma' \mathbf{x}_i + \sum_k \alpha_k d_{ki} + E(\zeta_i/R)$$

$$= \gamma' \mathbf{x}_i + \sum_k \alpha_k d_{ki} + \int_{\epsilon > -\beta_0} \frac{e(\epsilon) p(\epsilon) d\epsilon}{1 - F_\epsilon(-\beta_0)},$$

with the notational conventions as in the preceding. In particular, if the joint density $p(\zeta_i, \epsilon_i)$ is normal, it follows as for equation (8) that

$$E(y_i/R) = \gamma' \mathbf{x}_i + \sum_k \alpha_k d_{ki} + \sigma_{\zeta\epsilon} \frac{\phi(\beta_0)}{\Phi(\beta_0)}. \tag{11}$$

It is apparent by comparing (11) with the true structural expectation (10) that the only coefficient affected is the intercept γ_0. Fitting the given equation to the respondents ($i \in R$) would yield a new intercept tending almost surely to

$$\tilde{\gamma}_0 = \gamma_0 + \sigma_{\zeta\epsilon} \frac{\phi(\beta_0)}{\Phi(\beta_0)}$$

as the sample size (n, or equivalently n_R) becomes large. In this particular case, then, the contingencies of self-selection are rather innocuous, assuming of course that we have no specific interest in the intercept term γ_0.

Suppose, however, that the response decision depends upon a set of ancillary variables $\mathbf{z}_i$. Thus, instead of (2), we specify a more general dichotomy:

$$i \in R \Leftrightarrow \delta_i = \beta' \mathbf{z}_i + \epsilon_i > 0. \tag{12}$$

For example, levels of educational attainment or income are commonly held to be important in response rates to questionnaires. Corresponding to (11), we then have

$$E(y_i/R) = \gamma' \mathbf{x}_i + \sum_k \alpha_k d_{ki} + \sigma_{\zeta\epsilon} \frac{\phi(\beta' \mathbf{z}_i)}{\Phi(\beta' \mathbf{z}_i)}. \tag{13}$$

We may begin to perceive a problem. Suppose that the vector $\mathbf{z}_i$ shares some common elements (variables) with either $\mathbf{x}_i$ or the categorical dummies d_{ki}; or suppose that a strong correlation exists. For example, category 1, indicated by d_{k1}, might be the conservative category, and such people may be very short-tempered with questionnaires perceived as promoting the cause of women's liberation. Where a relationship between the categorical modifiers $\mathbf{z}_i$ and the structural independent variables exists, the estimated coefficients $\hat{\gamma}$ or $\hat{\alpha}$ can be expected to exhibit bias. Correspondingly, formal tests of significance based explicitly (regression) or implicitly (ANOVA) on these coefficients will exhibit bias and inconsistency: For example, with respect to the $\{\alpha_k\}$, there will be some set of values not all equal such that the estimated $\hat{\alpha}_k$ are equal, and for this set, we are less likely to reject a null hypothesis of equality than when true equality of the α_k is present. In other words, we could well end up accepting the null hypothesis of no categorical effect when there is in fact a difference or, vice versa, rejecting equality when the $\{\alpha_k\}$ are in reality the same.

In terms of the mathematical girls and the liberality of their fathers, suppose that the reality is no difference in performance ($\alpha_1 = \alpha_2 = \cdots = \alpha_r$ for r categories of "liberality"). But higher score girls have fathers who, other things being equal, are more likely to respond: $\sigma_{\zeta\epsilon} > 0$. Thus more able girls have more able fathers, and more able fathers (we shall suppose) are more willing to respond to the questionnaire. If the decision to respond is not correlated with the $\mathbf{x}_i$ or d_{ki} variables, the selection is nonneutral but innocuous – only the intercept γ_0 will be affected. Suppose, however, that, other things being equal, more liberal fathers tend to respond better to the questionnaire (by no means an implausible contingency!). In other words, $\beta' \mathbf{z}_i$ includes categorical variables d_{ki}. Over the domain of interest, the function $Q(x) = \phi(x)/\Phi(x)$ is roughly linear and declining in x. Hence to omit this function and fit equation (10) will result in an estimate of the liberality effect that is biased downward (in terms of coefficients of the relevant categorical dummies). More liberal fathers wrongly appear to be associated with less able daughters. Alternatively, suppose that more able fathers are less willing to respond (they are too busy), so that the covariance $\sigma_{\zeta\epsilon} < 0$. Then under the preceding assumptions on liberality, more liberal fathers would (wrongly) appear to be associated with more able daughters.

Violation of the Lawley selection criterion is clear in this example. Selection information is being passed to the score via the unsystematic, or "unmodeled," structural disturbance term ζ_i. The fact that both score and selection depend upon common variables (e.g., the liberality factor) is not in itself damaging. Thus selection information can be passed to the score: The potential for bias exists when selection information is passed to the score in a way not systematically modeled. Given the existence of unsystematic transfer, it becomes especially damaging when common or correlated structural variables are present in both the selection process and in the structure to be investigated.

Similar selection provisions apply to studies based upon factor analysis. The general model is

$$\mathbf{y}_i = \Gamma \mathbf{x}_i + \mathbf{u}_i$$

where Γ is a matrix of parameters, $\mathbf{y}_i$ contains the score of individual i on a set of items, $\mathbf{x}_i$ constitutes the factors of dimension less than $\mathbf{y}_i$, and $\mathbf{u}_i$ includes the specific and error influences. Let $\mathbf{z}_i$ be a set of influences determining selection into the sample. The $\mathbf{z}_i$ may be correlated with the factors $\mathbf{x}_i$. Provided, however, that $E\mathbf{u}_i/\mathbf{z}_i = E\mathbf{u}_i = \mathbf{0}$, selection bias will not be a problem. This does not in itself mean that the covariance structure of the density of u_i given $i \in R$ is the same as for $i \notin R$ or for the parent population as a whole (see, e.g., Gulliksen, 1950, chs. 12 and 13; Meredith, 1964). Nevertheless, restriction to the observed sample will preserve the mean structure $B\mathbf{z}_i$ and allow factor analyses on a consistent basis with the population as a whole.

Rectification (and testing) for selection bias is a substantial problem beyond the scope of this introductory survey. On occasion it may be achieved by simply including some of the systematic selection variables among the structural set and proceeding normally to tests based on regression or the analysis of covariance (Bowden, 1986, p. 322). On other occasions quick fixes of this kind will not work. We refer the reader to Heckman (1979) and Bowden and Turkington (1984, ch. 2) for more sophisticated approaches to testing for and possible rectification of self-selection bias, in general involving the application of maximum-likelihood and instrumental variables methods. Specific application to problems of nonresponse in sampling theory is as yet an undeveloped area.

2.3   Social information and coalitional behavior

In this section, we adumbrate a model of response or nonresponse cast in game-theoretic terms in which the role of the perceived social environment emerges as an important determinant of response. We shall use this sort of framework repeatedly in subsequent work. At the outset, however, we wish to stress the importance of social information in response, whether to a survey or to items within the survey, an importance that extends beyond the framework of the particular model that we construct. On a more informal level, social information has always been regarded as important in determining the fact and character of response, and it may be as well to begin by reviewing some examples from the political and sociological literature.

(a) One of the more visible manifestations of response is provided by voter turnout at elections. Of course, one might object that we are dealing with surveys and opinion polls rather than formal elections. Yet elections and opinion polls have this in common, that they represent an actual or implied vote by respondents on some particular issue or issues. Indeed, if the opinion poll is perceived to have a good chance of influencing some policy action, then the correspondence becomes quite close. Many authors have drawn attention to the expected closeness of the race as one of the determinants of voter turnout (e.g., Riker and Ordeshook, 1968, 1973; Ashenfelter and Kelley, 1975), and this is indeed part of the empirical folklore, as it were, of election behavior. In this case the social information is the expected majority, or vote proportions if there are more than two candidates, established on the basis of preelection polls or surveys of voter opinion. Some authors argue that if the race is close, an individual voter may feel that there is an increased probability of his or her personal vote swinging the result one way or the other – the last straw argument. An argument that is more compelling given the large number of voters is that noted by Olson (1965), namely, that the outcome of an election is a public good and that coalitional behavior is vulnerable to free riding. Free riding amounts here to a decision to save on the private costs of voting in terms of time, effort, or expense by not voting, relying on the votes of others of similar political persuasion (the implied coalition) to carry the day. Although we lack a formal theory of free riding in this and other contexts, one might anticipate that free riding would diminish if the result was expected to be close. In this way, social information would exert an influence on response rate, interpreted in this instance as voter turnout. This theory is developed further in what follows and is applied to the broader context of polls and surveys of all kinds.

(b) Information as to the attitudes of others might be regarded as carrying with it substantive information about the prospects for success of some mooted program about which the individual is in some doubt. He may be unsure whether candidate X has the economic expertise or political weight to be able to reduce the budget deficit. If a survey reveals that large numbers of other prospective voters support candidate X, the individual may revise (or even form) his view of the probability of the candidate's budgetary success. The support of specific interest groups constitutes public information of a similar kind, and indeed McKelvey and Ordeshook (1985a, b) have constructed a game-theoretic equilibrium in the presence of such information together with feedback to the candidates as to voter preferences. The general idea that knowledge of the attitudes or intentions of others may have informational content on a substantive issue has been influenced by work in the economics of rational-expectations equilibria, where observed prices correspond to the publicly available information. We shall return to matters of informational feedback in Chapters 4 and 5. However, we note here the following possibility. Suppose that people are unwilling to express an opinion – and therefore do not respond – because they feel that they do not know enough about the issue to do so. Suppose that social information does become available as to how others are thinking about the issue. Such information may, in good Bayesian fashion, refine the individual's prior beliefs to the point where he or she is now willing to take the action of expressing an opinion. In conveying information (even if ultimately wrong), social information as to the attitudes of others affects response.

(c) One possible rationale for the "silent-majority" phenomenon runs in terms of a nonresponse bias stemming from prevailing public expectations or information. People may be unwilling to express an opinion about apparently controversial or distasteful issues partly because the prospects of mooted attitudinal or legislative changes are viewed as having little chance of success should matters ever come to a direct or indirect vote. Underpinning this assessment is the individual's estimate that the proportion who oppose the proposal is in a majority. We observe that this is a variant of the free-riding argument broached under (a): The costs of response may be psychological as well as fiscal, and if the benefits from response are judged, as a matter of mathematical expectations, to be slender, then individuals will tend not to respond.

(d) In sociological research, the perceived social desirability of certain kinds of behavior has long been recognized as an influence in an individual's private readiness to admit to such traits. An instance is the controversy that exists with respect to studies that attempt to link the true incidence (untreated as well as treated) of mental illness to different social factors, including race. One criticism is that the readiness to admit to certain traits appearing in mental health inventory tests may be conditioned by the perceived prevalence of such traits in the individual's ambient social grouping (e.g., Dohrenwend, 1966). In investigating the existence or extent of resulting nonresponse biases, investigators have actually asked respondents for their personal estimates of social prevalence (Phillips, 1973, chs. 2 and 3). A similar social responsiveness occurs in such fields as education, where the embarrassment that subjects may feel at admitting the extent or consequences of their lack of education is occasioned by their perception that they are in a social minority. The influence from social desirability may be effected through the character and truthfulness of the individual's response or else through his or her refusal to respond altogether. Indeed, a refusal to respond could well be regarded as a way out of the moral dilemma as to whether to respond truthfully. In this way one could maintain that information as to the general social prevalence or desirability of the trait or subject can help to determine the decision as to whether to respond to a survey.

In a variety of contexts, therefore, the decision as to whether to respond has a social reference and is conditioned by individual perceptions of the attitudes of others in the community. Even with no further elaboration, the reminder that no man is an island may help to understand his reaction to a request for information: To give information is an act with social overtones that may well require a balancing acquisition of information.

Social information and private games

Issues of ignorance aside, it will be noted that costs of response play a fairly pervasive role in the preceding discussion. The costs may be pecuniary, psychological, temporal, actual, or implicit, but they are costs nevertheless. Our economic theory of response is founded on a balancing of the costs and returns from response. However, such a decision cannot be based myopically on individual balance sheets or profit and loss. The social reference is again essential, and we shall utilize the language, at least, of cooperative game theory to conceptualize the considerations that guide individual decisions.

To focus the discussion, let us imagine that the object of the survey is to reveal whether people are for or against some given issue or proposal. The payoff to any individual depends upon the individual's action – respond or refuse response – as well as his or her individual affectation from the collective outcome. The first element is his or her personal cost of response to the survey. As we have already indicated, this may be psychological (embarrassment, disruptive, mixing memory and desire, etc.), it may involve foregone time, or it may in some cases involve actual pecuniary costs. Let us write c_i as the monetary equivalent (see also Section 2.4) of the response cost for individual i.

The benefit to individual i is the personal payoff (gross of response cost) that results from the outcome of the survey. We shall imagine that two statistics result from the survey, namely, the manifested proportion in favor, ρ_m (loosely, the "vote"), and the response rate θ to the survey. Polls and surveys are typically done for a reason (although one wonders a bit these days) and represent, to a greater or lesser degree, an opportunity to influence policy decisions by governments or other executive bodies. The manifested majority is an obvious input in this respect. A further informational input to any policy decision is the response rate θ from the survey. Partly this is a question of the reliability (sampling variance) attached to the manifested majority. But the influence of the response rate has as much to do with the political economy of information. If the message from the survey is unpalatable to the decision makers, they will be looking for an opportunity to discount the results, and a low response rate provides such an opportunity. In summary, therefore, the manifested vote ρ_m and response rate θ may be taken as functionally related to the probability of policy action and, through this relationship, to determine the expected payoff to each individual. The payoff function for individual i may be written

$$p_i = \pi_i(\rho_m, \theta) - c_i \qquad (14a)$$

if he or she responds or

$$p_i = \pi_i(\rho_m, \theta) \qquad (14b)$$

if not.

The incentive to free ride is plain enough. If each individual among many thinks that his (or her) personal vote will not change the outcome (ρ_m, θ), then his personal payoff can only be improved by the deletion of his response cost c_i. In other words, the outcome is of the nature of a public good – no matter whether I vote or not, I enjoy the outcome if it is favorable and suffer if it is not. So why bother to record an opinion? We note in passing that we do not call on the "last straw" argument mentioned under (a) – the idea that each individual fears that his personal opinion may be the last one that sways the issue for or against. This becomes a progressively less convincing argument as the number of individuals becomes large. Instead, we have to examine the forces of social cohesiveness to explain why it is that people choose nevertheless to incur the private costs of response.

For if everybody took the easy way out and declined to respond, nobody would be around to record an opinion so that the ultimate outcome would be privately unfavorable, at least to a significant (on most issues) group of the population. Each individual knows that he or she is part of an unexpressed coalition of those of similar opinion on the issue. From the point of view of this implied coalition, the cooperative strategy is to incur the private cost of recording an opinion for all those whose payoff exceeds the cost of response. The payoff is in turn calculated from the equilibrium values of ρ_m, θ. More formally, suppose that there are N individuals with N large and let $\vartheta\{\cdot\}$ be the set indicator function. Then the cooperative equilibrium values ρ_m^*, θ^* are defined by the equations

$$\frac{1}{N} \sum_i \vartheta\{|\pi_i(\rho_m^*, \theta^*)| > c_i\} = \theta^*,$$

$$\frac{1}{N} \sum_i \vartheta\{\pi_i(\rho_m^*, \theta^*) > c_i\} = \rho_m^* \theta^*.$$

We shall assume that this solution is unique.

Now the cooperative solution is characterized not only by information about the equilibrium values of ρ_m^*, θ^* but also by the existence of some sanction that ensures no free riding. Most likely, the latter will itself be based on an additional piece of information, namely, who has not expressed an opinion or voted, together with moral or legal sanctions. For example, voting in Australian elections is compulsory, identifiable, and subject to a \$10 fine in its breach. Remove the information about who has not responded, and two things happen. The first is the possibility of free riding. The second is that individuals are no longer aware of the cooperative solution values ρ_m^*, θ^*. In other words, the values of ρ_m, θ upon which their personal payoff functions (14) are predicated are, for the purposes of decision making as to response, unknown.

Two contrary tendencies now exist. First, response assumes the character of a decision under risk. Suppose that the individual is able to form a subjective probability density for ρ_m, θ (a significant and questionable assumption we shall return to in due course). Then we might imagine the effect of risk to be replaced by a decision criterion cast in terms of the mathematical expectations $E_s(\rho_m), E_s(\theta)$ with respect to the subjective (s) probability distribution but one in which the response cost c_i has been inflated by a risk premium. In other words, the effect of risk is to raise the effective cost barrier to response. We shall analyze in the next section the effect of such cost barriers, but we may take it in anticipation that the extra response cost will lower the overall response rate θ and also affect the manifested majority ρ_m. Intuitively, if people do not know the true values of ρ_m, θ, they will gravitate more in their decision making to what is certain, namely, the cost of response.

The second tendency is to free riding. Sanctions aside, we might expect the tendency, statistically speaking, to free ride to increase as information about ρ_m, θ becomes better. Thus if people are fairly certain that ρ_m is high and they themselves support the measure or issue, then they are more liable to free ride, confident that things will get along fine without them. Electoral behavior supports this idea. If past experience has shown that their electorate is a safe Republican (conservative, liberal, etc.) seat, then those of like mind will feel less moral pressure to record their own vote. Conversely, suppose that no prior information about the likely value of ρ_m exists. In these circumstances, free riding becomes more dangerous, and those with much to lose will be correspondingly readier to vote or express an opinion, that is, to respond.

The net effect of social information – represented, say, in the form of greater precision of estimates of ρ_m and θ – can therefore be regarded as the resultant of the forces of cost of response, risk aversion, free riding, and the perceived individual benefits. Better social information would mean an increased response rate from risk aversion but a decreased response rate resulting from an enhanced disposition to free ride. If the proposal or issue is naturally in a majority, better social information is likely to yield a decreased manifest "vote" because of free riding and possibly also from decreased risk aversion.

The existence of free riding is something that we have presented as a statistical tendency rather than as an alternative game-theoretic equilibrium concept. If everybody indulged in free riding, the result would be a noncooperative and entirely suboptimal equilibrium. A state in which free riding exists is technically a state of disequilibrium; it does not appear to be amenable to a treatment as any kind of equilibrium. Yet free riding can exist only in the presence of a fair degree of residual cohesiveness. The knowledge of this basic cohesion may itself be regarded as a public good, binding together in an implicit rather then explicit fashion those of similar opinions or persuasions. Empirically, the task of any study of response to a given survey is to predict the strength of feelings on the issue, the cost involved in response, and the general salience of the proposed survey. In the next section we proceed to construct a formal model of response (drawing from statistical discriminant analysis) that represents an attempt to model response in the light of all these considerations.

2.4   Nonresponse bias

In this section we shall get down to brass tacks and construct a model of response, with the aid of which we are able to study in detail the biasing effects of nonresponse and its relationship to such influences as the costs of response, the strength of feelings, and the role of social information. To keep matters simple, we imagine a survey with just one issue and a dichotomous yes–no response or potential response. The basic model itself was developed in Bowden (1987b), where it is used to analyze real-time and volunteered response surveys. As indicated in the preceding, the strength of opinion will be an important consideration in the decision to respond; it will therefore be useful to begin with a model for attitudes and their strength.

Attitudes

We shall suppose the existence of a unidimensional scale of attitudes in the subject population. Linear attitudinal scales arise in a variety of literatures. If the survey is canvassing opinions on some development project (an increasingly common application), then the attitudinal scale could be given a monetary dimension corresponding to the equivalent or compensating variation idea of project analysis. The scale w could then represent the dollar amount w_i needed to compensate individual i if the project were not developed (the *equivalent variation*) or alternatively how much one would have to compensate individual i in order to achieve his or her consent to the development (the *compensating variation*). A unidimensional attitude scale is often assumed in social psychology and, with variations in treatment regarding cardinality or ordinality, forms the basis of empirical scales such as the Likert, Guttnam, latent structure, or unfolding types. For a review we refer the reader to Anderson, Basilevsky, and Hum (1983). Finally, linear dimensions such as "conservatism" or "liberalism" are, rightly or wrongly, still widely employed in empirical political science.

Thus let w be a variable whose values w_i are taken to indicate the attitudinal position of individual i along a unidimensional continuum. With no loss of generality, we shall, genuflecting to the economic imperatives of profit and loss, divide the scale at $w = 0$; if $w_i < 0$, the individual is taken to be against the proposal or have an unfavorable attitude, and if $w_i > 0$, the individual is for the proposal. With regard to the population of interest, we shall suppose that attitudes are normally distributed with mean μ and variance σ^2. Then the proportion in favor of the proposal, development, and so on, is given by

$$\rho = \text{prob}(w_i > 0) = 1 - \Phi(0; \mu, \sigma^2), \tag{15}$$

where the reader will recall that Φ is the normal distribution function and ϕ the corresponding density. For given proportion ρ, let r be defined by

$$\Phi(r) = \Phi(r; 0, 1) = \rho. \tag{16}$$

For brevity we shall often describe the proportion ρ as the "vote" – this should not be taken to imply that we necessarily have in mind a political poll or election.

For later purposes, it will be convenient to utilize ρ (or r) as one of the basic parameters of the attitudinal distribution. Note that given ρ, all combinations (μ, σ^2) such that $\mu/\sigma = r$ will give the same vote, where r is defined in terms of ρ by equation (15). Indeed, we may redefine the parameters of the distribution in terms of ρ and either μ or σ. Thus, instead of $\Phi(w; \mu, \sigma^2)$, we could describe the distribution function as

$$\Phi(w; \mu, \sigma^2) \equiv \Phi(w; \mu, \mu^2/r^2) \equiv \Phi(w; r\sigma, \sigma^2), \tag{17}$$

where in each case r is defined in terms of ρ by equation (16). We shall choose the parameterization in terms of σ rather than μ, although the same results are of course obtainable in terms of either. Although not central to our present purposes, we remark that the reparameterization is a useful way of referring to overall differences in attitudinal strength: for fixed ρ, a distribution characterized by a higher σ would be one in which people felt more strongly about the issue. [Some qualifications to this sort of statement exist where the distribution of attitudes is asymmetric, and the reader is referred to Bowden (1987b) for a further discussion of such matters.]

Models of response

As suggested in Section 2.3, the various costs of response interpreted as broadly as possible to incorporate psychological, temporal, and narrowly pecuniary pressures form a starting point for a model of response. Even if the costs are nonfiscal, we can (perhaps adopting the equivalent variational idea of the economists; see above) imagine that these response costs have been imputed to a dimension commensurate with w, the scale of attitudes. Given an actual or imputed cost c for response, we can imagine in the first instance that individual i will respond if and only if

$$|w_i| > c. \tag{18}$$

A dead zone applies with respect to his (or her) benefits w_i. If his benefit is positive but less than the cost of responding, then the individual will default. Likewise, if the worst he can do is to lose fifty cents (i.e., $w_i = -50$), then the individual will default if the imputed cost of response is a dollar. More realistically, we could specify that the cost of response c varies from individual to individual about some mean c and replace (18) by a corresponding stochastic statement in terms of the kind of censoring processes developed in what follows. As it stands, however, the implied decision process (18) is enough to capture the simple insight that whether an individual responds depends in the first instance upon the cost of response in relation to the benefits he is to derive from the subject proposal. Other things being equal, the higher the cost of response and the more indifferent people are to the subject, the lower the response rate.

On the other hand, we should not limit nonresponse entirely to considerations of actual or imputed cost in relation to benefits. As we have already pointed out, other motives for nonresponse may include moral judgments, ignorance, or general salience, not all of which can satisfactorily be imputed into a cost dimension. Collectively, we shall represent such motives in terms of a parameter β_0 that operates independently of perceived costs or benefits as a modifying factor in response. Thus even if $c = 0$, the response rate may be less than 100 percent. From the expositional point of view, the salience parameter β_0 represents a base response rate that encompasses all other response factors not expressly included.

In terms of the theory elaborated in Section 2.3, a response cost is likely to be associated with free riding especially if information is available concerning the attitudes of others. A simple stochastic model of the free-riding phenomenon may be constructed as follows. Consider first a potential respondent in favor of the proposal, that is, $w_i > 0$. We assume that the temptation to free ride is dependent upon the respondent's perceptions of the support for his or her position. Let $\hat{\rho}_i$ be the individual estimate of ρ, the proportion of the population in favor of the proposal. Then if $\hat{\rho}_i \gg 0.5$, individual i will be more ready to default. On the other hand, if the individual expects to benefit a great deal from the proposal, then he or she is less willing to place its support in jeopardy by free-riding behavior.

Imagine that individuals are characterized by inherent variation in their tendency to either default or free ride, reflecting moral virtue or particular circumstances; describe this variation in terms of a zero-mean random variable ϵ_i arranged so that more negative values correspond to increasing liability to free ride or default. Let β_0 be a constant indicating a general default threshold. In the first instance, let us say that individual i will default (not respond) if and only if

$$\beta_0 + \epsilon_i < 0. \tag{19}$$

By adjusting the parameter β_0, referred to earlier as a general salience parameter, we could raise or lower the general response rate. As indicated previously, however, the default threshold will be lowered as $\hat{\rho}_i > 0.5$ and raised as $w_i > c$. The default condition (19) is now adjusted to

$$\delta_0^+ = \beta_0 - \beta_1(\hat{\rho}_i - 0.5) + \beta_2(w_i - c) + \epsilon_i < 0. \tag{20}$$

The positive parameters β_1, β_2 are the free-riding parameter and the offset parameter, respectively. Notice that these parameters could well be regarded as themselves dependent upon the cost of response c. Finally, we augment the decision dichotomy (20) with that based upon the cost model (18). Considering response as the complementary event to default, a positively inclined individual i will respond if and only if

$$w_i > c \quad \text{and} \quad -\beta_0 + \beta_1(\rho_i - 0.5) - \beta_2(w_i - c) < \epsilon_i. \tag{21a}$$

Note that the two dichotomies of (21a) may be combined into the single statement

$$(+) \text{individual } i \text{ responds} \Leftrightarrow w_i > c + \tilde{c}_i^+,$$

where

$$\tilde{c}_i^+ = \min(0, c_i^+),$$

$$c_i^+ = -\frac{\beta_0}{\beta_2} + \frac{\beta_1}{\beta_2}(\hat{\rho}_i - 0.5) - \frac{\epsilon_i}{\beta_2}.$$

This version indicates that the effects of free riding and other systematic nonresponse tendencies incorporated in the constant β_0 may be regarded as equivalent to an individual-specific virtual increase in the cost of response. Such a reformulation has the virtue of homologizing the dimensions of the otherwise disparate or incommensurable dichotomies (18) and (20). However, the probability analysis is perhaps more straightforward using the original version (21a), and we shall employ this formulation in what follows. Finally, by following through the corresponding argument for the case of a negatively inclined subject ($w_i < 0$), we find that such an individual will respond to the proposal if and only if

$$w_i < -c \quad \text{and} \quad -\beta_0 - \beta_1(\hat{\rho}_i - 0.5) + \beta_2(w_i + c) < \epsilon_i. \tag{21b}$$

Finally, we may normalize the variance of ϵ_i to be unity with no loss of generality.

The way in which prevailing opinion influences the probability of response may not be quite as simple as the mechanism incorporated in inequalities (21). For instance, if $\hat{\rho}_i \ll 0.5$, a positively inclined individual may well consider that it is a lost cause and not bother to respond; in other words, the dependence on $\hat{\rho}_i - 0.5$ could be nonlinear. With regard to the individual estimates $\hat{\rho}_i$ of the majority (proportion in favor), we shall invoke the simplest assumption that $\hat{\rho}_i = \hat{\rho}$, some common value. A particular choice is $\hat{\rho} = \rho$, the true value. The latter could be taken as a rational-expectations type of assumption (see Chapter 5 and following) and will be referred to as such. In all cases it is possible to relax the commonality assumption by adding individual disturbance terms: For instance,

$$\hat{\rho}_i = \rho + \eta_i,$$

where η_i is a zero-mean random variable (individuals are on the average correct in their assessments of the prevailing state of opinion), a slightly more realistic version of the rational-expectations assumption. Mathematically, however, the price of this extra bit of realism turns out to be another integral sign, and in what follows we shall assume a common estimate $\hat{\rho}$.

Bias from simple cost censoring

Let us consider first the effects of the simple cost censoring incorporated in equation (18); in other words, we are not yet considering the model of response (19)–(21). Figure 2.2 is a graphical illustration. Cost censoring removes the distributional mass between the two vertical lines at $c, -c$, with effects upon both the response rate and the recorded or manifest majority. In terms of the diagram for the (cumulative) distribution function, the response rate is equal to $1 - AB$. The manifest majority is equal to $PB/(PB + 0A)$ as against the correct value $\rho = PR/(PR + OR)$.

Algebraically, the expected number of positively inclined respondents expressed as a proportion of the subject population is

$$M_c^+ = \text{prob}(w_i > c) = 1 - \Phi(c; r\sigma, \sigma^2)$$

$$= \Phi(r - c/\sigma), \tag{22a}$$

where we have employed the reparameterization in terms of r and σ. Similarly, the number of negative respondents is

$$M_c^- = 1 - \Phi(r + c/\sigma). \tag{22b}$$

The response rate is

$$\theta = M_c^+ + M_c^-,$$

and the recorded or manifest majority is given by

$$\rho_c = \frac{\Phi(r - c/\sigma)}{\Phi(r - c/\sigma) + 1 - \Phi(r + c/\sigma)}. \tag{23}$$

If the cost constant c is zero, then $\rho_c = \Phi(r) = \rho$. Given our earlier remarks on the significance of varying σ for a given ρ, the ratio c/σ may be taken as a cost–intensity ratio. The higher is this ratio, the lower is the response rate. Moreover, it can be shown (see Appendix 2) that the cost

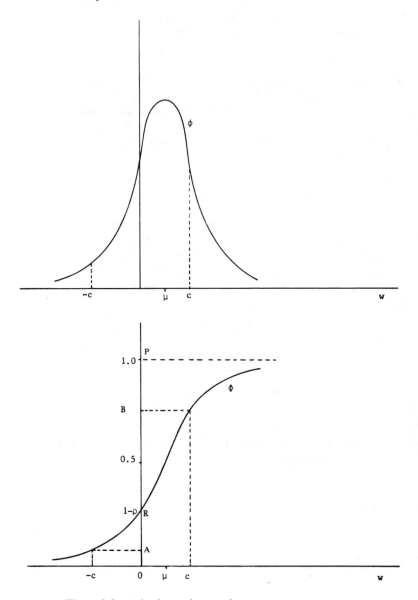

Figure 2.2. Attitudes and censoring.

parameter c exerts a biasing effect on the manifested majority $\rho_c > \rho$, and the overestimate increases with the cost parameter c. A corresponding result holds if $\rho < 0.5$, a minority proposal becomes accentuated in the respondents.

Free riding, salience, and so on

We may now proceed to incorporate the more complex model of response incorporated in equations (21a) and (21b). To do this, let us assume that ϵ_i and w_i are statistically independent. Then for fixed ρ, M_+ is given by

$$M_+ = \int_{w>c} \phi(w; r\sigma, \sigma^2) \int_{R_\epsilon(w)} \phi(\epsilon; 0, 1) \, d\epsilon \, dw,$$

where $R_\epsilon(w) = \{w: -\beta_2(w-c) + \beta_1(\hat{\rho}-0.5) - \beta_0 < \epsilon\}$.
    The preceding integral reduces to

$$M_+ = \int_0^\infty \phi(z; r\sigma - c, \sigma^2) \Phi[\beta_2 z; -\beta_0 + \beta_1(\hat{\rho}-0.5), 1] \, dz. \quad (24a)$$

A similar argument may be developed with respect to negative responses, yielding

$$M_- = \int_0^\infty \phi(z; -r\sigma - c, \sigma^2) \Phi[\beta_2 z; -\beta_0 - \beta_1(\hat{\rho}-0.5), 1] \, dz. \quad (24b)$$

The integrals in (24a) and (24b) cannot be evaluated analytically, but their general import may be seen as follows. According to the second mean-value theorem of integral calculus (e.g., Loomis, 1975, p. 389), there exists a number $z_0 > 0$ depending upon μ and the other parameters such that

$$M_+ = \Phi[\beta_2 z_0; -\beta_0 + \beta_1(\hat{\rho}-0.5), 1] \int_0^\infty \phi(z; r\sigma - c, \sigma^2) \, dz$$

$$= \Phi(\tilde{\beta}_0) \Phi(r - c/\sigma). \quad (25a)$$

where $\tilde{\beta}_0 = \beta_0 + \beta_2 z_0 - \beta_1(\hat{\rho}-0.5)$.
    Likewise, there exists $z_0' > 0$ such that

$$M_- = \Phi(\tilde{\beta}_0')[1 - \Phi(r + c/\sigma)], \quad (25b)$$

where $\tilde{\beta}_0' = \beta_0 + \beta_2 z_0' + \beta_1(\rho-0.5)$.
    Equations (25a) and (25b) are to be compared with the corresponding expressions (22a) and (22b) for the simple cost-censoring model. We observe that the general effect of free riding [the term $\beta_1(\hat{\rho}-0.5)$] is to lower the threshold for default in the case of positive potential respondents (partially offset by the term in β_2) and raise the default threshold for those negatively inclined. From equations (25), we derive the manifest majority as

$$\rho^m = \frac{\Phi(r - c/\sigma)}{\Phi(r - c/\sigma) + \lambda[1 - \Phi(r + c/\sigma)]}$$

$$= \frac{\rho_c}{1 + [\lambda(\hat{\rho}) - 1][(1 - \rho_c)/\rho_c]}$$

$$\triangleq H_c(\hat{\rho}), \quad (26)$$

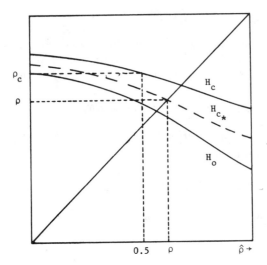

Figure 2.3. The function $H_c(\hat{\rho})$.

where

$$\lambda(\hat{\rho}) = \frac{\Phi(\tilde{\beta}_0')}{\Phi(\tilde{\beta}_0)} = \frac{\Phi[\beta_0 + \beta_2 z_0' + \beta_1(\hat{\rho} - 0.5)]}{\Phi[\beta_0 + \beta_2 z_0 - \beta_1(\hat{\rho} - 0.5)]}. \tag{27}$$

We observe that if $\beta_1 = \beta_2 = 0$ (no free riding or offset), then $\tilde{\beta}_0' = \tilde{\beta}_0 = \beta_0$ and $\lambda = 1$. The presence of a general salience effect alters the response rate [diminished by the factor $\Phi(\beta_0)$] but in a neutral way. Suppose, however, that the free-riding parameter β_1 is nonzero. Then if the estimated vote $\hat{\rho} \gg 0.5$ and there is only a limited offset ($\beta_2 \approx 0$), we might expect that $\tilde{\beta}_0' > \tilde{\beta}_0$ and hence $\lambda > 1$. From expression (26) we should then have $\rho^m < \rho_c$: The tendency of those in the majority to free ride means that the recorded majority is less than the majority resulting from simple cost censoring.

Figure 2.3 is a sketch of the function $H_c(\hat{\rho})$ defined by equation (26) with the particular assumption $\beta_2 = 0$ (no offset). Its shape and location are derived from a detailed discussion in Appendix 3 to this chapter. By reading the ordinate and comparing with the true value ρ, we can measure the bias corresponding to any state of prior expectation $\hat{\rho}$. We observe that if $\hat{\rho} = \rho$ (rational expectations), then the manifested $\rho^m > p$. Thus even if the individuals themselves on the average know the correct value, a positive bias will result. No bias would result only if individual expectations $\hat{\rho} = \hat{\rho}_1 > \rho$, the true value. In order for free riding to be able to offset the cost censoring, favorable agents have to be lulled into a false sense of security, imagining that more support exists than is really the case.

The function $H_0(\hat{\rho})$ in Figure 2.3 refers to the case $c = 0$. It is drawn under the supposition that even though response costs are zero, other motives are such that the response decision continues to be affected by peoples' perceptions of the vote $\hat{\rho}$; in other words, the parameter β_1 does not approach zero along with c, as a strict interpretation of the free-riding rationale would otherwise indicate. We note that as sketched, if $c = 0$, then rational expectations can result in an underestimate. This suggests that an optimal level of c might exist such that if expectations are rational ($\hat{\rho} = \rho$), then the resulting manifest vote $\rho^m = \rho$. In other words, the optimal c_* is such that ρ is the fixed point of the function $H_{c_*}(\hat{\rho})$. Thus if expectations were known to be rational, one would construct just the right barriers to response to yield an unbiased estimate of that figure. Of course, the practical implementation of this is highly problematical: One would have to know that expectations were rational (and yet not know what the actual vote is!) and also have a good appreciation of the parameters of the response structure. Yet the idea that optimal barriers to response might exist is not without interest.

Publication and dynamics

The social information that determines $\hat{\rho}$, the public's estimate of prevailing states of opinion, may well come from previous surveys. The replication of surveys is established practice in such areas as political polling. It may represent a planned temporal monitoring on the part of a single survey organization. Or it may arise more gratuitously because different survey firms are all addressing the same problem. We discuss further arrangements involving replication in the next section. At this point we note some of the consequences of a repeated sequence of surveys.

The publication aspect means that if an estimate ρ^m_{n-1} is taken after replication number $n-1$, this becomes absorbed, as it were, into individuals' information sets and hence influences their current estimates $\hat{\rho}_i$ of the prevailing state of opinion. Agents have two sources of information as to the underlying vote ρ: their own prior estimate, which incorporates their own private information together with any previously published estimate, and the estimate that has just been published. We could imagine individuals combining the two in Bayesian fashion, weighting each inversely with their respective estimated variances. A relatively tractable case is where the representative individual is responsive only to the current estimate: $\hat{\rho}_i = \rho^m_{n-1}$. Referring back to equations (26) and (27), we see that a dynamics is set up according to

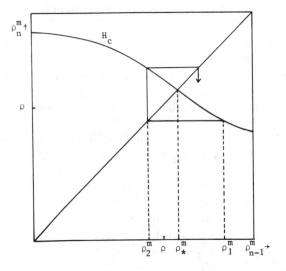

Figure 2.4. Publication and response dynamics.

$$\rho_n^m = H_c(\rho_{n-1}^m).$$

A possible phase plane is sketched as Figure 2.4.

After many iterations of the survey–publish cycle, a stationary point ρ_*^m obtains in the case illustrated. This stationary point is the fixed point of the function $H_c(\cdot)$. In the example of Figure 2.4, the final equilibrium ρ_*^m does not coincide with the true value ρ. It is in fact a little greater, although certainly closer than the initial value ρ_1^m. Suppose, however, that $c = c_*$, the optimum response barrier such that $H_{c_*}(\rho) = \rho$. Then the long-run equilibrium-manifested majority does equal ρ, the true value. Thus the possibility of replication (with publication) has meant that we could do away with the qualifying assumption that expectations are always rational: If one could somehow choose the optimal cost barrier c_*, then in the long run a self-fulfilling state would result in which people would come to achieve rational expectations along with and as a result of estimation by the statistician of the correct value ρ.

We note, finally, that an alternative dynamics involving a reaction function $H_c(\cdot)$ of steeper curvature could develop into a limit cycle rather than true convergence. Conditions that favor this alternative outcome are discussed in Appendix 3; they involve low overall response rates and a high degree of free-riding reactivity.

2.5 Extensions and evaluation

Covariance studies

It is quite possible to conceive of self-selective behavior with respect to correlational studies as well as the kind of simple measurement context considered in the previous section. We saw in Section 2.2 [cf. equation (12)] the general effects of nonneutrality in response on studies involving covariance-based techniques. Consider, for instance, the following model of score and response:

$$y_i = \gamma' x_i + \sum \alpha_k d_{ki} + \zeta_i, \tag{28a}$$

$$i \in R \Leftrightarrow \beta_0 + \sum_k \beta_k d_{ki} + \epsilon_i > 0, \tag{28b}$$

where $i \in R$ indicates that individual i is a respondent. Equation (28a) reproduces (12), the structural equation for the score. Equation (28b) indicates that the threshold parameter $\beta_0' = \beta_0 + \sum_k \beta_k d_{ki}$ depends upon the categories to which individual i belongs. Suppose that for some reason, $\sigma_{\zeta\epsilon} = E\zeta_i\epsilon_i \neq 0$. Utilizing equation (12), we have

$$E(y_i/R) = \gamma' x_i + \sum_k \alpha_k d_{ki} + \sigma_{\zeta\epsilon} \frac{\phi(\beta_0 + \sum_k \beta_k d_{ki})}{\Phi(\beta_0 + \sum_k \beta_k d_{ki})}.$$

In Section 2.2 we explained the bias that arises when $\sigma_{\zeta\epsilon} \neq 0$; we see here that the coefficients α_k of the structural categorical effects will be badly affected.

A role for social information may exist in this type of structure. Suppose that people were aware that a group 1 categorical influence existed. Those in group 1 might be especially unwilling to respond to the survey, whereas other groups would not exhibit a similar sensitivity. More generally, we might specify

$$\beta_k = \beta_k(\hat{\alpha}_1, \hat{\alpha}_2, \ldots, \hat{\alpha}_r), \quad k = 1, 2, \ldots, r.$$

The response dichotomy thus depends upon the perceived covariance parameters. In this way, people's awareness of the purpose or likely result of the survey might mesh with their social information to distort the result of regressions, ANOVAs, or factor analyses.

Evaluation

We have argued in this chapter that response to a survey or poll is not to be treated as a gratuitous or incidental event. It is instead to be treated in the light of a conscious decision, and the same philosophy of decision analysis that characterizes the economics of individual choice may yield some fruitful insights. Thus we have stressed the way in which the costs of response, imputed or otherwise, pecuniary or psychological, are balanced against the likely benefits from the outcome. On the other hand, we have stressed that this is not a simple matter of isolated optimization. A theory of group behavior that is implicit rather than explicit is needed: first, a theory of cohesiveness in the tacit coalition of those of like mind and, second, following the literature of public economics, an empirical hypothesis as to the statistical tendency to depart from the cooperative equilibrium by indulging in free-riding behavior. What results is ultimately an economic theory of response.

The role of social information, interpreted as information about the attitudes of others, is viewed as crucial to this theory of response, just as it has been found empirically useful in explaining instances of widespread nonresponse. Of course, social information does not materialize out of thin air. But man is after all a social animal. We can begin with transmission by word of mouth and other diffuse and informal means of communication. One important source of social information may well be the survey process itself. Indeed, we suggested that a dynamics can arise involving a repeated series of polls and publication at each stage. Individuals are therefore continually updating their information from a centralized source. One could extend this idea and develop a real-time survey scheme, featuring continuous feedback: As responses are received, the results are instantly disseminated while the recording of answers is still in progress. People who have not yet replied may have access to the latest information on how others are thinking, perhaps simply by watching a window on their television screen. Thus a dynamics (cf. Figure 2.4) could develop, perhaps with the possibility of a homeostasis or self-correcting behavior with respect to the self-selection bias.

Survey schemes administered by the media – television stations, radio, newspapers, and the like – have the power to reach a wide audience and to disseminate information very quickly to that audience. It is also true that the media have in recent years increasingly turned to polls and surveys. These are usually of the volunteered response (VR) type, involving unstructured dichotomous questions with the onus very much on the audience to respond. In such circumstances, self-selection phenomenon will assume almost overwhelming importance in the analysis of response. However, as Bowden (1987b) points out, the informational advantages associated with VR schemes administered by the media are such that good possibilities exist for homeostatic effects in real time or over a sequence of polls. Neutralities due to self-selection may therefore cancel out. We could say that the media are able to take advantage of the reactive nature of the sample space to administer on the cheap what may turn out in the long run to be a reasonably veracious investigation, no matter that a single administration considered in isolation may fall well short of such a standard. Note, too, the endogenous view of sampling error. One is accustomed to bias and sampling error as something cemented in place once the sample is drawn. However, one of the consequences of a replication facility with a reactive sample space is that things are not so final; from the viewpoint of self-selection bias, one loses a battle but wins the war.

Appendix 1. Some useful integration results for the normal distribution

A1: $\displaystyle\int_b^a \phi(x; \mu_1, \sigma_1^2)\,\phi(x; \mu_2, \sigma_2^2)\, dx$

$$= \phi(\mu_1; \mu_2, \sigma_1^2 + \sigma_2^2) \int_b^a \phi\left(x; \frac{\mu_1 \sigma_2^2 + \mu_2 \sigma_1^2}{\sigma_1^2 + \sigma_2^2}, \frac{\sigma_1^2 \sigma_2^2}{\sigma_1^2 + \sigma_2^2}\right) dx.$$

Special case:

$$\int_{-\infty}^{\infty} \phi(x; \mu_1, \sigma_1^2)\,\phi(x; \mu_2, \sigma_2^2)\, dx = \phi(\mu_1; \mu_2, \sigma_1^2 + \sigma_2^2).$$

Proof: Completing the square in the exponential term.

A2: $\displaystyle\int_{-\infty}^{\infty} \phi(x; \mu_1, \sigma_1^2)\,\Phi(x; \mu_2, \sigma_2^2)\, dx = \Phi(\mu_1; \mu_2, \sigma_1^2 + \sigma_2^2).$

Proof: Desired integral is equivalent to $\mathrm{prob}(s - x \le 0)$ for two independent normal variates s and x.

A3: $\displaystyle\int_{-\infty}^{\infty} x\phi(x; \mu_1, \sigma_1^2)\,\Phi(x; \mu_2, \sigma_2^2)\, dx$

$$= \mu_1 \Phi(\mu_1; \mu_2, \sigma_1^2 + \sigma_2^2) + \sigma_1^2 \phi(\mu_1, \sigma_1^2 + \sigma_2^2).$$

Proof: Use $x\phi(x; \mu_1, \sigma_1^2) = \mu_1 \phi(x; \mu_1, \sigma_1^2) - \sigma_1^2 (d/dx)\phi(x; \mu_1, \sigma_1^2)$ and integrate by parts using A1 and A2.

A4: $\displaystyle\int_b^a x\phi(x; \mu, \sigma^2)\, dx = \mu[\Phi(a; \mu, \sigma^2) - \Phi(b; \mu, \sigma^2)]$

$$+ \sigma^2[\phi(b; \mu, \sigma^2) - \phi(a; \mu, \sigma^2)].$$

Proof: Straightforward transformations of variables.

For the sake of ready reference we add also the basic differentiation results:

$$\frac{\partial}{\partial\mu}\phi(x;\mu,\sigma^2)=\frac{\tilde{x}}{\sigma}\phi(x;\mu,\sigma^2),\quad \tilde{x}=\frac{x-\mu}{\sigma},$$

$$\frac{\partial}{\partial\mu}\Phi(x;\mu,\sigma^2)=-\phi(x;\mu,\sigma^2),$$

$$\frac{\partial}{\partial\sigma}\phi(x;\mu,\sigma^2)=\frac{1}{\sigma}(\tilde{x}^2-1)\phi(x;\mu,\sigma^2),$$

$$\frac{\partial}{\partial\sigma}\Phi(x;\mu,\sigma^2)=-\tilde{x}\phi(x;\mu,\sigma^2).$$

Appendix 2. The simple cost-censored majority ρ_c as a function of c

From inspection of equation (23), it is apparent that the case $\sigma=1$ will lose no generality. Invert both sides of this equation and use the relationship $1-\Phi(x)=\Phi(-x)$ to obtain

$$\frac{1}{\rho_c}=1+\frac{\Phi(-c-r)}{\Phi(-c+r)}.$$

Differentiate with respect to the cost constant c to obtain

$$\frac{d}{dc}\left(\frac{1}{\rho_c}\right)=[\phi(-c+r)\Phi(-c-r)-\phi(-c-r)\Phi(-c+r)]/\Phi^2(-c+r),$$

from which

$$\frac{d}{d_c}\left(\frac{1}{\rho_c}\right)\leqq 0$$

according to whether

$$\frac{\phi(-c+r)}{\Phi(-c+r)}\lessgtr\frac{\phi(-c-r)}{\Phi(-c-r)}.$$

These are Quenouille functions (see Figure 2.1). The direction of the inequality depends upon the sign of r:

(a) If $r>0$ (meaning that the true vote $\rho>50$ percent), then

$$\frac{\phi(-c+r)}{\Phi(-c+r)}<\frac{\phi(-c-r)}{\Phi(-c-r)}$$

and hence

$$\frac{d}{d_c}\left(\frac{1}{\rho_c}\right)<0.$$

The manifested majority ρ_c is an increasing function of c.

(b) If $r<0$ ($\rho<50$ percent), the reverse conclusion holds.

Appendix 3. The function $H(\hat{\rho})$

From equation (26), we have

$$\rho^m = H_c(\hat{\rho}) = \frac{\rho_c}{1 + [\lambda(\hat{\rho}) - 1][(1 - \rho_c)/\rho_c]}, \tag{i}$$

where

$$\lambda(\hat{\rho}) = \frac{\Phi(\tilde{\beta}_0')}{\Phi(\tilde{\beta}_0)} = \frac{\Phi[\beta_0 + \beta_1(\hat{\rho} - 0.5)]}{\Phi[\beta_0 - \beta_1(\hat{\rho} - 0.5)]} \quad \text{(no offset, i.e., } \beta_2 = 0).$$

Differentiating with respect to $\hat{\rho}$, we have

$$\frac{d\rho^m}{d\hat{\rho}} = H_c'(\hat{\rho}) = -\beta_1 \rho^m (1 - \rho^m) \left[\frac{\phi(\tilde{\beta}_0)}{\Phi(\tilde{\beta}_0)} + \frac{\phi(\tilde{\beta}_0')}{\Phi(\tilde{\beta}_0')} \right]. \tag{ii}$$

The derivative is negative except where ρ^m attains its minimum and maximum values at zero or unity. Since $H_c(\hat{\rho})$ is continuous in $\hat{\rho}$, it follows that the function must be monotonically declining for $\hat{\rho} \in [0, 1]$. In general, the end points $\rho^m = 0, 1$ are never attained. Note also that by rearranging (i) evaluated at its fixed point ρ_*^m, we have

$$\lambda(\rho_*) = \frac{(1 - \rho_*^m)/\rho_*^m}{(1 - \rho_c)/\rho_c},$$

from which it must follow that $\rho_*^m < \rho_c$.

For stability purposes, we may bound the derivative $H_c'(\hat{\rho})$ as follows. Recall (see Figure 2.1) that the Quenouille function ϕ/Φ is monotonically declining and convex to the origin function of its argument. Over the possible range $0 \leq \hat{\rho} \leq 1$, we can use the convexity to bound the term of (ii) in square brackets by $2\phi(\beta_0 - \beta_1/2)/\Phi(\beta_0 - \beta_1/2)$. Then, since $\rho^m(1 - \rho^m) \leq \frac{1}{4}$, it follows that

$$|H_c'(\hat{\rho})| \leq \frac{1}{2}\beta_1 \frac{\phi(\beta_0 - \beta_1/2)}{\Phi(\beta_0 - \beta_1/2)}. \tag{iii}$$

A sufficient condition for dynamic stability is that the right side of (iii) is less than unity. This will certainly be the case if $\beta_0 \geq 0$ and $0 \leq \beta_1 \leq 1$, since $\phi(-0.5)/\Phi(-0.5) = 1.1409$. Figure 2.4 illustrates such a stable dynamics. Over a repeated cycle of VR call and publication of the results, the fixed point ρ_* of the reaction function $H(\cdot)$ is eventually obtained. The possibility of unstable behavior may also be noted. A limit cycle may obtain where β_0 is small (indicating low response rates) and β_1 is large, indicating pronounced tendencies to free-riding behavior in response to informational feedbacks. In this case the estimates cycle repeatedly without settling down.

Returning to comparative statics, we investigate the dependence on the cost constant c of the function $H_c(\hat{\rho})$. We have

$$H_0(\hat{\rho}) = \frac{\rho}{1+[\lambda(\hat{\rho})-1][(1-\rho)/\rho]}.$$

When $\hat{\rho} = 0.5$, note that $\rho^m = \rho$. Since $\rho_c > \rho$, we must have $(1-\rho_c)/\rho_c < (1-\rho)/\rho$. Thus $H_c(\hat{\rho})$ declines more slowly above $\hat{\rho} = \rho_c$ than $H_0(\hat{\rho})$ does above $\hat{\rho} = \rho$ and rises faster below these limits, motivating the curves of Figure 2.3. Note, however, that the comparison would be altered if the free-riding constant c and the free-riding parameter β_1 are mutually dependent. As remarked previously, to stick rigorously to the logic of the free-riding model would imply that both c and β_1 should tend to zero together (if $c = 0$, then no free riding is called for). Thus as $c \to 0$ and β_1 changes simultaneously, then the curve $H_c(\rho)$ tends to the horizontal line $\hat{\rho} = \rho$, reversing the preceding conclusions as to the relative steepness of $H_0(\hat{\rho})$ and $H_c(\hat{\rho})$ for $\hat{\rho} \neq \rho$.

CHAPTER 3

Response and strategic behavior

3.1 Introduction

Consider the following questions, all taken from the 1986 Australian Census:

Q.17: Does the person speak a language other than English *at home*?

Q.18: How well does the person speak English?

Q.24: What is the gross income (including pensions and/or allowances) that the person usually receives each week from all sources?

Q.33: In the main job held last week, how many hours did the person work?

Legal strictures notwithstanding, each of these questions is subject to the suspicion of untruthful responses for strategic reasons. Such questions have to be considered in their social context. Questions 17 and 18, which refer to aspects of migrant assimilation, have to be set against a continued and at times strident debate on immigration and its ethnic and social composition. Households continuing to speak Chinese or Italian at home might well choose not to reveal this. Question 24 should be set against prospective legislation on taxation policy or pension availability and general concern by social reformers with economic inequality as well as the traditional antipodean obsession with "tall poppies." Finally, those in the public service, including academics and schoolteachers, have a motive to overstate their hours of work in question 33 since salaries and other benefits are ultimately tied to the public's perception of the demands on the time of their servants.

Getting people to truthfully reveal their preferences or intentions has long been recognized as a problem in certain fields of economics, in particular in the theory of the provision of public goods. If certain kinds of facility are nonexcludable in their enjoyment, then incentives exist for individuals to dissemble their preferences, perhaps pretending not to want the good, opting out of payment, and subsequently enjoying its provision. This is the classic problem of free riding, and we have earlier drawn attention to its role in the response decision: There, the outcome from the poll or survey is of the nature of a public good, and the individual free rides by not incurring the private costs of a response, relying instead upon the response of others of a similar persuasion. In the present context we have in mind the situation where a response is provided but is of the wrong kind of magnitude, the individual deliberately dissembling true preferences, attitudes, or intentions. Moreover, the scope or incidence of nontruthful revelation is by no means limited to the context of public goods. For instance, one problem with forecasting visitor numbers for major events is that people will often overstate their intentions or likelihood of coming. There may be incentives for them to do so since provision of ancillary services such as additional entertainment, accommodation, or travel may depend upon the publication of favorable forecasts.

Some of the various motives for nontruthful response have received attention in the general statistical literature. One of the more acceptable – from the moral point of view – of these arises from the personally sensitive nature of questions. We have already referred to this in connection with models of response in Chapter 2: One tries to get subjects to reveal their true experiences or attitudes by a randomization device that assures them of complete anonymity. In other circumstances, anonymity may be less of a problem; one is concerned more with downright lying or dissimulation for strategic purposes. Thus a more common approach in written questionnaires is to insert trick questions or list some nonexistent alternatives among a set of choices, replies to which will determine whether the respondent is being completely truthful. If the respondent "fails" the truth test, even in a minor way, the usual recommendation is to discard the response completely, a practice commented on in Section 3.4. A general problem with such procedures is that they do not positively encourage respondents to tell the truth. Moreover, they do not distinguish minor falsehoods, which may stem from nothing more reprehensible than guessing out of simple forgetfulness, from a systematic desire to mislead. It would seem that a superior procedure could be twofold: (a) some device to encourage people to tell the truth and (b) a test, presumably based upon that device, for whether a substantial degree of untruthfulness remains, that is, whether or to what extent the encouragement has worked. So far as the econometric literature is concerned, the problem of truthful revelation has received only the most passing of mentions. Morgenstern (1963), in his classic study of the accuracy of economic observations, notes very early on the potential seriousness of the problem of strategic behavior but does not develop the issue any further. One is reminded of the old joke about the Scottish preacher who, having met the devil, "looked him firmly in the eye and passed on." The lack of formal treatment in the econometric literature seems surprising, for as noted previously, considerable attention has been devoted to the problem in general economic theory.

It could, of course, be remarked that if one suspects nontruthful revelation, then it might be better to reject the direct approach of actually asking subjects in favor of an indirect approach to try to deduce from their observed actions in related decisions their intentions or predispositions in the substantive matter. There is indeed a substantial empirical literature on such approaches in such areas as natural resource economics or the study of pollution or other externalities. The general difficulty with such techniques is simply that they are indirect; a host of influences, interpretations, and dubious maintained hypotheses may reflect adversely on the claimed link between the indirect measure and the variable of primary interest. In many instances, therefore, one is forced to some sort of reliance upon a direct approach to subjects. This said, the existence of possible indirect measures may be viewed in the light of corroborating or noncorroborating information. In other words, indirect information may be used to validate the direct information. From the statistical point of view, true attitudes, intentions, or a willingness to pay may constitute a latent variable, and anything that might have a bearing on identifying the probability density of the relevant latent variables is useful whether it be manifested values – what subjects report – or some indirect measure or proxy for the true variables.

In this chapter we shall review some of the problems of encouraging and testing for truthful revelation. In general, strategic behavior can take one of two principal forms. The first is nonresponse, in the knowledge of the biasing effects of nonresponse by one's peer group. In many respects this is the simplest form of behavior to analyze statistically, and Section 3.2 deals with such problems. A second reaction on the part of the subject is to respond but to lie or dissimulate out of strategic motives. Sections 3.3–3.5 deal with this aspect. It is convenient to organize this discussion in terms of a roughly decreasing amount of information concerning the probability of truthful revelation. The best information that one could hope for would be data available simultaneously on both the true preferences or intentions and the manifested values for at least one out of a series of similar experiments. This case is dealt with in Section 3.3, where we utilize data from a now famous experiment in the empirical application of the theory of public goods, namely, the Horicon goosehunter experiment. Section 3.4 considers the case where a discriminatory device can be utilized according to which some respondents can be held to tell the truth; one then tests for residual untruthful behavior with respect to the remainder. The most pessimistic case, where at best indirect measures or proxy variables are available, is dealt with in Section 3.5. Section 3.6 compares, in a sense, the outcome of Section 3.2 (nonresponse) with the sections immediately following. If there is pressure on a subject to act strategically, he or she may elect to lie or else to simply not respond. Bias will arise in both cases, in the first from untruthfulness, in the second from selectivity considerations. The question is which of the two outcomes produces the lesser bias. This is a matter of some importance for the design of national censuses: In this guise, the question is whether a given question should be made compulsory or whether subjects should be given the option of choosing not to respond to the item.

3.2   Strategic nonresponse

Probably the simplest – and morally least demanding – kind of strategic behavior is simply to refuse to respond or to delay indefinitely response to a request for information where it is perceived that supplying that information might damage the subject's interests or those of the peer group. For example, in income or wealth surveys, a material disincentive to disclosure might arise on the part of wealthier subjects. If it becomes evident that the distribution of income or wealth has recently resulted in a larger number of millionaires, public perceptions of income inequality may well lead to demands for more progressive tax scales, the penalizing of capital gains or even the imposition of wealth taxes. Thus even if a given subject has no objection on general grounds of privacy to the individual disclosure of wealth, it may well be perceived to be in the interests of the peer group and therefore of the subject not to respond. Notice the kind of argument here, one that we have used in the last chapter: Each individual realizes that personal disclosure (provided he or she is not a J. Paul Getty!) will have little effect on the aggregate outcome. Collectively, however, this is not so, and it behooves each individual in the interests of the peer group to behave in a certain way. No express collusion need be present. The motive force is simply a realization that everybody else in the implied peer group (the wealthy, say) will be thinking the same way. Arising out of this is an implicit coalitional imperative that may outweigh the kind of morality associated with individual or a broader social conscience. A refusal to respond to a question on income or wealth may be viewed as the easiest way of resolving the tension between the coalitional imperative and the demands of conscience as to truthfulness.

From the point of view of the statistician, the effects of such refusals are reasonably predictable and may be relatively easy to model. Following along the lines of the discriminant models of response of Chapter 2, let us suppose that individual i is characterized by a pair w_i, the variable of primary interest, and a zero-mean random variable ϵ_i, reflecting the individual's tendency to nonresponse, "conscience" say. Imagine that we are surveying wealth or income levels, both of which may be reasonably described in terms of the lognormal distribution. Thus if W_i is wealth,

$w_i = \log W_i$ is normally distributed. We shall assume that individual i will default, that is, refuse to respond, if and only if

$$\beta_0 - \beta_1(w_i - \mu) + \epsilon_i < 0, \tag{1}$$

where $\mu = Ew_i$. If W_i is lognormal, then μ locates (see Section 3.3) the median point M of the wealth distribution. Thus the threshold β_0 will be lowered if $w_i \gg \mu$, that is, if an individual perceives that he (or she) is well above the median wealth for the community. Conversely, if an individual perceives that he is poor, he will be anxious for the community to know that there are people like him and he will be more willing to respond. The latter is of course a particular supposition. Other motives may be at work, for instance, the embarrassment of some at having to report low incomes, which may be a matter of personal sensitivity. We note in passing the importance of social information: The parameter μ as it appears in the preceding decision dichotomy is in reality an estimate derived from some prior source of information available to the individual. Such response decision models therefore have a very close relationship with the decision models of Chapter 2, and the difference is really only a matter of motivation.

Given the censoring mechanism (1), we may easily derive the manifested distribution of wealth or incomes, that is, the density for those who do actually respond. Denote by R the event of a response. Then the joint density of w and the event R is given by

$$p(w, R) = \int_{-\beta_0 + \beta_1(w-\mu)}^{\infty} p(w, \epsilon) \, d\epsilon. \tag{2}$$

Suppose now that w, ϵ are independent and normal. From (1) we may evidently normalize the variance of ϵ to be unity with no loss of generality, serving as an identifiability requirement on the parameters β_0, β_1. Recall from Chapter 2 the notation $\Phi(x)$ for the unit normal distribution function with $\Phi(x; \mu, \sigma^2)$ the distribution function for general mean μ and variance σ^2 and corresponding notation for the density functions ϕ. From (2) it follows that

$$p(w, R) = \phi(w; \mu, \sigma^2) \Phi[\beta_0 - \beta_1(w - \mu)]. \tag{3}$$

Also, the probability of a response is given by

$$p(R) = p\{\beta_0 - \beta_1(w_i - \mu) + \epsilon_i > 0\}.$$

Since the term $\epsilon_i - \beta_1(w_i - \mu) + \beta_0 \sim N(\beta_0; 1 + \beta_1^2 \sigma^2)$, where $\sigma^2 = \text{Var}(w)$, the preceding probability is given by

$$p(R) = \Phi(\beta_0; 0, 1 + \beta_1^2 \sigma^2). \tag{4}$$

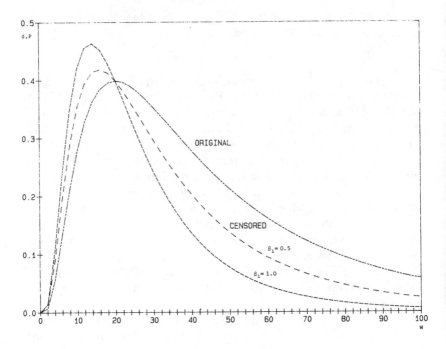

Figure 3.1. Effect of strategic response censoring.

Finally, dividing (3) by (4), we obtain the desired conditional density

$$p(w/R) = \frac{\phi(w; \mu, \sigma^2)\,\Phi[\beta_0 - \beta_1(w - \mu)]}{\Phi(\beta_0; 0, 1 + \beta_1^2\sigma^2)}$$

$$= \lambda(w)\,\phi(w; \mu, \sigma^2), \quad \text{say.} \tag{5}$$

Thus the density $p(w/R)$ of manifested responses differs from the true underlying density $\phi(w; \mu, \sigma^2)$ by a distortion factor $\lambda(w)$. We may write

$$\lambda(w) = \frac{\Phi[\beta_0 - \beta_1(w - \mu)]}{\Phi[\beta_0/\sqrt{1 + \beta_1^2\sigma^2}]}.$$

We observe that even if $w = \mu$, distortion arises at this point from the presence of the parameter β_1 except in the particular case $\beta_0 = 0$. Figure 3.1 plots the original lognormal density of wealth W and the corresponding manifested density $p(W/R)$ among the respondents. The parameter values are $\beta_0 = 0$ (hence a 50 percent response rate) and $\beta_1 = 0.5$ with income distribution parameters $\sigma = 0.858$ and a median income of \$20,000. The distribution has been bodily shifted to the left, and the degree of skewness has diminished. Notice also that the manifested mean has evidently declined.

Indeed, a correction is now necessary if it is desired to measure the central tendency of the true distribution. With a lognormal distribution there is room for debate about which measure of central tendency is most appropriate (see also Section 3.3). For our present purposes we shall take this as $\mu = E \log W$; $M = \exp(\mu)$ will then give the median of the W distribution. We may derive some insight into the nature of the necessary correction by considering the normal maximum-likelihood equation for the estimation of μ from a sample $w_1, w_2, \ldots, w_n$ of size n of (log) wealth figures. Considering the density (5), the log-likelihood function from an independent sample of size n is

$$\log L_R = \sum_{i \in R} \log \phi(w_i; \mu, \sigma^2) + \sum_{i \in R} \log \Phi(\beta_0 - \beta_1(w_i - \mu))$$

$$- n_R \log \Phi\left(\frac{\beta_0}{\sqrt{1 + \beta_1^2 \sigma^2}}\right). \tag{6}$$

We ought to be clear about the basis for this likelihood function: A sample of size n is drawn (e.g., n questionnaires administered) from which n_R people respond. The likelihood function (6) is then formulated from the observations w_i, $i \in R$, on these respondents so that it applies to independent sampling drawn from the conditional density (5). Taking the derivative with respect to the desired parameter μ and setting it equal to zero given the normal equation,

$$\mu = \bar{w}_R + \beta_1 \sigma^2 \frac{1}{n_R} \sum_{i \in R} \frac{\phi[\beta_0 - \beta_1(w_i - \mu)]}{\Phi[\beta_0 - \beta_1(w_i - \mu)]}, \tag{7}$$

where $\bar{w}_R$ is the recorded mean (log) wealth from among those who reply. Equation (7) shows that this recorded mean will be an underestimate of the true mean μ.

We can approximate the extent of the underestimate by replacing the sum $1/n_R \sum_i \phi/\Phi$ on the right side of (7) by its expectation, namely,

$$E\left(\frac{\phi[\beta_0 - \beta_1(w_i - \mu)]}{\Phi[\beta_0 - \beta_1(w_i - \mu)]} \Big| R\right). \tag{8}$$

The expectation (8) may be evaluated using the conditional density (5). The factor $\Phi[\beta_0 - \beta_1(w - \mu)]$ cancels, giving the required expectation as the integral

$$\frac{1}{\Phi(\beta_0; 0, 1 + \beta_1^2 \sigma^2)} \int_{-\infty}^{\infty} \phi(w; \mu, \sigma^2) \phi[\beta_0 - \beta_1(w - \mu)] \, dw.$$

This integral may be solved by using rule A1 of Appendix 1 to Chapter 2. The result is

$$E\left(\frac{\phi[\beta_0-\beta_1(w-\mu)]}{\Phi[\beta_0-\beta_1(w-\mu)]}\middle|R\right) = \frac{\phi(\beta_0;0,1+\beta_1^2\sigma^2)}{\Phi(\beta_0;0,1+\beta_1^2\sigma^2)}. \tag{9}$$

Finally, inserting the expectation (9) in place of the sum on the right side of equation (7), we obtain

$$\mu \simeq \bar{w}_R + \beta_1\sigma\frac{\phi[\beta_0/\sqrt{1+\beta_1^2\sigma^2}]}{\Phi[\beta_0/\sqrt{1+\beta_1^2\sigma^2}]}, \tag{10}$$

the approximation becoming exact with probability 1 as the sample size n becomes large. We observe that the size of the needed correction to the manifested mean $\bar{w}_R$ depends almost linearly upon the discriminant coefficient β_1 of (1).

We recall from Section 2.2 that the function ϕ/Φ is a monotonically declining, convex function of its argument. If the response threshold β_0 is negative, the value of this term in expression (10) can therefore also become large. The parameter β_0 governs the general level of response to the survey: If $\beta_0 < 0$, the response rate drops to less than 50 percent. The implication is that a survey that attracts a low response rate is particularly vulnerable to strategic nonresponse.

If strategic nonresponse is considered likely and if in addition the observed response rate is not high, a means of correction for strategic nonresponse has to be found. In most cases this will involve an attempt to actually model the response decision, perhaps along lines similar to the discriminant mechanism (1). If the latter is used, the maximum-likelihood estimator appears to be identified, although we have not checked in detail the concavity and other properties of the likelihood function (6).

Correlational studies

So far we have considered strategic nonresponse where the censoring is a simple matter of distortionary effects upon a variable of primary interest. In the preceding example, the problem was to measure some characteristic of the distribution of the $\{w_i\}$, and censoring consisted of an operation limiting the observations on the w_i. However, it is also conceivable that strategic nonresponse can affect the outcome of correlational studies. Consider, for example, the mathematical girls of Chapter 2. In that example we saw that if the fathers of more able daughters were less likely to respond, then one ended up with an apparent finding that daughters from more liberal fathers are superior in mathematics even though the underlying reality might be that the liberality of the home environment was immaterial. Now the more liberal and by assumption able fathers (of more able girls) might be able enough to see the consequences of their nonresponse. If they wished to encourage liberality in any way, then it could well be that nonresponse would be a perfectly rational action on their part.

As this example shows, however, it may take a fair amount of skill and understanding of statistics to be able to foresee the biasing effect of a response decision. In this respect one can contrast the correlational case with simple response censoring as discussed in the preceding, where the consequences of nonresponse are reasonably predictable to the subjects as well as to the statistician. Thus one could well argue that the informational requirements for strategic nonresponse in correlational studies are likely to be rather demanding. Still, the possibility must be noted.

We shall return in Section 3.6 to the problem of strategic nonresponse, treating it there as a problem in the design of censuses. In the next sections we consider what happens when people do respond but for strategic purposes may respond untruthfully. In other words we turn away from the fact of their response to the legitimacy of the volunteered information given a response.

3.3   Strategic revelation: direct testing

Suppose that individuals have responded to a survey. How can we be sure that the responses are truthful as to their content? In this and the following section we turn to the question of testing and, where applicable, to the encouragement of truthful revelation. The simplest or most unequivocal tests are available on the occasions where a direct comparison is available between true attitudes or intentions and those actually manifested. Accordingly, we shall begin in this section by supposing that data are available that allow a direct comparison between revelations on the one hand and true preferences or intentions on the other even though two different samples of individuals may be involved. Of course, it could well be asked why, if data on true preferences or intentions are available, one should bother with a second sample of manifest revelations. Two reasons come to mind: (a) The study might be one in which truthfulness in general is being investigated and the results as to truthfulness or otherwise are presumed to extend to other inquiries in the same field. (b) Obtaining the true figures may be costly. But a larger sample or census relying upon manifest revelations can be validated by testing against a smaller sample for which the true data are available. Thus although the availability of a direct comparison must be regarded as a relatively infrequent occurrence, it is useful for these and other reasons to consider methodological aspects in the context of an actual example.

The example to be considered in what follows is quite representative of a class of problems involving willingness to pay for a public good or facility. Suppose that an individual i is given the option of participating in a given facility. Let $u_i(\mathbf{p}, y_i; 1)$ denote the individual's indirect utility function given prices $\mathbf{p}$ and income y_i given that he or she participates and $u_i(\mathbf{p}, y_i; 0)$ the individual's utility when there is no participation. Willingness to pay for participation in the program or facility is defined as c_i, where

$$u_i(\mathbf{p}, y_i - c_i; 1) = u_i(\mathbf{p}, y_i; 0).$$

The magnitude c_i is referred to as the compensating variation. The problem is to find the distribution $F(c)$ of willingness to pay $\{c_i\}$ over different individuals or some appropriate summary measure thereof. A difficulty is that if the facility is a public good, meaning that nobody can be excluded from its enjoyment, then it may pay individuals not to manifest their true c_i but either a higher or lower figure depending upon arrangements for the financing of the facility. This is the well-known free-rider problem. The figure resulting from simply asking people their willingness to pay is often called contingent valuation or hypothetical valuation depending upon the particular context. An alternative to willingness to pay that is more appropriate in some contexts is the willingness to accept compensation, defined by

$$u_i(\mathbf{p}, y_i; 1) = u_i(\mathbf{p}, y_i + c_i; 0),$$

which corresponds to the equivalent variation rather than the compensating variation. Under certain circumstances, notably the absence of an income effect, the two are equal. Contingent or hypothetical valuations can also apply to the equivalent variation, and the same problem of revelation arises.

The specific example we shall consider comes from the general area of natural resource management, namely, the well-known Wisconsin goose-hunter study of Bishop and Heberlein (1979) and Bishop, Heberlein, and Kealy (1983). The reader may refer to these studies for full details, but the salient features so far as our purposes are concerned are the following. Goose hunters were approached with offers of money in exchange for their permits so that willingness to accept compensation is involved. A larger sample of 353 hunters was approached with a hypothetical offer of a stated amount of money. A second sample of 237 permit holders were actually sent checks with instructions to return either the check or

Table 3.1. *The Wisconsin goose-hunter experiment*

Amounts offered ($)	Cash offers		Hypothetical offers	
	Offers made	Number accepted	Offers made	Number accepted
1	31	0	15	0
5	29	3	17	2
10	27	6	20	3
20	25	7	20	4
30	23	9	23	9
40	21	13	27	14
50	19	17	30	13
75	17	12	34	13
100	15	11	36	20
150	15	14	41	30
200	15	13	43	24
Totals	237		306	

Source: Data courtesy of Richard C. Bishop.

the permit. The wordings of the two offers, real and hypothetical, were made as closely similar as possible. Table 3.1 summarizes the offers and the outcomes.

The principal aim of the experiment was to test whether the hypothetical valuations (HV) and actual valuations (AV) are the same, that is, the identity of the two distributions $\{c_i^m\}$ and $\{c_i\}$, where c_i is the actual valuation and c_i^m the manifest or hypothetical valuation. Other points of interest also arise. For instance, assuming that an empirical distribution of the $\{c_i\}$ has been established, the question arises as to the best or most appropriate summary measures, especially with respect to central tendency. Another question concerns the optimal design of an experiment aimed at establishing the distribution $F(c)$ of summary measures thereof.

Considering first the substantive question, let us assume that a preassigned set of offers d_i has been delivered either hypothetically or in reality, one to each individual. From their responses as to acceptance or rejection, we have to find the empirical distribution functions F_{HV} and F_{AV} and test for their equality.

Such a problem has not, to this author's knowledge, been considered in quite this way in the general statistical literature. Gnedenko and Korolyuk (1951/61) and others have considered the problem of testing the equality of two empirical distribution functions. However, the empirical distribution functions are obtained in the first place by means of the estimation procedure summarized by

$$F_n(c) = \frac{1}{n} \sum_{i=1}^{n} \vartheta(c_i \leq c)$$

where $\vartheta(\cdot)$ is the set indicator function with value unity if the indicated event occurs. In other words, $F_n(c)$ is the relative frequency of those c_i that are less than or equal to the given value c. The difficulty with the sampling theory of Kolmogorov–Smirnov tests, of which the Gnedenko-Korolyuk statistic is an example, is that the c_i must be directly observable and are also to be regarded as a random sample drawn from the underlying distribution function F (see Csáki, 1984). Neither of these contingencies is true in the present instance. A somewhat closer analogy occurs in the statistical theory of survival analysis, where the reservation price c_i would correspond to the time of death of individual i. In the censored survival model (see Miller, 1981) one observes the variables $\delta_i = \vartheta(d_i \leq c_i)$ and $h_i = \min(d_i, c_i)$; in other words, one observes whether individual i rejected ($\delta_i = 1$) or accepted ($\delta_i = 0$) the offer plus the minimum of the offer d_i and reservation price c_i. The difficulty here is again that actual reservation prices are never observed. The observations are δ_i and d_i. In summary, the existing nonparametric statistical literature, although suggestive in certain aspects, is not directly applicable.

Turning to parametric approaches, Bishop et al. (1983) in their own analysis utilize a logit model. Let π_i be the probability that individual i accepts the offer d_i. They begin by setting up a logit model,

$$\log\left(\frac{\pi_i}{1-\pi_i}\right) = \beta_0 + \beta_1 d_i + \beta'_2 \mathbf{X}_i + \epsilon_i, \tag{11}$$

where $\mathbf{X}_i$ is a vector of additional explanatory variables such as income and other hunter characteristics and ϵ_i a zero-mean random disturbance. Empirically, the probabilities π_i are established from the cells in Table 3.1 as the proportion of people responding at each d_i. Abstracting from the variables $\mathbf{X}_i$, the fitted value π as a function of d is interpreted as the probability that a hunter chosen at random will agree to sell at a given offer d. The desired distribution F of the $\{c_i\}$ is then estimated as $F(d) = \pi(d)$, and from this the desired summary statistics of F can be obtained.

One of the difficulties with such an approach is the implied lack of hierarchy, in that each cell (of Table 3.1) is essentially treated as a separate entry or observation in the regression. No reference is made to the fact that if rejection by an individual occurs at offer d_2, then if offered $d_1 > d_2$, the same individual would also reject d_1 with certainty. The logit model does not, therefore, use all the information that is available. Another way of making essentially the same point is to note that in estimating equation (11), we are estimating a density rather than a distribution function. Apart from the loss in information, the dependent variables themselves depend upon estimates $\hat{\pi}_i$, and this in turn places limits on the number of different d_i values that can be examined for a given overall sample size. In summary, although the logit model represents a sensible way of proceeding, it does have efficiency limitations.

We suggest the alternative approach of modeling more directly the decision process with respect to the acceptance or rejection of an offer d_i. Given the economics of the problem, the probability structure is quite simple: Given an offer d_i, individual i will accept (A) if $c_i \leq d_i$ and reject (R) if $c_i > d_i$. Thus, given a set of offers $\{d_i\}$ presented to a randomly selected sample of individuals, the likelihood function of the sample is

$$\prod_{i \in A} F(d_i) \prod_{i \in R} [1 - F(d_i)],$$

where $F(c)$ is the distribution function of the variations c_i. It is evident from this likelihood function and indeed the structure of the problem that this is a probit type of situation. All that remains is to choose candidates for the distribution function F. Since the dependent variable (i.e., the 0–1 probit dichotomy) is the same for all such candidates, the resulting likelihood values provide a ready means of model selection. Many possible candidates for the distribution function exist, such as the normal, lognormal, and various members of the extreme-value family such as the Weibull (see, e.g., Bury, 1975).

The normal and lognormal are especially convenient choices for $F(c)$ since probit programs based on the normal distribution are readily available. Considering first the normal case, we may write $c_i = \gamma + \epsilon_i$ with $\gamma = Ec_i$ and Var $\epsilon_i = \sigma_\epsilon^2$. Dividing through the preceding inequalities by σ_ϵ, the model can be written as

$$\text{individual } i \text{ accepts } (i \in A) \Leftrightarrow \tilde{\epsilon}_i \leq \beta_0 + \beta_1 d_i,$$
$$i \text{ rejects } (i \in R) \quad \text{otherwise,} \tag{12}$$

where Var $\tilde{\epsilon}_i = 1$ and $\beta_0 = -\gamma/\sigma_\epsilon$, $\beta_1 = 1/\sigma_\epsilon$. The probit [in the terminology of Finney (1977)] is $I = \beta_0 + \beta_1 d_i$ and standard probit programs apply. Given resulting estimates $\hat{\beta}_0$ and $\hat{\beta}_1$, we recover γ as $\hat{\gamma} = -\hat{\beta}_0/\hat{\beta}_1$ and $\hat{\sigma}_\epsilon = 1/\hat{\beta}_1$.

Comparisons between AV and HV, the actual and hypothetical valuations, are based in the first instance on the corresponding values of γ, the distribution means. In order to carry out appropriate tests of significance, we first need Var($\hat{\gamma}$). Following the usual asymptotic arguments, this can be obtained as

$$\text{Var}(\hat{\gamma}) = \frac{1}{\hat{\beta}_1^2} \text{Var } \hat{\beta}_0 + \hat{\gamma}^2 \text{Var } \hat{\beta}_1 + 2\hat{\gamma} \text{ Cov}(\hat{\beta}_0, \hat{\beta}_1).$$

Thus one will have to ask the probit program to print out the estimated asymptotic covariance matrix of $\hat{\beta}_0$ and $\hat{\beta}_1$. Assuming that the samples used to obtain $\hat{\gamma}_{AV}$ and $\hat{\gamma}_{HV}$ are independent, the test statistic is simply $(\hat{\gamma}_{HV} - \hat{\gamma}_{AV})/\sqrt{\text{Var } \hat{\gamma}_{HV} + \text{Var } \hat{\gamma}_{AV}}$, which is asymptotically unit normal.

The valuations AV and HV, being interpretable as equivalent variations, evidently have an income dimension. This being the case, it would seem advisable to fit as an alternative a lognormal probit model. This can be done very simply. If $F(c)$ is lognormal, then the distribution of log c_i is normal, and the relationships (12) are almost unchanged in form. The exception is that d_i must be replaced by log d_i (the switch is based upon log $c_i \leq$ log d_i, which is identical to $c_i \leq d_i$ but utilizes the normality of log c_i).

Introduction of the lognormal raises the rather interesting question of which measure of central tendency to compute. From the preceding development, when the lognormal model is fitted, we have $\gamma = E$ log c_i. Thus $m = e^{\gamma}$ (antilog γ) will yield the median rather than the mean of the distribution $F(c)$. If the mean μ is required, we have

$$\mu = Ec_i = E \exp(\log c_i) = \exp(\gamma + \tfrac{1}{2}\sigma_\epsilon^2)$$

in view of the normality of log c_i. In general, one could expect that $\mu \gg m$ from the skewness of the lognormal. It could be argued that the correct measure of central tendency is in fact the median m, for this represents the tie point in an implied vote on the adoption of any policy measure based upon the equivalent or compensating variations.

If desired, further concomitant variables $\mathbf{X}_i$ of hunter characteristics could be incorporated. In such cases, the variations c_i may be written $c_i = c_i(\epsilon_i, \mathbf{X}_i)$, and corresponding to dichotomy (12), we have

$$i \in A \Leftrightarrow \bar{\epsilon}_i \leq \beta_0 + \beta_1 d_i + \beta_2' \mathbf{X}_i$$

and $i \in R$ otherwise. The probit I is correspondingly extended to incorporate $\mathbf{X}_i$. Whether one wishes to incorporate these extra variables depends upon the purpose of the exercise. In the present instance, where the concern is primarily with measures of average willingness to pay or accept compensation, a case can be made for simply absorbing, as it were, the effects of the $\mathbf{X}_i$ variables in the overall distribution of the variations $\{c_i\}$. In choosing candidates for the distribution $F(c)$, one bears in mind the distributional influences exerted by presumed underlying $\mathbf{X}_i$ variables.

To illustrate all the preceding considerations, we fitted normal and lognormal probit models to the data of Table 3.1. The package used was

Table 3.2. *Probit fits for the distributions F and significance testing*

	F normal		F lognormal	
	AV	HV	AV	HV
I. Basic probit fits				
Number of observations	237	306	237	306
Average log-likelihood				
($1/n \times$ log-likelihood)	−0.5253	−0.6327	−0.4572	−0.6045
$\hat{\beta}_0$	−0.863	−0.697	−2.578	−1.968
	(−6.864)	(−5.730)	(−7.741)	(−6.356)
$\hat{\beta}_1$	0.0158	0.0063	0.752	0.451
	(7.350)	(5.489)	(8.108)	(6.160)
II. Derived statistics	$[\gamma = E(c_i)]$		$[\gamma = E(\log c_i)]$	
$\hat{\gamma}$	54.44	110.86	3.428	4.360
Var $\hat{\gamma}$	37.132	163.523	0.0169	0.0301
Distribution of c_i				
Mean (μ)	54.44	110.86	74.69	909.47
Median	54.44	110.86	30.83	78.25
III. Significance test on γ				
(H_0: $\gamma_{HV} = \gamma_{AV}$, H_1: $\gamma_{HV} > \gamma_{AV}$)	$Z = 3.983$		$Z = 4.293$	

Note: Asymptotic t values are in parentheses.

SHAZAM (White, 1978), and the PROBIT routine was executed by the author on a DEC-10 machine located at the Western Australian Regional Computing Centre. The results are summarized in Table 3.2. It will be observed that the lognormal model is to be preferred to the normal model since it is associated with higher likelihood values and sharper significance levels for all parameters. The point referred to in the preceding concerning the relative merits of the mean and median as summary measures of central tendency is vividly illustrated by the hypothetical mean of $909. Evidently there is a much longer tail on the hypothetical variations than on the distribution of the actual variations. This is a finding of some interest, although we do not speculate here as to what might produce it. The null hypothesis of equality between AV and HV is decisively rejected regardless of the model.

As remarked earlier, we have taken as given the sequence d_i of offers as presented in Table 3.1. However, since the covariance matrix of the various estimators depends upon the input sequence d_i, a question of interest concerns the optimal design of such a sequence of offers. The asymptotic covariance matrix is as follows. Suppose that the input sequence d_i is to obey some preassigned empirical distribution function F_d. For an arbitrary mean θ and variance σ^2, we recall the normal hazard function defined as

$$h(x; \theta, \sigma^2) = \phi(x; \theta, \sigma^2)/[1 - \Phi(x; \theta, \sigma^2)],$$

where $\phi(x; \theta, \sigma^2)$ denotes the normal density at x and $\Phi(\cdot)$ the corresponding distribution function. Define the function

$$H(x; \theta, \sigma^2) = h(x; \theta, \sigma^2) h(-x; \theta, \sigma^2).$$

Then by using standard asymptotic arguments based upon the strong consistency of probit estimators, we obtain the asymptotic information matrix I as

$$I = -E_d H(d; \gamma, \sigma_\epsilon^2) \begin{bmatrix} 1 & (d-\gamma)/2\sigma_\epsilon^4 \\ (d-\gamma)/2\sigma_\epsilon^4 & (d-\gamma)^2/4\sigma_\epsilon^8 \end{bmatrix},$$

where the expectation is taken over F_d. Since the asymptotic information matrix [of $\sqrt{n}(\hat{\gamma} - \gamma, \hat{\sigma}_\epsilon^2 - \sigma_\epsilon^2)$] is $-I^{-1}$, the objective is to make the elements of I, especially the diagonal elements, as large as possible. It is easy to show that the optimal choice for the mean of the input distribution F_d is just γ, the desired mean. We conjecture that the design problem has a Bayesian solution, where a prior on γ and σ_ϵ^2 can be employed to design an optimal input distribution F_d. In the meantime the information matrix as given in the preceding could be utilized to check out the appropriateness of different proposed input distributions according to the researcher's own prior ideas of the most likely values of γ and σ_ϵ^2.

Discussion

Quite obviously, considerable differences exist between the actual distribution of acceptable cash offers and the manifest distribution, or as we have called it, the hypothetical valuation distribution. It is difficult not to ascribe much, at least of this difference, to strategic behavior since the motives are so obvious. This example should be sufficient to dispel any lingering doubts that nontruthful revelation is a significant problem in empirical social science.

Nevertheless we should not jump to the conclusion that strategic motives account for *all* of the difference between the true and manifested figures. Some authors in this literature have referred to the possibility of a "hypothetical bias" that arises simply because individuals are constitutionally unable to make up their minds as to their valuations unless and until they are confronted by an actual decision exigency, in the preceding instance with hard cold cash. There is much to this idea, as any house hunter will attest; one conceives a figure that one is prepared to pay for a house, but any such figure has a way of becoming flexible when one faces up to the actual bargaining or auction process.

3.4   Strategic revelation: discriminatory testing

In most circumstances, the statistician will not have access to a sample of people whose replies can be regarded as categorically accurate or truthful. It would be useful to arrange some device that will assist in distinguishing truthful from untruthful responses even if only in the probabilistic sense that having replied in a certain way, a respondent is considered more rather than less likely to be revealing intentions or preferences accurately. It would also be useful if such a device positively encouraged people to tell the truth. The inspiration for the encouragement aspect comes again from public economics, this time in a body of work concerned with devices to ensure truthful revelation as an action in the individual's own best interests. One line of development originating with Lerner and Vickrey but applied and developed by Clarke (1971, 1972), Groves (1973), and subsequent authors imposes a tax on the individual according to the shift in supply of the public good to others that his or her demand occasions. A second class of procedures due to Thompson (1966) relies on an insurance scheme whereby people can insure against a win of the less favored alternative; the odds on a win or loss are announced by the government, which chooses that proposal for which the total of all insurance premiums received is minimal. A brief summary of two of these schemes is given for the reader's convenience in Appendix 1 at the end of this chapter. For a more detailed account see Mueller (1979, especially ch. 4). In all cases the schemes are designed to ensure that telling the truth is the dominant individual strategy in the implied game between the decision maker and the public.

A common criticism of such devices is that they are not terribly operational, in the sense that their administrative and informational requirements or assumptions are demanding, to say the least. It might however be possible to define less ambitious schemes that while being less perfect in screening out untruthful behavior nevertheless provide at least some encouragement to tell the truth and moreover enable probability assessments to be made as to whether residual untruthfulness remains. Thus in addition to the encouragement aspect, such a device would enable statistical discriminant analysis. In what follows we shall describe one particular approach to this problem. As we shall later remark, however, one could conjure up alternative discriminatory devices depending on the context, and the domain of the discriminant analysis described is correspondingly not limited to this particular scheme.

To fix ideas, it will be helpful to work in terms of a particular example. The statistician or forecaster is to conduct a survey with the object of forecasting visitor numbers to some major forthcoming event (expos, olympics, America's Cup, etc.). To this end he or she asks respondents for the likelihood π_i (on a scale of 1–10 or zero to unity) that they will attend the event. The researcher's task is to estimate the average probability of attendance $\pi = E\pi_i$ over the subject population, from which a forecast of visitor numbers can be derived.

As remarked in Section 3.1, a potential visitor to a major event may think that a higher published estimate $\hat{\pi}$ will draw forth additional supplies of accommodation, entertainment, or travel services associated with the event. Although it is realized that individual intentions carry only a miniscule weight in the aggregate, he or she will also realize that many others will think similarly so that implicitly the respondent is joining in a coalition of common interest playing against the forecaster, or beyond, the suppliers of services. Thus the individual's probability as manifested to the statistician is not the true probability π_i but $\pi_i^m \geq \pi_i$. In the aggregate this will yield an estimate $\pi^m > \pi$. So far as the individual is concerned, there is an expectation of benefit from the additional supply response if he or she does end up attending. In case of nonattendance, the individual will be no worse off. It might also be remarked that additional motives also exist for overstating one's intentions, such as approval seeking if the survey interview is of the face-to-face kind. This type of behavior cannot be described as strategic but evokes the same problem with respect to the manifestation of intentions.

In order to encourage the truthful revelation of intentions, the statistician might well consider some of the ideas mentioned in the preceding in connection with the public economics literature. Of the various ways of promoting truthful revelation, an insurance arrangement seems most promising for the kind of context considered here. The idea is to convince the respondent of the benefit from buying insurance against some adverse possibility associated with the event in question. Thus if a world fair is the event concerned, the respondent could be offered the opportunity to insure against the availability of accommodation of his or her choice or for the opportunity to purchase tickets for designated popular events. The insurance premium could be either refundable against the eventual purchase if he or she does come or not refundable in any event. In the former case, the organizers of the event would have to bear the cost of the premiums as a deduction on the purchase price (an expense that may be well recouped from the benefits of more accurate forecasting and planning). Similarly, in the case of a new product release, a prospective buyer could be offered the opportunity to insure for its earliest availability. Thus in the original release of the Ford Mustang, such an insurance offer would evidently have found many takers, especially if refundable as a deposit against the eventual purchase (see Iacocca, 1984, ch. 6).

The discussion in terms of insurance schemes that follows is intended to illustrate the way in which a particular discriminatory scheme satisfies the requirements of encouragement and discrimination. Much of the material may be adapted to a consideration of alternative forms of inducement to truthful revelation. Likewise it may be that in some particular context, strategic behavior leads to understatement of intentions or some other form of systematic bias rather than overstatement, and one may have to adapt the insurance or other scheme to such a contingency. In what follows we assume that the statistician suspects overstatement and utilizes the insurance scheme described.

The basic idea is that a person's behavior with respect to the insurance package will reveal information about his (or her) true probability π_i of attending or purchasing. In terms of a simple expository example, suppose that the organizer of the event announces a probability p that a customer with no insurance will be able to obtain his desired accommodation or places. A potential customer assesses his probability of attendance as π_i and his net benefit (economic surplus) from the insured event as B_i. (a) If the premium I is nonrefundable and he is risk neutral, he will insure if his expected gain from doing so $(\pi_i B_i - I)$ exceeds his expected gain from not insuring $(\pi_i p_i B_i)$, that is, if $\pi_i > I/(1-p)B_i$. (b) If the premium I is refundable against purchase, the net expected benefit is $\pi_i(B_i + I) - I$ if he insures and $\pi_i p_i B_i$ otherwise, leading to insurance purchase if the odds ratio $\pi_i/(1-\pi_i) > I/(1-p)B_i$. If we treat the assumed private benefit B as constant over different individuals, the manifested act of insurance purchase provides a clear cutoff point for the probability π_i of attendance. This cutoff point becomes less precise (see what follows) if the benefits B_i are not treated as identical across individuals.[1]

Suppose, then, that the option to purchase insurance is included along with or as part of the questionnaire intended to survey intentions of visiting or purchasing. Respondents will tend to be deterred from returning the combination of a high manifested probability π_i^m together with a rejection of insurance, for to do so would indicate that they are not prepared to "put their money where their mouth is." It might also be considered, depending on the precise context, that respondents who do elect

---

[1] One could argue that B_i and π_i are related – the possibility of attendance is higher if the perceived benefits B_i are also higher. Provided that the relationship is indeed one of positive correlation, this does not nevertheless diminish the informational content of the insurance purchase with respect to the probabilities π_i.

to purchase insurance will by that token have indicated their favorable leanings toward the event and have less additional motivation for exaggerating their true intentions or preferences. On all accounts, therefore, the insurance proposal appears likely to encourage truthful revelation.

There remains the question of testing for residual untruthful behavior. The basic idea in the various procedures to be considered is that if residual untruthfulness does remain, then it is unlikely to be neutral with regard to the insurance scheme. In other words, a wedge is driven between those who take insurance and those who do not. Two possible general approaches come to mind.

I.   *A split-half experiment.* Here, the survey sample is divided into two equal groups, one of which is given the opportunity to purchase insurance and the other not. Strictly speaking, this is not a design for testing residual untruthfulness but simply whether untruthful revelation is likely to arise in the first place. Given the two manifested distributions for π_i, one carries out tests for equality using standard nonparametric testing procedures such as those referred to in Section 3.3. Note that acceptance of the null hypothesis (H_0: the distributions from each half are the same) does not of necessity imply that everybody is being truthful; another possibility is that the insurance scheme is simply ineffective as a discouragement device for nontruthful behavior.

II. *Single treatment: discriminatory maintained hypotheses.* A somewhat less informative but more practical procedure would be to establish a pair of nonnested tests using alternative maintained hypotheses from the administration of the insurance scheme to the entire sample. The two possibilities are as follows:

A.   The maintained hypothesis is that accepters of insurance do not lie. One then tests

H_0^a: rejecters of insurance do not lie,

versus

H_1^a: rejecters do lie.

B.   The maintained hypothesis is that rejecters of insurance do not lie. One then tests

H_0^b: accepters of insurance do not lie,

versus

H_1^b: accepters do lie.

Depending upon a study of motivations for untruthful behavior in the specific context, one might have greater confidence in one or the other of the maintained hypotheses A or B. We would suggest that both be set up and tested. If no residual untruthfulness exists, then both H_0^a and H_0^b should be accepted. As for the split-half experiment, the procedure is not watertight. Its power in detecting any residual untruthfulness relies heavily on the presumed nonneutrality of such with respect to the given insurance scheme.

We have still to set up specific test statistics for the single-treatment procedure. The development outlined in what follows, which is suggested for this purpose, utilizes a common stochastic structure combined with specific variants according to the different maintained hypotheses, which in turn form the basis for an application of the Wu–Hausman testing methodology to this problem. Let us begin with the common probability structure.

We assume that a stochastic discriminant structure exists for determining whether or not an individual i accepts insurance. This is of the following form: The individual i purchases insurance if the log odds ratio

$$w_i = \log\left(\frac{\pi_i}{1-\pi_i}\right) \geq \alpha - \epsilon_i, \tag{13}$$

where α is a constant and ϵ_i is a $N(0, \sigma_\epsilon^2)$ disturbance. This is a logit-style discrimination structure with the logarithm of the observed odds ratio as dependent variable. Equation (13) will be taken as a more or less primitive assumption, but something of this form can be derived for several models of the underlying decision problems. For example, in terms of refundable premiums and risk-neutral individuals (see the preceding), agent i will purchase if

$$\log\left(\frac{\pi_i}{1-\pi_i}\right) > \log\left(\frac{I}{1-p}\right) - \log B_i. \tag{14}$$

If we assume that benefits B_i have a lognormal distribution with mean μ_B, then putting $\alpha = \log[I/(1-p)] - \mu_B$ yields the model (13). Finally we shall assume that the true (log) odds ratios w_i are distributed across the population as $N(\mu_w, \sigma_w^2)$.

Suppose that all intentions are correctly revealed ($w_i^m = w_i$) whether or not the individuals purchase insurance. The observed sample information for each individual then consists of the manifested probability π_i^m and corresponding log odds ratio w_i^m and also the dichotomous information as to whether that individual purchased insurance. For simplicity we assume initially that the random variables w_i and ϵ_i are independent.

Recall our notation for the normal density and cumulative distribution function ordinates as $\phi(x; \mu_x, \sigma_x^2)$, $\Phi(x; \mu_x, \sigma_x^2)$, respectively, where x may refer to either w or ϵ. The likelihood function is then of the form [2]

$$L(\mu, \alpha, \sigma_w^2, \sigma_\epsilon^2) = \prod_{i \in A} \phi(w_i^m; \mu, \sigma_w^2) \Phi(w_i^m; \alpha, \sigma_\epsilon^2)$$

$$\times \prod_{i \in R} \phi(w_i^m; \mu, \sigma_w^2)[1 - \Phi(w_i^m; \alpha, \sigma_\epsilon^2)], \qquad (15a)$$

where A denotes the accepters of insurance and R those who reject. The log-likelihood function is thus

$$\log L = \sum_i \log \phi(w_i^m; \mu, \sigma_w^2) + \sum_{i \in A} \log \Phi(w_i^m; \alpha, \sigma_\epsilon^2)$$

$$+ \sum_{i \in R} \log[1 - \Phi(w_i^m; \alpha, \sigma_\epsilon^2)]. \qquad (15b)$$

Under the null hypothesis, the maximum-likelihood estimates of μ and σ_w^2 are simply the overall sample mean and variance, as we should expect. The parameter estimates $\hat{\alpha}, \sigma_\epsilon^2$ must be solved numerically, but it is evident that with respect to these parameters, the relevant part of the likelihood function has a standard probit form. If the null hypothesis is correct, then the maximum-likelihood estimates $\hat{\theta}_u = (\hat{\mu}, \hat{\alpha}, \hat{\sigma}_w^2, \hat{\sigma}_\epsilon^2)$ are best asymptotically normal with the standard maximum-likelihood asymptotic covariance matrix V_u.

Suppose, on the other hand, that residual untruthfulness persists. Under our maintained hypothesis (A), such lying is confined to those who do not buy insurance. Formally, we may specify an alternative generation for manifested probabilities for $i \in R$ as

$$w_i^m = w_i + R(\alpha - \epsilon_i - w_i)\delta_i, \qquad (16)$$

where R is the unit ramp or indicator function for membership of this group $[R(x) = 1, 0$ according to whether $x > 0$ or $x \le 0]$ and δ_i is a semipositive random variable representing the biasing effect of untruthfulness. Even if systematic lying is present, some probability mass may nevertheless exist at $\delta = 0$ (some rejecters of insurance are still telling the truth). It is assumed that δ_i has a distribution function $F(\delta_i; \phi)$ depending upon certain parameters ϕ for which the density collapses on $\delta = 0$ as

[2] Proof: For $i \in A$, the representative likelihood element refers to the event

$$w_i^m \cap \{w_i^m > \alpha - \epsilon_i\} = \int_{\epsilon_i > \alpha - w_i^m} p(w_i^m, \epsilon_i)\, dw_i^m\, d\epsilon_i,$$

where p is the joint density. Under the independence assumption, this joint density factors directly into the product of the marginal densities, whence that part of formula (15a) referring to $i \in A$. A similar argument holds for $i \in R$.

ϕ tends to some specific value ϕ_0. The difficulty is that one may not have any very precise idea about the mechanism (16) beyond the apprehension that some such mechanism may exist. It is therefore difficult or impossible to construct classically nested tests of the null hypothesis. On the other hand, we can make use of a general procedure applicable to such situations developed by Hausman (1978); for a subsequent review see also Bowden and Turkington (1984, ch. 2).

Suppose that those who reject insurance are not in fact manifesting their intentions correctly. The observed sample of size n then contains n_A accepters with a manifested w_i^m equal to their true w_i and n_R rejecters whose manifested w_i^m may not necessarily be correct, that is, correspond to their true probabilities of attending or purchasing. The only admissible information from the latter group is taken to be the fact of their declining to purchase insurance. The likelihood function of the complete sample is therefore obtained as follows. If $i \in A$, the likelihood element remains as it appears in expression (15a). If $i \in R$, all that is recorded is that fact itself, and the probability of rejection is $\mathrm{prob}(\epsilon_i + w_i < \alpha) = \Phi(\alpha; \mu, \sigma_w^2 + \sigma_\epsilon^2) = 1 - \Phi(\mu; \alpha, \sigma_w^2 + \sigma_w^2)$. The complete restricted or limited (L) log-likelihood function under maintained hypothesis A is then

$$\log L^a(\theta_L) = \sum_{i \in A} \log \phi(w_i^m; \mu, \sigma_w^2) + \sum_{i \in A} \log \Phi(w_i^m; \alpha, \sigma_\epsilon^2)$$

$$+ n_R \log \Phi(\alpha; \mu, \sigma_w^2 + \sigma_\epsilon^2). \tag{17a}$$

Note that the limited information estimator of μ is not $\bar{w}_A^m = 1/n_A \sum_{i=1}^{n_A} w_i^m$ as one might expect. From the first-order maximization conditions, we derive

$$\mu_L^a = \bar{w}_A^m - \sigma_w^2 \frac{n_R}{n_A} \frac{\phi(\mu; \alpha, \sigma_w^2 + \sigma_\epsilon^2)}{1 - \Phi(\mu; \alpha, \sigma_w^2 + \sigma_\epsilon^2)}. \tag{18}$$

As it stands, the equation is implicit and the parameters must be solved numerically as part of the complete system, which is no longer decomposable in the way that the unrestricted likelihood function (15b) may be broken down. Equation (18) does indicate, however, that $\hat{\mu}_L < \bar{w}_A^m$, which means that simply throwing away the offending respondents and estimating μ for the remainder (those who accept) will not result in an unbiased or consistent estimate. This argument may have more general applicability since, as remarked in Section 3.1, discarding of respondents convicted, as it were, of lying is widely practiced.

However, our specific interest is with the process of testing for true revelation of intentions. We may summarize the argument thus. If H_0^a is correct, the unrestricted likelihood function (16) yields consistent and asymptotically efficient estimates of the parameters θ. If H_1^a is true (rejecters of insurance often lie), the unrestricted likelihood function will yield biased or inconsistent estimates of the parameters, especially of μ_w. Turning to the limited information estimator $\hat{\theta}_L$, if H_0^a is true, this estimator will yield consistent but inefficient estimates with the asymptotic covariance matrix [of $\sqrt{n}(\hat{\theta}_L - \theta)$] estimated in the standard way as $\hat{V}_L$. If H_1^a is true, the limited information estimator will (unlike the unrestricted estimator) continue to yield consistent estimates. Under the circumstances just described, Hausman's test statistic applies. Write $\mathbf{d} = \hat{\theta}_L - \hat{\theta}_u$ as the difference between the two estimators, and write $\Delta = \hat{V}_L - \hat{V}_u$, the difference between the estimated covariance matrices. The test statistic is

$$n\mathbf{d}\,\Delta^{-1}\mathbf{d}'. \tag{19}$$

Under the null hypothesis, this has a χ_4^2 distribution, whereas under the alternative hypothesis it is noncentral χ_4^2. Thus the rejection region for H_0^a will consist in high values of the computed statistic (19).

The testing procedure for maintained hypothesis B (rejecters of insurance presumed to be telling the truth) is a simple modification of the preceding development. Corresponding to (17a), we have the likelihood function

$$\log L^b(\theta_L) = n_A \log \Phi(\mu; \alpha, \sigma_w^2 + \sigma_\epsilon^2) + \sum_{i \in R} \log \phi(w_i^m; \mu, \sigma_w^2)$$

$$+ \sum_{i \in R} \log[1 - \Phi(w_i^m; \alpha, \sigma_\epsilon^2)]. \tag{17b}$$

Apart from this change, the testing procedure is as already described.

Finally we remark that restricted and unrestricted likelihood functions of similar form to (15) and (17) may be derived in the case where w_i and the discriminant disturbance ϵ_i are statistically dependent.[3] Recalling the rationalization of the discriminant mechanism (13) in terms of a decision process such as that represented by the inequality (14), the benefits B_i and the probabilities π_i could well be positively related, yielding a positive correlation between w_i and ϵ_i.

The limitations of the general single-treatment procedure should be understood. Rejection of one or both null hypotheses does not enable us

---

[3] Suppose w_i and ϵ_i have covariance $\sigma_{w\epsilon} = 0$, and write $\beta = \sigma_{w\epsilon}/\sigma_w^2$ as the theoretical regression coefficient of w upon ϵ. Then the conditional density of ϵ given w is $\phi[\epsilon; \beta(w_i - \mu), \sigma_\epsilon^2 - \beta^2 \sigma_w^2]$ (e.g., Cramér, 1961). Following a development similar to that of footnote 2, the first term of the unrestricted likelihood function corresponding to (15a) is

$$\phi(w_i^m; \mu, \sigma_w^2)\,\Phi\!\left(w_i^m; \frac{\alpha + \beta\mu}{1 + \beta}, \frac{\sigma_e^2 - \beta^2 \sigma_w^2}{(1 + \beta)^2}\right),$$

with similar expressions for the remaining term and the terms of the restricted likelihood function corresponding to expression (17). Note that the estimates of μ and σ_w^2 can no longer be derived as the overall mean and sample variance, even under H_0.

to say which group – the accepters or rejecters – is doing the lying, simply that some incongruity between the two groups exists. To be able to deduce anything more requires a prior judgment about which of the two maintained hypotheses A and B is more likely to be correct. This would in most instances depend upon a consideration of the possible motives for untruthful behavior. An appropriate estimate of the mean log-odds $\log[\pi_i/(1-\pi_i)]$ may be derived accordingly. For instance, if H_0^a is rejected and A is considered the more likely maintained hypothesis, then the appropriate estimate is not the overall mean $\bar{w}_m$ but μ_L^a as defined by equation (18). A corresponding expression exists if maintained hypothesis B is considered more likely and H_0^b is rejected.

3.5 Indirect concordance testing

Let W_i be some variable denoting the individual's true intentions, attitude, and so on, and let W_i^m denote that manifested to the statistician or policymaker. In Section 3.3 we assumed that observations on both W and W^m were available, although perhaps for different individuals, enabling a direct comparison between the two distributions. Section 3.4 considered the case where such a direct concordance was available only for a subset of the sample. In this section we consider the case where observations are available on the manifested variable W_i^m but not at all for the corresponding true attitudes W_i; instead the values of some indicator variable I_i related in some way to W_i are available. Concordance testing between W_i^m and W_i must be done indirectly between W_i^m and I_i. The problem then becomes one of (a) assuring oneself that there is indeed an unambiguous relationship between the index I_i and the true W_i and (b) investigating the conditions under which the validity or otherwise of the manifested W_i^m can be established by tests based on the available index I_i.

Some well-known instances of indirect proxy variables (I) arise in public economics. *Hedonic prices* represent a major source of indirect information about consumer willingness to pay. The general idea is that implicit prices of various attributes can be established in terms of coefficients in a regression relating the price consumers are willing to pay to measured variations in the physical characteristics, one of which will represent the item of primary interest. For instance, if residents of a major city were asked for hypothetical valuations of clean air, a potential for strategic overestimation could be said to exist depending, of course, upon who is to finance the cleanup. However, it ought to be possible to establish hedonic prices for clean air by examining variations in house prices across neighborhoods with (inter alia) different air pollution counts and examining the appropriate regression coefficient. Such a study has in fact been carried out by Brookshire et al. (1982), who compared hypothetic valuations (the W_i^m) of clean (or cleaner!) air in Los Angeles with hedonic prices (the I_i) as calculated from housing rent differentials. Similarly, in the case of public recreational facilities, another index of willingness to pay is to be found in the transport costs that individuals are willing to incur to travel to the facility concerned. In certain circumstances one might also be able to deduce information about willingness to pay from an observation of the effect upon demand for a related good available in the marketplace. For a complete review of such considerations we refer the interested reader to Mäler (1974) and Freeman (1979).

In general, the major difficulty with the use of proxy measures to corroborate or invalidate manifest revelations is simply that the measures are indirect. One would hope that the relationship between I_i and W_i is positive and monotonic, but this fact does not by itself suffice to test the relative characteristics of the distribution of W_i and the given W_i^m. On the other hand, theory or commonsense may yield further information about the relationship between the index and the individual's true preference or intention. Thus in the case of transport costs (TC) and willingness to pay (W) for a recreational facility, we should expect that (i) the inequality $TC_i \geq W_i$ and (ii) over different individuals, TC_i and W_i should be positively correlated. Likewise Brookshire et al. (1982) argued (i) $W_i \geq \Delta P_i$, where W_i represents the willingness to pay for an improvement in air quality and ΔP_i is the corresponding incremental hedonic price, and (ii) W_i and ΔP_i are positively correlated. In both cases, therefore, a test of whether (i) (the inequality) and (ii) (the correlation) are simultaneously true would be at least a partial test of the veracity of manifested survey responses.

Several problems arise in connection with suggestions of this kind. The first concerns the technical problem of setting up formal tests of hypothesis such as (i) and (ii), bearing in mind that they must be simultaneously true and with the complication that the relationship between direct and indirect measures usually has no natural or intrinsic parametric formulation. A second problem concerns how rigorously requirements such as (i) and (ii) should be interpreted. Suppose, for instance, that a minority of individuals actually enjoy travel on their way to goose hunting so that hunting and traveling are in the nature of joint outcomes. For such individuals we could observe $TC_i > W_i$, violating the requirement for a manifested W_i to satisfy (i). Evidently any proposed test should be robust enough to allow a minor degree of departure from universal observance of requirements imposed or suggested by strict theory. An alternative viewpoint is that to impose the inequality (i) would be inappropriate.

Instead, a sophisticated theoretical concordance should be established between, say, travel costs and the true W_i, which would take into account the contingency that some individuals actually enjoy the travel.

From the statistical point of view, the entire problem of revelation and truthfulness may be regarded as an unobservable variables problem. The true willingness to pay or intentions or preferences correspond to the latent variables, and the ultimate objective is to test hypotheses about these unobservable variables or structures involving them. The essential difficulty with the kind of concordance testing outlined here is that the information connecting the observables and the latent variables is usually qualitative in nature and no obvious parameterization may exist, suggesting that such problems are more naturally handled with methods of nonparametric inference yet to be developed.

3.6   Design: the census and compulsion

If one is forced to a reliance upon manifested responses or revelations, the question naturally arises as to what kind of rules for conducting surveys or constructing items in a survey should be applied in order to minimize the risk or extent of untruthful revelation. We have already considered one suggestion that attacks this problem in Section 3.4, where we considered an insurance scheme with a bit of in-built moral suasion. But in introducing moral suasion of any kind, we may well run up against a nonresponse problem: If individuals feel that they are being bullied (however gently), they may well choose simply not to respond. Since those so choosing will probably be more at risk with respect to untruthfulness, a selectivity bias would evidently arise. We may well be forced to decide which bias is likely to be the larger, that from untruthfulness or the bias from selectivity in nonresponse.

In fact, a similar sort of dilemma is apparent in the design of any national census. The laws relating to national censuses usually compel response, the fact of which is observable, and threaten penalties for untruthful response, the fact of which is only rarely verifiable. The result is very probably that people being compelled to respond on strategic questions will simply lie. A sample of questions on which this sort of behavior is probable was given in Section 3.1. Now an alternative might be to allow facultative rather than compulsory answers to a greater range of questions, especially those where strategic behavior is thought likely. Respondents unwilling to incur the risk or stigmatic conscience of lying would then simply not respond. However, this introduces the possibility of selectivity bias in response referred to in the preceding. The question that arises is which of the two, the bias from untruthfulness or that from selectivity, is likely to predominate? If it should prove that the bias from selectivity is less, then such a result would doubtless please those civil libertarians who argue that the less any citizen is forced to divulge to the state, the better.

The problem that we shall look at is therefore the following: Suppose questions are thought to be possibly and unavoidably strategic in nature. Is it better to make such questions compulsory or noncompulsory (optional)? Our primary line of attack concerns bias. In such terms, the technical question to be resolved is the following. A question that is optional is likely to entail censoring bias. If the question is compulsory, it will be subject to a bias from untruthfulness. Which of these biases is likely to prove the greater? One might expect that if the censoring point is less than the mean of the distribution of interest, then the censoring bias will be the smaller of the two, reasoning that if people lie, they will tend to gravitate toward the perceived mean in their response. Even if these perceptions are correct, however, the answer, rather surprisingly, is that the bias from untruthfulness is always less than the bias from censoring, indeed on reasonable assumptions only half as much. The somewhat depressing conclusion is that it is better to make questions compulsory rather than optional. It should be stressed that we are concerned primarily with considerations of bias in the application of standard censurial measurement techniques. As we later point out, other considerations and estimation possibilities may arise and may possibly affect the matter of compulsion.

Question 33 of the 1986 Australian Census (see Section 3.1) will provide an admirable if somewhat lighthearted paradigm to underpin subsequent discussion. We recall that this question asked how many hours the person worked per week. Actually the question is close-ended in that it lists a range of class intervals for hours one of which is to be ticked and the upper range of which is left open, but we shall for purposes of discussion suppose that the respondent is free to enter any figure. Prior questions in the census form had asked about the respondent's job, employer, and nature of duties. As a matter of personal observation, there is considerable variation in the working hours of Australian academics. Some work much longer than the 40 hours per week, others quite obviously work considerably less. However, if compelled to answer question 33, few if any of the leisurely academics would admit to anything less than the standard week, and most would claim more. The primary reason is strategic since salaries and other benefits are perceived as linked to the public image of the academic's life and work. In other words, the perceptive academic would be well aware of the public relations implications of his or her answer. Suppose, then, that the question is compulsory. The leisurely academic will answer but may very well lie [we shall euphemistically refer to this as being untruthful (U)]. The result is a bias in the published average hours worked. Suppose, on the other hand, that the question is optional, that is, need not be answered. (Perhaps it could be assembled with other such questions in a special optional part B of the census.) The indolent academic, whom we shall assume has been well brought up, is now relieved of the moral burden of untruthfulness and will simply not answer. Indeed, it is in his or her strategic interest not to answer. Since only the hard workers tend to answer, the mean computed from respondents' answers will tend to be higher than the true mean, introducing the selectivity bias referred to previously.

In order to achieve as close a degree of comparability between a response–nonresponse model and a strategic untruthfulness model, we have constructed a decision process in which not responding on the one hand and lying on the other represent two polar outcomes from a common branch point. It is possible to construct reactions intermediate between these two outcomes with correspondingly intermediate conclusions. In terms of our maintained example, let h be the hours worked by the individual. We assume that an individual (i) responds truthfully if and only if

$$h_i \geq h_0 + \epsilon_i, \tag{20}$$

where h_0 is some constant. The variability term ϵ_i is a random variable that for simplicity we shall assume is distributed as $\phi(\epsilon; 0, \sigma^2)$, where as usual ϕ is the normal density with indicated mean (0) and variance σ^2. The term $h_0 + \epsilon_i$ is of the nature of a random threshold. The mean h_0 of this threshold is left as arbitrary as possible. It may represent some industry standard, such as the 40-hour week, or it may simply indicate the average level at which individuals feel ashamed or worried enough to consider suppressing their true response. The distribution of working hours h_i across the population is assumed, for expositional brevity, to be independent of the threshold variability ϵ_i. We shall also assume that $h_0 < \mu$, where $\mu = Eh$ is the mean number of hours worked, and moreover that σ_ϵ is small in relation to $\mu - h_0$. The leading special case is where $\sigma_\epsilon = 0$, in which case deterministic censoring of responses occurs at the threshold value h_0. In summary the discrimination mechanism (20) indicates that individuals differ in their tendency to truthfully respond. Those with a very high h_i will usually respond truthfully. Those with a lower h_i may not depending on the associated value of the disturbance ϵ_i, which may be regarded as reflecting individual variations in veracity or other personal attributes or circumstances.

The polar reactions referred to in the preceding concern what happens when inequality (20) is not satisfied and reflect different assumptions about conditions attached to the question.

(a) Suppose that the question is not compulsory. Suppose also that people have an absolute aversion to lying. As a strategic reaction, they simply do not respond to the question. The complete model of strategic nonresponse is then

$$\text{Model C:} \quad \begin{aligned} &\text{observe } h_i \Leftrightarrow h_i \geq h_0 + \epsilon_i, \\ &\text{no response} \Leftrightarrow h_i \geq h_0 + \epsilon_i. \end{aligned} \tag{21}$$

We refer to this as model C (for censoring).

(b) Suppose that the question is compulsory. People now have to respond but the demands of strategy outweigh those of morality. The manifested response h_i^m may now differ from the true h_i. If inequality (20) is satisfied, the two are the same. Suppose, however, that the inequality is not satisfied. Two leading assumptions are possible for the value of h now manifested:

(i) Those working in the occupation presumably have a good appreciation of the average hours μ worked by their colleagues, and this value is entered as the manifested hours worked. We refer to this as model U (for untruthful):

$$\text{Model U:} \quad h_i^m = \begin{cases} h_i \Leftrightarrow h_i \geq h_0 + \epsilon_i, \\ \mu \Leftrightarrow h_i < h_0 + \epsilon_i. \end{cases} \tag{22}$$

We note a slight difficulty with this formulation: Depending on the value of ϵ_i, we could have $h_i < h_0 + \epsilon_i$ but $h_i > \mu$, in which case entering $h_i^m = \mu$ would not be sensible strategic behavior. We could get over this problem by the introduction of a second dichotomy, but it will be simpler to suppose that σ_ϵ is small in relationship to the distance $\mu - h_0$, thus ascribing only a small probability to such an anomaly.

(ii) The mean threshold h_0 may have some external reference as an industry standard (e.g., the 40-hour week). We could expect that the industry standard is less than μ, the mean number of hours actually worked. As a conservative approach – a more modest lie – we could imagine the respondent who works fewer hours simply listing the standard as his hours worked. A variable-threshold model is less suitable for this situation since it will suffer from the difficulty just mentioned. However the constant-threshold model remains logically unexceptionable:

$$\text{Model U':} \quad h_i^m = \begin{cases} h_i \Leftrightarrow h_i \geq h_0, \\ h_0 \Leftrightarrow h_i < h_0. \end{cases} \tag{23}$$

Further variants on either of the preceding models are possible. For example, in model U it could be assumed that a degree of random variation exists in respondents' perception of the mean μ. We do not investigate such finer points of detail.

Distributions and bias

Let us now consider the density of the observations actually available, namely, those who respond in the case of model C, and the manifested returns in the case of model U. We note that confining observations to those who have responded gives an incomplete account of the information available for model C since information is also provided by nonresponse as such; however we temporarily delay consideration of this aspect. The estimators considered here correspond to the arithmetic mean of the available observations considered as an estimator of the true mean, μ.

Model C

We are interested in the conditional density of hours given that a figure has been returned by the respondent. We denote this as $p(h/R)$, where R denotes the event of a response. Now the joint density

$$p(h, R) = \int_{-\infty}^{h-h_0} \phi(h, \epsilon)\, d\epsilon,$$

where $\phi(h, \epsilon)$ is the joint density of h and ϵ. In view of the assumed independence between h and ϵ, we may conclude that

$$p(h, R) = \phi(h; \mu, \sigma^2) \int_{-\infty}^{h-h_0} \phi(\epsilon; 0, \sigma_\epsilon^2)\, d\epsilon$$

$$= \phi(h; \mu, \sigma_h^2)\, \Phi(h - h_0; 0, \sigma_\epsilon^2)$$

$$= \phi(h; \mu, \sigma_h^2)\, \Phi(h; h_0, \sigma_\epsilon^2),$$

where as usual Φ is the (cumulative) distribution function corresponding to the density ϕ. Moreover

$$p(R) = p(h - \epsilon \geq h_0)$$

$$= 1 - \Phi(h_0; \mu, \sigma_h^2 + \sigma_\epsilon^2)$$

since h and ϵ are assumed independent. We conclude that the conditional density of h given response is given by

$$p(h/R) = \phi(h; \mu, \sigma_h^2)\, \Phi(h; h_0, \sigma_\epsilon^2)/(1 - \Phi_0), \tag{24}$$

where for brevity we write $\Phi_0 = \Phi(h_0; \mu, \sigma_h^2 + \sigma_\epsilon^2)$, with ϕ_0 the corresponding density value.

We shall now find the expectation of this distribution and hence evaluate the bias in estimating the mean number of hours μ by the arithmetic mean of the responses. The required conditional mean is

$$\mu_R = \int_{-\infty}^{\infty} hp(h/R)\, dh$$

$$= \frac{1}{1-\Phi_0} \int_{-\infty}^{\infty} h\phi(h; \mu, \sigma_h^2)\, \Phi(h; h_0, \sigma_\epsilon^2)\, dh$$

$$= \frac{1}{1-\Phi_0} \{\mu[1 - \Phi(h_0; \mu, \sigma_\epsilon^2 + \sigma_h^2)] + \sigma_h^2 \phi(\mu; h_0, \sigma_\epsilon^2 + \sigma_h^2)\}$$

$$= \mu + \frac{\sigma_h^2 \phi(h_0; \mu, \sigma_\epsilon^2 + \sigma_h^2)}{1 - \Phi(h_0; \mu, \sigma_\epsilon^2 + \sigma_h^2)}$$

$$= \mu + \frac{\sigma_h^2 \phi_0}{1 - \Phi_0} \quad \text{for brevity.} \tag{25}$$

(In carrying out the preceding integration, we use result A3 listed in Appendix 1 to Chapter 2.)

The bias function $H(h_0) = \phi_0/(1 - \Phi_0)$ has the form of the normal hazard function: although not normalized in the standard fashion of Figure 2.1, its general shape as a function of h_0 remains unchanged. Over the range considered, namely, $h_0 < \mu$, the hazard function increases slowly with h_0, suggesting that relatively large changes are needed in the threshold to produce an appreciable increase in the bias. We shall refer to the bias $\delta_c = \sigma_h^2 \phi_0/(1 - \Phi_0)$ as a censoring bias since the conditional density involved results from a relatively straightforward censoring process on the original or underlying values of h.

Model U

In deriving the density for model U [equation (22)], the arguments are very similar to those already employed with respect to model C. The probability structures of the two models are indeed virtually identical; instead of observing no response, one simply substitutes an observation to the value of μ (or h_0 in the case of model U'). Thus the required density is

$$p(h) = 1 - \Phi(\mu; h_0, \sigma_\epsilon^2 + \sigma_h^2) = \Phi_0, \quad h = \mu$$

$$= \phi(h; \mu, \sigma_h^2)\, \Phi(h; h_0, \sigma_\epsilon^2), \quad h \neq \mu. \tag{26}$$

One observes from result A2 of Appendix 1, Chapter 2, that

$$\int_{-\infty}^{\infty} \phi(h; \mu, \sigma_h^2)\, \Phi(h; h_0, \sigma_\epsilon^2)\, dh = \Phi(\mu; h_0, \sigma_h^2 + \sigma_\epsilon^2) = 1 - \Phi_0.$$

It follows from expression (26) that the density integrates to unity, as required. It has a mass concentration Φ_0 at the point $h = \mu$.

The expectation (first moment) of the distribution is given by

$$Eh = \mu\Phi_0 + \int_{-\infty}^{\infty} h\phi(h; \mu_h, \sigma_h^2)\Phi(h; h_0, \sigma_\epsilon^2)\, dh.$$

Utilizing result A3 of Appendix 1 to Chapter 2, we easily obtain

$$Eh = \mu - \sigma_h^2 \phi(h_0; \mu, \sigma_h^2 + \sigma_\epsilon^2)$$

$$= \mu + \sigma_h^2 \phi_0. \tag{27}$$

Since $h_0 < \mu$ by assumption, expression (27) indicates that the bias increases with h_0. This is as we should expect: A higher average threshold means that more people are becoming embarrassed at their working hours. We note also that increased variability (σ_ϵ) among the individual threshold levels implies a higher bias if $h_0 \ll \mu$.

Bias comparison

Equations (25) and (27) give the bias terms for the censored and untruthful models: $\delta_c = \sigma_h^2 \phi_0 / (1 - \Phi_0)$ and $\delta_u = \sigma_h^2 \phi_0$, respectively. It follows that

$$\delta_u / \delta_c = 1 - \Phi(h_0; \mu, \sigma_h^2 + \sigma_\epsilon^2) < 1. \tag{28}$$

In the important special case $\sigma_\epsilon = 0$ (the threshold is the same for all individuals) and $h_0 = \mu$ (the threshold is in fact the mean), we obtain $\delta_c = 2\delta_u$. The censoring bias is exactly twice that resulting from complete but possibly untruthful response. If $h_0 = \mu - \sigma_h$, that is, the threshold is set at one standard deviation below the mean, the gap is much smaller: The censored bias is only 16 percent greater than the untruthful bias. We note also that the effect of individual variability (σ_ϵ^2) in the response threshold h_0 is to worsen the comparison – a more variable threshold will tend to favor the untruthful model.

The preceding bias comparisons are a surprise and rather counter intuitive. Abstracting from the threshold variability ϵ, both models are in effect censored at h_0. In contrast to the censored model, however, the untruthful model yields no effective observations below μ. One might therefore have expected a higher calculated mean and therefore a higher bias for this model. The reason for the poorer performance of the censored model is evidently that values of $h \gg \mu$ are now receiving relatively more weight in the censored density. Thus the mean calculated on the basis of model C receives a weightier contribution from these high values, inflating the value of the mean calculated on the basis of those who actually respond. This effect outweighs the simple translation of density mass to the point $h = \mu$ in the case of the untruthful model.

Similar conclusions are reached if model U' [see equation (23)] is chosen rather than model U to represent untruthful revelations. In this case the biases are $\delta_c = \sigma_h^2 \phi(h_0; \mu, \sigma_h^2)/[1 - \Phi(h_0; \mu, \sigma_h^2)]$ and $\delta_u = \sigma_h^2 \phi(h_0; \mu, \sigma_h^2) - (\mu - h_0) \Phi(h_0; \mu_h, \sigma_h^2)$. It is evident that the conclusions drawn on the basis of model U are in fact reinforced since δ_u has further diminished relative to δ_c.

The relative bias (28) may be given a more operational interpretation as follows. Imagine that the question is optional and that N_R responses are received out of a total population of size N. From the dichotomy (20), it follows that $1 - \Phi_0$ can be interpreted as the proportion of the population that does respond, that is, $1 - \Phi_0 = N_R/N$. The relative bias is therefore given by

$$\delta_u/\delta_c = N_R/N. \tag{28'}$$

Thus, suppose that N_R out of N responses were received for the optional question. Assuming that model U applies, one could then assert that had the question been made compulsory, the bias would have been reduced by a factor of $1 - N_R/N = \bar{N}_R/N$, where $\bar{N}_R = N - N_R$. This provides statistical backing for the idea that if large numbers of defaults are considered likely, it is better to make the question compulsory in spite of the risk of untruthfulness that results.

Other considerations

In a situation where either censoring of responses or untruthfulness is expected, estimating μ or any other parameter by means of a simple average applied to the available observations might well be regarded as rather naive or else as a last resort. If alternative means of estimation are available, then it is premature to judge any matter of compulsion or other aspect of design on bias with regard to what may have been an inappropriate estimating procedure. For example, it might be noted that if attention is confined in the censored model only to those who respond, an available and important bit of information has not been utilized, namely, the number of people who do not respond.

To see that this might be useful, consider the maximum-likelihood estimator[4] for μ on the basis of the censored model. Partition the subjects into those who do respond (N_R) and those who do not respond ($\bar{N}_R$). The likelihood function is

---

[4] This is actually the likelihood function of a random *sample* of size $N = N_R + \bar{N}_R$ whereas we are taking $N, N_R, \bar{N}_R$ to refer to the entire population. Its usefulness for census work – which is essentially a curve-fitting type of context – rests on the presumed consistency properties of the resulting estimators as N becomes large.

$$\prod_{i \in N_R} \phi(h_i; \mu, \sigma_h^2) \prod_{i \in \bar{N}_R} \Phi(h_0; \mu, \sigma_h^2 + \sigma_\epsilon^2). \tag{29}$$

Taking the appropriate derivative gives the normal equation (first-order maximization condition) for μ as

$$\mu = \mu_R - \sigma_h^2 \frac{\bar{N}_R}{N_R} \frac{\phi(h_0; \mu, \sigma_h^2 + \sigma_\epsilon^2)}{\Phi(h_0; \mu, \sigma_h^2 + \sigma_\epsilon^2)}, \tag{30}$$

where μ_R is the mean computed from those who respond. To this we may add the relationship noted in connection with equation (28') that

$$\Phi(h_0; \mu, \sigma_h^2 + \sigma_\epsilon^2) = \bar{N}_R / N, \tag{31}$$

which may be taken as an additional equation for the determination of h_0. It may be remarked that the combination of (30) and (31) will yield equation (25), as we should hope. As they stand, equations (30) and (31) are not identified, the chief difficulty being the lack of identification of the threshold variability σ_ϵ. Suppose, however, that σ_ϵ is small in relation to σ_h. In Appendix 2 to this chapter, we show that the resulting normal equation for σ_h is given by

$$\sigma_h^2 = \sigma_R^2 + (\mu_R - \mu)(\mu_R - h_0), \tag{32}$$

where σ_R^2 is the variance computed from the respondents. Writing $\sigma_\epsilon^2 / \sigma_h^2 \simeq 0$ in equations (30) and (31), we end up with three independent equations in the three unknowns μ, h_0, σ_h^2 in terms of the observables μ_R, σ_R^2, and N_R / N. Thus if σ_h^2 is large in relation to the threshold variability σ_ϵ^2, then the true mean μ becomes estimable. In terms of equation (25) we use estimates of σ_h^2 and h_0 to adjust downward the mean μ_R computed from respondents.

On the other hand, the existence of compulsion would mean that a complete set of numerical observations is available rather than some numerical and others categorical in nature. If one introduces additional structural hypotheses, such as those of model U, additional parameters (in particular the threshold variability σ_ϵ^2) become identified, leading in turn to estimates of μ in the presence of significant threshold variability. Indeed, if something such as model U is applicable, then we should expect the observed empirical frequency function of hours to exhibit a sharp peak at $h = \mu$ [cf. the density (26)], which thereby becomes readily identifiable.

Summary

We may summarize the practical implications of the discussion of this section as follows. Strategic behavior in the answering of census or survey questions may manifest itself in two ways, a refusal to respond and untruthful response. If questions are optional, refusal will probably be the outcome; if questions are compulsory, untruthful behavior may result. If standard point estimators (such as the mean or proportion estimator) are used, then the optional question is likely to lead to censoring bias and the compulsory question to a bias from untruthfulness. We may expect the censoring bias to exceed the latter by a factor of up to 2. The bias is expressible in terms of the relative number of potential respondents and nonrespondents. Where appreciable censoring is expected from an optional question, one may expect that the compulsory alternative will entail considerably less bias. The applicability of more sophisticated estimation procedures may alter the preceding conclusion. Such procedures require more a priori structural assumptions or hypotheses about the nature of censoring, likely parameter values, and the nature of untruthfulness where it occurs.

3.7   Perspectives

Implicit in all the foregoing discussion is a gamelike interaction between the statistician (or at one remove, the policymaker) and the subjects. The game itself is a somewhat complicated one. Each individual agent realizes his or her own insignificance but realizes also the implied coalition of like-minded individuals. Thus the game is a compound one: on the macrolevel it is played between the statistician and coalitions trying collectively to influence the outcome in their favor; on the microlevel individuals may (as we saw in Chapter 2) be tempted to free-riding behavior with regard to their own coalition. Each individual has various possible approaches to the provision of information to the statistician, and these approaches constitute the strategy set for these individuals. The objective or payoff to the statistician is the correct appreciation of the true state of affairs: the intentions, opinions, willingness to pay, and so on, of the subjects, all of which are "states of nature" assumed to remain invariant while the survey process is going on.

In game-theoretic terms, the existence of bias indicates that an outcome has been reached that is unfavorable to the statistician. We have seen that different response strategies produce different biases. Not to respond is one possible strategy. It is indeed a strategy because individuals in a given implied coalition are well aware of the collective consequences of their nonresponse. The outcome is a selectivity bias since the response group is self-selected from among those who have something to gain by making their views known. A second class of strategies is to respond but to provide untruthful information. Comparison between the biases that arise depends upon precisely how the respondents will lie, if they do. If they tend to regress toward a perceived mean, then the rather surprising conclusion is that the bias from nonresponse is likely to be much more severe, a finding with implications for the design of censuses.

Faced with a potentially severe latent-variables problem of determining true attitudes or intentions, the statistician can try to alter either the rules or payoffs of the game. For example, schemes could be devised based on insurance or taxes aimed at inducing truthful revelation. If completely successful, the general purport of such schemes is that they render truthful revelation the dominant individual – and coalitional – strategy. Even if only partly successful, such procedures may nevertheless be enough to reassure the statistician that at least some of the subjects are behaving truthfully, enabling a test for residual untruthfulness among the population at large. It would appear that a degree of moral suasion would arise in such circumstances; devices that enable a test for the existence of untruthful behavior are ipso facto devices that tend to encourage truthful revelation.

It is difficult to know how pervasive and how serious is the problem of untruthful revelation or evasive nonresponse. Obviously this depends upon many things, not the least being exactly who is asking the questions and for what purpose; the way people respond to their income tax form may bear only a passing resemblance to their answers on the same sort of item on census night. But it may also be a problem that is evolutionary in nature. We have noted in Chapter 2 a secular downward trend in the willingness to provide information. The implication is that people are becoming more sophisticated in this respect. It needs only a little stretch of imagination to anticipate that this sophistication and reluctance will increasingly extend to the veracity as well as the fact of their answer. Information is the raw material of legislation. Given the increasing scope and in some cases intrusiveness of social and economic legislation, it might be increasingly – if depressingly – rational for subjects to exhibit such strategic behavior. The science of statistical inference in socioeconomic systems might increasingly become one of informational game theory.

Appendix 1. Processes for revealing preferences on public goods

As indicated in the text, the problem of encouraging truthful revelation has received much attention in the public economics literature. Here we outline two simple schemes chosen for their expositional simplicity. They do not represent current developments in the specialist literature, which are more demanding in their economic background. However, they should suffice to convey to the generalist or statistically oriented reader the basic gist of this kind of work.

A.   *Insurance schemes (Thompson, 1966)*

Suppose that the government announces a proposal for a new public facility together with details of the new tax needed to pay for it. Various incentives may exist, depending on exactly how the project is to be financed, for individuals not to state the true benefit that they would gain from the facility. Suppose that the government would build the facility if it knew that the arithmetic sum of individual benefits (net of the financing taxes that have been announced) would be positive. How could it come to such an assessment?

Suppose that the public believes that the probability that the project will be implemented is p. Such a figure could perhaps be announced by the government as its own preliminary assessment after a canvassing of public opinion. At any rate, the public is taken to believe uniformly in a fixed probability p that the project will go ahead. The government then announces an insurance scheme: By paying an insurance premium of p per dollar of insurance, people can insure against the victory of the given proposal; or by paying a premium of $1-p$ per dollar of insurance, people can insure against the victory of the status quo, that is, nothing happening.

Now if an individual i stands to gain, in monetary equivalent terms, a quantity C_i if the proposal goes ahead, then the individual will be willing to pay up to $(1-p)C_i$ to insure against the status quo. Likewise if another individual j stands to lose a quantity E_j by the proposal, he or she will be willing to pay up to pE_j to insure against its victory. Note that individuals are assumed to be risk neutral so that the preceding sums are actually paid for insurance.

The payment of premiums represents a signal of true costs or benefits. The decision rule for the government is therefore to go ahead with the proposal if

$$\sum_i C_i > \sum_j E_j, \tag{i}$$

that is, if the insured sums against the status quo exceed the insured sums against the proposal. The government chooses the proposal for which the dollar compensation to the losers is smaller.

This rule has also the happy consequence that the government will run a profit on its insurance scheme. Suppose that (i) is true. Then the government has to pay out $\sum_j E_j$. Its net revenue is then

$$\pi = (1-p)\sum_i C_i + p\sum_j E_j - \sum_j E_j$$

$$= (1-p)\left(\sum_i C_i - \sum_j E_j\right)$$

$$> 0.$$

Table 3.A.1. *Payoffs and taxes from truthful revelation*

	Issue		
Voter	P	S	Tax
A	30	0	20
B	0	40	0
C	20	0	10
Total	50	40	30

This net revenue can be subsequently distributed, although the government will have to be careful not to do so in a way that will arouse people's anticipations of a dividend and thereby disturb the original insurance-selling game.

B. *Voting taxes*

We consider a simple example from Mueller (1979, p. 72). Three voters A, B, and C have to choose between the proposal P and the status quo S. The payoffs (ignore the tax column) to each voter are given in Table 3.A.1.

Let us take it initially that the payoffs in the table are those manifested to the government by the individual. Thus they may not in the first instance represent *true* payoffs. The government announces that it will determine the issue by adding up all the dollar votes (payoffs). Thus with Table 3.A.1 as it stands, proposal P would win since it has 50 dollar votes as against 40 for S.

The government also announces a voting tax calculated in the following way. A voter pays tax only if his or her vote would be decisive in changing the outcome, the manifested dollar votes of all other individuals being taken as given. In that case the amount of the tax the voter pays is assessed as equal to the net gains accruing to the other individuals in his or her absence as a voter and as a determining voter in particular. Under this rule, individual B would clearly pay no tax since B never casts a deciding vote. Individual A would pay 20, for if absent, the issue would go to B with a net gain of 20. Similarly individual C would pay a tax of 10.

We may now see how such a voting tax encourages truthful revelation. A voter pays the tax only with a vote that is decisive in changing the outcome, and the amount that he or she pays is always less than the true benefit received. Suppose an individual felt tempted to manifest 51 dollar votes from proposal S. This would indeed shift the outcome in the desired direction, but the tax cost to the individual would be 50, resulting in a net loss of $50 - 40 = 10$ dollars. Or, individual A might consider it better to understate his or her preferences to 25. This plainly changes nothing, neither the tax nor the outcome. In all cases that one can devise, no positive incentive exists for individuals to do anything other than state their true preferences and intensity of those preferences. Similar to the insurance scheme (A), the voting tax is designed to make truthful revelation the individually dominant strategies in the implied game against each other and the government.

Appendix 2. The normal equation for σ_h in Section 3.6

Differentiating the likelihood function (29) with respect to σ_h gives

$$\sigma_h^2 = \frac{1}{1+\theta} \frac{1}{N_R} \sum_{i \in N_R} (h_i - \mu)^2,$$

where

$$\theta = \sigma_h \frac{\bar{N}_R}{N_R} \frac{h_0 - \mu}{\sqrt{\sigma_h^2 + \sigma_\epsilon^2}} \frac{\phi_0}{\Phi_0}.$$

Utilizing the identity

$$\sum_{i \in N_R} (h_i - \mu)^2 = \sum_{i \in N_R} (h_i - \mu_R)^2 + N_R(\mu_R - \mu)^2,$$

we obtain

$$\sigma_h^2 = \frac{1}{1+\theta} [\sigma_R^2 + (\mu_R - \mu)^2].$$

Now if $\sigma_\epsilon^2/\sigma_h^2$ is small,

$$\theta \simeq (h_0 - \mu) \frac{\bar{N}_R}{N_R} \frac{\phi_0}{\Phi_0}$$

$$= (h_0 - \mu) \frac{\Phi_0}{1 - \Phi_0} \frac{\phi_0}{\Phi_0}$$

$$= (h_0 - \mu)(\mu_R - \mu)/\sigma_h^2,$$

utilizing equation (25). Substituting this value into the expression for σ_h^2 yields

$$\sigma_h^2 \simeq \sigma_R^2 + (\mu_R - \mu)(\mu_R - h_0),$$

which is equation (32).

CHAPTER 4

Publication and the political economy of prediction

4.1   Introduction

In previous chapters we considered the role of social information in such matters as the response to surveys or polls. The possession of information about the attitudes of others did not, in this work, affect the underlying individual attitudes, which were assumed to be immutable with respect to social information. Suppose, however, that knowledge of the attitudes or intentions of others affects our own intentions. Then the purveyors of social information evidently acquire considerable power to influence events. Such a contingency has long been noted by political pollsters, for instance. The bandwagon influence of surveyed intentions upon election outcomes is one such effect. Moreover, campaign money and activity is heavily dependent upon the performance in current opinion polls of the competing candidates, and the effects of such campaigning will in turn materially affect voter intentions. That many commentators – and indeed legislators – have expressed grave disquiet at the consequential effects of polls as news events is ample testimony to the pervasiveness and importance attached to the nonneutral effects of surveys of voter opinion. More recently it has been realized (see Section 4.3) that opinion polls may have a social function in transferring information about candidates to the electorate and vice versa so that the results of a cycle of polling and publication may be socially beneficial, a cause for encouragement rather than disquiet.

The behavior-modifying influence of published predictions is by no means confined to the political arena. As we point out in Section 4.2, forecasts of intentions with respect to major events can have a major influence upon the actual outcome through a variety of causal channels. Since the forecaster may very well be aware of the effects of his or her forecasts, an obvious incentive exists for strategic behavior. What results is a political economy of prediction, with publication and gamelike behavior forming a nexus determining the final outcome. The game theory model involved is that of a dominant player, the forecaster, and those who react to the predictions, namely, the public.

In considering the nature of the games involved, it is perhaps easiest to start by abstracting from stochastic considerations such as sampling in order to consider strategic motives and to establish certain basic models of the prediction process in terms of myopic or anticipative behavior on the part of the forecaster. This problem is addressed in Section 4.2, which also covers, together with Section 4.3, some of the applications mentioned in the preceding. Consideration of the game involved, or of game-like behavior, cannot be limited on the other hand to deterministic models. It is of course the feature of most surveys that they are subject to sampling error; moreover, if further replications of the forecasting exercise are to be undertaken, then the underlying state of the system may be perturbed by additional innovational or noisy elements. In either case, therefore, one has to extend discussion to allow for stochastic influences and the way in which these might affect the game "solution." From Section 4.4 to the end of the chapter various aspects of sampling error and/or additional sources of stochastic noise are investigated. Section 4.4 considers, in the presence of sampling error alone, a problem that in some respects is prior to the forecasting problem, namely, the problem of state estimation in the presence of reactive influences from published estimates of the current state. Such state estimates are frequently used for predictive purposes. Thus if the current survey reveals that 200,000 people intend to come to Perth for the America's Cup festivities, this estimate could be considered as a forecast of the final attendance. Whatever the merits of the implied forecast, it is certainly true that if people react above all to the current state estimates, then the forecasting problem becomes essentially one of state estimation in the presence of reactive effects. One has then to consider the limiting behavior of such state estimates, which involves a consideration of the various fixed points and invariant distributions that arise.

From state estimation we proceed in Section 4.5 to consider explicitly the problems of forecasting. If people react to current state estimates, then the forecasting problem becomes a more or less immediate corollary of the problem of state estimation. But if people start to react to the published forecasts – as forecasts rather than as estimates of the current states – then the problem of forecasting takes on new life and far stronger results can be obtained. These results are presented (somewhat mechanically) in Section 4.5, and their interpretation in terms of game-theoretic equilibria are explained in the first part of Section 4.6. It turns out that given forecast reactions (i.e., people react to forecasts), a whole class of consistent forecasts can be derived that are homologous to stochastic approximation estimators so that the immense body of literature on stochastic approximation becomes potentially applicable.

In terms of the consistency of outcome with the prediction, such forecasts may be reckoned a success. But it is by no means clear that the pursuit of a game-theoretic equilibrium is to maximize social welfare: It may be that the cycle of prediction and publication drives the system off in directions that conflict with any reasonable interpretation of public welfare. Such considerations are part of the job for any forecaster who appreciates the impact of his or her predictions, and they are discussed with more brevity than we should like in Section 4.6.

Up to this point we shall work exclusively in terms of surveys of a conventional kind; replications, where applicable, are simple repetitions of the original survey. Now the replication of surveys is presumably a costly exercise. In Section 4.7 we discuss the problem of correcting or allowing for reaction effects in the context of a single survey. After briefly considering informal questionnaire-based ways of anticipating publication response, we turn to the novel area of real-time surveys, by which we mean those in which by some device or other respondents have access to progress results from the same survey. It could of course be remarked that a replicated series of primary surveys can itself be regarded as a supersurvey with feedback and in a sense is therefore real time. However we have in mind the kind of arrangement that is increasingly feasible with modern communications technology (viatel, minitel, etc.) in which respondents can make up their mind from progress scores to which thus far they have not themselves contributed. Real-time survey schemes have already been mentioned in Chapter 2 in connection with selective response. The aspect of primary interest in the present context concerns reactivity phenomena: By monitoring progress results, the decisions by participants as to when and how to respond can guide the system toward a fixed point, assuming that such a property is desirable. (An incidental result is that the statistician may also be enabled to test for the presence of reaction effects, although we do not develop this point.) In keeping, perhaps, with the somewhat speculative nature of the technology, our discussion is itself rather speculative, not least in the absence of formal results. Nonetheless the real-time proposal is a good example of the active design of informational experiments and is worth pursuing.

4.2 Reflexive forecasting of "hallmark" events

The theory of prediction from stationary or near-stationary time series has over the years received intensive scrutiny, and the associated techniques such as Box–Jenkins identification or Kalman filtering are widely practiced in a variety of social and economic contexts as well as the technical or engineering problems for which many of these methods were originally designed. The ongoing and in a sense repetitive nature of such tasks means that the past of the series and of related series can provide a considerable amount of information about the likely future course of the variable or variables of substantive interest. In many circumstances, however, it may be necessary to forecast in a situation where very little prior experience is available and such information that can be utilized is at best of an indirect nature. Although such situations are less frequent in the sense that they do not recur on a month-to-month or even a year-to-year basis, they often have an economic or political aspect such that the implied loss function with respect to forecast errors can assume spectacular proportions. Instances are major new product launches (e.g., the Edsel or, on the other hand, the Mustang) or major occasions such as world fairs or Olympic Games. For such events mistakes can be expensive on a scale that transcends the consequences of poor forecasting in the day-to-day operations of the ordinary enterprise. Yet such has been our preoccupation with classical time series forecasting that little if any systematic effort has been directed to a consideration of the kinds of principles that should guide the forecasting of "one-off" events of the preceding type.

As already remarked, hallmark events are characterized by a dearth of information based on previous experience. This is, of course, a matter of degree rather than kind depending upon the particular application. Nevertheless, it has a definite bearing on the type of information utilized in the forecasting process. Of necessity, the statistician is forced to become a somewhat more active data gatherer, and typically a large part of the hard evidence will consist of a sample survey, perhaps replicated one or more times. In such surveys potential visitors, purchasers, and the like (the public) are asked about their intentions with respect to the event concerned. Such survey information is then amalgamated with what circumstantial or inferential evidence is available from other sources: the size of the subject population (e.g., 60 million people within a day's journey of Scuba, Tokyo, the site of the 1985 World Fair), attendance ratios at previous such events, the appeal of the prospective product, and other such specific but indirect pieces of supporting evidence.

Because the projects are usually large, they are very often of public concern. This being the case, the forecasts become matters of public information or interest. In turn, this serves to introduce one of our principal themes. If a forecast becomes public information, this will itself influence the public's intentions toward the event in question. It may do so via a simple bandwagon effect. Or it may – as was reputedly the case with the Los Angeles Olympics – induce apprehension about the availability of services, especially of accommodation. Alternatively, publication may affect public intentions indirectly via a supply response associated with the event. Thus in the forthcoming festivities for the America's

Cup in Perth, Australia, it could well be argued that ancillary announcements such as the construction of a large casino, running of a million dollar horse race, and attempts to schedule a world heavyweight boxing challenge were predicated upon the prior announcement by the Western Australian Tourist Commission of forecasts of expected visitor numbers. Such attractions would in turn be expected to augment visitor numbers. In all cases, the effect is the same: The publication of forecasts itself affects public intentions and therefore the outcome of the event forecasted. We shall refer to this phenomenon as reflexivity and a forecast subject to such reactions as a reflexive forecast.

The 1984 Summer Olympics in Los Angeles provides a case study of the effects of publication. Widespread national media reporting in 1983 and early 1984 of potential congestion and possibly exorbitant visitor travel and accommodation pricing was based upon various surveys of visitor intentions, including one commissioned and presented in 1982 by the LAOOC, the organizing committee. In the event, visitor numbers over the 28-day-period were less than what was expected. Disneyland reported the worst summer for 10 years. And spare a tear for Shoreline Park:

Shoreline Park in the City of Long Beach, with the only camping in the city, raised its rates from $18, $14, and $6 a day to $40, $30, and $15 a day. The result was below normal traffic. Park management indicated that maintenance of the usual rates would have been better for business and revenue because the park would have filled up.

> Economic Research Associates: Community Economic Impact
> of the 1984 Olympic Games in Los Angeles (undated), p. 58.

It is difficult to ascribe the displacement of normal tourist, business, and convention traffic that occurred to factors such as the unusual strength at the time of the U.S. dollar; or even more tenuously, to ascribe the fewer than expected visitor numbers to the withdrawal from the games of the Eastern Bloc countries. More probably, forecasts of visitor numbers fell short because of the adverse effects of publication upon visitor intentions.

Historically, forecasts of major events have often been proven wrong to an extent well outside the range of standard error associated with that prediction. The phenomenon of reflexivity and associated strategic behavior may help to account for this, although we do not pretend that these are the only perturbing influences. In what follows we shall review some of the problems arising from the phenomenon of reflexivity in forecasting. It will help to be specific. Thus, suppose that a forecast θ_0 has been prepared, say, of visitor numbers to some major event. For expositional convenience, we shall in the present section suppose that this forecast is based on a complete enumeration of a well-defined subject population each member of which actually responds, so that we shall assume away problems of nonresponse bias. Note that complete enumeration means that we shall be abstracting from sampling considerations; this and other sources of stochastic behavior do make a difference but will be considered in due course.

With regard to the survey of intentions, respondents simply indicate whether they will come (we can easily generalize this to an indication of probabilities that they will come). The forecast θ_0 is formed (for present purposes) as the summary of those intentions and is now published. In becoming public knowledge, this information affects the public's view of the event in one of several ways. As noted previously, a bandwagon effect might exist so that θ_0 visitors might connote a festive atmosphere to the prospective visitor; this is an example of a stimulus from the demand side. Or, the revelation of θ_0 may help to generate further planned activities associated with the event. Additional accommodation might be constructed, further entertainment facilities planned, or the supply of services – airline flights, charter services, new taxi licenses, and the like – stimulated. All of these activities might be expected, once made public knowledge, to encourage further attendance. Thus if the supply of these number-generating activities is denoted by S, we may write $S = S(\theta_0)$ with $S' > 0$. The new demand for visits could be represented as $\theta_1 = D(S, \theta_0) = D[S(\theta_0), \theta_0] = H(\theta_0)$ for brevity, a reduced-form relationship.

A possible form of the reaction function H is sketched in Figure 4.1. As we have drawn it, it embodies some specific assumptions about the form of the constituent elements of H. If we set $S = 0$ (no additional number-generating activities), we obtain a function $D(0, \theta)$ indicating pure attitude or bandwagon effects to an announced θ. We assume that the initial effect of increasing θ upon this function is strongly stimulatory but that beyond a certain point, concern about overcrowding or expensive facilities arises. The function $S(\theta)$, representing the supply of new services, may offset such fears; this will be the case if the second-order partial derivative $D_{12} > 0$ (e.g., extra accommodation relieves fear of overcrowding). The net effect of all these forces is portrayed according to our assumptions in Figure 4.1. The reaction function crosses the 45° line at some point θ_*.

Figure 4.1 can be turned into a phase plane. After publication of the initial estimate θ_0, the state of public intentions becomes θ_1, as illustrated. If the surveys should be replicated and the reaction function G remains stable, the dynamics are generated by the recursion $\theta_r = H(\theta_{r-1})$, with a fixed point θ_*, as indicated. Thus if θ_* were announced by the forecaster, the resulting reaction would generate exactly the same value so that the

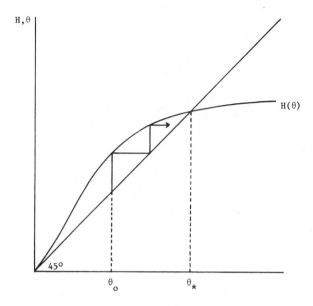

Figure 4.1. Reaction function.

forecast and subsequent intentions would agree. This kind of publication–reaction dynamics was employed by Grunberg and Modigliani (1954) and Simon (1954).

Strategic behavior

The potential advantages of strategic behavior on the part of the forecaster are illustrated in Figure 4.2, which incorporates different assumptions about the constituent elements of the reaction function H. The zone $0F$ is a failure zone: If an initial canvassing of opinion falls in this zone, a reverse bandwagon effect will hold. Thus if θ_0 indicates the initial announcement, the subsequent state of intentions $\theta_1 < \theta_0$. On the other hand, if θ_0' is the initial announcement, the subsequent state θ_1' exceeds this initial value. In terms of a replicated set of surveys or polls, the point U is an unstable equilibrium node.

The returns from strategic behavior on the part of an interested forecaster should now be clear. Having obtained θ_0, such a forecaster dissimulates either lying directly or creating otherwise the impression that the true value is in the vicinity of θ_0'. The next survey yields the value θ_1'. The forecaster can then claim with apparent truthfulness that his (or her)

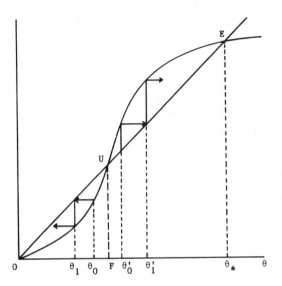

Figure 4.2. Unstable node.

forecast has been validated; indeed, it was evidently a conservative fore-cast since $\theta_1' > \theta_0'$, the announced value! Now, of course, the forecaster does not usually know the form of the reaction function H. In many in-stances, however, he may suspect that over certain crucial regions – the breakeven points for success, as it were – public reactions are strongly sloping. It will then pay him to interpret and present his evidence in as favorable a light as possible, even to lie or to suppress unfavorable indi-cations. Post hoc, the outcome may well prove him to be right. Indeed, by choosing to replicate the surveys, he would drive the outcome right up to the stable fixed point θ_* at E.

Even if the forecaster feels a professional obligation not to lie or fudge, he (or she) nevertheless has the option of simply not publishing a fore-cast that he or his employer does not like. But if this is the case, it follows that over a sample space of all forecasts, a biased selection procedure exists for those that are actually published. Later we show that the biased nature of forecasts exists in another sense, even with perfectly honest forecasters, so we ought to be a little more precise at the present junc-ture: Over a sample space of all forecasting exercises, *any published sur-vey of current intentions is biased.* We are not being altogether frivolous here. There are depressingly few people who go to the trouble of prepar-ing forecasts out of a dispassionate and correctly informed view of the public interest. Indeed, it might even be that in some circumstances it is in the public interest for the forecaster to lie. We shall return to consider such welfare evaluations later in the chapter.

What sort of defense mechanisms are available to the public against strategic behavior on the part of a forecaster? It is true that any published assessment θ may be treated with a certain amount of skepticism, arising variously from the nature of the methodology or from any perceived incentive for the forecaster to view the world through rose-tinted spectacles. But a basic difficulty arises. In a reflexive forecasting situation, the outcome depends not only upon what each agent thinks of the published $\hat{\theta}$ and the actual or implied forecast, but also upon what other agents think and therefore what each agent thinks about what other agents think. This is the "expectations-about-expectations" problem discussed in detail in Section 6.6. Implicitly, agents are involved in a second-guessing game. It may well be that agents view θ as published by the statistician with private skepticism. However, if other people believe it, then the published θ will acquire credibility ex post. A built-in weakness therefore exists. Each agent reads the published θ and knows his or her own mind; but the agent needs and does not have a third bit of information, namely, the opinions of other agents.

Much also depends upon whether the forecaster and his (or her) public share a similar welfare function with respect to the given event. If they all share common attitudes, then the public will tend to be less discriminating with respect to the published forecast. In such circumstances there may indeed be little motivation for the statistician to fudge things, and his forecast becomes more credible. If a forecaster feels a need to exaggerate, this may imply a measure of divergence between his welfare (or that of the employer) and the welfare of the public that he is trying to persuade.

It should also be remembered that incentives may exist for the public to exercise their own strategic behavior by dissimulating their responses to the survey of intentions. Such incentives have been reviewed in Chapter 3, where some possible tests for such behavior were suggested. It will be evident that in complete generality, the problem of public forecasting becomes a game played between the statistician or forecaster as the dominant player and the members of the public as the reacting players. Its treatment in the present chapter is of necessity somewhat stylized, and we cannot claim to have done full justice to all the dimensions and possible strategies involved in many real-life applications.

Some invariance considerations

Up to this point we have been working in terms of a model that might be formalized thus: The statistician prepares an estimate θ_{n-1} (at survey number $n-1$) of current intentions and utilizes this as a forecast of ultimate intentions, for example, how many visitors will actually come. Thus the forecast at stage $n-1$ is

$$f_{n-1} = \theta_{n-1}. \tag{1a}$$

Faced with this forecast, the public reacts:

$$\theta_n = \tilde{H}(f_{n-1}) = H(\theta_{n-1}). \tag{1b}$$

Equation (1b) yields the kind of dynamics represented in Figure 4.1 or 4.2.

The preceding model contains an implicit assumption that each survey is regarded as terminal. Given that attitudes θ_{n-1} have been surveyed, these are assumed to stick thereafter. But it could reasonably be objected that if the statistician expects to conduct further surveys or expects other investigators to do the same, then the forecast f_n should take this information into account. Our forecaster does not know the nature of any reaction function, but if any such function is presumed to be stable, then it seems reasonable to forecast by trying to forecast the fixed point θ_*. Perhaps this could be done by imagining that a stable H function exists; as successive surveys reveal $\theta_0, \theta_1, \theta_2, \ldots$, this information might be used to identify the nature of H and its parameters. At any rate, suppose that the statistician forecasts according to some function

$$f_{n-1} = f_{n-1}(\theta_{n-1}, \theta_{n-2}, \ldots, \theta_0). \tag{2a}$$

Then the underlying reaction is

$$\theta_n = \tilde{H}(f_{n-1}) = H_{n-1}(\theta_{n-1}, \theta_{n-2}, \ldots, \theta_0). \tag{2b}$$

We may now see the difficulty. The reaction function of expression (2b) is in general no longer a stable (i.e., time-invariant) function of the published estimates $\theta_{n-1}, \theta_{n-2}, \ldots, \theta_0$. Thus in conceiving of the forecasting problem as estimating a fixed point of some kind, the statistician may be hunting a snark. From the game-theoretic point of view, the statistician is trying to play a dominant player's game with no prior knowledge of the reaction function.

Remarkably enough, the kind of objection encapsulated in equations (2a) and (2b) can be overcome by a suitable decision rule on the part of the forecaster. In Section 4.5 we introduce a class of estimators of the form (2b) and predicated on recognition by the forecaster that agents will react to the forecasts rather than merely to revelation of the current state of opinions or intentions. Application of this rule leads with repeated surveys to the fixed point θ_* of the function H. However, a satisfactory treatment of such dominant-player games must take into account stochastic considerations such as sampling, where complete enumeration is not possible, or stochastic evolution of the state vector θ. Before turning to such matters, it is useful to consider a further example of publication-reaction dynamics.

4.3 Informational dynamics of political polls

An interesting and potentially important instance where a systematic dynamics of publication and reaction may exist originates in the informational content of political polls. Suppose that many prospective voters are in fact rather ignorant about the positions or prospects of candidates. Such voters may be seeking guidance from published polls as to the opinions of other voters. This is a familiar enough idea: If we are uncertain about any course of action, we often like to consult others to see what they think. One social function of polls may well be to convey information of this kind. In a recent series of contributions McKelvey and Ordeshook (1984, 1985a, b; see also Ordeshook, 1987) have formalized the kind of dynamics and equilibria involved, drawing on ideas concerning the informational content of rational-expectations equilibria. We study such equilibria in Chapter 5; however, the resulting disequilibrium dynamics falls quite naturally into the framework of the present chapter.

Let us imagine that on the issue at stake, the positions of both candidates and voters can be represented along a continuum of one dimension. Thus B could be the conservative candidate and A could be the liberal or social-democratic candidate. Voters inclined to the right along the continuum would vote (in the presence of perfect information) for B and those to the left for candidate A. We may represent the position of candidate A as x_A along the continuum and that for B as x_B. The choices of perfectly informed voters could then be rationalized by imagining for each voter i an ideal point x_i in the continuum. Supposing that voters have welfare or utility functions $u_i(x) = -|x_i - x|$, voter i will then choose the candidate whose position $x = x_A$ or $x = x_B$ is closest to that voter's own ideal point x_i. Such spatial models of elections are discussed by Enelow and Hinich (1984). We observe that the point $\frac{1}{2}(x_A + x_B)$ is a natural break point along the continuum; any perfectly informed voter i would vote for A if $x_i < \frac{1}{2}(x_A + x_B)$ and for candidate B otherwise.

Now suppose that some of the voters are not too well informed about x_A or x_B, that is, precisely where the two candidates stand on the issue. Call these the uninformed (u) voters. Others are called the informed voters (I). Let us suppose that the electorate is divided in proportions $\beta, 1 - \beta$ into the uninformed and the informed. For the purposes of Figure 4.3, we assume that $\beta = \frac{1}{2}$ so there are equal numbers of informed and uninformed. The axis and probability distributions in this diagram refer to

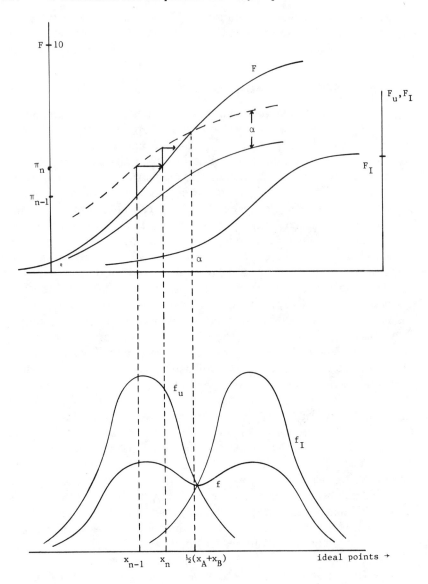

Figure 4.3. Informational dynamics.

ideal points x_i and the frequency distributions of the x_i. The lower part of the graph refers to the densities f_u and f_I of the uninformed and informed and the aggregate density f, which is obtained as the mixed density $f = \frac{1}{2}f_u + \frac{1}{2}f_I$. The upper half portrays the corresponding cumulative frequency distributions F_u, F_I and the aggregate F. The diagram is basically that of Ordeshook (1987, Figure 1), but we have added a phase plan dynamics similar to that employed in the foregoing predictive discussion.

To see how this dynamics is established, we specify that uninformed voters know with respect to candidates' positions, only that $A < B$; that is, they know that candidate A is the "liberal" and candidate B the "conservative," but they do not know precisely where the candidates stand (x_A or x_B) relative to their own ideal points (x_i). However, all voters do have an additional bit of information; they know where they stand relative to other voters. In other words they know the position of their ideal points x_i in the distribution $F(x)$ of ideal points in the electorate: For example, "I know that I am in the upper 10 percent for conservatism."

Let us now see how voters will poll. Imagine that a previous poll, poll number $n-1$, has given a vote of π_{n-1} percent to candidate A and $1-\pi_{n-1}$ to candidate B. Assume away any nonresponse problems. This information will not change at all the intentions of the informed voters. A proportion

$$\alpha = F_I\left(\frac{x_A + x_B}{2}\right) \tag{3}$$

will continue to support candidate A. But the reported π_{n-1} does have informational content capable of affecting the attitudes of the uninformed voters. If 40 percent of the poll supports A, this means that 40 percent of the electorate have ideal points closest to A. Thus, if an uninformed voter i regards himself or herself as in the 40 percent decile from the left, he or she will expect to vote for A. More generally, if a fraction π_{n-1} voted for A, the marginal critical point is x_{n-1} such that

$$F(x_{n-1}) = \pi_{n-1}; \qquad F(x) = \beta F_u(x) + (1-\beta)F_I(x). \tag{4}$$

So if his or her ideal point $x_i > x_{n-1}$, uninformed voter i will vote for A in the next round of polling. With proportions $\beta, 1-\beta$ of uninformed and informed, the fraction voting for A in poll n will then be

$$\pi_n = \beta F_u(x_{n-1}) + \alpha(1-\beta). \tag{5}$$

Equations (4) and (5) define a recursive dynamics for π_n in terms of π_{n-1}: $\pi_n = H(\pi_{n-1})$; $n = 1, 2, \ldots$. Figure 4.3 represents this dynamics in a phase plane of π against x. The stationary point is given by

$$F(x_*) = \pi_*,$$

$$\beta F_u(x_*) + \alpha(1-\beta) = \pi_*.$$

It follows from these equations and equation (3) that

$$F_I(x_*) = \alpha,$$

whence $x_* = \frac{1}{2}(x_a + x_b)$.

Thus with respect to the uninformed, the proportion voting for candidate A becomes $F_u[(x_a + x_b)/2]$, the "correct" proportion. In other words, in the final stationary point or equilibrium, the uninformed voters have become perfectly informed. The sequence of polls has transferred information from the group of informed voters to the uninformed.

As Ordeshook (1987) points out, the preceding dynamics involves several assumptions of the "heroic" kind, notably the unidimensional structure of preferences and that voters know their placement on the issue relative to others. If these assumptions are relaxed in various ways, different dynamics can result; for instance, it is possible that no convergence occurs so that information is never completely transmitted. The outcome from such modeling is obviously of importance for any study of the publication effects of polling or surveys. In what follows we shall assume a well-behaved dynamics in the sense that convergence can occur to some stationary state, not necessarily globally unique. Such an assumption should not however mask the necessity for a detailed study of the likely dynamics resulting from a cycle of survey and publication and bearing in mind the particular or special features of the application that one has in mind.

4.4   State estimation under reaction: Markovian structure and convergence

Although considerations of uncertainty were implicit in some of the discussion of Section 4.2, we have not so far introduced sources of ignorance regarding either the state of opinion or intentions θ or else the nature of the reaction function H. Let us now drop the assumption that θ is perfectly observable. Instead it must be estimated at each stage, for example, by means of a sample survey. We shall continue to suppose that some underlying reaction function H exists, which is unknown to the statistician. In this and the following section we shall consider the following problem: Suppose that the statistician estimates the current state θ of the system (e.g., intentions) by means of a sampling statistic e and publishes the results. The reactions of the public to the published statistic induce a new state. What are the effects of this on the validity of the statistic e; and over a sequence of replications of this basic experiment, what are the convergence properties, if any, of the resulting sequences both of estimates e and states θ? We shall call this the problem of state estimation under reaction effects. Of course it may be that the state estimates e can be utilized as forecasts, in which case they would clearly correspond to the myopic forecasts of the deterministic treatment. This is indeed the way in which such estimates have often been used in the past.

However, it turns out that the current state estimate is not the only possible forecast; the distinction rests not only upon whether forecasts are myopic or anticipative, but also upon how the public are presumed to react. For this reason we shall delay an explicit treatment of the forecasting problem until Section 4.6, concentrating in the interim upon the prior questions of state estimation under sampling. However, before we consider the complications due to sampling, it will be useful to start with the stability properties of the deterministic dynamics (1) generated by a reaction function $H(\cdot)$.

The stability properties of H

Let us consider the convergence properties of the deterministic process $\theta_{r+1} = H(\theta_r)$, that is, the stability properties of the function $H(\cdot)$. A fixed point θ_* is such that $\theta_* = H(\theta_*)$, and we shall usually assume that at least one fixed point of the function H exists. The classical result concerning existence is Brouwer's fixed-point theorem: In Euclidean space, if H is a continuous function from the bounded closed interval I to itself, then there is at least one fixed point. If in addition H obeys a Lipschitz condition $|H(\theta_1) - H(\theta_2)| \leq K|\theta_1 - \theta_2|$ for $0 < K < 1$ for every $\theta_1, \theta_2 \in I$, then the fixed point θ_* is unique and moreover the iterative routine $\theta_{r+1} = H(\theta_r)$ will yield $\theta_r \to \theta_*$ as $r \to \infty$. The requirements of Brouwer's theorem are sometimes not met in the kind of problem we shall be concerned with. For instance, it may be known that a population proportion can adopt only a small number of possible values; yet the sample estimate adopts a very much denser set and may for all practical purposes be treated as a continuum. Likewise a Lipschitz condition may be unduly restrictive for stability analysis, and we shall adopt in the following the method of Liapounov: Given a fixed point θ_*, suppose that $V(\theta - \theta_*)$ is a positive definite function and define $Q_\lambda = \{\theta : V(\theta - \theta_*) \leq \lambda\}$. Let θ_0 be an initial value. If $\theta_1 = H(\theta_0)$ and $V(\theta_1) - V(\theta_0) = -k(\theta_0) \leq 0$ for $\theta_0 \in Q_\lambda$, then $\theta_r \to \{\theta : k(\theta) = 0\} \cap Q_\lambda$, a limit set, as $r \to \infty$. Somewhat less precisely, one has to show that V is decreasing given the dynamics $\theta_{r+1} = H(\theta_r)$. Figure 4.4 is a simple illustration of a well-behaved reaction function where the limit set is the unique point θ_*. Thus if sampling were in fact complete enumeration of the population, the cycle of repeated survey and publication would ultimately yield the fixed point θ_*, with the rate of convergence exponential in the case illustrated.

Sampling and transition probabilities

We shall imagine that the object is to estimate the value of a parameter θ referring to some attribute of a population. For expositional reasons we

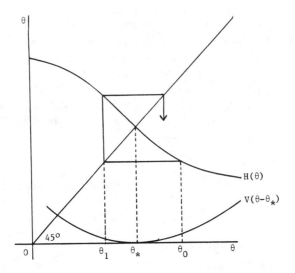

Figure 4.4. Publication dynamics; deterministic.

shall treat this as a scalar, but many results extend immediately with obvious modifications to the vector parameter case. Consider then a framework of repeated samples of fixed size n. Given that the population parameter at stage r is θ_r, we shall estimate this by a statistic e_r, which is a function of the sample observations. The estimate e_r is announced or published. People react to this announcement, modifying their behavior in such a way that the new parameter is θ_{r+1}. In the simplest specification we shall assume that

$$\theta_{r+1} = H(e_r), \tag{6}$$

some unspecified function[1]; an alternative is

$$\theta_{r+1} = H(e_r, \theta_r), \tag{7}$$

and both formulations may be further generalized (see Section 4.5) in the form of conditional probability statements about θ_{r+1} given e_r and θ_r. We shall assume that given a population parameter θ_r, the estimate e_r is

---

[1] It could reasonably be objected that any reaction function should include higher sampling moments of e_r from risk aversion or similar motives. Suppose, however, that $e = \hat{p}$, the sample estimate of a population proportion; then $\sigma_{\hat{p}}^2 = \hat{p}(1-\hat{p})/m$, where m is the sample size, assumed fixed in repeated surveys. Thus any reaction function of the form $\tilde{H}(e, \sigma_e^2) = H(e)$ in this case. Hence, in some cases, the objection can be handled by an appropriate specification of H. In others one may be able to augment e_r with say $\sigma_{e_r}^2$ to form a state vector and work out the dynamics of such a state vector.

a sufficient statistic for θ_r. Thus if a random sample of observations $\mathbf{X}_r$ of size m_r is taken at stage r, then $e_r = e(\mathbf{X}_r)$ and

$$P(\mathbf{X}_r; \theta_r) = g(e_r; \theta_r) h(\mathbf{X}_r) \tag{8}$$

where $g(e; \theta)$ is the density of e given θ and $h(\mathbf{X})$ is the conditional density of $\mathbf{X}$ given e and is independent of θ. The sufficiency property is important because it means that all information about the state (θ) of the system is carried over from one replication to the next by the statistic e; without the sufficiency assumption one would have in addition to consider explicitly the transmission of information by the vector of observations $\mathbf{X}$, a far more complicated task. For expositional simplicity we assume the existence of continuous probability densities, but in all cases Riemann integrals may be replaced by Lebesgue–Stieltjes integrals for more general state spaces and distribution functions, and the results do not depend upon continuity assumptions except where otherwise stated.

Equations (6) and (7) indicate a Markovian structure for e_r, with the one-stage transition relationship

$$f_{r+1}(e_{r+1}) = \int_{e_r} g[e_{r+1}; \theta_{r+1}(e_r)] f_r(e_r) \, de_r \tag{9}$$

where $\theta_{r+1}(e_r) = H(e_r)$ and $f_r(e_r)$ is the stage r density for e_r. Under the preceding sufficiency conditions, all information about θ_r is contained in e_r and the Markovian structure of the latter generates a corresponding process for the population parameters θ_r, which are now themselves random variables. The one-stage transition mechanism is of the form

$$\nu_{r+1}(\theta_{r+1}) = \int_{\theta_r} G(\theta_{r+1}; \theta_r) \nu_r(\theta_r) \, d\theta_r \tag{10}$$

where $G(\theta_{r+1}; \theta_r) = g(e_r^-; \theta_r)/H'(e_r^-)$ is the transition density with $e_r^- = H^{-1}(\theta_{r+1})$ the functional inverse of H.[2]

The stationary or invariant distribution

In general, suppose that $\phi(x; y)$ is the one-stage transition probability in a discrete-time Markov process with a continuous state space. Then

---

[2] To see this make the transformation $\theta_{r+1} = H(e_r)$. The integral on the right side of equation (9) may be written as

$$\int_{e_r^-} g(e_{r+1}; \theta_{r+1}) \frac{f_r(e_r^-)}{H'(e_r^-)} \, d\theta_{r+1}.$$

Making the transformation $\theta_{r+2} = H(e_{r+1})$, the left side may be written $f_{r+1}(e_{r+1}^-) = \nu_{r+2}(\theta_{r+1}) H'(e_{r+2}^-)$. Equating the two sides yields equation (10).

given a marginal distribution $p_{n-1}(y)$ at time $n-1$, the marginal distribution at time n is given by

$$p_n(x) = \int_y \phi(x; y) p_{n-1}(y) \, dy.$$

One is often interested in conditions on the transition probabilities $\phi(x; y)$ that will ensure that as time $n \to \infty$, the density $p_n(x)$ approaches a stationary state independent of n. Such a density $p_*(x)$ would be invariant in the sense that it satisfies the stationary condition

$$p_*(x) = \int_y \phi(x; y) p_*(y) \, dy.$$

Turning to the transition mechanisms (9) and (10), the stochastic version of the fixed-point property is that as $r \to \infty$ the densities $f_r(\cdot)$ and $\theta_r(\cdot)$ tend to stationary or invariant densities $f^*(\cdot)$ and $v^*(\cdot)$. The conditions under which this is true are somewhat technical and are discussed in detail in Appendix 1 to this chapter. Basically they fall into three categories, corresponding to properties of the sampling procedure and estimation at each stage; the nature of the transition density function; and the stability of the underlying dynamics as represented by the stability properties of the reaction function H. With regard to the first of these requirements, convergence will be true if the successive samples $r = 1, 2, 3, \ldots$ are independently drawn and the estimation procedure at each stage is unbiased with a finite sampling variance. The second aspect is covered by requiring that the transition probabilities are always positive, so that all values of either e_r or θ_r can communicate with all values e_{r+1} and θ_{r+1}, respectively. Finally it is required that the dynamics represented by the deterministic function H is stable in the sense described in the preceding (e.g., Figure 4.4), and indeed we suppose that a deterministic Liapounov function V applies. Thus the stochastic stability in the sense of the existence of a limiting probability distribution is tied to the deterministic stability associated with the reaction function H as a necessary requirement. Moreover the rate of convergence is exponential in the sense that any suitable norm of the difference between the densities $f_r(\cdot)$ and $f^*(\cdot)$ approaches zero exponentially as $r \to \infty$. The preceding conditions are sufficient rather than necessary; it is possible to significantly weaken them in specific examples and perhaps even in general.

As a matter of dynamics, two counterbalancing forces are at work with respect to the convergence of the densities $f_r(\cdot)$ of the estimates e_r. The deterministic dynamics $e_{r+1} = H(e_r)$ pulls e toward e^*, the fixed point, especially for values of e far from e^*. As e_r approaches e^*, the inward dynamics become less important relative to the diffuseness created by the sampling fluctuation. The stationary distribution represents a long-run balance between these inward and outward forces. Note also that the requirement that H yields a globally stable deterministic dynamics about a unique fixed point may perhaps rule out some phenomena of interest. One possibility is that the system is ergodic but periodic; there are cyclically moving subsets of states (see Doob, 1953, Section V.5). In other words, the cycle of repeated sampling and publication may, with certain types of reaction function, tend to stochastically cyclic behavior for the population parameter. In the ensuing discussion we shall usually suppose that the stationary or invariant distributions f^* and ν^* that solve equations (9) and (10) are unique. We shall also suppose that the fixed point x_* of $H(x)$ is unique. This is not however a necessary condition for the existence of a unique stationary distribution (see the example that follows).

Finally it may be pointed out that the convergence results continue to hold if the reaction mechanism (7) is assumed to hold rather than the basic case (6). The stochastic dynamics are those of the joint system

$$e_{r+1} = H(\theta_r, e_r) + \epsilon_{r+1},$$

$$\theta_{r+1} = H(\theta_r, e_r),$$

where ϵ_{r+1} represents a sampling fluctuation given θ_r. The corresponding deterministic dynamics is obtained by simply dropping the sampling variation ϵ_{r+1} and is of the form $x_{r+1} = H(x_r, x_r)$. Provided the latter dynamics in (θ_r, e_r) is asymptotically stable with an appropriate Liapounov function, the convergence results continue to hold under the kind of assumptions quoted before concerning the transition mechanisms for the joint density of θ and e.

Fixed-point properties under sampling

Given a purely deterministic dynamics, the concept of a fixed point is quite straightforward: e^* is a fixed point if $e^* = H(e^*)$. Of course, there may be multiple fixed points or they may not even exist, but the idea is clear enough. However, once we invoke sampling considerations, *two* more invariant points arise.

(a) Recalling that $\theta_{r+1} = H(e_r); \theta_r$, let $\gamma(\theta) = E(H(e); \theta)$, so that $\gamma(\theta_r) = E(\theta_{r+1}; \theta_r)$. Then we define θ^* such that $\theta^* = \gamma(\theta^*)$, the fixed point of the conditional mean function $\gamma(\theta)$. Thus if $\theta_r = \theta^*$, then the population parameter θ_{r+1} generated for the ensuing period is on the average equal to the given value $\theta^* = E(\theta_{r+1}; \theta_r = \theta^*)$. On the other hand, even if H has a fixed point e^*, it is not necessary that a fixed point θ^* for the conditional expectation function exists (in the example that follows it does not); nor is it necessary that θ^* is unique even if e^* is.

(b) The second fixed point is the mean π^* of the stationary or invariant distributions. In fact, if the statistic e is unbiased, then

$$E^*e = E^*H(e) = E^*\theta = E^*\gamma(\theta) = \pi^*, \tag{11}$$

where the asterisk denotes expectations with respect to the stationary distributions. In other words, the means of the distributions $f^*(e)$ and $\nu^*(\theta)$ have the same value π^*. The proof of this property is quite straightforward and relies on the iterated expectation: Given a function $f(x, y)$ of two random variables x, y,

$$E_{x,y} f(x, y) = E_y[E_x f(x, y); y]$$

where the semicolon denotes conditioning. In the present instance, note first that

$$E(e_{r+1}; e_r) = \theta_{r+1} = H(e_r),$$

since e_{r+1} is unbiased. Hence $Ee_{r+1} = E_{e_r}E_{e_{r+1}}(e_{r+1}; e_r) = E_{e_r}H(e_r)$. Since e_{r+1} and e_r have the same invariant distribution, it follows that $E^*e = E^*H(e) = \pi^*$, say. Then $E^*\theta = E^*H(e) = \pi^*$ and

$$\pi^* = E^*\theta_{r+1} = E^*_{\theta_r}E^*_{\theta_{r+1}}(\theta_{r+1}; \theta_r) = E^*_{\theta_r}E^*_{e_r}[H(e_r); \theta_r] = E^*\gamma(\theta_r),$$

so that $\pi^* = E^*\theta_{r+1} = E^*\theta = E^*\gamma(\theta)$ since θ_{r+1} and θ_r have the same stationary distribution and the result follows.

Whereas the mean π^* of the invariant distributions $f^*(e)$ and $\nu^*(\theta)$ is not itself a fixed point of any function, it does have an invariance property of its own, namely, as the almost sure limit of the time average $\bar{e}_n = 1/n\sum_{r=1}^{n} e_r$ as the number of surveys $n \to \infty$. This result can be shown to follow from the central limit theorem for Markov processes (Doob, 1953, Section 7.5), which states also that (i) $\lim_{n \to \infty} En(\bar{e} - \pi^*)^2$ exists equal to σ^2, say, and (ii) $\sqrt{n}(\bar{e} - \pi^*)$ is asymptotically normal $(0, \sigma^2)$. Thus one can actually estimate the mean of the invariant distribution by taking a running mean $1/n\sum_{r=1}^{n} e_r$ of the sample estimates e_r of the underlying state of intentions θ_r at each stage. This running mean will be important in the next section.

We turn now to discuss the relationship between the different fixed or invariant points e^*, θ^*, and π^*. This turns out to depend upon the functional form of H. Suppose first that the reaction function H is linear in e. If this is the case, then $\gamma(\theta) = E[H(e); \theta] = H(Ee; \theta) = H(\theta)$. Thus the fixed points e^* and θ^* are identical, so that $\theta^* = e^*$. Moreover, $\pi^* = E^*e = H(E^*e) = H(\pi^*)$, so that $e^* = \pi^*$. In summary, if the reaction function is linear, all invariant points coincide.

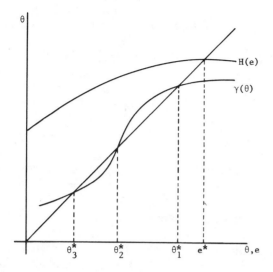

Figure 4.5. Functions γ and H: concave H.

This coincidence is not in general true if H is nonlinear. However, it is possible to draw some conclusion for general classes of function. Suppose that H is concave, so that $H(e)$ lies below its tangent line (see Figure 4.5). It must then follow that

(i) $\gamma(\theta) \leq H(\theta)$,   all $\theta \in S_\theta$,

(ii) $\theta^* \leq e^*$ and $\pi^* \leq e^*$.   (12)

To see property (i), take expectations conditional upon θ. Then $\gamma(\theta) = E[H(e); \theta] \leq H(Ee; \theta) = H(\theta)$ if H is concave (Jensen's inequality). To see property (ii), recall first that if the deterministic dynamics based upon H are stable, it must be true that $|H^*(e^*)| < 1$. Now since H lies beneath its tangent plane at e^*, it must be true that

$$H(e) \leq e^* + (e - e^*)H'(e^*).$$

Taking expectations conditional on θ and putting $\theta = \theta^*$, we obtain

$$\theta^* = \gamma(\theta^*) \leq e^* + (\theta^* - e^*)H'(e^*), \tag{13}$$

whence $\theta^* \leq e^*$ if $|H'(e^*)| < 1$. Taking unconditional expectations of each side of (13) with respect to the stationary distribution, we have

$$\pi^* = E^*H(e) \leq e^* + (\pi^* - e^*)H'(e^*),$$

whence also $\pi^* \leq e^*$. Note also that the inequalities in (12) may be reversed in the case where H is convex to the origin rather than concave (i.e., $-H$ is concave).

We note that nothing definite can be said about the relationship between θ^* and π^* even for functions known to be globally concave or convex. In Bowden (1987a) it is suggested, based on a Taylor series approximation, that if H is only mildly concave, then it is likely that $\pi^* < \theta^* \leq e^*$ (reversed if H is convex to the origin).

This concludes our detailed discussion of the fixed and limit points associated with the sampling–publication sequence. The relationship between the functions H and γ and their fixed points is interpreted graphically in Figure 4.5. In this example, $\gamma(\theta)$ has multiple fixed points $\theta_1^*, \theta_2^*, \theta_3^*$; all must be less than e^*.

We conclude this section with an example in which the invariant distribution and fixed points are worked out explicitly. Although it is not a fixed point, the mean of the invariant distribution can act as guide to the correct action or decision to be made on the basis of repeated sampling.

Example

Suppose that a local authority is contemplating building a new marina. To help its decision process, it commissions a survey of public intentions about owning boats over some coming horizon. Reflexivity arises because these intentions may well depend upon the existence of the new marina, and this in turn will be perceived to depend upon the survey results.

Let π_c represent a critical proportion unknown to the statistician such that the public anticipates that a new marina will be built if the announced sample value $e > \pi_c$, where e is the sample proportion who plan to own a boat. If the marina is to be built, a proportion p_1 of the population will plan to own a boat; if not, a smaller proportion $p_2 < p_1$ will plan boat ownership. Thus the state space S_θ consists of just two points p_1, p_2. The reaction function H is discontinuous:

$$\theta_{r+1} = p_1 \leftrightarrow e_r \geq \pi_c$$

$$= p_2 \leftrightarrow e_r < \pi_c.$$

Given the proportion θ_r at stage r, the sample number planning ownership has a binomial distribution, and the sample proportion has mean θ_r and variance $\theta_r(1-\theta_r)/m$, where m is the size of the sample. Denoting by Φ the (cumulative) distribution function of e_r, the transition probabilities in S_θ may be worked out as follows. Given that $\theta_r = p_1$, we get $\theta_{r+1} = p_1$ if $\hat{e} > \pi_c$, so

$$p^{11}=1-\Phi\left(\pi_c; p_1, \frac{1}{m}p_1(1-p_1)\right)=1-\Phi_1$$

for brevity. Then

$$p^{21}=\text{prob}(\theta_{r+1}=p_2; \theta_r=p_1)=\Phi_1$$

and similarly

$$p^{22}=1-\Phi\left(\pi_3; p_2, \frac{1}{m}p_2(1-p_2)\right)=1-\Phi_2 \quad \text{and} \quad p^{12}=\Phi_2.$$

Working out the stationary probabilities as the appropriate normalized eigenvector of $p=(p_{ij})$ (e.g., Cox and Miller, 1965, Section 4.5), we obtain

$$\nu^*(p_1)=\frac{\Phi_2}{\Phi_1+\Phi_2}, \qquad \nu^*(p_2)=\frac{\Phi_1}{\Phi_1+\Phi_2}$$

as the stationary density for θ with expectation

$$E^*(\hat{e})=E^*(\theta)=\pi^*=(p_1\Phi_2+p_2\Phi_1)/(\Phi_1+\Phi_2).$$

The conditional expectation function $\gamma(\theta)$ is given by

$$\gamma_1=\gamma(p_1)=p_1(1-\Phi_1)+p_2(\Phi_1),$$

$$\gamma_2=\gamma(p_2)=p_1\Phi_2+p_2(1-\Phi_2).$$

We note also that $\pi^*=(\Phi_2\gamma_1+\Phi_1\gamma_2)/(\Phi_1+\Phi_2)$, or

$$\frac{p_1-\gamma_1}{\gamma_2-p_2}=\frac{\Phi_1}{\Phi_2}.$$

These latter relationships enable us to fix the various points in graphical interpretations. Figure 4.6 is a possible configuration.

In this configuration, both p_1 and p_2 are fixed points for the H function; if sample r yields precisely p_1, then $\theta_{r+1}=p_1$, and if it yields p_2, then $\theta_{r+1}=p_2$. We note that the existence of two fixed points does not preclude the existence of a stationary distribution. There are no fixed points for the $\gamma(\theta)$ function. The long-run expectation $\pi^*>\pi_c$.

A policy of announcing the current estimate e_n as the official estimate will evidently result in instability, with the underlying θ continually switching between the values p_1 and p_2. On the other hand, if the running mean $\bar{e}_n$ (defined in the preceding) were announced as the official estimate, then as the number of polls became large, this value would tend to the constant π^*, and the authority could eventually rest assured that another round of sampling would not result in a reversal of their decision with respect to building. The present example is of course highly stylized rather

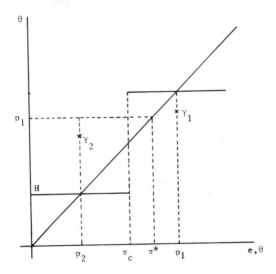

Figure 4.6. Functions γ and H: discrete state space.

than realistic. However, the advantages of presenting a running mean as the official estimate are taken up in a predictive context in the next section.

4.5   The forecasting problem: reactions, myopia, and anticipation

In the preceding section we have considered in detail the problem of state estimation in the presence of reactive behavior. Naturally enough, there is a strong connection between state estimation and forecasting. Consider, for instance, the interpretation of a repeated sequence of polls, say of the Gallup or ABC–Harris type. Suppose that the nth poll has just been taken yielding a statistic e_n. The correct interpretation of this value might be worded thus: "Had an election been held today (just before this poll is announced) the estimated majority for candidate x would be e_n." Put this way, the problem is clearly one of state estimation; one is estimating current intentions. The problem is, of course, that the public is very often more interested in a forecast of how the election will actually turn out. In such circumstances, the state estimate e_n is often interpreted as a de facto forecast. The conventional expert reaction is to deprecate such an interpretation, for as we have seen, the presence of publication effects means that the preceding statement is no longer valid if the words in parentheses are replaced by "after this poll." A more complete approach to the problem would recognize that the current estimate e_n can indeed represent a forecast, but perhaps not a particularly good one, and that it may be possible to design a forecasting procedure that improves upon the current state estimate. This is especially true if one expects to take further polls (say) before the time of the election. Thus in the present section we shall explicitly consider the problems of prediction as distinct from the somewhat more limited context of state estimation.

At the outset, we should recognize that the predictive performance of any forecasting function should depend upon the nature of public reactions. Two polar cases arise (combinations are possible but are not considered here). In the first, people react to the publication of the current state estimate:

$$\theta_{n+1} = H(e_n). \tag{6}$$

This is the kind of supposition that we have hitherto been using as equation (6). However, it might be that once a forecast f_n is prepared, people react to this rather than to the current state estimate. Thus suppose that the forecast f_n is of the form

$$f_n = f_n(e_n, e_{n-1}, \ldots, e_0), \tag{14}$$

generalizing equation (2a) of Section 4.2 to the sampling context. Then instead of reacting to the current state estimate e_n, people react as

$$\theta_{n+1} = H(f_n). \tag{15}$$

In what follows we shall consider both of these contingencies in turn under the headings of state reactions and forecast reactions.

State reactions

The statistical dynamics of model (6) have already been considered in some detail in Sections 4.4 and 4.5. The forecaster's task is essentially to estimate where the system will be at some designated date (value of n) in the future. Suppose that the election will be held after period N, the horizon, that is, N polls in all will be taken prior to the election. If N is large in relation to n, then the distribution of θ_N given information up to the current period n will approximate the stationary distribution with expectation π^*. The central-limit theorem given in Section 4.5 suggests that given $\ldots, e_{n-1}, e_n$, a better prediction would then be the current estimate of π^*, namely, $\bar{e}_n = 1/n \sum_{r=0}^{n} e_r$. Thus over successive polls, the statistician would record two bits of information: (a) the current estimate e_n measuring the current state of opinion and (b) the running means $\bar{e}_1, \bar{e}_2, \bar{e}_3, \ldots$. These would represent predictions of the final outcome.

The resolution of whether e_n or $\bar{e}_n$ is a better predictor of θ_N depends upon the absolute value of n as well as the difference $N - n$. In particular, if n is small, the early dynamics of the reaction function H are likely to predominate, and if this (deterministic) dynamics is monotonic, the current figure e_n is to be preferred. Thus in the 1980 U.S. presidential election, a series of 13 ABC–Harris polls taken between June and November showed that support for the third candidate (Anderson) declined in roughly exponential fashion from 25 to 9 percent. Of course, we should not attribute all of this movement to a publication–reaction dynamics; the real world is a multivariate place. In such circumstances the use of a running mean for predictive purposes is clearly not justified (the final result was 6 percent). On the other hand, where trends or reactions are either less well defined or appear to be cyclical, the running mean will perform better. Thus in the poll sequence referred to in the preceding, the running means $\bar{e}_n$ were almost uniformly closer than were the current estimates e_n to the final result for the eventual winner, Reagan. The difference hinges also upon the expected magnitude of the sampling variances of each estimate e_n; the running mean will constitute a better smoothening of such fluctuations.

We have noted that where public reactions are to the state estimates e_n, the ensuing statistical dynamics are essentially those of the state estimation problem considered in the previous section. One implication of this is that no matter how many replications have occurred, the one-period-ahead forecasts are always biased: given e_n, then $\theta_{n+1} = H(e_n) \neq e_n$ or $\bar{e}_n$ unless either happens to be equal to the fixed point of H. The latter contingency can occur only by chance since no property ensures – for this model – that for n either large or small, e_n or $\bar{e}_n$ are even approximately equal to that fixed point. The most that one can assure oneself of is that predictions (as $\bar{e}_n$) may be unconditionally unbiased referring to the stationary distribution to be established as the result of a large number of future replications of the survey–forecast experiment. This is rather unsatisfactory. One would like to know of one's forecasting procedure that if a large number of replications had already been incurred, then the one-period-ahead forecast is somewhere close to the resulting state so that the incentive to conduct a further survey–forecast replication should be small. This particular contingency corresponds to an equilibrium concept (see Section 4.6). What we are effectively saying here is that if the public reacts to the current state, then a satisfactory equilibrium to the resulting forecasting game does not exist. As we shall shortly point out, things are quite different where the public reacts to the published forecast rather than merely to the estimated current state.

Forecast reactions

It would seem quite possible, as a matter of applications, that if the statistician prepares a forecast f_n, then people will react to the forecast rather than to the current state estimate e_n. After all, both the forecaster and the public are presumably interested in the same thing, namely, the final outcome – the number of people who will end up attending, the actual result of the election, and so forth. Accordingly let us turn to consider the dynamics entailed by reaction (15), in which the state of the system depends upon the announced forecast.

The very simplest example of a forecast function is

$$f_n = e_n, \tag{16}$$

which is of the form (14) with zero contributions from past state estimates. We might call this a *myopic* forecast for reasons that will later be apparent. The resulting state dynamics are those of equation (6) and have already been analyzed. It will be recalled that although a stationary distribution for both the state and the forecast (in this case e_n) are attained, both state and forecast continue to move around from period to period. No matter how large is n, the *conditional* expectation of θ_{n+1} given the forecast f_n is never (except by chance) equal to f_n. Thus myopic forecasts will always be biased whether they refer to one, two, or any number of periods into the future.

Suppose, on the other hand, that the forecaster decided to utilize as a forecast the running mean of the sufficient statistics e_i:

$$f_n = \bar{e}_n = \frac{1}{n} \sum_{i=1}^{n} e_i.$$

An alternative recursive representation of the running mean forecast is

$$f_n = f_{n-1} + \frac{1}{n}(e_n - f_{n-1}). \tag{17}$$

Recalling that $e_n = \theta_n + \epsilon_n$ and combining this with equation (15), we obtain also

$$e_n = H(f_{n-1}) + \epsilon_n. \tag{18}$$

Equations (17) and (18) now constitute a dynamics in f_n, e_n and, by implication, the current state θ_n. Provided that the reaction function $H(\cdot)$ is stable in the sense of Liapounov, it may be shown (Bowden, 1987) that the sequence of forecasts f_n tends almost surely to the fixed point of the reaction function H. The latter point we shall designate here as f_* (rather than e_* as in Sections 4.4 and 4.5, where the reaction was to current state estimates e_n). Thus

$$f_n \to f_*, \quad \text{where } H(f_*) = f_* \text{ almost surely.}$$

It follows immediately that

$$\theta_n \to H(f_*) = f_* \text{ almost surely.}$$

Thus the limiting forecast f_* forecasts the state of the system exactly. The existence of an exact forecast is a far stronger state of affairs than for the myopic forecast (16).

Moreover we may turn things around. Suppose that we bend our efforts to finding a forecasting function (14) that, with probability 1, attains the fixed point f_* of the reaction function $H(f)$. It would seem not unreasonable to aim for such a forecasting function, for if the forecaster knows that the survey and forecast will be replicated into the future, he or she ought to try to anticipate future reactions, in effect moving along a phase diagram such as that of Figure 4.1. We might therefore term such a forecasting function an *anticipative* forecast.

Various ways exist of preparing anticipative forecasts. We might, for instance, try to actually estimate the reaction function $H(f)$ and hence calculate its fixed point or points. As an estimator of the latter, the procedure will fall into the class (14), assuming of course that no prior information as to the nature of H exists. The difficulty with such a procedure is that it inevitably has to be parametric, involving some sort of guesswork as to the functional form of the reaction function and requiring also a fair number of replications of the basic survey–forecast experiment. Less demanding are the nonparametric techniques, where one need not make any guesses as to the nature of the reaction function and indeed may remain in ignorance as to the precise nature of this function throughout the series of replications. Of these nonparametric techniques, the method of stochastic approximation, which generalizes the running mean forecast (17), appears to be especially promising.

Forecasting by stochastic approximation

Given the forecast reaction (15), let us consider the following forecasting procedure: Having surveyed or sampled to obtain the estimate e_n of the current state, define the recursive forecast

$$\begin{aligned} f_0 &= e_0, \\ f_n &= f_{n-1} + a_n(e_n - f_{n-1}), \quad n = 1, 2, \ldots, \end{aligned} \tag{19}$$

where the nonnegative sequence a_n of "gains" modifies the quasi-error correction process $e_n - f_{n-1}$. The gain sequence may itself be stochastic, but we shall suppose that it is a nonstochastic sequence chosen in advance. The forecasts f_n are published at each stage. Equation (19) thus represents a series of recursively defined forecasts and as a forecast function is of the general form (14).

Substituting (15) and $e_n = \theta_n + \epsilon_n$ into equation (19), we obtain

$$f_n = f_{n-1} + a_n M(f_{n-1}) + a_n \epsilon_n, \tag{20}$$

where $M(f_{n-1}) = H(f_{n-1}) - f_{n-1}$. Now equation (20), as a stochastic difference equation, is precisely of the form considered in the stochastic approximation literature. For readers unfamiliar with this literature, a brief account is given in Section 7.3. Although the physical or experimental interpretation of equation (19) differs a little from the classical stochastic approximation problem, the latter is certainly concerned as we are with estimating the zero of the function $M(f)$. In particular, the classical Robbins–Monro procedure results in equations homologous to (19) and (20). Under suitable conditions on the choice of gain, the stochastic errors ϵ_n (or $\epsilon_n + \zeta_n$), and the reaction function H, it is true that $f_n \to f_*$ almost surely, where the fixed point is such that $M(f_*) = H(f_*) - f_* = 0$. Moreover, as we shall see, asymptotic distributional results are available for the forecast f_*.

For general surveys of stochastic approximation convergence properties, we refer the reader forward to Section 7.3 and especially to Dupac (1984), from which the material that follows is adapted for the present context. With respect to the reaction function, let us suppose that for $f \neq f_*$,

$$[H(f) - f] \operatorname{sgn}(f - f_*) < 0. \tag{21}$$

Such a condition is implied by the existence of a Liapounov function for the deterministic stability of the function $H(\cdot)$ and graphically means that the reaction function crosses the 45° line from above. Then if the gain sequence is chosen so that $\sum_n a_n = \infty$ and $\sum_n a_n^2 < \infty$, we have $f_n \to f_*$ almost surely. The condition $\sum_n a_n^2 < \infty$ can be replaced by $a_n \to 0$ as $n \to \infty$ for mean-square convergence $[E(f_n - f_*)^2 \to 0]$, which is in fact quite sufficient for the present context.

The gain sequences a_n most commonly chosen are of the form

$$a_n = an^{-\alpha}, \quad a > 0, \quad 0 < \alpha \leq 1. \tag{22}$$

It will be noted from equation (17) that the particular choice $a = 1$, $\alpha = 1$ corresponds to the running mean $f_n = \bar{e}_n = 1/n \sum_{i=1}^{n} e_i$ as forecast. However, as remarked in what follows, the choice $a = 1$ is not usually optimal.

Distributional results may be derived as follows. Assume that the sequence of estimation variances (or estimation plus state noise variances for the noisy state model) is bounded and that $\lim_{n \to \infty} \sigma_n^2 = \sigma^2$. For brevity, write $m_* = |M'(f_*)| = |H'(f_*) - 1|$. Then under the preceding convergence conditions.

$$\sqrt{n}(f_n - f_*) \sim N\left(0, \frac{a^2\sigma^2}{2m_* a - 1}\right) \tag{23}$$

asymptotically. Note that from the asymptotic variance point of view, the minimal variance choice for the "powering" constant a is $a = 1/m_*$, giving a minimal asymptotic variance of σ^2/m_*^2. Although the equilibrium gradient m_* is not known a priori, its value can be progressively estimated (Lai and Robbins, 1979): Let $Y_n = e_n - f_{n-1}$ and define the running means

$$\bar{f}_n = \frac{1}{n}\sum_{i=1}^{n} f_n \quad \text{and} \quad \bar{Y}_n = \frac{1}{n}\sum_{i=1}^{n} Y_i.$$

Let

$$W_n = \frac{\sum_{i=1}^{n}(f_i - \bar{f}_n)(Y_i - \bar{Y}_n)}{\sum_{i=1}^{n}(f_i - \bar{f}_n)^2}.$$

Suppose that it is known a priori that $r_1 \le m_* \le r_2$, some bounded interval, and define the monitored estimate $\hat{m}_* = \max[r_1, \min(|W_n|, r_2)]$. Then $\hat{m}_* \to m_*$ with probability 1, and moreover if $H''(f_*)$ exists, then $(\log n)^{1/2}[\hat{m}_* - m_*]$ is asymptotically $N(0, m_*^2)$. In general, the prominence of $a = 1/|M'(f_*)|$ is not too surprising since we are essentially finding the root to $M(f) = 0$ based upon a stochastic version of the Gauss–Markov algorithm while the additional factor $1/n$ is responsible for smoothening stochastic fluctuations in the observed output from the iterative convergence experiments. Finally we note that the asymptotic distributional result (23) may be used to construct confidence intervals for f_* of increasing accuracy as n becomes large. One estimates σ^2 as $1/n \sum_{i=1}^{n}(Y_i - \bar{Y}_n)^2$, where $Y_i = e_i - f_{i-1}$ and $\bar{Y}_n$ is defined in the preceding.

Since the number of replications n is typically far short of what is required for true asymptotic considerations, we should also like to know something about the likely rate of convergence of f_n to f_*. Some insight is available in the case where $V(f) = (f - f_*)^2$ is a Liapounov function for the deterministic stability of the recursion $f_n = H(f_{n-1})$, corresponding to classic monotonic or cobweb convergence in the phase plane: Thus $V(f_n) = [H(f_{n-1}) - f_*]^2 < (f_{n-1} - f_*)^2$. It follows by simple algebra that $[H(f) - f_*](f - f_*) < -\frac{1}{2}(f - f_*)^2$, so that $K = \frac{1}{2}$ in Theorem 3.3 of Dupac (1984, p. 518). For gains of the form (22), the rate of mean-square convergence is given by

$$E(f_n - f_*)^2 = O \begin{cases} n^{-\alpha}, & 0 < \alpha < 1, \\ n^{-1}, & \alpha = 1, \ a > 1, \\ n^{-1} \log n, & \alpha = 1, \ a = 1, \\ n^{-a}, & \alpha = 1, a < 1. \end{cases}$$

Thus if it is suspected that the reaction is a Liapounov-stable one, convergence is encouraged by the use of a long basic step length ($a > 1$), with the gains subsequently decreasing at the rate $1/n$.

Some extensions

Once it is realized that stochastic approximation forecasts are applicable, the underlying reaction models can be extended to some degree.

(a) Perhaps the simplest generalization is to allow the state to be contaminated with extraneous noise, reflecting the impact of factors unconnected with reactive phenomena but arising in the course of time over replications. Instead of (15) we might then specify

$$\theta_n = H(f_{n-1}) + \zeta_n, \tag{15'}$$

where ζ_n is an uncorrelated sequence of zero-mean noise variates. With this change, the underlying stochastic difference equation resulting from the stochastic approximation forecasting procedure (19) becomes

$$f_n = f_{n-1} + a_n M(f_{n-1}) + a_n(\epsilon_n + \zeta_n). \tag{20'}$$

Under our temporal independence assumption on the sampling error ϵ_n and the state noise ζ_n, the convergence properties of (20') are the same as those of (20), and all the results given in the foregoing continue to apply, replacing where necessary ϵ_n and its variance by the compound disturbance $\epsilon_n + \zeta_n$ and its variance. Thus $f_n \to f_*$ almost surely. The resulting state is given by

$$\theta_n = H(f_*) + \zeta_n = f_* + \zeta_n \tag{24}$$

and is therefore a proper random variable. Thus for the noisy-state model, exact limiting equality between forecast and state no longer applies. Note however that as $n \to \infty$, $E(\theta_n/f_{n-1}) = E(\theta_n/f^*) = f_*$ so that the forecast f_* represents an unbiased estimate of the state resulting from its publication. We shall comment further on such aspects in the next section.

(b) Although we have assumed that the reaction functions $H(\cdot)$ are stable over time, some possibility does appear to exist that the assumption may be relaxed. In the dynamic Robbins–Monro stochastic approximation process (see Lai and Robbins, 1979; Dupac, 1965, 1984), it is assumed that (in our terminology) the functions $M_n(f) = H_n(f) - f$ are time dependent in such a way that the fixed points $f_{*n} = \phi_0 + \phi_1 n$ constitute a linear function of time n with unknown parameters ϕ_0, ϕ_1 and that $M_n(f) = M(f - f_{*n})$, an otherwise invariant function with respect to time. A forecasting process that is convergent under suitable regularity conditions may be obtained as follows. Having obtained f_{n-1}, correct it in a first estimate of f_n as $\tilde{f}_n = (1 + 1/n)f_{n-1}$. Announce $\tilde{f}_n$ as the forecast so that $\theta_n = H(\tilde{f}_n)$. Then f_n is formed as

$$f_n = \tilde{f}_{n-1} + a_n(e_n - \tilde{f}_{n-1})$$

and the process is replicated. Then $f_n \to f_n^*$ as $n \to \infty$, and announced forecasts are, for large n, not subject to revisions stemming from the announcement itself. A linear reaction function with its intercept following a simple time trend would fall into this kind of temporal framework.

(c) One problem that we have not explicitly considered is that of testing whether publication effects are actually occurring. From the point of view of inferential theory, this starts to become an interesting problem only in the noisy-state model, where the task is to filter out from changes in the state induced by other effects the particular contributions due to reactions to publication of the previous replication. In keeping with the kind of data and specificational limitations apparent in practice, one would want such testing to continue to be based on the nonparametric approach. A possible intermediate specification is where systematic factors depending on a limited number of parameters augment the reactive effect in the determination of the state. Thus one might specify

$$\theta_n = H(f_{n-1}) + \mathbf{X}'_n \boldsymbol{\beta} + \zeta_n$$

where $\boldsymbol{\beta}$ is a vector of unknown parameters and $\mathbf{X}_n$ is a vector of observable concomitant variables of low dimension. The nature of the reaction function $H(\cdot)$ continues to be unknown: One is interested only in testing whether *some* reaction exists and if so in designing procedures that would identify the resulting dynamic fixed-point equilibrium forecasts in an appropriate generalization of the dynamic Robbins–Monro procedure. In general, one of the interesting aspects of the testing problem is that it is not necessary to follow automatically a continued cycle of estimation, forecasting, and publication. One strategy open to the forecaster is to decide not to publish after the survey results have been prepared. One is then able to compare changes following a published forecast with those manifested in a subsequent survey with no prior forecast. One might expect that this facility should sharpen inference as to the existence of publication effects and, in general, strengthen the hand of the forecaster as a dominant player.

4.6   Equilibrium and the social optimality of repeated sampling

Equilibrium

Let us consider the dominant-player game in which restrictions are based upon the published forecast f so that model (15) or its corresponding noisy-state version (15′) are to apply. Implicit in our discussion of the anticipative forecast (e.g., the running mean or the stochastic approximation forecast) is a search for some kind of equilibrium to the implied dominant-player game. As with other game-theoretic equilibria, the equilibrium should be a characterization of the strategies, which here correspond to the forecast or the forecast function. Thus consider as a possible candidate for an equilibrium strategy the forecast f_*. Note first with respect to the basic reaction model (15) that if $f_{n-1} = f_*$, then $\theta_n = H(f_*) = f_*$, so that f_* retains its property of being an exact forecast of the state resulting from its own publication. In other words, a forecaster who had located the fixed point of $H(\cdot)$ would know that no further forecast is needed and indeed that the exact value of the state has been located that has its own equilibrium value $\theta_* = f_*$. Thus the fixed point of the reaction function, once arrived at, would constitute a full forecasting equilibrium.

A similar property continues to hold, but in the weaker expectational sense, for the noisy-state model (15′). Suppose that the fixed point f_* of the reaction function $H(\cdot)$ has been located. Then

$$\theta_n = H(f_{n-1}) + \zeta_n = H(f_*) + \zeta_n = f_* + \zeta_n,$$

and hence

$$E(\theta_n; f_{n-1} = f_*) = f_*.$$

Thus the forecast f_* continues to be an unbiased estimate of the state resulting from its publication. As a forecast, it corresponds to a "rational expectation" in the terminology of economists, meaning a reflexive forecast that is unbiased, although the underlying game is very different from the kind of game to which the traditional rational-expectations equilibria of economics apply (see especially Chapter 6). Exegetical matters aside, the forecast f_* has in this instance the property that the forecaster has no incentive (at least assuming a quadratic loss function) to proceed to a further replication, for on the average he or she can expect to do no better by doing so.

In both cases therefore – models (15) and (15′) – the fixed point f_* has the property that once it is evaluated and released, the forecaster will be prepared to rest on his laurels. No incentive exists for any further action to counter reactive effects. In the case of model (15), the deterministic state space, the forecasting variance is zero; for the noisy-state space (15′), the forecasting variance is minimal and is equal to the variance of the innovations in the state process, with no contribution from functional biasedness with respect to the reaction mechanism.

The social optimality of repeated sampling

Implicit in the foregoing discussion is that a forecasting equilibrium is a consummation devoutly to be wished. However it is by no means clear that, given the power of a forecaster to influence events, it is at all desirable to attempt to achieve an equilibrium. Indeed, the very ability of a forecaster to influence the outcome, from even one survey let alone several or many, has been viewed as a source of disquiet. Thus legislators in a variety of countries, states, and provinces have grappled with the problem of restricting electoral opinion polls, in some cases absolutely, in others immediately before an election. The problem is by no means confined to electoral polls; in the Los Angeles Olympics, for example, it might have been better not to release forecasts of expected visitor numbers rather than conduct just one major forecasting exercise. The difficulty in all cases is the same. Once an estimate or forecast is published, with the *imprimatur* either of expertise or officialdom, one can in general expect this to modify subsequent behavior.

Two issues are in fact involved. In the first place, the statistician who publishes an estimate will in general be wrong, in the kind of sense dealt with in the foregoing. As we have seen, the forecaster's predictive performance – or assessment of the postsurvey state of the world – can be improved by replicating the survey. In time he or she *may* achieve an equilibrium, or something in the neighborhood of an equilibrium, depending on a dynamic nexus between the nature of the forecast and the reaction by the public to the forecast. If an equilibrium is achieved, the forecaster will feel more at peace and more secure in the public esteem attached to the professional performance.

At this point, the second issue becomes troublesome. Assuming that a fixed point of some kind is achieved, there is nothing inherently socially desirable in doing so, indeed society as a whole may end up much worse off. Implicitly, we are thinking of some kind of social welfare function $W(\theta; \theta_0)$ in terms of the current state θ and the initial presampling state θ_0. When the statistician publishes his (or her) estimate e, this alters through the reaction function H, the current state θ, and hence the level of community welfare. Evidently there is nothing objective any more about the role of the statistician. When he decides to publish his estimate, he becomes part of the system he is attempting to study. Assuming that he can correctly assess the welfare function, his is now a control problem, stochastic because of its sampling aspects. His control variable is the number of samples to take, and his objective is to maximize W subject to the stochastic dynamics generated by the reaction function H. Alternatively we could say that he is acting as a dominant player in a formal game. A complication is that only rarely will he ever have anything more than a vague notion of the nature of the reaction function involved. At any rate, by pushing the number of replications to infinity (presuming a long-suffering or maniacally interested public), he could achieve an equilibrium in one of the senses discussed in the preceding. But it is by no means necessary that this would achieve an optimum for his presumed welfare function.

In practice, things are never quite as clear-cut or as well defined as the preceding analysis suggests. But it does provide some clues as to procedure. Consider the case of the Los Angeles Olympics: Should the surveys of expected visitor numbers have been replicated? The answer is probably yes, given that the first had been published. One can construct a simple reaction function analysis that suggests an overreaction by potential visitors to forecasted visitor numbers. If further polls had been taken and published, the situation would have corrected itself with gains to both potential visitors and the inhabitants of Los Angeles. This is a case in which it might have been better to chase, as it were, the fixed point for the good of all, including the statistician. Likewise, it could be argued, following the analysis of Section 4.3, that it is surely beneficial to disseminate information about candidates or their positions, and if polls are thought to fulfill such a function, then we should arrange as many replications as are thought necessary and convenient. We should not conclude from these examples, however, that the fixed point is the vade mecum of statistical social dynamics. It is equally possible to construct examples where it is desirable, in terms of the general good, to conduct no polls at all or at least not to publish.

This concludes our study of formal forecasts in the presence of reaction effects. As we have remarked, the underlying model is a dominant-player game in which the statistician is the dominant player attempting to predict an outcome, either proximal or ultimate, in the presence of reactions to his or her estimates or predictions. The precise outcome depends upon the details of the reactions and upon the formulation of the prediction function. The most favorable outcome – judged only from a methodological point of view – is where a state of equilibrium exists in which the statistician's predictions are at least unbiased, so that no further incentive exists to replicate the survey/forecast. In such a state, the forecaster's actions and the reactions of the public will display a mutual consistency in the sense that no systematic surprises will perturb either side. In Chapters 5 and 6 we shall analyze in depth the equilibrium properties of a more decentralized kind of game in which no single player occupies the center stage in the dissemination of information. A state of equilibrium, called a rational-expectations equilibrium in this literature, is one in which the expectations of all agents are again mutually consistent and unbiased. Such equilibria therefore share a generic similarity with the dominant-player equilibria considered in the present chapter, although their establishment appears to be considerably more demanding in terms of their informational requirements.

4.7   Reflexivity and real-time survey schemes

All the preceding analysis assumed that the reactions due to publication effects worked themselves out in the course of a repeated series of distinct surveys. The question naturally arises as to whether one could hope to design a survey that would in its construction effectively anticipate reactions to its own publication; presuming, in the light of previous discussion, that one does wish to achieve the predictive fixed point. By doing so, the statistician and society as a whole could hope to save themselves the costs of a repeated series of otherwise distinct surveys. Of course the difficulty is that one rarely has any firm appreciation of the nature or form of the reaction function involved. One might consider inserting questions aimed at establishing likely reactions to publication of a range of visitor numbers (to invoke our earlier example). Although we should not wish to minimize the potential for such interrogatory procedures, two general problems arise. The first is that such reactions will be conjectural on the part of respondents. We have already referred (Section 3.3) to the "hypothetical bias" that can arise in such contexts. A second point is that motives may arise for strategic behavior on the part of respondents, so that the veracity of response becomes a problem. Thus we shall not follow the interrogatory line of attack. Instead we shall consider a rather more radical alternative.

Real-time surveys, as remarked in Chapter 2, are surveys in which progress results are made known to participants as they are received. For example, one could imagine an intelligent television set at which respondents can key in their answers, or "votes," while progress results are displayed on the screen. Although the development of such schemes may seem conjectural, the technology is quite feasible as of the time of this writing, and we understand that one or two trial experiments of simple key-in survey systems (one part at least of the proposed system) have been conducted in Western Europe and the United States. At first sight, a facility for inspecting progress results prior to committing oneself to a recorded opinion seems to violate every known canon of scientific sampling. Yet as we shall see, real-time surveys can provide a natural and cost-efficient way of minimizing prediction errors arising from reflexivity.

Let us suppose that individuals are given a fixed time within which to respond. Each individual has access to the number of those who have so far responded and the progress result in terms of the statistic of interest. (One could of course arrange for the conveyance of more information than this, but questions of confidentiality and context arise that will only confuse the issues at this point.) As a matter of taxonomy, two leading possibilities arise:

(a) Each individual is allocated a specific response time by means of some random queuing and cueing device. The order of response may be drawn as a random permutation of the numbers $1, \ldots, N$, where N is the size of the audience. Equivalently after the nth person has been drawn, the $(n+1)$th person is drawn by sampling without replacement from the remaining $N-n$. We shall call this the *random-access* model.

(b) Individuals are advised of a physical (calendar) time limit but are allowed to decide the point of response for themselves. Thus given that the nth person has responded, remaining respondents have the choice of entering a response or of waiting until others have responded (while watching the clock). We shall refer to this as the *self-selection* model.

Many more possibilities arise. For instance individuals may be allowed to "recontract," that is, change their mind, a prespecified number of times either during the course of the experiment or once all "draft" responses are in, after the fashion of the Delphic model of prediction. Or the temporal arrangements may combine elements from (a) and (b): Individuals are randomly assigned a specific time limit within which they must respond rather than a specific point of response. In what follows, however, we shall consider in detail only the polar models (a) and (b).

In order to focus discussion a little, we shall use as an example of reactivity the McKelvey–Ordeshook model of information transference by political polling (see Section 4.3). Let N be the total number of individuals and π_n be the recorded majority for candidate A after n people have responded. We assume away any nonresponse problems, although as suggested in Section 2.5, real-time survey schemes may exert an ameliorating effect in this respect. In the framework of the McKelvey–Ordeshook model, let us consider in turn the performance of the random-access and self-selective variants of a survey in real time.

(a) The random-access model: Given that N individuals have to respond, we may identify time with the indexing set $n = 1, 2, ..., N$. At each step a draw is made from among those who have not so far responded. Thus sampling is without replacement of ideal points x_i from the parent distribution function $F(x) = \beta F_u(x) + (1-\beta) F_I(x)$, where F, F_u, and F_I now necessarily refer to empirical distribution functions of the overall, uninformed, and informed ideal points. When the ideal point x_i is drawn, this may correspond to either an informed or an uninformed individual. If the former is drawn, the informed individual knows precisely which candidate he (or she) will "vote" for, so his voting behavior is independent of π_{n-1}, the progress score. On the other hand, if an uninformed respondent is drawn, the progress vote π_{n-1} will now affect his response. Following the analysis of Section 4.3, we may assume that in the absence of knowledge concerning just who has responded thus far, the best estimate he can make is that the proportions of informed–uninformed follow the aggregate distribution F and that the progress score π_{n-1} is the result of simple sampling from this distribution: Thus if his personal $x_i < F^{-1}(\pi_{n-1})$, he will, when asked, record a preference for A, and for B otherwise. In other words, to such individuals π_{n-1} is a "critical value" in the language of hypothesis testing. Thus, given π_{n-1}, π_n becomes determinate, established in terms of the contingent event: either I (informed) or U (uninformed) being drawn. The recursion may be summarized as follows. Write $x_s = \frac{1}{2}(x_a + x_b)$, the true switch point between candidates, known only to the informed. Then given π_{n-1}, π_n has values

$$\frac{1}{n} + \frac{n-1}{n}\pi_{n-1} \quad \text{if either (i)} \quad n \in I \text{ and } x_n \leq \pi_s$$

$$\text{or (ii)} \quad n \in U \text{ and } \beta F_u(x_n) + (1-\beta)F_I(x_n) \leq \pi_{n-1}, \tag{25}$$

$$\frac{n-1}{n}\pi_{n-1} \quad \text{if either (i)} \quad n \in I \text{ and } x_n > x_s$$

$$\text{or (ii)} \quad n \in U \text{ and } \beta F_u(x_n) + (1-\beta)F_I(x_n) > \pi_{n-1}.$$

Brief reflection shows that this process is not Markovian; it is in fact quite complex since the sequence of observed π_n depends on the exact order with which respondents are drawn, and this in turn is a matter not only of their points of preference (x_i) but whether they are informed or uninformed. As yet we have no formal insights to offer on the moments of π_N, the terminal vote, or the expected course of voting. On an intuitive level, one might expect the convergence behavior of the sequence π_n as $n \to N$ to depend upon N, the size of the audience. For suppose that the current respondent number $n-1 \ll N$. Then so far as drawing voter n is concerned, sampling is effectively with replacement (i.e., the relevant finite population correction factor is very small). The probability that an uninformed respondent n will vote for candidate A can therefore be treated as stable, in fact as $(1 - \beta)F_I(x_s) + \beta F_u[F^{-1}(\pi_{n-1})]$ and the probability that he or she will vote for B as derived from the complementary event. One can construct a stochastic Liapounov function argument to show that under such "stationarity" sampling conditions, the dynamics (22) does converge almost surely to the fixed point π_* defined by $F(x_s) = \pi_*$ so that information has been correctly transferred to the uninformed. Consider now what happens as n nears N. Nonreplacement effects start to become significant. By this time, however, the weight of numbers has built up to such an extent that π_n is very little affected by the remaining accumulation. Thus if nonreplacement effects are noticeable only over the last 50 respondents and 10,000 have already responded, one should not expect the last 50 to change things much.

Some preliminary simulation experiments appear to support the preceding conjecture with some important qualifications. It was found that if one set $\pi_0 = 0$, to start up the process convergence was extremely slow and biased from beneath (i.e., $\pi_n \to \pi_*$ systematically from below). Recursion (22) shows why. Suppose $n = 1$, that is, we are drawing our first respondent. If this individual happens to be uninformed, then the "critical value" upon which his or her vote is based is zero. So such an individual will never vote for candidate A. Only if an informed individual who happens to favor A is drawn can the process effectively start up. It takes a long time for the recursion to recover from this initial "snooker." On the other hand, if we arranged it so that up to $n = 10$ (say) uninformed individuals (if drawn) assumed simply that the critical value of π was an uninformative 0.5, then the recursion was considerably accelerated. This procedure proved superior to the alternative of simply feeding in $\pi_0 = 0.5$ as the initial condition; this latter procedure is still somewhat subject to the "snookering" problem for $n = 2$.

Our discussion with respect to the McKelvey–Ordeshook process suggests some lessons for the random-access scheme in general. First, a fairly large sampling population may be needed to obtain reasonable convergence. Second, convergence is facilitated if in the early stages respondents do not cleave entirely to the progress results in their estimation of the substantive population parameter or forecast. Things work better if they start with an uninformative prior and give this progressively less weight in favor of the progress result as n gets larger; in other words, respondents should display "reasonable" learning behavior.

(b) The self-selected scheme: Suppose that individuals can please themselves as to when they respond subject to an overall time limit. In general

terms the possibility now arises of the individuals influencing by the timing as well as the value of their response the subsequent course and final outcome of the survey.

Some of the considerations involved may be illustrated with further reference to the McKelvey–Ordeshook polling model. Time will now be calendar time. Suppose that $n-1$ individuals have responded up to the current point in time, and let π_{n-1} be the progress vote. Consider an uninformed individual with preference point x_i who has not yet responded. We may view the individual as setting up a statistical decision problem with null hypothesis:

$$H_0: \pi^* \geq F(x_i).$$

Three actions are available: (a) On the basis of π_{n-1} (perhaps also the entire history $\pi_1, \pi_2, \ldots, \pi_{n-1}$) accept H_0 and vote for candidate A; (b) reject H_0 and vote for B; and (c) take no action and wait until more information becomes available before committing oneself. Viewed this way, the problem so far as uninformed voters are concerned is one of sequential hypothesis testing. However, the problem has a few additional wrinkles. If the respondent elects to vote on the basis of π_{n-1}, he (or she) could well do so incorrectly. Thus suppose with respect to a given voter that H_0 really is correct but that $\pi_{n-1} < F(x_i)$. The respondent voting on the basis of π_{n-1} will incorrectly vote for B. In doing so, he will not only "lose" his personal vote but he will push π_n further to the left and induce other voters to make a similar mistake. On the other hand, suppose that such a respondent elects to take no action, that is, wait. Then if $\pi_{n-1} > F(x_i)$, he will have missed an opportunity to correctly vote for A and in doing so drive π_n even further to the right, influencing subsequent voters. Moreover, he must fear that those favoring B will take advantage of his abstention, driving π_n to the left. It is therefore true that so far as the uninformed voters are concerned, there are potential losses not only from responding incorrectly but also from not responding at any given point in time. And the assessment by any such voter of these losses depends in part on what he expects other respondents will do.

So far as the informed voters are concerned, things are a little more predictable. Since they know the correct "critical value," namely, $x_s = \frac{1}{2}(x_a + x_b)$, the possibility of an incorrect response (type I or type II error) does not arise. They will in fact be concerned to register their preferences as quickly as possible in order to influence subsequent voters. Thus the third strategy, that of waiting, is dominated by those of immediate response one way or another. The result is that early voting will be heavily dominated by the responses of the informed with value $\pi = F_I(x_s)$. This value may be considered as a natural initial value for the uninformed.

For it may reasonably be presumed that a temporary equilibrium strategy set for the latter is to wait for the predictable responses of the informed.

If the preferences of the uninformed are identical to those of the informed and the fact is widely known or supposed to be the case, then the votes of the informed, once recorded, effectively end the game; for they have identified the desired stationary point $\pi_* = F(x_s)$. If, however, this is not the case, then the game earlier outlined begins in earnest among the uninformed. As yet we have no results or even conjectures as to an equilibrium set of strategies or indeed whether the process continues to convergence on the correct stationary value π^*.

In summary, the self-selective model appears to involve genuine gamelike behavior with respect to the nature and timing of response. Precisely what difference this makes (vis-à-vis the random-access model, say) remains to be elucidated. The study of real-time survey schemes is virtually virgin territory. However, such schemes do offer within a single sample frame, as it were, ways of handling reflexivity. Since they also appear to be nearing technical feasibility (and one presumes will ultimately be media driven), real-time surveys may come to constitute a viable field of survey research.

Appendix 1. Markov convergence results

The subject of stochastic stability is very large, and we can only refer the reader to the very readable account by Kushner (1971) and other books on stochastic control and stability. Basically one wants to extend the deterministic Liapounov function approach to the stochastic context. Suppose that for any given initial value X the outcome X_1 is a random variable defined according to some stochastic Markovian mechanism. Then we simply verify that $EV(X_1) < V(X)$. More precisely, the following result may be constructed from the various results of Kushner (Section 8.6, especially paragraphs 4 and 7) and discussion.

Let (X_i), $i = 0, 1, 2, ..$, constitute a Markovian process on a continuous state space S with n-step transition densities $p^{(n)}(y; x)$, which are such that (a) $p^{(1)}(y; x)$ is continuous in y, x and for each x, $p^{(1)}(y, x) > 0$ on some open set of y points and (b) $p^{(n)}(y; x) > 0$ for some n independent of x, y. Let $X = X_0$ and let $V(\cdot) \geq 0$ satisfy

$$EV(X_1) - V(X) = -k(X) + c,$$

where the expectation is conditional upon X, $k(X) \geq 0$, and $k(X) \geq c+1$ on $S - A$, where the set A is compact. [If the state space S is discrete, conditions (a) and (b) may be replaced by the assumption that all states communicate, i.e., the resulting system is aperiodic, and the set A is specified to be finite.] Then X_i tends in distribution to a unique invariant distribution.

The convergence result referred to in Section 4.4 follows quite readily by imposing on the transition mechanism (9) conditions that will certainly satisfy those listed in the preceding. A more precise statement of the convergence of the sequence $f_r(\cdot)$ to a stationary or invariant density is as follows.

Suppose that:

(a) Successive samples are independently drawn. For each θ_r the corresponding estimate e_r is unbiased and the estimation variances $\sigma_{e_r}^2 = E(e_r - \theta_r)^2$; θ_r are all positive and uniformly bounded in r; $\sigma_{e_r}^2 > c$, some constant.

(b) The density g and reaction H are such that transition densities $g(e_{r+1}; e_r)$ are always strictly positive; if the state space is continuous, each transition density is continuous in both arguments.

(c) Let e^* be the unique fixed point of the function $H: e^* = H(e^*)$. Considering the deterministic dynamics $e_r = H(e_{r-1})$, suppose that $V(e) = (e - e^*)^2$ is a Liapounov function such that $-k(e) = V(e_1) - V(e) \le -(1+c)$ for $e_0 = e \in S - A$, where A is a compact set including e^*. Then the stochastic sequence of estimates (e_r) converges in distribution to a unique invariant distribution: As $r \to \infty$,

$$f_r(e) \overset{d}{\to} f^*(e),$$

independent of r.

The proof is quite easy and is given in Bowden (1987a).

CHAPTER 5

Rational expectations and socioeconomic modeling

5.1 Introduction

In this and the next chapter, we shall study different aspects of rational-expectations equilibria, a notion that lies at the heart of invariance phenomena in socioeconomic systems. The basic idea originated in economics with the work of Muth (1961) and is concerned with the way in which individuals form their expectations or predictions of future variables. One of the drawbacks of the several popular expectational schemes used in empirical work at the time was that predictions formed by using such schemes were in general biased. Muth was actually concerned to show that under certain circumstances one such scheme, namely, the adaptive expectations scheme, could result in unbiased forecasts if the parameter of this scheme was correctly chosen. Later authors, however, seized on and developed the methodology of Muth's paper, dispensing altogether with adaptive or other simple expectational schemes. Such methods could be used to develop forecasting formulas that were inherently model based and unbiased. In this way, an awkward and unappealing implication of the mechanistic schemes could be avoided: For if such schemes were recognized to be biased, it would surely pay individuals to improve things or even to take private advantage of the bias and in doing so change the way in which in the aggregate expectations were formed.

We should be a little clearer about the invariance aspect of such equilibria. Individuals are assumed to form subjective probability distributions of future variables and to formulate decisions based upn those distributions. In the simplest case, the decisions will be based upon the mean, that is, expectation, of the subjective densities, but we shall temporarily remain more general. Once those decisions are carried out, an ex post distribution of the realized values results. In general this could well be different from the ex ante subjective distributions originally supposed by agents. The invariance property of a rational-expectations equilibrium is that for all time periods, the ex ante subjective and ex post objective distributions are equal. In the weaker form, the respective means are equal. (One often sees the word *expectations* used either with respect to the entire distribution or just the mathematical expectations thereof.)

Such an invariance property may be regarded as the stochastic equivalent of a perfect-foresight assumption as it might be used in deterministic analysis. In the present context, people cannot foresee precisely the outcome, but they do know (in the mooted equilibrium) its probability distribution. Of course it could well be asked how it is that they come to know enough about the system in which they are embedded to be able to form such expectations. This is an aspect of learning that we shall consider in Chapter 7. However, if it is true that people have acquired such expertise or can acquire it, then the consequences are far-reaching. Among other things, it implies that for important classes of macroeconomic problems economic policy may be quite ineffective.

Not surprisingly, therefore, the hypothesis that states of rational expectations might exist empirically acquired considerable importance and attracted much controversy, in the course of which the properties, problems, and empirics of such systems came to be better understood. In this and the next chapter we shall study and develop these matters. The present chapter has more of an introductory flavor, laying out the various kinds of rational-expectations equilibria that have been proposed and surveying some of the empirical work on the issue. Further such material may be found in book-length surveys such as Begg (1982), Sheffrin (1983), and Shaw (1984). However, the chapter does contain some developmental work, especially with respect to invariance under publication (Section 5.3) and the influence of extraneous expectational influences (Section 5.5). Apart from a few doubts raised on the empirical work, we shall adopt the rational-expectations hypothesis somewhat uncritically, deferring until Chapter 6 a critical examination of the meaning and the very possibility of rational-expectations equilibria.

5.2   Rational-expectations equilibria: the homogeneous case

The best way to convey the essential features of basic rational-expectations equilibria is to start with a simple example. We may use this to establish some methodology for later use and also to illustrate some of the shortcomings of the mechanistic and correctible modes of expectations formation that were characteristic of the older literature. Most economists will doubtless be quite familiar with the material to be covered and may simply wish to skip straight on to the following section. However, the economics of the example is undemanding, and the noneconomist is urged to stick with it.

Consider a simple model of the market for some commodity in which price constitutes an observable outcome obtained as an equilibrium in each period t between forces of supply S and demand D. The demand schedule [equation (1b)] is a function of the current price p_t and a set $\mathbf{x}_{dt}$ of exogenous variables, meaning that they are determined outside the model; in particular they are statistically independent of the structural disturbances ζ_{dt}, ζ_{st}. The supply schedule [equation (1a)] depends upon producers' expectations of the price that will rule in the market period. Producers have to plan their production now for delivery in the coming period. Conceptually this means that they have to form an expectation or forecast $\hat{p}_{t/t-1}$ of price at time t using information available to them as of time $t-1$. Later on we shall be a bit more explicit about exactly what this information set consists of. In addition to the expected price, supply depends upon a vector of exogenous variables $\mathbf{x}_{st-1}$ where the timing follows from the preceding view of the production process. Finally we allow zero-mean random disturbances ζ_{st}, ζ_{dt} to affect both final supply and demand. These schedules are thus of the form

$$S_t = \beta_1 \hat{p}_{t/t-1} + \gamma_1' \mathbf{x}_{st} + \zeta_{1t}, \tag{1a}$$

$$D_t = -\beta_2 p_t + \gamma_2' \mathbf{x}_{dt} + \zeta_{2t}. \tag{1b}$$

Any necessary intercept terms (e.g., to prevent demand from becoming negative) are included in the vectors of exogenous variables.

In addition to the supply-and-demand schedules, we specify a market equilibrium condition:

$$S_t = D_t = q_t, \tag{2}$$

where q_t is the transacted quantity. Price moves to clear the market; there is no rationing or, on the other hand, unsold stocks in any period. To keep matters simple, we shall suppose that observations on the market quantity q_t are not available to individual participants in any period. We shall also suppose in this particular example that all producers have equal access to information usable in prediction and that each producer is small and without significant market power. The effects of removing these assumptions will be explored at various points in this and the following chapter.

The dynamic system governing the evolution of price is obtained as

$$p_t = \frac{\beta_1}{\beta_2} \hat{p}_{t/t-1} + \frac{1}{\beta_2} \gamma_2' \mathbf{x}_{dt} - \frac{1}{\beta_2} \gamma_1' \mathbf{x}_{st} + \frac{1}{\beta_2} (\zeta_{2t} - \zeta_{1t}). \tag{3}$$

Thus the actual outcome for price depends explicitly upon producers' prior expectations.

So far we have not been very explicit about the nature of these expectations or forecasts. The simplest specification is that the forecast $\hat{p}_{t/t-1}$ is formed as the mathematical expectation of the producers' subjective distribution function for p_t, conditional upon the available information in period $t-1$. A rationale for the use of mathematical expectations is the Simon–Theil certainty equivalent result (see Theil, 1957): If producer objective functions are quadratic and the system dynamics is linear, then optimal decisions may be cast in terms only of the mathematical expectation of the unknown future state variables, conditional upon the available information. This is often referred to as first-order certainty equivalence. In fact higher order certainty equivalents can be defined for nonlinear dynamics or objective functions (e.g., Bowden, 1985), and approximations to these have been used empirically in certain foreign exchange contexts. However, for the moment we shall stick to first-order certainty equivalence and work with the mathematical expectation as the appropriate forecast.

The mathematical expectation $\hat{p}_{t/t-1}$ of the agents' subjective probability distributions of p_t has evidently to be conditional upon the information available to them. The values $\mathbf{x}_{st-1}$ are by assumption always available, as are values of this vector for the more distant past. Previous realized prices $p_{t-1}, p_{t-2}, \ldots$ also qualify for inclusion in the individual's information set. Other possible qualifiers are the past values $\mathbf{x}_{dt-1}, \ldots$ of exogenous variables affecting demand. Denote by $\mathcal{I}_{t-1}$ the manifold of all potentially relevant information available to producers. Thus we may write

$$\hat{p}_{t/t-1} = E_s(p_t/\mathcal{I}_{t-1}),$$

where the expectation is taken over the producers' subjective probability distribution.

Now from the dynamics (3), the true or objective mathematical expectation of price given $\mathcal{I}_{t-1}$ is

$$E(p_t/\mathcal{I}_{t-1}) = -\frac{\beta_1}{\beta_2} E_s(p_t/\mathcal{I}_{t-1}) + \frac{1}{\beta_2} \gamma_2' E(\mathbf{x}_{dt}/\mathcal{I}_{t-1})$$

$$-\frac{1}{\beta_2} \gamma_1' \mathbf{x}_{st-1} + \frac{1}{\beta_2} E[(\zeta_{2t} - \zeta_{1t})/\mathcal{I}_{t-1}]. \tag{4}$$

The crucial consistency condition that identifies a rational-expectations equilibrium is that subjective and objective expectations are equal for all t:

$$E_s(p_t/\mathcal{I}_{t-1}) \equiv E(p_t/\mathcal{I}_{t-1}). \tag{5}$$

This consistency condition means that the solution to the dynamic system is determinate. Provided that only one-period-ahead expectations are involved (but see Section 5.4), there is only one time path for p_t that is consistent with this condition, in a sense to be described. We shall now show how to find this path.

Let us begin by writing

$$v_t = v_{t/t-1} = p_t - \hat{p}_{t/t-1}$$

as the prediction error from an arbitrary prediction $\hat{p}_{t/t-1}$. Substituting for $\hat{p}_{t/t-1}$ in equation (3) and writing $u_t = \zeta_{2t} - \zeta_{1t}$, the dynamics may be written in terms of the prediction error as

$$p_t = \frac{\gamma_2}{\beta_1+\beta_2} x_{dt} - \frac{\gamma_1}{\beta_1+\beta_2} x_{st-1} + \frac{\beta_1}{\beta_1+\beta_2} v_t + \frac{u_t}{\beta_1+\beta_2}.$$

The reader will notice that to economize on otherwise awkward notation, we have dropped the explicitly vector terminology with respect to x_{dt} and x_{st-1}, regarding them as scalars, with no violence to the resulting conclusions. Now write

$$p_t = \frac{1}{\beta_1+\beta_2}[\gamma_2 E(x_{dt}/\Im_{t-1}) - \gamma_1 x_{st-1} + E(u_t/\Im_{t-1})]$$

$$+ \frac{1}{\beta_1+\beta_2}\{\gamma_2[x_{dt}-E(x_{dt}/\Im_{t-1})] + [u_t - E(u_t/\Im_{t-1})] + \beta_1 v_t\}. \qquad (6)$$

Impose the requirement that the system is in a continuing or dynamic rational-expectations equilibrium. From the preceding definition of v_t it must be that

$$E(v_t/\Im_{t-1}) = E[p_t - E(p_t/\Im_{t-1})]$$
$$= 0.$$

Equation (6) therefore illustrates a decomposition of p_t into two parts. The term in square brackets depends upon the information set $\Im_{t-1}$. The term in curly brackets is a residual that is statistically independent of $\Im_{t-1}$. The first term is predictable given (as we shall always assume in the present chapter) that agents know enough about the system dynamics and parameters to be able to form such unbiased predictions. The second term is not predictable from $\Im_{t-1}$. For a rational-expectations solution path it must therefore follow from the definition of the prediction error v_t that

$$v_t = \frac{1}{\beta_1+\beta_2}\{\gamma_2[x_{dt}-E(x_{dt}/\Im_{t-1})] + [u_t - E(u_t/\Im_{t-1})] + \beta_1 v_t\},$$

whence

$$v_t = \frac{\gamma_2}{\beta_2}[x_{dt}-E(x_{dt}/\Im_{t-1})] + \frac{1}{\beta_2}[u_t - E(u_t/\Im_{t-1})]. \qquad (7)$$

Hence from equation (6), the rational-expectations solution path is given by

$$p_t = \pi_2 E(x_{dt}/\mathcal{I}_{t-1}) + \pi_1 x_{st-1} + \pi_3 E(u_t/\mathcal{I}_{t-1}) + v_t, \tag{8}$$

where $\pi_2 = \gamma_2/(\beta_1 + \beta_2)$, $\pi_1 = -\gamma_1/(\beta_1 + \beta_2)$, $\pi_3 = 1/(\beta_1 + \beta_2)$, and v_t is defined by equation (7). Moreover the sequence v_t is serially uncorrelated and statistically independent of the information set $\mathcal{I}_{t-1}$. Technically, v_t constitutes a martingale difference process with respect to $\mathcal{I}_{t-1}$.

Equations (7) and (8) constitute a general solution for this model. The actual time path depends upon the particular specifications of the exogenous process (x_{dt}) and of the disturbance process u_t (recall that this is derived from the structural disturbance ζ_{1t}, ζ_{2t}) and may be illustrated with a particular case. Suppose that

$$x_{dt} = \lambda x_{dt-1} + \xi_t, \quad 0 < \lambda < 1, \tag{9}$$

and

$$u_t = a u_{t-1} + \eta_t - b \eta_{t-1}, \quad 0 < a_1 < 1, \ 0 < b < 1,$$

where ξ_t and η_t are white-noise innovation processes. Now it is apparent from equation (3) that u_t is observable with respect to the manifold

$$\mathcal{I}_t = \{p_t, p_{t-1}, \ldots; x_{dt}, x_{dt-1}, \ldots; x_{st}, x_{st-1}, \ldots\} \tag{10}$$

and the same is obviously true of x_{dt}. We therefore have

$$\xi_t = x_{dt} - E(x_{dt}/\mathcal{I}_{t-1})$$

and

$$\eta_t = u_t - E(u_t/\mathcal{I}_{t-1}).$$

From (7) it follows that

$$\eta_t = \beta_2 v_t - \gamma_2 \xi_t.$$

Hence

$$\hat{u}_t = E(u_t/\mathcal{I}_{t-1}) = a u_{t-1} - b \eta_{t-1}.$$

Lagging one period, multiplying by a, and subtracting yields

$$\hat{u}_t = a \hat{u}_{t-1} + (a - b) \eta_{t-1}$$
$$= a \hat{u}_{t-1} + (a - b)(\beta_2 v_{t-1} - \gamma_2 \xi_{t-1}). \tag{11}$$

Inserting (11) into (8), following through the same lagging multiplying process as in the preceding, and utilizing $\xi_t = x_{dt} - \lambda x_{dt-1}$, we obtain

$$p_t = [a p_{t-1} + \theta_1 x_{dt-1} + \theta_2 x_{dt-2} + \theta_3 x_{st-1} + \theta_4 x_{st-2} - \rho v_{t-1}] + v_t, \tag{12}$$

where

$$\theta_1 = \frac{\gamma_2}{\beta_1 + \beta_2} (\lambda - a + b), \qquad \theta_2 = \frac{\lambda \gamma_2}{\beta_1 + \beta_2} (a - b - a\lambda),$$

$$\theta_3 = -\frac{\gamma_1}{\beta_1+\beta_2}, \qquad \theta_4 = \frac{a\gamma_1}{\beta_1+\beta_2},$$

and

$$\rho = \frac{a\beta_1+b\beta_2}{\beta_1+\beta_2}.$$

The term in square brackets in (12) is the unbiased predictor $\hat{p}_{t/t-1} = E(p_t/\mathcal{I}_{t-1})$, where the sequence of forecast errors may be established recursively from the equation. Alternatively, equation (12) is equivalent to a possibly infinite-horizon distributed lag of the form

$$p_t = \sum_{i=1} a_i p_{t-i} + \sum_{i=1} \varphi_{1i} x_{st-i} + \sum_{i=1} \varphi_{2i} x_{dt-i} + v_t. \tag{13}$$

From (13) it is apparent that the information set $\mathcal{I}_{t-1}$ must be as defined in (10). Note also that an infinite distributed-lag formulation will exist only if

$$|\rho| = \left| \frac{a\beta_1+b\beta_2}{\beta_1+\beta_2} \right| < 1$$

so that stationarity of the underlying input stochastic processes is not a sufficient condition for the existence of a distributed-lag form or for the stationarity of the resulting solution path for p_t. Finally we note that alternative methods are available for obtaining the rational-expectations solution path. One such method is to start with equation (13) in terms of arbitrary coefficients $\{a_i, \varphi_{1i}, \varphi_{2i}\}$ and solve for these parameters by imposing a rational-expectations requirement with respect to $\hat{p}_{t/t-1}$ in the dynamics (3), in other words, a method of undetermined coefficients.

Model-based forecasts and unbiasedness

The rational-expectations forecast is an example of what Phelps (1983) has called a "model-based," or "model-theoretic," forecast. In the preceding example the forecasts were based upon equation (8), which is the very equation that would be produced by such forecasts, as an invariance procedure. The rational-expectations forecast is in this sense a correct one.

Model-based forecasts in the preceding sense may be contrasted with automatic or mechanistic forecasting schemes characteristic of the older literature. Consider, for instance, the still widely used adaptive expectations forecasting methodology. For brevity, write $p_t^e = \hat{p}_{t/t-1}$ as the one-period-ahead forecast. Given a parameter λ, simple adaptive expectations are defined by any one of the following equivalent formulas:

$$p_t^e = p_{t-1} + \lambda(p_{t-1}^e - p_{t-1}), \quad 0 \le \lambda \le 1, \tag{14a}$$

$$= p_{t-1}^e + \mu(p_{t-1} - p_{t-1}^e), \quad \mu = 1 - \lambda, \tag{14b}$$

$$= (1 - \lambda)(p_{t-1} + \lambda p_{t-2} + \lambda^2 p_{t-3} + \cdots), \quad 0 \le \lambda < 1. \tag{14c}$$

Formulas (14a) and (14b) incorporate different rationales in terms of error correction, and version (14c) illustrates the equivalence with exponential smoothening. All formulas are in turn equivalent to

$$\hat{p}_t^e = p_{t-1} - \lambda v_{t-1} \tag{15}$$

where v_t is the one-period-ahead prediction error $v_t = p_t - \hat{p}_{t/t-1}$.

Suppose that forecasts (15) are inserted in the dynamics (3). Will the outcome mean that the forecast is unbiased? In general, the answer is no, as will immediately be apparent by comparing (15) with the forecast based upon equation (8) (by dropping the term v_t). The most sympathetic special case is the particular example given in the foregoing based on the specification (9). The resulting forecast is given by the square brackets of equation (12). It will be evident that if $\gamma_1 = \gamma_2 = 0$ (no exogenous variables), $a = 1$, and the constant λ is chosen equal to $\rho = (\beta_1 + b\beta_2)/(\beta_1 + \beta_2)$, then the adaptive expectations forecast will be unbiased. In all other cases we shall have

$$p_t^e \ne E(p_t/\mathcal{I}_{t-1})$$

for the adaptive expectations forecast.

Similar remarks are applicable to other mechanistic forecasting rules. The general implication is that if rules are systematically biased, then an incentive exists for individuals to detect this bias and change their methods of forecasting. In this sense, agents who stick with the old rule would not be exhibiting rational behavior, hence the name *rational expectations*.

Invariant distributions

As we have seen, the characteristic feature of rational expectations *as expectations* is the property (5), which it will do no harm to reiterate:

$$\hat{p}_{t/t-1} = E_s(p_t/\mathcal{I}_{t-1}) = E(p_t/\mathcal{I}_{t-1}).$$

Forecasts are based on subjective expectations, meaning expectations of the subjective distribution functions that individuals have of future prices (in this case). Rational expectations, or weak rational expectations as we may call it, refers to the property that subjective and objective mathematical expectations coincide.

Alternatively, decisions may be based not merely upon the expectation of the subjective distribution function, but upon higher order moments as well, or in complete generality on the entire distribution so that decision functionals are involved. As in the preceding, the outcome depends on these decisions. Thus we may write, analogous to dynamics (3),

$$P_t = \pi[\phi_t^s(P/\mathfrak{I}_{t-1}), x_t, u_t] \tag{16}$$

where x_t represents the exogenous variables and the disturbance u_t is as already defined. Since the subjective probability density ϕ^s may also depend upon exogenous variables, it has to be time indexed. Now the property

$$\phi_t^s(P/\mathfrak{I}_{t-1}) = \phi_t(P/\mathfrak{I}_{t-1}) \tag{17}$$

is obviously a basic consistency property: Agents know enough about the system to be able to base their decisions on the mathematically correct probability density, given the available information set, in each period. This clearly corresponds to the weaker condition (5) with respect to the expectations of the relevant distribution function, and we may refer to it as a *strong* rational-expectations equilibrium. Notice that both versions, strong and weak, are hardly trivial requirements; agents have to correctly form their expectations or subjective distributions in the presence of reflexivity; the outcome depends upon actions predicated on those expectations or distributions. As remarked in Section 5.1, the word *expectations* is often used loosely to refer to either E_s or ϕ_s, that is, either expectations in the strict sense or the entire distribution; we shall on occasion adopt this usage when the context is clear.

5.3   Heterogeneous information and publication

In the previous section we implicitly considered the case where information possessed by all agents was the same and expectations were conditional upon the common set. In the present section we relax this assumption, allowing agents to have heterogeneous information sets. In the process, we shall introduce an alternative kind of rational-expectations equilibrium and investigate also the effects on the system of publication, say, by an external statistician, of the equations governing its evolution.

The Lucas informational model

In Section 4.2, we saw how information could be passed from individuals with superior information sets – we called them the informed voters – to those with inferior information, the uninformed voters. The information transference process took place not by direct personal communication, but by the results of a polling procedure. The intellectual origins of this kind of model lie in work by Lucas (1972b) and later authors concerned with the informational signaling function of prices in the financial marketplace. The context is actually quite straightforward, and it requires little economic insight to understand how this sort of model works.

Suppose that individuals are interested in predicting the return θ on some asset. We shall not be specific with the definition or nature of this return, but we shall suppose that it depends upon some state of nature in the coming period that cannot be perfectly foreseen now. Suppose that the asset is traded in the market. Then the resulting equilibrium price P may reveal information about its likely return θ. This will be true if people think that there are certain people who have more expert, or even "inside," information. A higher price will then be taken as a signal that the experts have an optimistic view of θ. In this way information can be passed indirectly via an observable price from the informed to the uninformed. The analogies with the McKelvey–Ordeshook polling process of Chapter 4 will be clear.

So far, however, we have not indicated the connection with or precise role of rational expectations. Adopt the notation t for now and $t+1$ for the future time period, more natural for present purposes than the dating used in the previous section. Assume that θ_{t+1} is a random variable with variance components as follows:

$$\theta_{t+1} = \eta_t + \epsilon_{t+1}. \tag{18}$$

Consider now the conditional distribution of θ_{t+1} given the component η_t. We have $\text{Var}(\theta_{t+1}/\eta_t) = \sigma_\theta^2(1-r^2)$, where r is the correlation coefficient between θ and η (we have temporarily assumed stationarity, but the reader will observe that the argument is unaffected). Thus an individual who had prior knowledge of η_t would be in possession of better information about θ_{t+1}; call this an informed individual. Such individuals are assumed to predicate their demand for the asset upon the subjective density

$$\Phi_I^s(\theta_{t+1}/P_t, \eta_t, \mathcal{I}_t^c) \tag{19}$$

where the conditioning terms indicate the information available to such agents and are as follows:

P_t = currently observed price;
η_t = value of component observed by informed; and
$\mathcal{I}_t^c$ = residual information set, which is presumed to be common to all individuals.

Uninformed individuals, on the other hand, have only the price P and the residual information set to guide them: they form

$$\Phi_u^s(\theta_{t+1}/P_t, \mathcal{I}_t^c). \tag{20}$$

Equivalently we might say that the information sets are defined by

$$\mathcal{I}_t^I = \{P_t, \eta_t, \mathcal{I}_t^c\}, \qquad \mathcal{I}_t^u = \{P_t, \mathcal{I}_t^c\}. \tag{21}$$

Assume temporarily a fixed number of informed and uninformed individuals. Let S_t be the (exogenous) supply of the asset. Then by equating the demand, which is predicated on the distributions (19) and (20), to the supply S_t, we obtain a solution for the price P of the general form

$$P_t = f[\Phi_I^s(\theta_{t+1}/P_t, \eta_t, \mathcal{I}_t^c), \Phi_u^s(\theta_{t+1}/P_t, \mathcal{I}_t^c), S_t]. \tag{22}$$

Note that the function f and the distributions Φ may depend explicitly upon time, but we shall not adopt any special notation for this. Note also the simultaneity aspect of equation (22), incorporating the reflexivity referred to in earlier sections. Under suitable regularity conditions, we may solve for P_t to give

$$P_t = \pi(\eta_t, S_t, \mathcal{I}_t^c). \tag{23}$$

The function π is referred to as a rational-expectations equilibrium price function.

For a rational-expectations equilibrium we must have simultaneously

$$\Phi_u^s(\theta_{t+1}/P_t, \mathcal{I}_t^c) = \Phi_u(\theta_{t-1}/P_t, \mathcal{I}_t^c), \tag{24a}$$

and

$$\Phi_I^s(\theta_{t+1}/P_t, \eta_t, \mathcal{I}_t^c) = \Phi_I(\theta_{t+1}/P_t, \eta_t, \mathcal{I}_t^c). \tag{24b}$$

The subjective and objective probability distributions are equal for all t for each class of agent. So far as informed agents are concerned, no additional content arises beyond the considerations of the last section. In fact,

$$\Phi_I = \Phi_I(\theta_{t+1}/\eta_t, \mathcal{I}_t^c)$$

since prices convey no information additional to the known η_t for such agents.

The equilibrium price function (23) is incorporated into the consistency condition (24a). Suppose initially that the supply S_t is fixed, that is, constant. Prior to the start of each trading period, we could imagine agents as having formed a prior density, in the Bayesian sense, for η_t. Given that the price P is established in the trading process, the agent may now invert the function (23) to solve for the signal η_t. The equilibrium price would then reveal the signal η_t deterministically to all parties. Now suppose that the supply factor S_t is random and that the uninformed agents are never apprised of its value. In this case, the signal η_t will be revealed to such agents only in the probabilistic sense that, given (23), a Bayesian posterior density may be derived for η (perhaps as the marginal corresponding to a joint posterior for η_t, S_t) that will be more informative than the prior density. Thus the information on P_t changes prior ideas about η_t, and hence θ_{t+1}, on the part of the uninformed agents. In turn, their demand, predicated on this posterior density, combines with the demand of the informed agents to generate again the equilibrium price P upon which these posteriors are predicated. Equilibrium is characterized by complete consistency in this respect. We do not at this point investigate how it is that uninformed agents come to form their appreciation of the rational-expectations equilibrium price function.

We may summarize all the preceding by saying that an informational rational-expectations equilibrium can exist in which an observed outcome (price in this instance; votes in the example of Chapter 4) conveys information between agents. In general, however, agents will not end up with exactly the same posterior distribution function for the unknown events or characteristics. It is in principle therefore possible to have a rational-expectations equilibrium with heterogeneous conditioning or information sets, some elements of which may be endogenous. In equilibrium the subjective distribution of each agent, given the agent's own conditioning set, coincides with the objective distribution, again given that information set. Finally we remark that various assumptions can be removed from the model as previously outlined. For example, Grossman and Stiglitz (1980) have endogenized the number of informed and uninformed participants: If individuals end up with different posterior distributions for θ_{t+1}, then an incentive exists for those with relatively diffuse densities to acquire information by actually paying to obtain the signal η_t. Given a certain cost for obtaining this information, an equilibrium number of informed and uninformed agents may eventually exist.

Structural models with heterogeneous information

The market model of Section 5.2 was a structural model in which the expectations or forecasts of a future variable – in this case price – drove the dynamics of the price actually realized subsequently. Thus the future state of nature was not independent of the actions of agents. A general linear paradigm for such a structure is of the form

$$A\mathbf{y}_t = B\hat{\mathbf{y}}_{t/t-1} + \Gamma\mathbf{x}_t + \epsilon_t \tag{25}$$

where A, B, Γ are coefficient matrices such that both A and $A-B$ are nonsingular and $\mathbf{y}_t$ is an endogenous state vector. In the ensuing discussion, we shall assume that the disturbance term ϵ_t is vector white noise, that is, $E\epsilon_t = 0$ and $\mathrm{Cov}(\epsilon_t) = E\epsilon_t\epsilon_t' = Q$, a constant independent of time. It is easy to see that given the exogenous vector x_t, the rational-expectations forecast is given by

$$\hat{y}_{t/t-1} = (A - B)^{-1}\Gamma x_t,$$ (26)

with error

$$v_t = y_t - \hat{y}_{t/t-1} = A^{-1}\epsilon_t.$$ (27)

The resulting model dynamics is given by

$$(A - B)y_t = \Gamma x_t + (A - B)A^{-1}\epsilon_t.$$ (28)

Thus if all individuals have access to current information x_t, the forecasting task is in principle straightforward and the forecast error vector is as given by equation (27).

Now let us abandon the assumption of homogeneity across information sets. To focus discussion, partition the individuals whose behavior is collectively represented by (25) into two distinct groups. The informed group knows the whole of the exogenous vector x_t. The uninformed group knows only a subvector x_{1t}. Even here various possible assumptions are possible: We could assume, for instance, that it is only current information x_{2t} on the variables in x_2 that the uninformed lack. To turn matters into starker relief, we shall assume that the uninformed have no knowledge, either past or present, of the variables x_{2t}. Finally, let us suppose that a fixed proportion w of the agents are informed and that with this supposition, the dynamics (25) becomes

$$Ay_t = B[w\hat{y}_{t/t-1}^I + (1-w)\hat{y}_{t/t-1}^u] + \Gamma x_t + \epsilon_t,$$ (29)

where the notation should be clear.

Several problems now arise. The resolution of these is rather technical and is relegated to Appendix 1 at the end of the chapter; only the conclusions are presented here. Because a subset of individuals do not know a portion x_{2t} of the potential information set, the dynamic behavior becomes much more complicated than solution (28). If uninformed individuals do not have observations on x_{2t}, they may to some extent be able to compensate if the series x_{2t} is serially correlated. For in this case, the serial correlation will be reflected in the solution path of the endogenous variables y_t, which are certainly observable. Thus past values of y_t and x_{1t} become substitutes, as it were, for the unknown x_{2t}. Such a conjecture turns out to be true: In the resulting dynamic rational-expectations equilibrium, uninformed agents are able to form expectations that coincide with mathematical expectations given their limited information sets. These uninformed expectations are simply less efficient as predictors, that is, have a greater residual variance.

On the other hand the problem becomes much more difficult for the informed agents. If all agents are informed, then the optimal predictor is quite simple, namely, (26). However, if some agents are uninformed, then as we have seen in the preceding, a more complex serial correlation structure is introduced. Informed agents have to come to grips with this structure. Moreover, the actions and expectations of informed and uninformed agents have to remain consistent with each other.

A game-theoretic interpretation is possible. Since the informed possess superior information, they can in effect know the mechanism that arises from the actions of the uninformed. It is as though given any prediction $\hat{y}^u_{t/t-1}$ for the uninformed, the informed agents can formulate their own best predictor $\hat{y}^I_{t/t-1}$. And the latter feeds into the system to constitute part of the environment for the uninformed. As the development in Appendix 1 suggests, this is a dominant-player (leader–follower) game. In equilibrium the two sets of predictions $\hat{y}^u_{t/t-1}$ and $\hat{y}^I_{t/t-1}$ must be consistent with one another.

So far as the informed agents are concerned, the efficiency of forecasting remains unchanged relative to the model with homogeneous information. The error in these forecasts is still given by

$$\mathbf{v}^I_t = A^{-1}\epsilon_t,$$

just as in equation (27). We should not be surprised at this. Informed agents possess the complete information set, excluding only the white-noise term ϵ_t. Whatever actions the uninformed agents take, the results of such actions must appear in variables that belong in the informed agents' information sets. All that does happen, as indicated previously, is that the rational-expectations forecasting formula becomes a much more complicated [cf. formula (A.17) of Appendix 1] function of present and past variables, involving either recursive elements or an infinite distributed lag.

In the first instance, then, we have shown that a rational-expectations equilibrium can exist for structural models with heterogeneous information sets. For each class of individual, a coincidence exists in rational-expectations equilibrium between subjective and objective mathematical expectations given their specific information sets. Individuals have different expectations, but correct ones, given their own information sets. Some individuals are simply better at forecasting than others.

More disturbing is a second implication. If information sets differ, then the problem of forecasting can become extremely difficult, as Appendix 1 shows for even a simple heterogeneity. Perhaps it might get simpler if there exists a large number of different information sets and individuals are individually of little significance in the scheme of things. Some version of the law of large numbers might apply to the functional specification to be derived from such a setup, according to which the aggregate exhibits quite simple behavior. We leave the issue of the practical feasibility of a structural rational-expectations equilibrium with heterogeneous information sets as an unresolved issue.

Information and publication

Suppose that an external observer, having estimated a system already in rational-expectations equilibrium, publishes the findings. These findings possibly constitute a new information set for the participating individuals depending on the nature of the findings and the precise model. Let us assume that our external observer is in any case an inspired statistician, so good that if estimating any probability density, he or she gets the parameters and other characteristics correct with no sampling error.

If the equilibrium he (or she) is observing is characterized by completely homogeneous information sets, then provided he utilizes no additional elements (keeps to the same information set, a natural assumption since he is merely studying the system), the statistician will have no effect upon the system that he is studying. For instance, if the model were (25) and the statistician published the parameters A, B, and Γ, then the forecasting behavior of people would continue unchanged. In this sense, a rational-expectations equilibrium with homogeneous information is invariant to publication.

Suppose, on the other hand, that information is heterogeneous. Whether the model concerned is an informational or a structural one, the principles governing the outcome are similar. Suppose that the statistician estimates a system based on the minimal information set. For example, in the Lucas information model the statistician could estimate and publish the conditional density $\phi(\theta_{t+1}/P_t, \mathcal{I}_t^c)$. Or in the structural model as discussed in Appendix 1, he or she could estimate and publish a forecasting formula such as (A.12), which is of the kind used by the uninformed individuals. In either case, nothing happens. The statistician has given nothing new to the uninformed. Nor will it make any difference to the informed, with their superior information sets and inferior forecasting error variances.

If the statistician publishes a structure or forecasting procedure predicated on the maximal information set, things may or may not be different. To start with, publication may reveal that the additional elements η_t (or x_{2t}) are involved, but uninformed individuals may simply be denied access to these variables. In this case publication will make no difference to behavior. However, it may be that individuals in the uninformed set were previously unaware of the importance of the additional elements in the information set. They can obtain data on η_t (the Lucas model) or x_{2t} (the structural model), but it never occurred to them that there might be a stable relationship between this data and the outcome they seek to predict. Publication of $\phi(\theta_{t+1}/P_t, \eta_t, \mathcal{I}_t^c)$ would certainly change things in the Lucas model for those whose information set did not previously include η_t; the uninformed would become the informed. Likewise, publication of the informed forecasting equation for the structural model [see Appendix 1, equation (A.17)] would also change things for that system.

Here again, however, we have a problem. If the uninformed switch to modes previously characterizing the informed, the outcome cannot be a rational-expectations equilibrium! If the external statistician publishes the informed forecasts equation (A.17) of the structural model, this equation will immediately become incorrect, for since information sets are now homogeneous, the only correct forecast is based upon the equilibrium defined in equations (25)–(28). Likewise in the Lucas informational model, the density $\phi(\theta_{t+1}/P_t, \eta_t, \mathcal{I}_t^c)$ arising from an initially heterogeneous informational dynamics will now be incorrect when all information becomes homogeneous.

We may therefore conclude the following impossibility principle:

> *In a rational-expectations equilibrium characterized by heterogeneous information sets, publication by an external observer of models or distributions will in general result in changed behavior. The external observer's findings will be invalidated by publication.*

The point has obvious importance for econometric studies that purport to reveal a structure characterized by rational expectations. If information sets are heterogeneous, the statistician had better not publish the findings. We return to such matters in Chapter 8.

5.4   Multiperiod and ex ante expectational equations

The structural models considered in preceding sections were characterized by ex post expectational dynamics: The current value y_t is determined by expectations $\hat{y}_{t/t-1}$ put into place in a previous period. Moreover, only one-period-ahead expectations were involved. In the present section we shall relax both these assumptions.

We shall start by looking at models in which expectational dynamics are still ex post, as described previously, but multiperiod expectations are involved. In many contexts, agents have to look further ahead, beyond the next period. For example, economic decision makers often have to view an entire future stream of input variables: expectations about the course of interest rates, wages, or inflation, perhaps over the entire lifetime of a plant or project. The full complexity of such applications is beyond the scope of the present book. However, it is useful to begin with a simple example in which two-period-ahead prediction is involved.

Example 1 (ex post, two-period expectations): The following model has been used by Taylor (1977) and others to describe the outcome or reduced form of a simple macroeconomic model for the determination of the aggregate price level:

$$y_t = \beta E(y_t/\mathcal{I}_{t-1}) + \alpha E(y_{t+1}/\mathcal{I}_{t-1}) + \delta m_t + \eta_t, \tag{30}$$

where y_t is the endogenous variable of interest, m_t is an exogenous variable (in this context, the log of the money supply), and η_t is a white-noise disturbance process. The information set $\mathcal{I}_{t-1}$ will consist of past values of y_t and m_t:

$$\mathcal{I}_{t-1} = \{y_{t-1}, y_{t-2}, \ldots; m_{t-1}, m_{t-2}, \ldots\}. \tag{31}$$

Thus the expectations are formed before information on m_t becomes available. In general, it will be apparent that the model of equations (30) and (31) is homogeneous in its expectational basis with the structural model of Section 5.2: Current values are determined by expectations formed last period; the difference is that those expectations may refer to more distant periods as well as the current period. With no real loss of generality we shall set the parameter $\delta = 1$ in what follows.

We turn now to the solution procedure for (30). What is sought is a solution path for y_t expressed perhaps as a stochastic difference equation along which it is true that (30) holds. In solving such expectational equations, the following superposition rule due to Gourieroux, Laffont, and Monfort (1982) is highly useful. Suppose that the processes m_t and η_t as inputs to the stochastic difference equation (30) are statistically independent. Let y_t^1 and y_t^2 be solutions to the separate equations:

$$y_t^1 = \beta E(y_t^1/\mathcal{I}_{t-1}^1) + \alpha E(y_{t+1}^1/\mathcal{I}_{t-1}^1) + m_t,$$
$$\mathcal{I}_{t-1}^1 = \{m_{t-1}, m_{t-2}, \ldots\}, \tag{32a}$$

$$y_t^2 = \beta E(y_t^2/\mathcal{I}_{t-1}^2) + \alpha E(y_{t+1}^2/\mathcal{I}_{t-1}^2) + \eta_t,$$
$$\mathcal{I}_{t-1}^2 = \{\eta_{t-1}, \eta_{t-2}, \ldots\}. \tag{32b}$$

Then

$$y_t = y_t^1 + y_t^2 \tag{33}$$

is a solution to the complete equation (30). Note that we have to be a little careful about necessity and sufficiency here: The solution (33) is not the only solution, as we shall see in the next section. However, the result does give us a way of constructing solutions, and that is all that is required at this stage. The proof of the preceding superposition principle is quite straightforward and follows by noting that since m_t and η_t are statistically independent, it must be true that

$$E(y_{t+1}^1/m_{t-1}, m_{t-2}, \ldots) = E(y_{t+1}^1/m_{t-1}, m_{t-2}, \ldots; \eta_{t-1}, \eta_{t-2}, \ldots)$$

with a similar statement for the conditional expectation for y_t^2. Adding each case, it must be true that $y_t^1 + y_t^2$ satisfies (30), as required. Notice that superposition is a linearity property; the inputs m_t and η_t have to be additively separable as well as statistically independent. Thus the property may be regarded as an extension of the well-known superposition rule in the analysis of solutions to dynamic linear systems.

Accordingly, we may start by considering equation (30) without the independent disturbance η_t. Let $v_{1t} = y_t^1 - E_{t-1}y_t^1$ and $v_{2t+1} = y_{t+1}^1 - E_{t-1}y_{t+1}^1$. Substituting into (32a) and lagging one period, we obtain

$$y_t^1 = \frac{1-\beta}{\alpha}y_{t-1}^1 - \frac{1}{\alpha}m_{t-1} + v_{2t} + \frac{\beta}{\alpha}v_{1t-1}. \tag{34}$$

Now equation (32a) implies that

$$y_t^1 = f_t(y_{t-1}^1, y_{t-2}^1, \ldots; m_{t-1}, m_{t-2}, \ldots) + m_t \tag{35}$$

for some function $f_t(\cdot)$. It follows immediately from its definition that

$$v_{1t} = m_t - E_{t-1}m_t = \epsilon_{mt}, \quad \text{say.}$$

The ϵ_{mt} may be regarded as basic innovations in the variable m_t.

Notice also from (34) that since $v_{1t-1} = \epsilon_{mt-1}$ is known as of time $t-1$, it must follow by subtracting $E_{t-1}y_t^1$ from y_t^1 that

$$v_{2t} = E_{t-1}v_{2t} + \epsilon_{mt}. \tag{36}$$

By comparing (34) with (35), we observe that v_{2t} must be measurable with respect to $m_t, m_{t-1}, \ldots$ yet independent of $m_{t-2}, m_{t-3}, \ldots$ since it is a two-period prediction error. For a linear solution with time-invariant coefficients, we must therefore have

$$v_{2t} = \theta\epsilon_{mt} + c\epsilon_{mt-1}$$

for some constants θ and c. But combining this with (36), we must have $v_{2t} = c\epsilon_{mt-1} + \epsilon_{mt}$, whence $\theta = 1$. Thus

$$v_{2t} = c\epsilon_{mt-1} + \epsilon_{mt}$$

for some arbitrary constant c. In summary, the linear, time-invariant solutions to (32a) must be of the form

$$y_t^1 = \frac{1-\beta}{\alpha} y_{t-1}^1 - \frac{1}{\alpha} m_{t-1} + c_1 \epsilon_{mt-1} + \epsilon_{mt} \tag{37a}$$

for some arbitrary constant c_1.

We may now turn to the second input η_t and the solution of (32b). The reader will see that, in fact, (32a) and (32b) are homologous. The only differences are now that the innovations in the input sequence η_t coincide with the series itself. The solution is therefore

$$y_t^2 = \frac{1-\beta}{\alpha} y_{t-1}^2 + c_2 \eta_{t-1} + \eta_t. \tag{37b}$$

Adding (37a) and (37b) as in (33), we get the complete solution

$$y_t = \frac{1-\beta}{\alpha} y_{t-1} - \frac{1}{\alpha} m_{t-1} + c_1 \epsilon_{mt-1} + \epsilon_{mt} + c_2 \eta_{t-1} + \eta_t. \tag{38}$$

It may be checked that (38) is indeed a solution path; that is, it satisfies equation (30). Along with (38) we have

$$\alpha E(y_{t+1}/\mathfrak{I}_{t-1}) = (1-\beta) E(y_t/\mathfrak{I}_{t-1}) - E(m_t/\mathfrak{I}_{t-1}).$$

Hence

$$\alpha E(y_{t+1}/\mathfrak{I}_{t-1}) + \beta E(y_t/\mathfrak{I}_{t-1}) + m_t + \eta_t$$

$$= E(y_t/\mathfrak{I}_{t-1}) + \epsilon_{mt} + \eta_t$$

$$= \frac{1-\beta}{\alpha} y_{t-1} - \frac{1}{\alpha} m_{t-1} + c_1 \epsilon_{mt-1} + c_2 \eta_{t-1} + \epsilon_{mt} + \eta_t$$

$$= y_t,$$

as required. Thus the path (38) does indeed satisfy the expectational properties incorporated in equation (30).

Note that two arbitrary constants c_1, c_2 have entered into the solution, which is therefore not unique. Indeed, as we shall see in Section 5.4, additional solution elements may enter. As the next example shows, apparently arbitrary solution constants may have a physical interpretation in reflecting different modes of forecasting, all of which are unbiased.

Example 2 (ex ante expectational dynamics): In our second example, expectations drive the system dynamics in a different way: Current values depend upon expectations held now with respect to future values. Models of this kind have been used extensively in studying various aspects of speculation, for in such contexts a current asset price is very much determined by what investors think of its future prospects. (For

references on speculative bubbles analyzed in such terms see Section 5.5.)
The same sort of expectational dynamics is thought to occur in phases of
hyperinflation, where the demand for money may be heavily – and negatively – dependent upon the prospect of its exponentially declining value
in the hands or wheelbarrows of the consumer [on this, see Sargent and
Wallace (1973), and for a broad survey of such applications of rational
expectations, see Shiller (1978)]. The general model studied by these and
other authors is of the form

$$y_t = aE(y_{t+1}/\{y_{t-1}, y_{t-2}, \ldots; m_t, m_{t-1}, \ldots\}) + \delta m_t + \eta_t, \qquad (39)$$

with the notation as described for model (30). A variant of (39) is

$$y_t = aE(y_{t+1}/\{y_t, y_{t-1}, \ldots; m_t, m_{t-1}, \ldots\}) + \delta m_t + \eta_t. \qquad (39')$$

The difference is that the current value y_t occurs among the informational
conditioning variables on the right side so that the model is effectively
simultaneous in y_t. This has some appeal in models of stock market prices
and similar contexts, where the current price is posted continuously and
so always available. On the other hand, appending a disturbance η_t to
such an equation entails some awkward interpretative problems: The logic
would indicate that in forming their expectations, individuals know the
current value y_t, yet this cannot be so if a disturbance η_t is subsequently
added. Nevertheless, solutions to the formulation (39') do exist (see what
follows) and are in fact closely similar to those for the nonsimultaneous
model.

The solution to equation (39) may be obtained very easily. Following
the same procedure as for Example 1, we abstract initially from the random disturbance term and consider the reduced system

$$y_t = aE(y_{t+1}/\{y_{t-1}, y_{t-2}, \ldots; m_t, m_{t-1}, \ldots\}) + \delta m_t. \qquad (40)$$

Defining $u_{t+1} = y_{t+1} - E_t y_{t+1}$ as the one-period-ahead prediction error,
we may substitute into equation (40), lag one period, and obtain

$$y_t = \frac{1}{a} y_{t-1} - \frac{\delta}{a} m_{t-1} + u_t. \qquad (41)$$

Note that the prediction error u_{t+1} will be independent of $\{y_{t-1}, y_{t-2}, \ldots;$
$m_t, m_{t-1}, \ldots\}$. Hence, lagging one period, we have

$$E(u_t/y_{t-2}, y_{t-3}, \ldots; m_{t-1}, m_{t-2}, \ldots) = 0. \qquad (42)$$

Now equation (40) is of the form

$$y_t = f_t(y_{t-1}, y_{t-2}, \ldots; m_t, m_{t-1}, \ldots). \qquad (43)$$

Comparing (41) and (43), it must be true that u_t is of the form

$$u_t = u_t(y_{t-1}, y_{t-2}, \ldots; m_t, m_{t-1}, \ldots)$$
$$= u_t(y_{t-2}, \ldots; m_t, m_{t-1}, \ldots),$$

where we have solved recursively for y_{t-2} from (43). Applying (42), it must then be true that

$$E[u_t(y_{t-2}, y_{t-3}, \ldots; m_t^*, m_{t-1}, \ldots)/\{y_{t-2}, y_{t-3}, \ldots; m_{t-1}, m_{t-2}, \ldots\}] = 0. \tag{44}$$

The asterisk on m_t indicates that conditional on the given information, the only random variable involved is m_t^*. As in Example 1, the only linear invariant solution to (44) is of the form

$$u_t = c(m_t - E_{t-1}m_t/m_{t-1}, m_{t-2}, \ldots) = c_1 \epsilon_{mt}, \quad \text{say,}$$

where c is an arbitrary constant and ϵ_{mt} is the innovation in the m_t process. The resulting solution may be written as

$$y_t = \frac{1}{a}y_{t-1} - \frac{\delta}{a}m_{t-1} + c_1\epsilon_{mt}, \tag{45}$$

where the constant c_1 is arbitrary.

Next we turn to the input η_t and the solution of

$$w_t = aE_t w_{t+1} + \eta_t, \tag{46}$$

where the conditioning is in terms of $\eta_{t-1}, \eta_{t-2}, \ldots$. Following through an argument very similar to that just given, we find the solution to (46) as

$$w_t = \frac{1}{a}w_{t-1} + c_2\eta_{t-1} + \eta_t, \tag{47}$$

where the constant c_2 is arbitrary. By the superposition rule, since m_t and η_t are statistically independent, we may add solutions (45) and (47) to obtain the solution to (39) as

$$y_t = \frac{1}{a}y_{t-1} - \frac{\delta}{a}m_{t-1} + c_1\epsilon_{mt} + c_2\eta_{t-1} + \eta_t. \tag{48}$$

It is straightforward to verify that along the proposed solution path (48) the expectational equation (39) holds, as desired. As with Example 1, the solution contains two arbitrary constants, one corresponding to the m_t input and the other to the disturbance η_t.

Turning to the "simultaneous" model (39'), which incorporates the current value y_t as part of the information set for predictive purposes, it may be noted that the derivational argument used in the preceding may not be used directly to find the solution since equation (43) is now simultaneous. However, a suitable modification of the argument indicates as the solution

$$y_t = \frac{1}{a} y_{t-1} - \frac{\delta}{a} m_{t-1} - \frac{1}{a} \eta_{t-1} + c_1 \epsilon_{mt} + c_2 \eta_t, \tag{48'}$$

where, again, c_1 and c_2 are arbitrary constants. It will be observed that this differs from the solution (48) to the nonsimultaneous form only in the placement of the arbitrary constants. In particular, if the structural equation contains no disturbances η_t, then the two models coincide in their solutions. Thus for many of the applications of model (39) that are discussed in the ensuing pages, current values y_t may enter the conditioning set with little or no adverse effect upon our conclusions.

Forecasting models and the arbitrary constants

We have noted with respect to both the ex post and ex ante expectational models considered in the preceding that arbitrary constants appear in the solution. A useful physical interpretation of such constants is that they refer to the results of different forecasting procedures. We have in fact said very little up to this point about the actual techniques of forecasting beyond the requirement that they shall be unbiased, so this is a good point at which to take up such matters. In doing so, we shall use the ex ante expectational model (Example 2), but for simplicity we shall suppose $\eta_t = 0$, that is, consider as an input series only m_t, and put the constant $\delta = 1$. The equation to be considered here is thus

$$y_t = aE(y_{t+1}/\{y_{t-1}, y_{t-2}, \ldots; m_t, m_{t-1}, \ldots\}) + m_t \tag{49}$$

with solution

$$y_t = \frac{1}{a} y_{t-1} - \frac{\delta}{a} m_{t-1} + c\epsilon_{mt}, \tag{50}$$

where c is an arbitrary constant. Note that on occasion we shall write the preceding conditional expectation as E_t for brevity.

Let us consider some of the solutions of (49) that have been proposed in the econometrics literature.

1. The forward solution: Start with equation (49) and successively substitute "forward." Using the iterated expectations rule [e.g., $E_t E_{t+1}(\ ) = E_t(\ )$], we derive

$$y_t = m_t + aE_t m_{t+1} + a^2 E_t m_{t+2} + \cdots \tag{51}$$

provided the sequence converges, with probability 1, to a proper random variable. A necessary condition is $|a| < 1$. Introduce the backward lag operator z such that, for example, $zy_t = y_{t-1}$. Write m_t in terms of its innovations as

$$m_t = \epsilon_{mt} + \theta_1 \epsilon_{mt-1} + \theta_2 \epsilon_{mt-2} + \cdots = \theta(z)\epsilon_{mt}, \quad \text{say,}$$

where $\epsilon_{mt} = m_t - E_{t-1}m_t$. Then the value of (51), if it exists, is

$$y_t = \sum_i \varphi_i \epsilon_{mt-i}, \qquad \varphi_i = \sum_{j=1} \theta_j a^{j-i}.$$

Lagging one period and dividing both sides of the resulting equation by the constant a, we obtain

$$y_t = \frac{1}{a}y_{t-1} - \frac{1}{a}(\epsilon_{mt-1} + \theta_1\epsilon_{mt-2} + \theta_2\epsilon_{mt-3} + \cdots) + (1 + a\theta_1 + a^2\theta_2 + \cdots)\epsilon_t$$

$$= \frac{1}{a}y_{t-1} - \frac{1}{a}m_{t-1} + \theta(a)\epsilon_{mt}. \tag{52}$$

We observe that (52) is of the form (50) with $c = \theta(a)$.

    2. *The "backward" solution:* Suppose that y_t is a linear function of $m_{t-1}, m_{t-2}, \ldots$. In this case $E_t y_{t+1} = y_{t+1}$ and

$$y_{t+1} = \frac{1}{a}y_t - \frac{1}{a}m_t. \tag{53}$$

This corresponds to (50) with $c = 0$. What is happening here is that (53) generates the process deterministically and (49) is trivially true.

    3. *The ARMA–ARIMA solution of Gourieroux et al. (1982):* Suppose that m_t obeys an ARMA or ARIMA scheme of the form

$$A(z)m_t = B(z)\epsilon_t, \tag{54}$$

where $A(z)$ and $B(z)$ are polynomials of finite order in the lag operator z (such that $zm_t = m_{t-1}$) and $B(z)$ has no roots on or inside the unit circle. The solution of Gourieroux et al. is given by

$$B(z)y_t = C(z)m_t, \tag{55}$$

where

$$C(z) = \frac{1}{z-a}\left[zB(z) - a\frac{B(a)}{A(a)}A(z)\right]m_t.$$

From equation (55) we have

$$y_t = \frac{z}{z-a}m_t - \frac{1}{z-a}a\frac{B(a)}{A(a)}\epsilon_t$$

$$= \frac{z}{z-a}m_t - \frac{1}{z-a}a\frac{B(a)}{A(a)}(m_t - E_{t-1}m_t).$$

Multiplying both sides by $z - a$ and rearranging yields (50) with $c = B(a)/A(a) = \Theta(a)$, say.

A perusal of the preceding examples will show that they all differ in the specification or type of the input series m_t and/or the nature of the generating equation for y_t: The forward solution requires $|a| < 1$; the backward solution treats the process as deterministically generated by equation (53); the solution of Gourieroux et al. requires $|a| > 1$ and an ARMA or ARIMA process for m_t. For each of the preceding specifications, a different forecasting procedure is called for. Each of these forecasting procedures is unbiased and obeys the rational-expectations imperative. Each is associated with a particular value of the solution constant c.

The arbitrary solution constants may therefore be viewed as a manifestation of ignorance about the underlying mode of generation of y_t: An expectational equation such as (49) does not contain in itself sufficient information about the generation of the endogenous variables to be able to determine the appropriate forecasting procedure. Some authors have tried to resolve this indeterminacy by imposing, on a more or less arbitrary basis, criteria such as stationarity or forecasting efficiency. Reference back to solution (38) for the ex post expectational model will show that the choice $c_2 = 0$ for the arbitrary constants yields forecasting efficiency among all choices of c_2. Likewise, choosing $c = 0$ in solution (50) will yield the best forecasts. However, the difficulty in this procedure is obvious: Such choices amount to a very definite statement about the underlying generation of the y_t process, statements that might be incompatible with one's a priori ideas. Thus to choose $c = 0$ on grounds of forecasting efficiency for solution (50) will imply that y_t is generated as in (53), which amounts to a very special view of the world. In general, then, choices of the arbitrary constants on grounds such as stationarity or forecasting efficiency are fraught with hazard. The only way to resolve such indeterminacies is to impose at the outset additional a priori information, to realize that equations with multiperiod or ex ante expectations do not contain in themselves sufficient information to uniquely identify the underlying structure.

Finally we remark that the solution of multivariate models with multiperiod or ex ante expectations is the subject of a growing econometrics literature. A basic reference is Blanchard and Kahn (1980); see also Whiteman (1983). The procedure is usually based on the method of undetermined coefficients mentioned in Section 5.2. The basic object is to reduce the number of arbitrary constant matrices (corresponding to our arbitrary constants) appearing in the solution. A second line of work (see, e.g., Fourgeaud, Gourieroux, and Pradel, 1984) considers systems with a bounded or truncated "memory" so that expectations are formed in terms of a set number of past lags rather than a potentially infinite regression. Any judgment of the importance or usefulness of these lines of work is as yet premature for it depends in part upon the intellectual fate of the rational-expectations hypothesis itself. That sort of assessment is a subject to which we shall return in Chapters 6 and 7.

5.5   The homogeneous solution: fundamentals versus expectations

An often helpful distinction widely used in the analysis of markets or trends is that between "fundamentals" and "expectational forces." Fundamentals are supposed to reflect the underlying structure of the system generating the data of interest. However, it is by implication recognized that expectations of market participants can perturb or distort the fundamental outcome to the profit or loss of the actors involved. Suppose, however, that expectations are formed in terms of all variables entering into the structure, and only in terms of those variables, and moreover that expectations are rational. The distinction between fundamentals and expectations loses force for in this case the expectations simply embody the mathematical expectations of the fundamentals; rational expectations constitute a neutrality proposition so far as the formation of expectations are concerned. But suppose that expectations depend in part upon variables that are essentially extraneous to the true structure. Such a possibility might arise if a commentator, having gained influence in the past for essentially fortuitous reasons or by virtue of his or her position in the market, thinks that certain variables are important that are in reality not part of the true structure. Or it may be that market sentiment is sensitive to strikes, sunspots, elections, editorials, weather, political pronouncements or events, and the like; but the true structure is more robust with respect to such stochastic influences than observers imagine. Then it is quite possible for expectations involving such extraneous elements to become self-fulfilling; the endogenous variable of interest does become influenced by those elements, reinforcing the credibility of the commentator or of market opinion generally.

The possibility is much more than academic, as the following newspaper quote indicates:

The Dow Jones index slumped 86.61 points on Thursday night, sending shock waves through the international investment community.

The record drop, equivalent to 4.6 per cent of the market's capital, was triggered by a blanket-sell recommendation from economic guru Mr. Robert Prechter and a computer-generated selling program by leading investment house Salomon Bros.

Mr. Prechter, an advocate of the Elliott Wave theory of stock market performance, advised his clients to sell their entire portfolio.

Many took his advice and with the computer-driven programs of Salomon and other brokers feeding off each other, the selling frenzy gathered momentum.

Turnover was 237.56 million shares, surpassing the previous record of 236.57 million set on August 3 1984, with the Dow Jones index finally settling at 1792.89 points.

At day's end, stunned dealers were looking for reasons why the market had fallen such an extent – second only to the Great Crash of October 28 1929 when almost 13 per cent of the market's value was wiped out.

Thursday's fall easily eclipsed the previous record set on July 7 this year when 61.87 points was slashed off the index.

It further demonstrated the extraordinary influence of the small clutch of experts whose soothsaying can move markets and which, if enough people heed the call, becomes a self-fulfilling prophecy.

The Weekend Australian, September 13–14, 1986.

Taylor (1977, p. 1382) drew attention to the possibility of such a phenomenon in the particular context of a macroeconomic model explaining the price level, interpreting it as an instance of nonuniqueness of a rational-expectations solution path. He pointed out that even though the extraneous elements are white noise, if agents believe forecasts based upon them, the extraneous elements will become incorporated into the price level in a self-fulfilling rational-expectations equilibrium. Such extraneous but self-fulfilling elements are characteristic also of the later work on speculative "bubbles" in areas such as the study of hyperinflations or foreign exchange markets (see, e.g., McCallum, 1977; Flood and Garber, 1980; Blanchard and Watson, 1982). Such bubble elements constitute particular solutions of the general class constructed in what follows. Ideally one would like to solve a system in which the extraneous inputs can exhibit any deterministic or stochastic structure (e.g., it is most unlikely that a market commentator would produce a forecast consisting purely of white noise). Moreover we should plainly allow for the contingency that market opinion could incorporate proper structural variables as well as processes that are in reality extraneous.

In this section we show how such problems may be approached, essentially by demonstrating that all extraneous elements may be viewed as inputs to the homogeneous part of the expectational difference equations describing the evolution of the endogenous variable. The resulting rational-expectations solution path can be decomposed into a *fundamental part* and an *extraneous part*. The extraneous elements do indeed come to influence the endogenous variable, and forecasts based upon or simply incorporating them will be credible. But the influence of such terms can be separated from that of the fundamentals. In a sense this separation principle reinforces the popular view of the role of fundamental and expectational dynamic contributions. One substantive implication is that a market subject to influences from extraneous elements is always more variable than one that is not. Forecasting variances are higher. Thus a case can be made that purely expectational as distinct from fundamental influences exist but constitute a public bad.

Although we have a variety of markets and forecasting problems in mind – foreign exchange, interest rates, commodities, consumer or producer prices, and the like – we choose to remain general, partly in order to avoid getting into arguments over models of particular applications. The structure that we shall use for illustrative purposes is the ex ante expectational model (39) (Example 2 of section 5.4); as we have pointed out, this structure has been widely used in the analysis of the markets mentioned previously, and it is simple enough so that the essential lessons will not become bogged down in mathematical detail. Again, however, we should not wish to limit discussion to such models, and it will be apparent that both the methodology and the conclusions apply more generally. One point of principle ought to be commented on at the outset. In order to give a degree of determinacy to our methods and results, we assume throughout that rational-expectations solutions will result and will persist. It could be objected that if agents know enough to be able to form expectations that are rational, that is, conditionally unbiased, then they should also know enough to be able to recognize that any forecasts proposed to them contain extraneous elements and therefore discount such forecasts. The question of precisely what individuals need to know in order to be able to form rational expectations is raised in the next two chapters, and we shall not dwell on such matters here. We shall simply assume that some empirically based technique is available that has enabled agents to form unbiased forecasts and that the informational requirements for such forecasts fall short of full knowledge of the system structure. Likewise, it could be objected that eventually people would wake up to the fact that their forecast variances were higher than they needed to be. This argument, however, is based on collective rather than private considerations; if everybody else believes commentator X, then it is plainly foolish for any single participant, whatever the private reservations, to ignore the influence of X. Yet again, it is true that the influences of false doctrines decay and the most fashionable of market pundits sooner or later stand revealed in sackcloth rather than silk. Our argument is that, empirically, such market influences persist long enough to make it meaningful and useful to study their effects in the kind of framework we envisage.

The model: extraneous information

Suppose that the underlying model, the fundamentals, can be represented, perhaps in reduced form, as

$$Y_t = aE_t Y_{t+1} + \delta m_t, \tag{56}$$

where E_t denotes the expectation conditional upon an information set that includes m_t and past values $Y_{t-1}, Y_{t-2}, \ldots$. Now imagine that an index I_t is published, which is believed by market participants to influence the outcome of Y_t. In other words, agents do not realize that the structure is as simple as equation (56). (This needs a fair stretch of imagination, but as we shall later see, the methodology and conclusions are quite general.) Instead they heed the pronouncements I_t of a market commentator, which they think contains information about future values of Y_t. Since the structure contains the expectations of these participants, it is now of the form

$$Y_t = aE(Y_{t+1}/\{Y_{t-1}, Y_{t-2}, \ldots; m_t, m_{t-1}, \ldots; I_t, I_{t-1}, \ldots\}) + \delta m_t. \tag{57}$$

Now the index I_t may have any stochastic form or temporal dependence. However, it is easier to begin by supposing that it is stochastically independent of the m_t process, reserving the relaxation for later. Thus we are initially considering the rather extreme case of a public forecast or index that contains no real information about fundamentals, the pure snake oil case. In what follows we shall assume that both m_t and I_t are stochastic processes with zero mean. Additional deterministic elements are very easy to handle by using the kind of separability properties outlined in what follows (one simply adds the deterministic solution).

Since the m_t and I_t processes are statistically independent, we can use the superposition property of Section 5.4 to break the solution process down into two constituent problems as follows:

$$x_t = aE(x_{t-1}/\{x_{t+1}, x_{t-2}, \ldots; I_t, I_{t-1}, \ldots\}), \tag{58a}$$

the extraneous solution, and

$$y_t = aE\{y_{t-1}, y_{t-2}, \ldots; m_t, m_{t-1}, \ldots\} + \delta m_t, \tag{58b}$$

the fundamental solution. The latter provides the path that the solution would take if there were no extraneous elements and the public had correctly identified the structural variables involved and the form of the structure. The form of equation (58a) indicates that there are no exogenous inputs into the extraneous solution; this part of the overall solution is entirely generated in terms of the published index I_t.

(a) The extraneous solution: The reader will note that equation (58a), which gives the extraneous solution, may be referred to as the homogeneous solution. As with the models of Section 5.4, we seek linear time-invariant solutions to the homogeneous form.

Suppose that we can write

$$I_t - E(I_t/I_{t-1}, I_{t-2}, \ldots) = i_t,$$

an innovations process. The structure of i_t need not be stationary, but successive i_t are by definition uncorrelated. Define

$$v_{t+1} = x_{t+1} - E_t x_t, \tag{59}$$

where the conditional expectation E_t is defined as in equation (58a). Combining (58a) and (59) and lagging one-period, we obtain

$$x_t = \frac{1}{a} x_{t-1} + v_t. \tag{60}$$

Now from equation (58a) we must have, along the solution path for x,

$$x_t = f_t(x_{t-1}, x_{t-2}, \ldots; I_t, I_{t-1}, \ldots) \tag{61}$$

for some function f_t of the indicated arguments. For (59) and (60) to coincide, it must in turn be true that

$$v_t = v_t(x_{t-1}, x_{t-2}, \ldots; I_t^*, I_{t-1}, \ldots) \tag{62}$$

with $E(v_t/\{x_{t-1}, x_{t-2}, \ldots; I_{t-1}, I_{t-2}, \ldots\}) = 0$ following from definition (59). The asterisk indicates that the only random variable, given the conditioning set, is the current value of I. Note also from equation (61) that v_t can be expressed in the form $v_t(I_{t-1}, I_{t-2}, \ldots)$ along any solution path.

The general solution to equation (62) takes the form of any martingale difference sequence defined on the process I_t. That is, $v_t = H_t - H_{t-1}$, where H_t is a function of the I_t process such that $E_{t-1}H_t = H_{t-1}$. Many such solutions exist, but the only linear time-invariant solution is given by

$$v_t = \gamma(I_t - E_{t-1}I_t) = \gamma i_t$$

for an arbitrary constant γ. The extraneous solution is therefore

$$x_t = \frac{1}{a} x_{t-1} + \gamma i_t. \tag{63}$$

(b) The fundamental solution: We have already obtained in Section 5.4 the solution to the fundamental part (58b). It is given by the solution path (45), which we reproduce here:

$$y_t = \frac{1}{a} y_{t-1} - \frac{\delta}{a} m_{t-1} + c\epsilon_{mt}$$

for some arbitrary constant c.

We may add solutions (63) and (45) to give the complete solution:

$$Y_t = \frac{1}{a} Y_{t-1} + \frac{\delta}{a} m_{t-1} + c\epsilon_{mt} + \gamma i_t. \tag{64}$$

For future reference we note from (64) that $E_t Y_t = Y_t$, where the information set is given in equation (57). Along the path (64), the optimal forecasts are

$$E_t Y_{t+1} = \frac{1}{a} Y_t - \frac{\delta}{a} m_t \tag{65}$$

since the innovations ϵ_{mt+1} and i_{t+1} are unpredictable. The forecast error is

$$Y_{t+1} - E_t Y_{t+1} = c\epsilon_{mt+1} + \gamma i_{t+1}. \tag{66}$$

Note that the optimal forecast (65) is not what agents would actually employ since they are not supposed to have direct or current knowledge of Y_t. Substituting for Y_t from (64), we derive one possible operational version as

$$E_t Y_{t+1} = \frac{1}{a^2} Y_{t-1} - \frac{\delta}{a} \left(\frac{1}{a} m_{t-1} + e_{t-1} m_t \right)$$
$$+ \frac{c-\delta}{a} (m_t - E_{t-1} m_t) + \frac{\gamma}{a} (I_t - E_{t-1} I_t). \tag{67}$$

We may now proceed to relax our initial assumption that the index I_t is wholly extraneous. Suppose that I_t contains some information about fundamentals and decompose it as follows:

$$I_t = I_{1t} + I_{2t},$$

where I_{1t} is based upon fundamental variables and I_{2t} is based upon wholly extraneous variables. Suppose also that I_{1t} contains only the fundamental information otherwise available to market participants, namely, Y_{t-1}, m_t, and lagged values thereof. In such circumstances, the element I_{1t} makes no difference to the fundamental solution as described in the foregoing. The reason is quite simple: The information set $\{Y_{t-1}, Y_{t-2}, \ldots; m_t, m_{t-1}, \ldots; I_{1t}, I_{1t-1}, \ldots\}$ is the same as the original $\{Y_{t-1}, Y_{t-1}, \ldots; m_t, m_{t-1}, \ldots\}$. All that does happen is that the extraneous solution becomes defined in terms of I_{2t} and its innovations i_{2t}. Thus the solution is defined by equation (64) with i_{2t} replacing i_t. Equation (65) for the optimal predictor is unchanged.

On the other hand, the operational version (67) is now changed. The reason is that I_{2t} is not separately observable; only the observed index I_t can appear in the operational version of the forecasting equation. For example, suppose that $I_{1t} = \beta_1 Y_{t-1} + \beta_2 m_t$ represents the systematic part of a guru's forecast for some parameters β_1, β_2. Then

$$E_{t-1}I_{1t} = \beta_1 E_{t-1}Y_{t-1} + \beta_2 E_{t-1}m_t$$

$$= \beta_1 Y_{t-1} + \beta_2 E_{t-1}m_t$$

in view of the property $E_t Y_t = Y_t$ previously noted. Hence

$$I_{2t} - E_{t-1}I_{2t} = I_t - E_{t-1}I_t - (I_{1t} - E_{t-1}I_{1t})$$

$$= I_t - E_{t-1}I_t - \beta_2 \epsilon_{mt}.$$

It follows by replacing I_t by I_{2t} in (67) that

$$E_t Y_{t+1} = \frac{1}{a^2}Y_{t-1} - \frac{\delta}{a}\left[\frac{1}{a}m_{t-1} + E_{t-1}m_t\right]$$

$$+ \frac{1}{a}(c - \delta - \beta_2\gamma)\epsilon_{mt} + \frac{\gamma}{a}(I_t - E_{t-1}I_t) \tag{68}$$

is the operational version of the forecast, replacing equation (67). Thus the equation actually used for prediction will not remain unchanged. On the other hand, the prediction error (66) continues to hold if we substitute i_{2t} for i_t.

Separation, volatility, and self-fulfillment

As we have seen, the market digests the sequence of indexes or forecasts $I_t, I_{t-1}, \ldots$ by taking into account only the innovations (i_t or i_{2t}) in the flow of this information. The rest has already been absorbed into Y_{t-1} to become part of the basic information set. Thus the market reacts only to the essential news conveyed by the index or forecast I_t. From the point of view of market participants, past values of I_t are embedded in Y_{t-1}, and from this aspect it is indeed true that the index sequence becomes part of the model. Consider, for instance, the application of the Granger causality criterion (discussed in more detail in the next section): Y_{t+1} can be better predicted knowing I_t (in addition to Y_t and m_t), but I_{t+1} cannot be better predicted by utilizing observations on Y_t. Thus $I_t \rightarrow Y_{t+1}$; the index or forecast I_t causes Y_{t+1}. One could indeed build this into a formal testing procedure for the existence of extraneous expectational influences from a published series (I_t).

From the point of view of an external, omniscient observer, on the other hand, the solution exhibits a separation principle. For brevity, we reintroduce the lag operator z (e.g., $zy_t = y_{t-1}$). Referring to the solution path (64), one may decompose Y_t as follows:

$$Y_t = y_t + x_t \tag{69}$$

where

$$y_t = \frac{1}{1-(1/a)z}\left(-\frac{\delta}{a}m_{t-1}+c\epsilon_{mt}\right)$$

and

$$x_t = \frac{\gamma}{1-(1/a)z}i_t.$$

The sequence y_t is the fundamental solution and x_t is the extraneous solution. The innovations i_t may represent i_{2t}, the extraneous part of a published index or forecast I_t. It is clear from the decomposition (69) that a system with extraneous elements may be considerably more volatile than the fundamental solution. In the present model the addition to the system variance is given (under stationarity) by

$$\text{Var } x_t = \frac{a^2\gamma^2}{a^2-1}\sigma_i^2, \qquad \sigma_i^2 = \text{Var } i_t, \qquad |a| > 1.$$

This may be substantial if $|a|$ is close to unity.

Nevertheless, it is easy to see why the influence of a market commentator, once established, may persist. He or she can claim with some justification that the published index I_t does have genuine predictive power for it is certainly true that, post hoc, I_t and Y_{t+1} are correlated. Suppose, to take a worst case scenario, that the index I_t is in reality quite uncorrelated with fundamentals. From (69) we then have

$$EY_{t+1}I_t = Ex_{t+1}I_t \neq 0.$$

Indeed suppose that I_t can be expressed in terms of i.i.d. innovations i_t with common variance σ_i^2 as follows:

$$I_t = i_t + \theta_1 i_{t-1} + \theta_2 i_{t-2} + \cdots = \Theta(z)i_t, \quad \text{say,}$$

where z is the lag operator. Then

$$Ex_{t+1}I_t = \gamma E\left(i_{t+1}+\frac{1}{a}i_t+\frac{1}{a^2}i_{t-1}+\cdots\right)(i_t+\theta_1 i_{t-1}+\theta_2 i_{t-2}+\cdots)$$

$$= \frac{\gamma}{a}\Theta\left(\frac{1}{a}\right)\sigma_i^2.$$

Thus if, for example, $I_t = \lambda I_{t-1}+i_t$, then

$$\text{Cov } Y_{t+1}I_t = \frac{\gamma}{a-\lambda}\sigma_i^2.$$

Similar conclusions apply if I_t contains fundamental as well as extraneous elements; the prediction error variance is lower if I_t is incorporated in addition to the fundamentals. Thus once the market starts believing a commentator, any individual participant would be foolish not to take into account the commentator's prognostications.

We may summarize our conclusions as follows:

(a) A common supposition in the analysis of social or market behavior is that "expectations" acquire an influence independent of fundamental forces. This distinction cannot be sustained as a rational-expectations equilibrium if market expectations are based only upon information already incorporated in the fundamentals. But expectations can acquire causal status if they have credibility, that is, if people believe them, and are based at least in part upon factors that do not appear in the fundamentals.

(b) Where this happens, a separation principle applies. The rational-expectations solution can be split into two parts, one reflecting the fundamentals and the other the extraneous part of the published indexes or forecasts.

(c) These indexes or forecasts are, however, self-fulfilling in that they do acquire genuine predictive power. An individual participant would be foolish to ignore them if everybody else believes them.

(d) The published forecasts or indexes, if believed, do acquire genuine causal status. A possible test for their extraneity with respect to the fundamental influences may be based upon the Granger causality notion.

(e) A dynamics with such extraneous influences may be much more volatile than one based only upon fundamentals. From this point of view, the influence of elements that are really extraneous could be regarded as a public bad. Participants may become locked into a system paying too much heed to an influential commentator or to public or market sentiment. The result is excessive system volatility. The social desirability of such commentators thus hinges upon whether they do in fact provide genuinely new and fundamental information.

In the preceding analysis it was assumed that all agents (participants, excluding the social commentator) are homogeneous in their information sets. However, a possibly useful social role for a commentator or guru may exist where information sets or abilities are heterogeneous. The information conveyed by social commentators may then include an assessment of "average" opinion. The role of average opinion is explored in detail in Section 6.7. We remark here that a social commentator may end up performing a social service merely by explicitly or implicitly reporting average opinion even though he or she may be quite ignorant as to the fundamentals that drive the market or system dynamics at issue.

Endogenous bubbles: implicit extraneity

Solution (69) is

$$Y_t = y_t + x_t$$

where

$$y_t = \frac{1}{a}y_{t-1} - \frac{\delta}{a}m_{t-1} + c\epsilon_{mt} \tag{69a}$$

$$x_t = \frac{1}{a}x_{t-1} + \gamma i_t. \tag{69b}$$

Consider now the expectational equation

$$Y_t = aE(Y_{t+1}/\{Y_t, Y_{t-1}, \ldots; m_t, m_{t-1}, \ldots\}) + \delta m_t, \tag{57'}$$

which differs from equation (57) in the presence of the current value Y_t among the conditioning set and in the absence of the explicit informational series I_t. Now if Y_t is available, it can readily be verified from (69a) and (69b) that i_t can be recovered from Y_t, m_t, and their past. This means that the formal absence of I_t and its past from the conditioning set of (57') is, for this particular model, not crucial since agents implicitly know it. Moreover (69) continues to be the solution to (57') at the cost perhaps of the interpretative difficulties noted in Section 5.4.

In such circumstances, solution (69) – and (69b) in particular – becomes a model of endogenous bubbles in which the observed process Y_t itself contains the seeds of its own bubble. This is indeed the way that most previous commentators have defined and approached the general problem of extraneous influences. Moreover the interesting solutions may not all be linear. Thus Blanchard and Watson (1982) note the following possibility (in our terminology):

$$x_t = \begin{cases} (1/\pi)(1/a)x_{t-1} + (1/\pi)i_t, & \text{with probability } \pi, \\ 0, & \text{with probability } 1 - \pi. \end{cases}$$

In other words there is a probability π that the bubble will collapse at any time.

It will be observed that in its full generality, testing for endogenous bubbles is the problem of filtering out the implied extraneous solution x_t or, equivalently, its innovations i_t. This may be difficult, especially when the expectational equation (57') is overlain with additional sources of noise (as an equation disturbance). "Variance bounds" tests (e.g., Shiller, 1981; Blanchard and Watson, 1982) attempt to infer bubbles indirectly by relating the variance of Y_t to what one would expect on the basis of an estimated fundamental solution (69a). Other tests, not all of which are convincing, are based nonparametrically on runs and on distributional properties of changes in Y_t (see, e.g., Evans, 1986).

5.6 Identification and inference

On any interpretation of the rational-expectations hypothesis, individuals are assumed to know an awful lot about the world they live in. It is true that information sets may differ and that some may be poorer rather than better; even so, to be able to form conditionally unbiased forecasts implies a measure of statistical expertise on the part of participating agents. It is not surprising, therefore, that a considerable degree of disbelief has attended the advancement of the rational-expectations equilibrium as an empirical hypothesis describing the current state of certain socioeconomic systems. One approach to the defense of the hypothesis has been to try to show that empirically the hypothesis cannot be rejected, more or less as a matter of formal statistical hypothesis testing. Typically this consists of a time series test or more rarely a cross-sectional test of actual data with respect to some maintained hypothesis about the nature of the system structure. Now there are all sorts of problems, logical and otherwise, concerning the setting up of such historical "experiments" and the amount of guidance that such tests would give for the future use or interpretation of the models in which the rational expectations are embedded. However, we shall defer consideration of such matters to Chapter 6 and in the present section take the tests that have been proposed at face value.

The vast amount of empirical literature on various aspects of the rational-expectations hypothesis creates many problems for a survey as condensed as the present one has to be, not the least in organizing it into a coherent expositional framework. At the outset, however, we may recognize that in no instance is one testing the rational-expectations hypothesis in and of itself. Expectations, or at least the *true* (rather than manifested) expectations of individuals, are of the nature of latent variables, never directly observed. Instead the expectations are typically embedded in a more or less explicit structural framework so that one is testing a compound hypothesis involving not only the rationality or otherwise of expectations but also the veracity of the structural model in which the expectations appear as arguments. Indeed it is very possible that one could end up accepting the rationality of expectations out of some confounding process in which expectations are not rational but the model is misspecified. Be this as it may, the structural dimension will nevertheless yield us an organizing principle for the purposes of present discussion. Thus we shall commence with tests based on actually reported expectations series. The only structure involved here revolves around the problem of whether

individuals can actually perceive their expectations correctly or are prepared to report them truthfully. The next stage of structural complexity
is represented by simple models of securities or foreign exchange markets, where observed prices are held to reflect expectations in a more or
less simple manner. The final stage of structural complexity is one of
formal model building, and the bulk of our survey is devoted to this topic.

Reported expectations

The best known of the series of reported expectations is the Livingstone
survey of U.S. business, which reports a number of series of economic
importance. The consumer price index series has been analyzed with regard to implied mechanisms of expectational formation by a number of
authors, starting with Turnovsky (1970), Pesando (1975), Carlson (1977),
and Figlewski and Wachtel (1981). As another example, Friedman (1980)
has examined a survey of reported interest rate expectations among a
panel of money market dealers.

Assume that the one-period-ahead forecast series y_t^e is available on a
historical basis consistent with the corresponding actual figures y_t. The
first question to be resolved is how one tests whether the observed series y_t^e
is consistent with rational-expectations formation. To answer this question, we should have some additional information, namely, the information set $\mathcal{I}_{t-1}$ upon which the predictions y_t^e are assumed to have been
predicated (note the implied structure creeping in already). In the empirical testing, $\mathcal{I}_{t-1}$ is always supposed to be the same for all agents and
typically to consist of, in the actual past, $\{y_{t-1}, y_{t-2}, \ldots\}$ together with
any other series $\{x_{t-1}, x_{t-2}, \ldots\}$ that individuals might reasonably be assumed to use in forecasting the series y_t of primary interests. The implied
structure is thus schematically

$$y_t = y_t^e(\mathcal{I}_{t-1}) + \eta_t, \tag{70}$$

where η_t is a residual. If we regress y_t upon y_t^e, we should – if expectations are unbiased and truthfully or accurately reported – observe a zero
intercept and a unit coefficient on y_t^e. Moreover, if we form $\eta_t = y_t - y_t^e$,
then the elements of $\mathcal{I}_{t-1}$ should yield no information about the residual
η_t and a corresponding regression should reveal statistically insignificant
coefficients.

The test procedure is thus reasonably straightforward, but in spite of
this, a minor controversy has arisen with respect to the Livingstone price
series referred to in the preceding, with the bulk of opinion unfavorable
to the rational-expectations hypothesis. We note the difficulty arising out
of the vagueness of the presumed information set $\mathcal{I}_{t-1}$, the choice of

which is left very much up to investigators. Almost certainly, real-life expectations are predicated upon information – newspaper commentaries, political pronouncements, and the like – that do not appear among the officially recorded economic series usually taken by investigators as the raw material for $\mathcal{I}_{t-1}$. A further difficulty lies with the way expectational series are often reported. Respondents in surveys are usually asked for simply dichotomous or polychotomous responses: Prices will rise, will fall, or stay the same. To get from a reporting of such data to a numerical measure of the movement of expectations takes an additional bit of implicit model building, usually of the "heroic" variety. Finally an incentive may exist for respondents to indulge in strategic behavior and misrepresent their true expectations. As we have seen in Chapter 2, response to any survey is better if the subject is regarded as salient or important; but by the same token, the very importance of the subject may evoke temptations to influence the result in favor of the respondent's interest group. Thus suppose that at time t, business views π_t^* as a desirable rate of price inflation. Let π_t^e represent true expectations. Then the reported series may be of the form $\pi_t^R = f_t(\pi_t^e, \pi_t^*)$. One then has the latent-variables problem of inferring something about π_t^e from the observed response π_t^R, and to do this, some implicit hypothesizing about π_t^* and f_t will be necessary. In general, then, we may conclude that whereas at first sight direct data on expectations seems the obvious way of testing for the ability of respondents to form rational expectations, exactly what we can infer from such survey data is by no means obvious.

Expectationally conditioned observables: financial markets

A large body of empirical work in the finance literature is concerned with verifying the efficient capital market theory, which says that prices of traded securities reflect all available information about the securities or the economy generally. It is not possible, on this view, by using *publicly* available information to systematically outguess the market. In particular, since such information certainly includes the past history of stock prices (say), schemes based upon chart behavior or mechanical trading rules can never hope to beat the "fair-game" character of the market. It is not denied that those with insider knowledge can and do make money; but in a manner corresponding to the Lucas informational model of Section 5.3, the resulting movement of the stock conveys such inside information to the public resulting in an equilibrium price that once again reflects all available information. The resulting proofs by Samuelson (1965) and Mandelbrot (1966) that given efficient capital markets, stock prices fluctuate randomly (see what follows) can be regarded as the theoretical underpinning of empirical work by Bachelier (1900/64) in his *Theorie de la Speculation* and half a century later by authors such as Granger and Morgenstern (1963), Moore (1964), and Fama (1965). For a general review of this theoretical and empirical work we refer the reader to Fama (1965) and finance textbooks such as Lev (1974).

The essence of the efficient capital markets hypothesis may be conveyed by a homogeneous structure of the form

$$P_t = E(P_{t+1}/\mathfrak{I}_t). \tag{71}$$

The variable P_t is usually in logarithms. The information set $\mathfrak{I}_t$ available at time t is of the form

$$\mathfrak{I}_t = \{P_{t-1}, P_{t-2}, \ldots; I_t, I_{t-1}, \ldots\}. \tag{72}$$

Here I_t is a schematic catch-all representing any nonprice information flows: announcements on dividends, stock splits, bonus issues, market sentiment, market commentators, and general economic conditions. Now the structure (71) is of the homogeneous form considered in detail in Section 5.5. To find the solution, one simply puts the constant $a = 1$ in the model of that section to derive

$$P_t = P_{t-1} + \gamma i_t, \tag{73}$$

where $i_t = I_t - E(I_t/\mathfrak{I}_{t-1})$ and γ is an arbitrary constant. Equation (73) is the famous "random walk of stock market prices" referred to in the preceding. The random walk is driven by innovations in market innovation: essentially unpredictable news events or simply new information. Technically, prices thus represent a martingale difference series with respect to the flow of information I_t.

Early empirical work was in the main directed at showing that prices did indeed behave according to the random-walk model (72) using one of the many nonparametric tests available (e.g., runs tests) for testing pure randomness in the price differences $\Delta P_t = P_t - P_{t-1}$. Such tests were almost always supportive of the random-walk hypothesis. However, they needed to be supplemented by a further demonstration that the difference ΔP_t constituted a martingale difference sequence with respect to the flow of information I_t so that ΔP_t should be statistically independent of $\{I_{t-1}, I_{t-2}, \ldots; P_{t-1}, P_{t-2}, \ldots\}$. Additional empirical tests were based on the imputed or actual performance of mechanistic trading rules such as filter rules (see, e.g., Lev, 1974, p. 219). Generally all such testing procedures confirm the efficient capital markets hypothesis with respect to stock market prices.

It could be objected that at best, expectations are only indirectly incorporated into stock market prices, at least of the usual spot market kind.

Foreign exchange and commodity markets have long been characterized by futures trading in which speculators or hedgers can establish a price now for future delivery. This is the *forward* price, to be contrasted with the *spot* price for current delivery. Let f_t be the forward price for delivery one period hence. In this literature, prices are always expressed in logarithms, which turns out to create desirable symmetries between alternative expressions of prices (e.g., p_{dollars} in terms of the pound or p_{pounds} in terms of the dollar). If agents are risk neutral and temporal discounting is neglected, then we should have

$$f_t = E(s_{t+1}/\mathcal{I}_t). \tag{74}$$

Also,

$$s_t = E(s_{t+1}/\mathcal{I}_t) + \epsilon_{t+1}, \tag{75}$$

where the innovation ϵ_{t+1} is independent of the current information set $\mathcal{I}_t$. From (74) and (75) it follows that in this case

$$\dot{s}_{t+1} = f_t + \epsilon_{t+1}. \tag{76}$$

The forward price should thus constitute a rational expectation of the future spot price. Equation (76) forms the basis of much empirical work aimed at testing the rational-expectations hypothesis in foreign exchange and commodity markets. It may be noted that in some of this work an intercept is added to (74) to represent a systematic aversion to risk (e.g., more risk-averse buyers of dollars in the forward market than sellers), and this is carried through to equation (76) as an allowable negative intercept. Most authors have set up the problem in regression format,

$$s_{t+1} = -\alpha + \beta f_t + \epsilon_{t+1}, \tag{77}$$

and tested whether $\beta = 1$ together with tests for the absence of serial correlation in the residual (see, e.g., Baillie, Lippens, and McMahon, 1983, who in fact find some evidence of serial correlation). Note, however, that a complementary testing procedure could be constructed as suggested in the preceding: Let I_t be any element or index in $\mathcal{I}_t$. Then once f_t is included in the regression (77), the additional inclusion of I_t should not improve the residual sums of squares, with standard F tests applicable.

Several authors have considered that the risk premium α referred to in the foregoing should be treated as a random variable, α_t, say, although nevertheless serially uncorrelated. Let $\alpha = E\alpha_t$, that is, the process is assumed to have a constant mean, and write $\tilde{\alpha}_t = \alpha_t - \alpha$. Equation (77) is replaced by

$$s_{t+1} = -\alpha + \beta f_t + u_{t+1}, \qquad u_{t+1} = \epsilon_{t+1} - \tilde{\alpha}_t. \tag{78}$$

Since f_t and the redefined disturbance term u_{t+1} are now correlated (α_t is reflected in f_t as a risk premium), ordinary least-squares methodology applied to (78) will not result in consistent estimation or tests of hypotheses. Frenkel (1981) utilized an instrumental-variables technique with instruments based upon variables formally external to the model (74)–(78) to test $\beta = 1$, again failing to reject the null hypothesis.

Whereas the preceding testing procedures, whether for the stock market or the foreign exchange or commodity markets, do provide a fair measure of support for the rational-expectations hypothesis, one is forcibly struck by a common defect: To a greater or lesser degree the studies involved represent correctly the model under the null hypothesis, as it were, of rational expectations; but they do not attempt to test this null hypothesis against any properly formulated alternative. The difficulty is twofold: (a) apart from rather trivial and clearly unacceptable models such as simple adaptive expectations, no very clearly formulated alternative to rational expectations and market efficiency exists and (b) even if it did, the rational-expectations hypothesis may not be naturally nested within such a class of alternatives in the sense of classical hypothesis testing theory. Nonnested procedures would be more appropriate. We shall return to this general point in what follows.

In spite of these and other empirical and methodological doubts, it seems clear that the rational-expectations hypothesis as a description of expectational formation in the analysis and description of market behavior has gained wide credence. According to this view, all foreseeable information has historically been incorporated, and nothing systematic remains in the observed movement of prices, which reflect only the flow of unanticipated information. One should in conclusion remark that most of the tests referred to are concerned with rational expectations in the mean. It has more recently been suggested that the past may provide information about the variance, rather than the mean, of future innovations. Thus in the case of the random-walk hypothesis, regressing *squared* differences $(p_t - p_{t-1})^2$ on past values of the innovations (e.g., $\epsilon_{t-1} = p_{t-1} - p_{t-2}$) sometimes does result in statistical significance. Such considerations motivate Engle's autoregressive conditional heteroscedastic (ARCH) models; we refer the reader to Engle (1982) and for a recent survey to Engle and Bollerslev (1986).

Expectations in structural models

The final degree of structural complexity that we shall consider is the embedding of one or more rational expectations in a more or less complete system of stochastic equations of the general linear form

$$Ay_t = By_t^e + \Gamma x_t + \epsilon_t, \tag{79}$$

where the conventions are as in Section 5.3. The general methodological problem attached to a system such as (79) has several facets:

(a) The structural identification problem: Assuming that the model (79) is a correct description of the behavior of the endogenous variables y_t, are the parameters A, B, Γ and the distributional parameters of the disturbance vector all identifiable?

(b) The model identifiability problem: It may be that a competing structural model with an alternative mode of expectations formation is empirically indistinguishable, that is, generates the same joint distribution for (y_t, x_t) as does the rational-expectations model (79).

(c) The optimal estimation procedures for model (79).

(d) The problem of testing whether expectations are rational; which as we shall see also involves (a)-(c).

These four aspects will serve to organize the discussion that follows.

(a) The identification problem: To see that one might have problems with the statistical identification of the structural parameters $\{A, B, \Gamma\}$, suppose in the first instance that the information set $\mathcal{I}_t$ available to agents for the formation of their predictions includes all current values x_t of the exogenous variables. As in Section 5.3, the optimal predictor is then given by $y_t^e = (A-B)^{-1}\Gamma x_t$, and the model (79) is equivalent to

$$(A-B)y_t = \Gamma x_t + u_t, \qquad u_t = (A-B)A^{-1}\epsilon_t. \tag{80}$$

Now model (80) is recognizable as a standard linear simultaneous system of stochastic equations. Those familiar with the identification theory of such systems will see immediately that a great deal of additional a priori information on the elements of A and/or B will be necessary to identify the separate elements of A, B given only the equation (80).

Suppose, on the other hand, that the agents whose behavior (or the consequence of whose behavior) the model describes do not have access to current information on all the exogenous variables but only a subset x_{2t}. The remaining variables x_{1t} must themselves be predicted in order to be able to predict y_t. In other words,

$$y_t^e = (A-B)^{-1}\Gamma \hat{x}_t, \tag{81}$$

where $\hat{x}_t' = (\hat{x}_{1t}', x_{2t}')$.

The subset x_{1t} is to be predicted on the basis of whatever information is available for the purpose; typically past values $\{x_{1t-1}, x_{1t-2}, \ldots\}$ and past (perhaps also present) values of the remaining exogenous variables x_{2t}. The predictions y_t^e as given by (81) may now be substituted back into (79). The reader may verify that the endogenous vector y_t is now "explained" by the variables x_{1t}, $\hat{x}_{1t}$, and x_{2t}.

In estimation terms, this means that an additional set of instruments $\hat{x}_{1t}$ is now available, augmenting the basic set x_t. The possibilities for the identification of the structural parameters $\{A, B, \Gamma\}$ are correspondingly enhanced. Suppose that all a priori information on these parameters takes the form of exclusion restrictions, that is, that only certain parameters are known to be zero. Write $\bar{K}_1 = \dim(\hat{x}_{1t})$ and, considering the ith equation of the system (79), let G_i be the number of endogenous variables y_t appearing on the right side, let L_i be the number of expectations y_t^e appearing, and let K_i be the total number of exogenous variables appearing. Turkington and Bowden (1988) have shown that a necessary condition for the statistical identifiability of the ith equation of (79) is that

$$K + \bar{K}_1 \geq G_i + L_i + K_i. \tag{82}$$

This condition is usually sufficient as well as necessary. Its meaning is as follows. The left side gives the total number of independent (for sufficiency) instruments available, all the exogenous variables plus the $\bar{K}_1$ predictions for the x_1 variables. The right side represents the number of variables in equation i for which instruments are needed, or equivalently the number of coefficients to be estimated. The condition is that there must be at least as many instruments as the number of coefficients to be estimated.

We observe from condition (82) that the possibilities for statistical identification of any equation improves with the number $\bar{K}_1$ of variables in x_1, those about which no current information is available to agents for the purposes of prediction. An interesting inverse-correspondence principle first noted by Wegge and Feldman (1982) therefore holds: In structural models with rational expectations, the less current information available to agents whose behavior the model represents, the greater the possibilities for identification of the system by an external observer. Or putting it differently, there is a trade-off between internal efficiency in forecasting and external efficiency in the study of system parameters.

(b) Model identification: Consider the following structural model, which relates unemployment u_t to expectations π_t^e of the rate of inflation π_t:

$$u_t = \alpha z_t + \beta(\pi_t - \pi_t^e) + \epsilon_{1t}, \tag{83a}$$

$$\pi_t = \gamma_1 \pi_{t-1} + \gamma_2 m_t + \epsilon_{2t}. \tag{83b}$$

Here z_t is an exogenous variable and $\epsilon_{1t}, \epsilon_{2t}$ are white-noise disturbances. In forming their expectations π_t^e agents do not have access to current values of m_t, the other exogenous variable (representing in the present context the logarithm of the money supply). Instead they are constrained to predict m_t as $\hat{m}_t = \lambda m_{t-1}$; we shall suppose that this is an unbiased predictor, equivalent to assuming that the process m_t is itself generated as a first-order Markov process with autoregressive parameter λ. In the terminology of structural identification $x_t' = (z_t, \pi_{t-1}, m_t)$ and $\hat{x}_{1t} = \hat{m}_t$. Although the a priori restrictions on equation (83a) (involving "structural neutrality" in the effect of π_t on u_t) are not of the simple exclusion type considered in the discussion of structure identification [(a) in the preceding], it is easy to show using the Wegge–Feldman criterion that all parameters of the model (83) are identified, provided, as we have assumed, that current observations on m_t are unavailable to the agents whose collective behavior the model represents.

Utilizing (83b) and $\hat{m}_t = \lambda m_{t-1}$, we find that

$$\pi_t - \pi_t^e = \gamma_2(m_t - \lambda m_{t-1}) + \epsilon_{2t}.$$

Substituting in equation (83a) we derive

$$u_t = \alpha z_t + \gamma_1 m_t - \gamma_2 m_{t-1} + v_t, \tag{84}$$

where $\gamma_1 = \beta\gamma_2$, $\gamma_2 = \beta\lambda\gamma_2$, and $v_t = \epsilon_{1t} + \beta\epsilon_{2t}$ remains a white-noise disturbance process. Equation (84) exhibits u_t as a distributed lag of present and past m_t. As such, this equation has quite different policy implications for the control of the money supply m_t than has the rational-expectations structure (83). We shall consider such matters in Section 6.2. For the moment we only note that the observed behavior of a set of endogenous variables may be generated by more than one model or set of explanatory hypotheses, each of which is identified as a structure in its own terms. Then the fact that a rational-expectations structure is identified does not mean that the statistical task of testing rational expectations should begin and end with such a structure. We return to this point in what follows.

(c) Estimation: Given that the structure is identified, its estimation theory is a reasonably straightforward adaptation of the standard theory for linear simultaneous stochastic models (for which, see any econometrics textbook). The maximum likelihood and instrumental-variables theory of the structural model (79) has been considered by Wallis (1980), Wickens (1982), Turkington (1986), Pesaran (1987), and other authors. The principal econometric difficulty lies in specifying what information agents are assumed to have available for predicting current values of the exogenous

variables in x_t where these are not immediately available. In general this means that such components have themselves to be modeled. By the definition of exogeneity, the resulting likelihood function is recursive and therefore separable, decomposing into the conditional likelihood of the endogenous variable given the exogenous variables or their predictions and, as a second factor, the marginal likelihood for the exogenous variables. Finally we should point out that the paradigm (79) by no means exhausts the possibilities for structural specification. For some alternatives we refer the reader to the econometric studies collected in Lucas and Sargent (1981).

(d) Testing the rational-expectations hypothesis in structural models

Nested tests: Let us consider the following system:

$$u_t = \alpha z_t + \beta \pi_t^e + \epsilon_{1t}, \tag{85a}$$

$$\pi_t = \gamma_1 \pi_{t-1} + \gamma_2 m_t + \epsilon_{2t}, \tag{85b}$$

where the conventions are as for model (83). Our objective is to test whether expectations π_t^e are formed rationally. To make things simple, we shall assume always that current values m_t are known as agents.

Perhaps the simplest test for the unbiasedness of expectations would concentrate on equation (85b). If expectations are rational, we should then have

$$\pi_t^e = \gamma_1 \pi_{t-1} + \gamma_2 m_t \tag{86}$$

given that current values m_t are assumed available to agents.

Suppose that instead of (86) expectations are formed as

$$\pi_t^e = \delta_1 \pi_{t-1} + \delta_2 m_t \tag{86'}$$

for arbitrary δ_1, δ_2. Substitute (86') into (85a) to obtain a two-equation system in terms of the observables as

$$u_t = \alpha z_t + \theta_1 \pi_{t-1} + \theta_2 m_t + \epsilon_{1t},$$

$$\pi_t = \gamma_1 \pi_{t-1} + \gamma_2 m_t + \epsilon_{2t}, \tag{87}$$

where $\theta_1 = \beta \delta_1$ and $\theta_2 = \beta \delta_2$. Now if expectations are rational, the coefficients of the model (87) should satisfy the following:

$$\frac{\theta_1}{\gamma_1} = \frac{\theta_2}{\gamma_2} \quad (=\beta). \tag{88}$$

Condition (88) is an example of the cross-equation parameter constraints that characterize simultaneous systems containing rational expectations.

Testing procedures based on such cross-equation constraints are explored in detail by Hoffman and Schmidt (1981), who suggest standard Wald-type or likelihood ratio tests of the restrictions [in this case equation (88)]. The advantage of the Wald tests, as always, is that one need fit only the unrestricted model in order to be able to execute the test. The disadvantage is that Wald tests are not invariant to different ways of expressing the equalities to be tested.

In the language of classical hypothesis-testing theory, tests of the preceding kind are based on the nesting principle: The observable model (87) with rational expectations is a particular case of the model with general expectations provided the latter are of the class (86′). The last proviso is important. It might be highly restrictive to suppose that expectations are always formed as some parametric variant of (86′). For example, adaptive expectations [equation (14)] do not belong to this family. Moreover one may have a quite different overall structure in mind so that the question of model identifiability [see (b) in the preceding] will also arise. More complete tests of the rational-expectations hypothesis must therefore be based upon the principle of nonnested hypothesis testing.

Nonnested tests: Various procedures are available in the general statistical literature for testing nonnested alternative models or hypotheses. For a good survey with a structural slant the reader is referred to McAleer and Pesaran (1986). In particular, Cox's procedure (1961) has found some application in the literature on testing rational expectations. In general, this procedure is based upon the likelihood difference. Let $l_{RE}(\hat{\theta})$ denote the (maximum) log-likelihood for the rational-expectations model incorporating a set of parameters θ. Let $l_A(\hat{\varphi})$ denote the log-likelihood of a proposed alternative model evaluated at the parameter estimate $\hat{\varphi}$. The Cox test statistic is

$$T_{RE/A} = l_{RE}(\hat{\theta}) - l_A(\hat{\varphi}) - E_{\hat{\theta}}[l_{RE}(\hat{\theta}) - l_A(\hat{\varphi})]. \tag{89}$$

The expectation $E_{\hat{\theta}}$ indicates that the rational-expectations model is assumed to be correct and that the parameters are evaluated at the maximum-likelihood estimate $\hat{\theta}$. The Cox statistic represents a centering of the log-likelihood difference on the assumption that the rational-expectations model is the correct model. If this hypothesis (H_0: rational expectations) is correct, then the statistic $T_{RE/A}$ is asymptotically normal with variance $V_{\hat{\theta}}(T_{RE/A})$, say, which may (often with some difficulty) be worked out. A second statistic $T_{A/RE}$ is constructed on a similar basis except that now the alternative model is assumed to be the correct one. One then draws conclusions by examining any asymmetry between rejections based upon $T_{RE/A}$ and those based upon the complementary Cox statistic $T_{A/RE}$.

In practice, the evaluation of the various expectations and variances involved are often difficult. However, Pesaran (1974) has given a relatively simple expression for the two Cox statistics for competing linear models of nonsimultaneous form. In a later contribution (Pesaran, 1982) he applied the Cox procedure to the rational-expectations context, testing a version of the "structural neutrality" model [similar to the model (83)] with rational expectations against a more Keynesian version of the Phillips curve, which does allow a trade-off between inflation and unemployment. His results are somewhat inconclusive: Neither model rejects the other.

Informal tests: Finally, it may be pointed out that a variety of more informal tests have been proposed based upon special features of the model under consideration. Consider, for instance, the following model with structural neutrality:

$$u_t = \sum_{i=1}^{\infty} \theta_i u_{t-i} + \beta(\pi_t - \pi_t^e) + \epsilon_{1t},$$

$$\pi_t = \gamma_1 \pi_{t-1} + \gamma_2 m_t + \epsilon_{2t}.$$

The disturbances $\epsilon_{1t}, \epsilon_{2t}$ are, as before, specified to be white noise. Suppose that agents in forming their predictions π_t^e have access to information on current m_t. It will be apparent that the best predictor of u_t given all available information is simply its own past $\{u_{t-1}, u_{t-2}, ...\}$. In the terminology, m_t or past values of π_t do not "cause" u_t. The notion of causality is that of Granger (1969): x_t causes y_t if y_t can be better predicted by adding $x_{t-1}, x_{t-2}, ...$ to the last of all predicting variables. One could then test the combined hypothesis of rational expectations and structural neutrality by drawing on a test due to Sims (1972); for a review see also Pierce and Haugh (1977). The test that, for instance, m_t does not cause u_t is carried out by regressing m_t against the manifold $\{u_{t+r}; -\infty < r < \infty\}$. If statistical insignificance attaches to the coefficients u_{t+r} for $r > 0$, this is interpreted as supporting the hypothesis that m_t does not cause u_t, with similar remarks with respect to π_t. In general, the disadvantage of this type of test should be clear: Since the series involved are generally highly collinear, one would expect problems of multicollinearity to result from the proposed regression. Pierce and Haugh (1977) discuss in detail a prewhitening procedure to overcome such problems by reducing (in terms of the preceding example) both u_t and m_t to their basic uncorrelated innovational components.

5.7   Evaluation

In this chapter we have introduced the idea of a rational-expectations equilibrium as a state of affairs where people's subjective expectations or forecasts are in fact identical with the objective mathematical expectations given their respective information sets. In the next two chapters we shall enlarge on this theme and in the process examine much more closely the idea of equilibrium that is involved and the very possibility that a rational-expectations equilibrium can either exist or maintain itself once established. Pending such developments, an evaluation of what the present chapter has accomplished is perhaps a little premature, but a few general remarks may be made at this point.

Rational expectations may in one sense be taken as a neutrality proposition with respect to the way people are assumed to view the future. It is probably fair to say that most dynamic models – those involving time in an essential way – in the social sciences entail some hypothesis, either explicit or implicit, about people's expectations of what is to come. The difficulty with mechanistic formulations such as adaptive expectations is that they introduce into such dynamic discussion an additional source of systematic bias. By hypothesizing expectations to be unbiased, or rational in the terminology, we can concentrate on the fundamentals, as it were. On the other hand we have seen that the rational-expectations hypothesis is not strong enough to shield the basic dynamics from infection by extraneous influences. The verdicts of market commentators or social gurus can acquire self-fulfilling status even though expectations are rational; their pronouncements become part of people's information sets, and the fundamentals have therefore to be redefined to include this new information. The discussion of Section 5.5 showed also that unbiasedness has nothing to do with social efficiency in forecasting. A market with influential commentators may be much more volatile, but expectations continue to be unbiased. One cannot therefore claim that rational expectations are neutral in the sense that expectations have no effect on the dynamics of the system.

As we have seen, it is not necessary to assume that everyone necessarily has the same expectations in a rational-expectations equilibrium. Expectations are conditional upon individual information sets, which is one way of formalizing the idea that some people are better at predicting than others. Of course, there may be other reasons; perspicuity may be a skill, inborn or otherwise, regardless of the information set. However, the idea that information sets may differ does have some implication for the stability or invariance of rational-expectations equilibria. We saw, for instance, that publication effects might be entailed: If an external statistician published a model of a system in a state of rational-expectations equilibrium, a new equilibrium would in general arise that would nullify the model. More generally the social flow of information would then impose a new tier of structure. One related aspect that we shall consider in the next chapter is that in forming their expectations, people might in the process have to think about the way that others are forming their own expectations: Flows of social information about such expectational states would have an obvious modifying effect.

As this remark suggests, we have so far said very little about the way people are presumed to form their expectations: One simply assumes that they are able to do so in a way that is mathematically unbiased. This rather curious "black-box" attitude is thoroughly characterisic of the empirical literature on estimating and testing models with rational expectations. Some lip service is paid to the problem more or less as a matter of necessity in postulating the existence of a certain information set that agents are supposed to use. However, the empirical literature typically presumes homogeneity of forecasting skills and information sets. Since we know that this is not likely to be the case and does not even have to be the case, a specification error is already being introduced. Presumably the models used for such testing purposes refer to a representative agent, the result of some aggregation process not made clear. But in that case one wonders about the predictive status of such a model once fitted. This is not just a matter of publication effects. As we have seen, the dynamics of price or voting may depend in an essential way upon information heterogeneity. To assume homogeneous information may therefore be like the late-night drunk looking for his watch at the corner. He knows he lost it down the street, but the light is better under the lamp at the corner.

On the other hand it would be foolish to ignore a body of apparently corroborative evidence, in particular in the operations of securities and foreign exchange markets. The rational-expectations hypothesis must therefore be taken seriously as an empirical finding. As pointed out in Section 5.6, much depends upon what kind of alternative hypothesis one has in mind. There is surely no contest between rational expectations and simple mechanistic alternatives such as adaptive expectations. But the available empirical evidence that apparently supports the rational-expectations hypothesis may nevertheless be consistent with other alternatives. To understand what these might be requires in the first instance a much closer look at the idea of a rational-expectations equilibrium. This is the task of the next chapter.

Appendix 1. The statistical dynamics of structural models with heterogeneous information

See Section 5.3. Our strategy is as follows. (a) First we look at model (25) with a partitioning of the exogenous vector into x_{1t}, x_{2t}. We suppose that individuals have homogeneous information, namely, x_{1t} but not x_{2t}, and obtain the form of the optimal predictor, in the process drawing attention to various efficiency matters. (b) Next we assume two kinds of individuals, those who have information on the full vector x_t (the informed) and those with information only on the subset x_{1t} (the uninformed). We look at the problem in sequence first from the point of view of the uninformed using the results from part (a) and then from the point of view of the informed given the rules followed by the uninformed.

A.   *Individuals need not know everything*

Consider model (25) assuming that all participants know x_{1t} but not x_{2t}. Utilizing $\hat{y}_{t/t-1} = y_t - v_t$, where v_t is a prediction error, we obtain

$$y_t = (A-B)^{-1}\Gamma_1 x_{1t} + (A-B)^{-1}\Gamma_2 x_{2t} + (A-B)^{-1}(\epsilon_t - Bv_t), \qquad (A.1)$$

where here and in what follows we simply assume that the various inverses exist without further qualification. Introducing the lag operator z such that $zw_t = w_{t-1}$ for any w_t, let us assume that the series x_{2t} is generated by a regular stationary stochastic process of the form

$$x_{2t} = \Theta(z)x_{2t-1} + \eta_{2t}, \qquad (A.2)$$

where η_{2t} is a vector white-noise innovation process and $\theta(z)$ is a polynomial of finite order in the lag operator z. Assume that the generating function $I - \theta(z)$ contains no determinantal zeros on or inside the unit circle so that the autoregressive process (A.2) is invertible to a moving-average process. Thus we write

$$[I - \theta(z)]^{-1} = \frac{1}{1 - z\mu(z)}\Psi(z)$$

where $1 - z\mu(z) = \det[I - \theta(z)]$ is a polynomial of finite order in z and $\Psi(z)$ is the adjoint matrix of $I - \theta(z)$. Thus

$$x_{2t} = \frac{1}{1 - z\mu(z)}\Psi(z)\eta_{2t} \qquad (A.3)$$

is the moving-average process corresponding to (A.2). Applying (A.3) to (A.1) and multiplying by $1 - z\mu(z)$, we obtain

$$y_t = \mu(z)y_{t-1} + (A-B)^{-1}\Gamma_1(1 - z\mu(z))x_{1t} + (A-B)^{-1}$$
$$\times [\Gamma_2\Psi(z)\eta_{2t} + (1 - z\mu(z))\epsilon_t] - (A-B)^{-1}B(1 - z\mu(z))v_t. \qquad (A.4)$$

According to a result of Granger and Morris (1976), the sum of the finite-order moving-average processes that appears in the square brackets can be written as

$$\Gamma_2 \Psi(z) \eta_{2t} + [1 - z\mu(z)] \epsilon_t = \Delta(z) \bar{\epsilon}_t$$

$$= [I + zD(z)] \bar{\epsilon}_t \tag{A.5}$$

for some matrix polynomial-generating function $D(z)$, again of finite order in z, with the series $\bar{\epsilon}_t$ being vector white noise. Hence

$$\mathbf{y}_t = \mu(z)\mathbf{y}_{t-1} + (A - B)^{-1}\Gamma_1(1 - z\mu(z))\mathbf{x}_{1t} + (A - B)^{-1}$$

$$\times (D(z)\bar{\epsilon}_{t-1} + B\mu(z)\mathbf{v}_{t-1}) + (A - B)^{-1}(\bar{\epsilon}_t - B\mathbf{v}_t). \tag{A.6}$$

Turning now to a rational-expectations requirement for $\hat{\mathbf{y}}_{t/t-1}$, it must be true by an argument similar to that used in the market example of Section 5.2, that

$$\mathbf{v}_t = (A - B)^{-1}(\bar{\epsilon}_t - B\mathbf{v}_t)$$

whence

$$A\mathbf{v}_t = \bar{\epsilon}_t.$$

Substituting this into (A.6), we get

$$\mathbf{y}_t = [\mu(z)\mathbf{y}_{t-1} + (A - B)^{-1}\Gamma_1(1 - z\mu(z))\mathbf{x}_{1t}$$

$$+ (A - B)^{-1}(D(z)A + B\mu(z))\mathbf{v}_{t-1}] + A^{-1}\bar{\epsilon}_t. \tag{A.7}$$

Evidently the rational-expectations prediction may be formed recursively as the term in the square brackets of (A.7), with error as the residual term $A^{-1}\bar{\epsilon}_t$.

As a predictor, $\hat{\mathbf{y}}_{t/t-1}$ formed as in the preceding is less efficient than the predictor (26), which utilizes the full-potential information set, incorporating in addition the actual values of $\mathbf{x}_{2t}$. The prediction error of the latter is given by $A^{-1}\epsilon_t$, to be compared with $A^{-1}\bar{\epsilon}_t$ for the limited-information model.

From (A.5) we observe from the independence of ϵ_t and η_{2t} that

$$\text{Cov } \bar{\epsilon}_t > \text{Cov } \epsilon_t,$$

in the usual sense of positive semidefinite differences. It follows immediately that

$$\text{Cov } A^{-1}\bar{\epsilon}_t > \text{Cov } A^{-1}\epsilon_t. \tag{A.8}$$

In other words, the limited-information predictor $\hat{\mathbf{y}}_{t/t-1}$ defined in the square brackets of (A.4) is a less efficient predictor than that based on the full model. The preceding development is based on Wallis (1980).

B.   *Heterogeneous information*

Now suppose that some individuals know $\mathbf{x}_{2t}$ as well as $\mathbf{x}_{1t}$; these are the informed agents. For brevity, write $\hat{\mathbf{y}}^I_{t/t-1} = \hat{\mathbf{y}}_{t1}$ as the predictions of the informed and $\hat{y}^u_{t/t-1} = \hat{y}_{t2}$ as the predictions of the uninformed. Given the proportion w of the informed, the structural model is then equation (28), reproduced here:

$$Ay_t = B[w\hat{y}_{t1} + (1-w)\hat{y}_{t2}] + \Gamma x_t + \epsilon_t. \tag{A.9}$$

Consider first the informed agents. Take expectations of both sides of (A.9), conditional upon their information sets, which include x_t. Since the expectations $\hat{y}_{t2}$ of uninformed individuals are conditional upon information already available to the informed (i.e., $\mathcal{I}^u_t \subset \mathcal{I}^I_y$), we have

$$E_I(\hat{y}_{2t}/\mathcal{I}^I_t) = \hat{y}_{2t}.$$

Notice that no claim is made that the prediction $\hat{y}_{2t}$ is passed directly from the uninformed to the informed: Simply that however $\hat{y}_{2t}$ is formed, the results are predictable to the informed. Hence for the informed, it is as though they form $\hat{y}_{t1}$ by substituting $\hat{y}_{t2}$ into (A.9) to yield

$$\hat{y}_{t1} = (1-w)(A-wB)^{-1}\hat{y}_{t2} + (A-wB)^{-1}\Gamma x_t. \tag{A.10}$$

Now let us turn to the uninformed. Substituting (A.10) into (A.9), we obtain the model as it faces the uninformed:

$$Ay_t = \tilde{B}\hat{y}_{2t} + \tilde{\Gamma}x_t + \epsilon_t, \tag{A.11}$$

where

$$\tilde{B} = (1-w)B[I + w(A-wB)^{-1}]$$

and

$$\tilde{\Gamma} = [I + wB(A-wB)^{-1}]\Gamma.$$

The analysis of part (a) now applies to the model (A.11). Uninformed individuals have to form the prediction $\hat{y}_{2t}$ knowing only the portion x_{1t} of the vector x_t. Corresponding to equation (A.7), the optimal predictor for the uninformed is

$$\hat{y}_{2t} = \tilde{\mu}(z)y_{t-1} + (A-\tilde{B})^{-1}\tilde{\Gamma}_1(1 - z\mu(z))x_{1t}$$
$$+ (A-\tilde{B})^{-1}(D(z)A + \tilde{B}\mu(z))\tilde{v}_{2t-1} \tag{A.12}$$

with $\tilde{v}_{2t} = y_t - \hat{y}_{2t} = A^{-1}\tilde{\epsilon}_t$, where $D(z)$ and $\tilde{\epsilon}_t$ are again defined by (A.5). From (A.12) and (A.11), the stochastic behavior of the uninformed predictor is given by

$$\hat{y}_{2t} = y_t - A^{-1}\tilde{\epsilon}_t$$
$$= y_t - A^{-1}\Delta^{-1}(z)(1 - z\mu(z))(x_{2t} + \epsilon_t). \tag{A.13}$$

Substituting (A.13) into (A.11), the stochastic model as it faces the informed predictor (who can observe x_{2t}) is, after a little rearrangement, given by

$$[A-(1-w)B]\mathbf{y} = wB\hat{\mathbf{y}}_{t1}+\Gamma_1\mathbf{x}_{1t}+[\Gamma_2-(1-w)BA^{-1}\Delta^{-1}(z)(1-z\mu(z))\mathbf{x}_{2t}]$$
$$+[I-(1-w)BA^{-1}\Delta^{-1}(z)(1-z\mu(z))]\epsilon_t. \qquad (A.14)$$

Now writing $\Delta^{-1}(z)(1-z\mu(z))=I+zG(z)$ and taking expectations conditional upon the information sets of the informed, we obtain

$$(A-B)\hat{\mathbf{y}}_{t1} = \Gamma_1\mathbf{x}_{1t}+[\Gamma_2-(1-w)BA^{-1}(I+zG(z))]\mathbf{x}_{2t}$$
$$-(1-w)BA^{-1}G(z)\epsilon_{t-1}. \qquad (A.15)$$

From (A.14) it must be true that the prediction error for informed individuals is given by

$$\mathbf{v}_{1t} = [A-(1-w)B]^{-1}[I-(1-w)BA^{-1}]\epsilon_t$$
$$= A^{-1}\epsilon_t. \qquad (A.16)$$

Thus the optimal predictor error is exactly the same for the informed individuals as in the undifferentiated model [cf. equation (27)]. We should not expect otherwise. However, the optimal predictor is quite different. Substituting (A.16) into (A.15), the predictor is given by

$$\hat{\mathbf{y}}_{t1} = (A-B)^{-1}\Gamma_1\mathbf{x}_{1t}+(A-B)^{-1}[\Gamma_2-(1-w)BA^{-1}(I+zG(z))]\mathbf{x}_{2t}$$
$$-(A-B)^{-1}BA^{-1}G(z)A\mathbf{v}_{1t-1}. \qquad (A.17)$$

The forecasting needed by informed agents is therefore considerably more complicated than where all information is homogeneous. Even informed individuals now have to adopt error correction modes and smooth the sequence of the $\mathbf{x}_{2t}$ variates.

The preceding development forms the basis for the remarks in the text.

CHAPTER 6

Games, beauty contests, and equilibrium: the foundations of structural invariance

6.1 Introduction

In the previous chapter we described the idea of a rational-expectations equilibrium. The reader will recall that such an equilibrium is characterized by equality between the subjective expectations of participants and mathematical expectations given their respective information sets. All predictions are in this sense self-fulfilling. One might suspect from the anticipatory nature of such systems that some problems might arise for the theory of social or economic policy. This does turn out to be the case, and the early part of this chapter is concerned with the resulting problems. To begin with, a degree of care must be exercised that policy rules are based on the real invariants of the system and not upon the kind of reduced form that is usually taken to govern the system's evolution. Moreover an anticipatory system implies a fair measure of interdependence between the action of the policymaker and the actions that he or she is trying to influence, introducing the possibility of game-theoretic interactions between policymaker and subjects. The additional complexity of the resulting control problems together with the necessity of identifying those parameters that remain invariant under different controls impose an estimation task of considerable magnitude for the policymaker. All the preceding issues are discussed in Sections 6.2 and 6.3. Even if these problems can all be satisfactorily resolved, an additional difficulty arises for the application of standard control-theoretic methods: the problem of time inconsistency, discussed in Section 6.4. With some degree of foresight, actions for this period are determined by policy settings for next period as well as those for this period. If this is the case, the resulting optimal policy does not satisfy the Bellman efficiency principle of dynamic programming, and this in turn leads to a temptation on the part of the government to revise a previously announced or understood policy.

At this point, the determinate character of rational expectations begins to break down, for each party will, with the possibility of time inconsistency, be trying to second guess the others. Section 6.5 gives a game-theoretic resolution of the problem, pointing out the prisoner's dilemma nature of the situation. It goes on to consider some of the empirical difficulties that beset the estimation of structures in the presence of game-theoretic elements, introducing the notion of argument instability. From here on, the chapter increasingly becomes an exploration of the relationship of the rational-expectations equilibrium to game-theoretic equilibria. The formal equivalence of a classic many-agent rational-expectations equilibrium with the Nash equilibrium of noncooperative game theory is developed in Section 6.6. Incidental to any behavioristic account of such equilibria is the necessity to forecast the actions or opinions of others, knowing that these opinions will in their turn depend upon yet other opinions. This kind of infinite regress is familiar from game theory.

The noncooperative Nash equilibrium corresponds to the classic rational-expectations equilibrium of competitive economic theory, in which individually insignificant agents act in accordance with well-defined mathematical expectations of their environmental variables. Other kinds of game-theoretic solutions that might arise are also characterized in equilibrium by perfect foresight or rational expectations, but agents may not actually be using these forecasts to determine their actions. In Section 6.7 we attempt an evaluation of all these game-theoretic notions and their relationship to rational-expectations equilibria and indeed whether rational expectations can exist in disequilibrium states.

In summary, the chapter starts with the idea of rational expectations as reasonably well defined if empirically somewhat tendentious. What appear at first sight to be a few minor wrinkles in its application to problems of policy lead to a full-scale inquiry into the meaning and applicability of the rational-expectations equilibrium. We end up with the rational-expectations idea as shaky but relatively intact as a description of certain kinds of game-theoretic equilibria but not at all well defined out of equilibrium.

6.2   Invariance and policy

In explaining the kinds of difficulty that arise in the control of an anticipatory system, it is useful to begin with an example already utilized in Chapter 5, namely, a Phillips curve relating unemployment proximally to inflation and expectations of inflation and ultimately to the government's policy rules for determining the stock of money in the economy. Let u_t denote the rate of unemployment at time t and $\bar{u}_t$ the "natural rate." It is not the purpose of the present study to examine economic issues such as the meaning and existence of the natural-rate concept or indeed the concept of the Phillips curve itself. For present purposes we simply assume that a natural rate exists and that it is a predetermined and known function of time not controllable by the policymaker. Let π_t be the rate of price inflation and let π_t^e be its expected rate given observations on variables up to time $t-1$. Finally let m_t be the (logarithm) money supply and let ϵ_{1t} and ϵ_{2t} be unobservable white-noise disturbances or innovations. The model is

$$u_t = \bar{u}_t + \alpha \pi_t + \beta \pi_t^e + \epsilon_{1t}, \tag{1a}$$

$$\pi_t = \gamma_1 \pi_{t-1} + \gamma_2 m_t + \epsilon_{2t}. \tag{1b}$$

The most important special case for the parameters is the structural neutrality assumption $\alpha + \beta = 0$, which means that people react only to the unanticipated component of inflation as $\alpha(\pi_t - \pi_t^e)$.

Suppose that prior to the establishment of the control rules to be examined, the money supply m_t has followed some stochastic evolutionary path with an autoregressive representation of the form

$$m_t = \alpha_1 m_{t-1} + \alpha_2 m_{t-2} + \alpha_2 m_{t-3} + \cdots + \epsilon_{mt}, \tag{2}$$

where ϵ_{mt} is the innovations process in the stock of money. We may conveniently represent the preceding autoregressive process by using the lag operator z such that $zm_t = m_{t-1}$ and defining $\alpha_m(z) = \alpha_1 + \alpha_2 z + \alpha_3 z^2 + \cdots$; $A_m(z) = 1 - z\alpha_m(z)$. Then

$$A_m(z)m_t = \epsilon_{mt}$$

is the shorthand representation of the autogressive process (2). We can take it that the variable m_t represents some deviation about a long-term mean, so that the process (2) represents a regular stationary stochastic process of zero mean. It may be that the process represents the operations of some previous control rule with a stochastic component or it may be that the money supply has in the past been left very much to its own devices. The prior period during which the scheme (2) is assumed to have been operating will be referred to as the "sample period" for reasons that will shortly become apparent.

From equations (1a) and (1b) we must have

$$u_t = \bar{u}_t + (\alpha + \beta)\pi_t - \beta(\pi_t - \pi_t^e) + \epsilon_{1t}, \tag{3}$$

and

$$\pi_t - \pi_t^e = \epsilon_{2t} + \gamma_2(m_t - m_t^e) = \epsilon_{2t} + \gamma_2 \epsilon_{mt} = \epsilon_{2t} + \gamma_2 A_m(z)m_t. \tag{4}$$

For future reference we note that according to a result by Granger and Morris (1976) noted in Chapter 5, we may write

$$(\alpha + \beta \gamma_1 z)\epsilon_{2t} + (1 - \gamma_1 z)\epsilon_{1t} \equiv \eta_t + \theta \eta_{t-1}, \tag{5}$$

where η_t is some white-noise innovation process. Substituting (4) into (3) and utilizing (5), we derive

$$u_t - \bar{u}_t = \gamma_1(u_{t-1} - \bar{u}_{t-1}) + \gamma_2[\alpha + \beta - \beta(1 - \gamma_1 z)A_m(z)]m_t + \eta_t + \theta\eta_{t-1}. \tag{6}$$

We shall refer to this equation as the *policy-reduced form* of system (1). Its importance lies in the fact that it gives us the effect upon the target u_t (or $u_t - \bar{u}_t$) of m_t regarded as a potential policy variable, or "instrument" in the terminology of Tinbergen (1952).

Imagine, then, that the policy-reduced form (6) is estimated over the sample period. On the strength of the estimated coefficients, an optimal control policy is designed. If, for example, the aim is to minimize $\mathrm{Var}(u_t - \bar{u}_t)$, that is, to track as closely as possible the natural rate $\bar{u}_t$, the optimal policy is very easily obtained. Rearrange the policy-reduced form in terms of a simple white-noise disturbance η_t as

$$u_t - \bar{u}_t = \frac{\theta + \gamma_1}{1 + \theta z}(u_{t-1} - \bar{u}_{t-1}) + \frac{\gamma_2[\alpha + \beta - \beta(1 - \gamma_1 z)A_m(z)]}{1 + \theta z}m_t + \eta_t. \tag{7}$$

Then the optimal setting of m_t is obtained by destroying the autocorrelation in equation (7), that is, by making

$$(\theta + \gamma_1)(u_{t-1} - \bar{u}_{t-1}) + \gamma_2[\alpha + \beta - \beta(1 - \gamma_1 z)A_m(z)]m_t = 0.$$

The money supply m_t is therefore to be set according to the recursive scheme

$$m_t = \phi_1 m_{t-1} + \phi_2 m_{t-2} + \phi_3 m_{t-3} + \cdots + \phi(u_{t-1} - \bar{u}_{t-1}), \tag{8}$$

where

$$\phi_1 = -\frac{\beta}{\alpha}(\alpha_1 + \gamma_1), \qquad \phi_i = -\frac{\beta}{\alpha}(\alpha_i - \gamma_1\alpha_{i-1}) \quad \text{for } i \geq 2$$

and

$$\phi = -\frac{\theta + \gamma_1}{\alpha\gamma_2}.$$

The resulting path of u_t is simply

$$u_t = \bar{u}_t + \eta_t, \tag{9}$$

so that unemployment follows the natural rate $\bar{u}_t$ with a simple white-noise residual.

The use of a reduced form for control purposes in the preceding fashion, with many technical variations and developments, has been quite characteristic of the application of techniques from the theory of optimal control to problems of economic policy. Indeed it has often been suggested in the literature of econometrics and time series analysis that since only reduced forms are employed to resolve the important policy questions of prediction and policy, the specification and estimation of a structural form model such as (1) is unnecessary and possibly even dangerous since it may be more subject to misspecification problems. The only valid role for the structural form, on such a view, is to suggest possible a priori restrictions, the "overidentifying restrictions" in the jargon, to improve the efficiency of the estimation of the reduced form.

Now suppose that the previous sample period generation of m_t is replaced by the control rule (8). Since the latter is nonstochastic, we must then have $m_t - m_t^e = 0$. Reference back to the structure (1) will show that in this case $\pi_t - \pi_t^e = \epsilon_{2t}$, and one derives a new policy-reduced form relating m_t to u_t as

$$u_t - \bar{u}_t = \gamma_1(u_{t-1} - \bar{u}_{t-1}) + \gamma_2(\alpha + \beta)m_t + \eta_t + \theta\eta_{t-1}. \tag{10}$$

Application of policy rule (8) to this reduced form will no longer yield the minimal-variance system (9). Indeed if equation (10) is the policy-reduced form, then the best control is the simple feedback

$$m_t = -\frac{\theta + \gamma_1}{\gamma_2(\alpha + \beta)}(u_{t-1} - \bar{u}_{t-1}), \tag{11}$$

which does attain the minimal-variance system (9).

What has happened here? The structural system (1) has stayed the same, that is, is invariant. But the reduced form (6) upon which the policy is predicated is not invariant to the generation of the m_t process, which changes with the existence or type of control law in operation. Things get even worse in the case of the structural neutrality contingency referred to in the preceding: $\alpha + \beta = 0$. As equation (11) suggests, in this case *no* control is possible. All deterministic policies such as (8) yield a policy-reduced form that is independent of m_t. Thus any policy is impotent.

It is easy to see how a policymaker could be led into error. Suppose that he or she is unaware of the true underlying structural form (1) but formulates perhaps an alternative structure that leads to the same policy-reduced form (6). Or else he or she may simply establish equation (6) directly by Box–Jenkins techniques or other methodologies from time series analysis. Over the sample period, all such structures or descriptions are observationally equivalent. But as we have seen, the implications for policy of the structural form (1) are very different from those of, say, equation (6), regarded as a primitive assumed reaction. Moreover, the same difficulties apply to problems of prediction as well as control. Imagine a once-and-for-all change in A_m at time t. According to the reduced form (6), the effects of this change become gradually reflected in $u_t - \bar{u}_t$ according to the operation of the distributed lag $A_m(z)$, building up after a long period of time to the ultimate or steady-state effect. But according to the structural form (1), the effects of the change A_m are instantly translated in full via the rational expectation m_t^e and hence π_t^e. That the same difficulties should apply to prediction as well as control is not surprising since the two are closely related. Control can be viewed as designing a predicted path in accordance with some given objective. Conversely, prediction is the process of assigning a certainty equivalent to future values of variables in accordance with some given optimality criterion, such as least squares: The prediction is therefore a control solution.

All of the foregoing insights are quite general and do not depend upon the particular model that we have used for illustration. The noninvariance of the reduced-form coefficients under policy changes is the essence of the critique by Lucas (1976) of econometric policy evaluation. Lucas notes that Marshak (1953) had earlier warned of the dangers in assuming the invariance of reduced-form parameters. For detailed implications of observational equivalence in the presence of structural neutrality and rational expectations we refer the reader to Sargent and Wallace (1975), who build on the work of Lucas (1976; also 1972a, b).

The preceding example shows that the reactions of the public, as embodied in the policy-reduced form, depend upon what is assumed about the policy rules of the government. Under the rational-expectations assumption, the public (the "private sector") are supposed to be privy either to these rules or else to the dynamics resulting from these rules. The problem may be put in terms of classical control theory as follows. Assume a system of stochastic equations governing the evolution of an endogenous state vector $\mathbf{y}_t$:

$$\mathbf{y}_t = \alpha + A\mathbf{y}_{t-1} + B_p\mathbf{x}_{pt} + B_g\mathbf{x}_{gt} + \epsilon_t, \tag{12}$$

where $\mathbf{x}_{pt}$ and $\mathbf{x}_{gt}$ are action vectors of the two sets of agents (p for the private sector and g for the government). The vector α may be either a constant or a function of time and ϵ_t is a white-noise innovation vector. Classical control theory would have the government choose its policy vector $\mathbf{x}_{gt}$ by maximizing a suitably defined objective function (see, e.g., Section 6.3) subject to a reaction function for the private sector of the form

$$\mathbf{x}_{pt} = R\mathbf{y}_{t-1} + \rho, \tag{13}$$

where R and ρ contain constants known to the government. The classical control solution (see Section 6.3) to such problems is of the form

$$\mathbf{x}_{gt} = G_t\mathbf{y}_{t-1} + \mathbf{g}_t, \tag{14}$$

where G_t and $\mathbf{g}_t$ depend upon A, B_p, B_g, R, ρ, and the parameters of the government's objective function. Suppose, however, that the government estimates (12) and (13) from a prior sample period. On this basis, it designs a control (14). Feeding (14) into the dynamics (12), the environment facing the decision maker is

$$y_t = \tilde{\alpha}_t + A_t \, y_{t-1} + B_p x_{pt}, \tag{15}$$

where $\tilde{\alpha}_t = \alpha + B_g g_t$ and $\tilde{A}_t = A + B_g G_t$. Under the rational-expectations assumption, the public can correctly identify the dynamics (15) for any government policy rules G_t, g_t. Referring back to (13), the reaction function, it must therefore be true that

$$R = R(\alpha + B_g g_t, A + B_g G_t) \tag{16}$$

with a similar expression for f.

Thus the parameters of the reaction (13) are not in fact invariant to policy changes. Strictly speaking, this kind of reduced-form parameter instability does not really require that the private sector have perfect knowledge either of the government's new rules, when they change, or of the new system dynamics. All that is needed is to assume that private agents become aware of *some* change in the laws governing the system in terms of which they formulate their own actions. However, if expectations are rational, in the sense described in the preceding, then Chow and others (see what follows) have shown how control theory might be resurrected. The government abandons the idea of an invariant reaction function (13) and recognizes instead that the reactions of the private sector depend upon the government's own actions, that is, that equations such as (16) apply to these reactions. In this approach the invariants are pushed back to the parameters of the objective functions of the private sector (and possibly also of the government) together with the basic dynamics (12). How this is done is considered in the next section.

6.3 Estimation of decision invariants

If nothing else exists that corresponds to an invariant structure under policy changes, an alternative is to look at the presumed decision problem of the agents involved and to locate invariance among the parameters of this problem. This line of attack has been considered by Sargent (1978, 1979), Hansen and Sargent (1981), Taylor (1979), Chow (1980, 1981), and other authors. Because it is relatively context free and bears a close familial resemblance to classical control problems, we shall follow here Chow's formulation. In his earlier contribution, he considers a group of identical private agents with a common decision problem of minimizing some quadratic penalty function describing the consequences of deviations from some target over time. Thus let the agent now be at time zero and index planning time as τ. Let a target sequence be some given time function a_τ, $\tau = 0, 1, 2, \ldots$, representing a desirable path for the state vector $\mathbf{y}_\tau$. Finally denote by E_0 the expectation operator given the information available at time $\tau = 0$. The decision problem on the part of the agents is then

$$\min E_0 \sum_{\tau=0}^{N} (\mathbf{y}_\tau - \mathbf{a}_\tau)' K_\tau (\mathbf{y}_\tau - \mathbf{a}_\tau) \tag{17}$$

subject to a perceived dynamics

$$\mathbf{y}_\tau = A\mathbf{y}_{\tau-1} + C\mathbf{x}_\tau + \mathbf{b}_\tau + \epsilon_\tau. \tag{18}$$

Here $K_\tau = \beta^\tau K$, where β is a discount factor for future time $(0 < \beta < 1)$ and K is a constant matrix; it is also assumed that $\mathbf{a}_\tau = \phi^\tau \mathbf{a}$, where ϕ is again a discount factor. The parameters of the dynamics (18), including any parameters of the time function $\mathbf{b}_\tau$, are assumed to be known by the agents. Assuming that they are suitably clever, the agents solve the decision problem (17) and (18) by methods of dynamic programming. Ignoring temporarily any problem of parameter instability, the optimal solution (e.g., Chow, 1975; Bertsekas, 1976, ch. 3) has the feedback form

$$\hat{x}_\tau = G_\tau \mathbf{y}_{\tau-1} + \mathbf{g}_\tau, \tag{19}$$

where the coefficient matrices G_τ and vector $\mathbf{g}_\tau$ are established recursively. If the horizon N is long, then for low values of τ the solutions G_τ and $\mathbf{g}_\tau$ approach a stationary state: $G_\tau = G^*$ and $\mathbf{g}_\tau = \mathbf{g}^*$ as the recursion proceeds backward. These values are defined by the set of implicit Riccati equations:

$$G^* = -(C'H^*C)^{-1}C'H^*A,$$
$$H^* = K + (A + CG^*)'H^*(A + CG^*), \tag{20}$$

with corresponding equations to describe the evolution of g_τ^*. The parameter matrix H^* is an auxiliary set with a duality aspect.

With the preceding problem and solution procedure for the private agents, we may now turn to the government's estimation and control problem. Considering again the private agents; let the current period be denoted by t so that the individual is looking forward in his or her planning to time $t + N$, where N is large. From (19) and (20), the current decision is given by

$$\mathbf{x}_t = G^* \mathbf{y}_{t-1} + \mathbf{g}_t^*, \quad (\tau = 0). \tag{21}$$

According to the critique of Section 6.2, the government cannot use the reaction (21) for purposes of control since neither G^* nor $\mathbf{g}_t^*$ will remain invariant to changes in the control regime. However Chow tackles the problem of estimating K and $\mathbf{a}$, which (in addition to A, C, and parameters in $\mathbf{b}_t$) *are* invariant with respect to different control regimes. Suppose that a given policy regime has been in operation over a prior sample period. Then G^* will be constant and likewise so will be any parameters in $\mathbf{g}_t^*$. The sets of equations (18) and (21) – the latter treated as stochastic – are fitted by any suitable statistical technique as a more or less standard problem in the estimation of simultaneous linear models. Having obtained estimates $\hat{A}$, $\hat{C}$, and $\hat{G}$, it is suggested that the unknown K can then be recovered from equations (20), with similar equations for the invariants $\mathbf{a}, \beta, \phi$. The form of these equations suggests that this may not be particularly easy, with problems of both identification and overidentification to consider, but such a procedure is at least in principle possible. Thus the emphasis has shifted away from the estimation of the potentially treacherous policy-reduced form or reaction function (21) as representing a presumed invariant to the use of this function as an ancillary device for the estimation of the true underlying invariants, in this case the decision constants $K, \mathbf{a}$ and associated discount factors. The latter may safely be employed by the policymaker for the purposes of optimal control.

So far we have not considered the precise optimal control rules that will be utilized by the government, even assuming as we now do that it knows the parameters of the private sector's decision problem. As we pointed out in Section 6.2 [see especially equation (16)], the reaction functions of the private sector will depend upon the government's policy, and this dependence must be taken into account in designing optimal control solutions. Conceptually perhaps the most natural approach is to view this as a formal game of the dominant-player (or Stackelberg) variety. The private sector takes as given any strategy of the government and reacts to this. The government takes this reaction into account.

Thus suppose that the government follows some decision rule of the form

$$\mathbf{x}_{gt} = G\mathbf{y}_{t-1} + \mathbf{g}_t, \tag{22}$$

recognizable as equation (14) with G constant. The dynamics of the state vector $\mathbf{y}_t$ are as given by equation (12), which we reproduce here:

$$\mathbf{y}_t = \alpha + A\mathbf{y}_{t-1} + B_p\mathbf{x}_{pt} + B_g\mathbf{x}_{gt} + \epsilon_t.$$

The equations governing the private sector are then

$$\mathbf{y}_t = (A + B_g G)\mathbf{y}_{t-1} + B_p\mathbf{x}_{pt} + \alpha + B_g\mathbf{g}_t + \epsilon_t. \tag{23}$$

The private sector optimizes according to some criterion (17), subject to (23), which for this problem replaces the arbitrary dynamics (18). It derives thus the optimal policy feedback rule

$$x_{pt} = Ry_{t-1} + \rho_t, \tag{24}$$

where R, ρ_t are defined in terms of the Riccati equations (20) with A re-defined as $A + B_g G$ and C as B_p. This gives the concrete representation of the dependence illustrated by equation (16). The government's task as the dominant player is to choose G in (22) subject to the reaction process embodied in equation (24), to maximize its own welfare function. The resulting solution has been solved in its steady-state form by Chow (1981).

An alternative solution concept is that of the Nash equilibrium. A pair G^*, R^* (also g_t^*, ρ_t^*) will be a Nash equilibrium for this problem if, given that the government utilizes the rule G^*, it is optimal from the private sector's viewpoint, taking G^* as given, to utilize the proposed feedback R^*; and vice versa. No behavioral interaction or assumptions are invoked. Each player simply takes as given and immutable the control rule to be used by the other; if the two rules happen to have the consistency property, the result is an equilibrium one, with no temptation for either party to diverge from the "solution." Chow (1981) shows how to obtain the unique Nash equilibrium pair for this problem and adds some remarks on estimation in the case where it is necessary to estimate the decision parameters of the government as well as those of the private sector.

Some "heroic" assumptions are clearly involved in the preceding approaches to the problem of invariance and control, and in a sense it is unfair to burden with objections what are clearly exploratory forays. However a few of these problems should be mentioned at this point. Players are supposed to possess welfare functions that can be approximated in quadratic terms, and this approximation will have to remain invariant over a considerable range of values of the arguments y_t, a_t. The process of estimation will work only if a relatively long sample period is available during which control rules remain the same. An unsatisfactory aspect of the implied game is that the private sector is assumed to react as one mind. In reality every individual is faced with a personal game situation in which he or she is trying to guess not only what the government will do but what everybody else is doing (we return to such aspects in due course). A more serious objection than any of the preceding, however, concerns the property of time consistency that is presumed by classic control rules. This is the subject of the next section.

6.4   Policy inconsistency

One of the most substantial objections against the application of classical control theory to models with perfect or rational expectations is that such situations exhibit what has been termed *dynamic inconsistency*. Actually we shall see that the problems that stem from this property equally give rise to a further problem that can be laid at the door of the rational-expectations hypothesis itself. However, let us begin by outlining in this section the notion of policy inconsistency, which in the present context is due to Kydland and Prescott (1977), whose basic model we follow.

Consider the following simple decision problem for the government or policymaker. It has to maximize some welfare function W_G, which we might take as the public interest as opposed to the individual private interests that determine the collective reaction of the private sector. Thus the government's problem is

$$\max_{\pi_1, \pi_2} W_G(x_1, x_2, \pi_1, \pi_2) = w_1(x_1, \pi_1) + w_2(x_2, \pi_2) \tag{25}$$

subject to a state dynamics in x_1, x_2 determined by the reactions of the private sector:

$$x_1 = X_1(x_0; \pi_1, \pi_2), \tag{26a}$$

$$x_2 = X_2(x_1; \pi_2). \tag{26b}$$

Equation (26a) indicates that period 1 decisions by the private sector depend not only upon the policy decisions π_1 in period 1 but also upon the policy decisions in period 2. This is the "perfect-foresight" assumption, although whether or not it *can* be perfect is something that we shall return to in due course.

Now the first-order, or stationary, conditions for the maximization of the criterion (25) subject to (26) are

$$\frac{\partial w_1}{\partial \pi_1} + \left(\frac{\partial w_1}{\partial x_1} + \frac{\partial w_2}{\partial X_2} \frac{\partial X_2}{\partial x_1} \right) \frac{\partial X_1}{\partial \pi_1} = 0, \tag{27a}$$

$$\frac{\partial w_1}{\partial x_1} \frac{\partial X_1}{\partial \pi_2} + \frac{\partial w_2}{\partial x_2} \left(\frac{\partial X_2}{\partial x_1} \frac{\partial X_1}{\partial \pi_2} + \frac{\partial X_2}{\partial \pi_2} \right) + \frac{\partial w_2}{\partial \pi_2} = 0. \tag{27b}$$

Equation (27b), the stationary condition with respect to the policy variable π_2, will be of special concern to us. As a general point, the solutions π_1, π_2 of equations (27) (assumed unique and indeed a maximum) correspond to *open-loop* control, in the jargon of control theory. This simply means that the maximizing π_1, π_2 are completely laid out at the start of the horizon, as opposed to *feedback* or *closed-loop* control, where the optimizing π_2 would be given in terms of the then current state variable x_1 resulting from the application of π_1.

Feedback control, which underpins most classical control theory, is based upon Bellman's principle of dynamic programming or upon procedures such as the calculus of variations or Pontryagin's maximum principle, which can be derived from the dynamic programming principle. The original references are Bellman (1957) and Bellman and Dreyfus (1962), but most books on control theory and its applications discuss the principle, which reads as follows: Whatever the state resulting from past decisions, the decisions from then on must be optimal taking that state as given. Let us apply this principle to the maximand (25). Given x_1, the government's welfare function from then on is $w_2(x_2, \pi_2)$, where x_2 is described in terms of the given state x_1 by equation (26b). Thus for the given x_1, whatever it is and whatever past decisions have been taken to get there, the maximizing π_2 must satisfy the first-order condition

$$\frac{\partial w_2}{\partial x_2}\frac{\partial X_2}{\partial \pi_2} + \frac{\partial w_2}{\partial \pi_2} = 0. \tag{28}$$

Notice the implied feedback rule: Given x_1, we then solve for π_2 in terms of x_1 (see, e.g., the feedback rules of the preceding two sections).

Unfortunately if a true optimal solution π_1^*, π_2^* does satisfy equations (27), it will not in general satisfy the Bellman condition (28). To see this, let $x_1^* = X_1(x_0, \pi_1^*, \pi_2^*)$ be the corresponding state vector at the start of period 2 or end of period 1. Comparing (27b) and (28), we observe that π_2^* will not satisfy (28) for the given $x_1 = x_1^*$ unless

$$\left(\frac{\partial w_1}{\partial x_1} + \frac{\partial w_2}{\partial x_2}\frac{\partial X_2}{\partial x_1}\right)\frac{\partial X_1}{\partial \pi_2} = 0 \tag{29}$$

when evaluated at the optimum ($*$). An equivalent formulation in view of (28) is

$$\left(\frac{\partial w_1}{\partial x_1} - \frac{\partial w_2}{\partial \pi_2}\right)\frac{\partial X_1}{\partial \pi_2} = 0, \tag{29'}$$

again at the optimum. Apart from very special cases in which the bracketed terms are zero, conditions (29) or (29') will be true only if $\partial X_1/\partial \pi_2 = 0$. This may be interpreted as lack of foresight – current decisions are not affected by perceived future policy settings. If we explicitly rule this out under the rational-expectations hypothesis, we see that the optimal π_1^*, π_2^* as solved from (27) does not satisfy the Bellman principle of optimality. Cruz (1975) notes that this kind of situation is quite general for leader–follower (Stackelberg) decision paradigms, of which the preceding is an example. Decision problems involving Nash equilibria, on the other hand, are consistent with the use of the dynamic programming principle by the participants.

If the Bellman principle is not satisfied, an inconsistency may result in real time. Suppose that the government solves the optimality problem [i.e., equations (27)] to obtain optimal two-period policies π_1^*, π_2^*. These policies are announced at the outset, that is, the start of period 1. The private sector believes that these policy settings will indeed be invoked in the respective periods. Time rolls by and period 1 has ended, with state vector $x_1^* = X_1(x_0; \pi_1^*, \pi_2^*)$. This becomes the initial state for period 2. The government now decides to renege on its commitment to π_2^*. For it is profitable (in the once-off situation that we are envisaging) for it to do so. To see this, note that the government's new policy problem is

$$\max_{\pi_2} w_2(x_2, \pi_2) \quad \text{subject to} \quad x_2 = X_2(x_1^*; \pi_2) \tag{30}$$

given now that $x_1 = x_1^*$. The first-order conditions for the revised problem (30) are just the Bellman optimality conditions (28). The optimal solution to problem (30) is now given by (c for "cheat")

$$\pi_2^c = R(x_1^*) \tag{31}$$

for some revision function R. As we have already remarked,

$$\pi_2^c \neq \pi_2^*,$$

the promised policy. The time inconsistency has resulted. Of course, there is no real suggestion that the government has intended all along to cheat; the inconsistency could simply result from the installation of a new government. Similar time inconsistencies arise in situations of intergenerational planning (e.g., Pollak, 1968). Kydland and Prescott use the suboptimality of control-theoretic or feedback policies – which are by definition consistent – to argue for simple rules of thumb for macroeconomic policy (e.g., "the money supply should grow at a constant 4 percent per annum") rather than rules based upon feedback or discretion.

We shall not follow these and other authors further into matters of economic policy. As we have noted, there is a built-in temptation for the policymaker to cheat or at least start afresh as the planning period develops in real time. If agents indeed have perfect foresight, this is not really a problem; for reasons that will shortly be apparent, the government would never cheat in such a contingency. But if perfect foresight is not possible in such circumstances, what are the implications of this for the policy problem? It turns out that to discuss such matters deepens our understanding both of the nature and limits of the rational-expectations hypothesis and ultimately of the possibility of structural inference in the social sciences.

6.5   Consistency and prisoner's dilemma: solutions and argument instability

In a world driven by human actions and reactions, perfect foresight is a possibility only for a system in which the flow of awareness is fully recursive. It is possible for a guru viewing the world from the fastness of a

Himalayan cave to "look into the seeds of time and say which grain will grow and which will not" only if no one else is aware of the guru's existence and omniscience. For if the guru's predictions or ability to make predictions were communicated to any other person, such powers of foresight would plainly be at an end. As the book of Genesis tells us, the capability for wilful contradiction is above all what distinguishes human beings from obedient machines. As we saw in Section 6.4, the possibility that the policymaker may later cheat or perhaps renege for circumstances beyond control introduces an element of uncertainty into the control problem. The nature of this uncertainty turns out to yield a good deal of insight not only about the particular problem of policy, but also about the very nature of probability assessments as a behavioral characteristic and through this into the stability or invariance of behavioral equations.

We begin by recalling the basic problem: The government has to maximize a welfare function

$$W_G[X_1(\pi_1, \pi_2), X_2(x_1, \pi_2), \pi_1, \pi_2], \tag{32}$$

where we have condensed equations (25)–(26) into a simple unconstrained problem and suppressed dependence upon the initial state x_0. Likewise, there exists a corresponding decision problem for the private sector. Abstracting from aggregation problems (e.g., by the "representative member" assumption), we write the private sector welfare function as

$$W_p[X_1(\pi_1, \pi_2), X_2(x_1, \pi_2), \pi_1, \pi_2]. \tag{33}$$

(At first sight it may seem rather odd that a hiatus should arise between the preceding two welfare functions, but this is no more than a reflection of the discrepancy between the public interest and the private pursuit of gain given constraints imposed in the public interest, a discrepancy that lies at the heart of the science of public economics.)

Let us now look at the various possible outcomes over the complete horizon of two periods. These depend upon whether the government "cheats" (or reneges for any better reason beyond its control) and whether the private sector believes that the government will remain true to its period 1 promise. Notice with respect to the private sector that all agents are assumed to hold the same belief as part of the representative agent assumption. Matters arising from independent action and possibly diverse beliefs are reserved for discussion in later sections. Four different possibilities arise, and we shall discuss these in turn.

(a) Believe, not cheat: The private sector believes the government, and the government does not cheat or renege. The ex ante optimal open-loop policy π_2^* as announced by the government in period 1 is preserved. The welfare outcomes are

$$W_G^{(a)} = W_G[X_1(\pi_1^*, \pi_2^*), X_2(x_1^*, \pi_2^*), \pi_1^*, \pi_2^*],$$

$$W_p^{(a)} = W_p[X_1(\pi_1^*, \pi_2^*), X_2(x_1^*, \pi_2^*), \pi_1^*, \pi_2^*],$$

where $x_1^* = X_1(x_0; \pi_1^*, \pi_2^*)$.

(b) Believe, cheat: The government announces π_1^*, π_2^* in period 1. Individuals take action x_1^* as in the preceding. When period 2 rolls around, the government reneges with a new control $\pi_2^c \neq \pi_2^*$. The revised setting π_2^c solves problem (30), that is,

$$\max_{\pi_2} W_G((x_1^*, X_2(x_1^*, \pi_2), \pi_1^*, \pi_2),$$

giving from equation (31) the new setting

$$\pi_2^c = R(x_1^*) = R[X_1(\pi_1^*, \pi_2^*)],$$

where we recall that in this context R denotes a revised policy function rather than a reaction. The welfare outcomes are

$$W_G^{(b)} = W_G[X_1(\pi_1^*, \pi_2^*), X_2(x_1^*, \pi_2^c), \pi_1^*, \pi_2^c],$$

$$W_p^{(b)} = W_p[X_1(\pi_1^*, \pi_2^*), X_2(x_1^*, \pi_2^c), \pi_1^*, \pi_2^c].$$

Comparing the welfare outcomes to those under contingency (a), we should certainly expect that

$$W_G^{(b)} > W_G^{(a)} \quad \text{(government's incentive to cheat)},$$

$$W_p^{(b)} < W_p^{(a)} \quad \text{(public will be worse off)}.$$

(c) Not believe, not cheat: The private sector thinks that the government will cheat, but in fact the government remains true to the promised π_2^*. This is a rather harder contingency since we have to answer the question as to what the private sector nevertheless does assume about the actions of the government if the latter is to cheat. Let $\pi_2^e \neq \pi_2^*$ (the announced value) be any value assumed by the private sector in period 1. Then $x_1^e = X_1(\pi_1^*, \pi_2^e)$ is the corresponding private decision. Now the public thinks that if the policymaker does cheat in period 2, then the government will know by that time the π_2^e assumed by the private sector. Hence the private sector knows what the second-period decision π_2 will be from the formula (31), and it must be true that

$$\pi_2^e = R[X_1(\pi_1^*, \pi_2^e)], \tag{34}$$

that is, the private sector assumes that the government will, if it cheats, select the fixed point of the function R. The resulting decision for the private sector is

Table 6.1a. *Payoff matrix; form*

	Government	
Public	Not revise	Revise (cheat)
Believe	$W_p^{(a)}, W_G^{(a)}$	$W_p^{(b)}, W_G^{(b)}$
Not believe	$W_p^{(c)}, W_G^{(c)}$	$W_p^{(d)}, W_G^{(d)}$

$$x_1^e = X_1(\pi_1^*, \pi_2^e). \tag{35}$$

Evidently the assumption of π_2^e as defined by (34) and the associated decision (35) correspond to a kind of limited-foresight assumption on the part of the private sector. The outcome is

$$W_G^{(c)} = W_G[X_1(\pi_1^*, \pi_2^e), X_2(x_1^e, \pi_2^*), \pi_1^*, \pi_2^*],$$

$$W_p^{(c)} = W_p[X_1(\pi_1^*, \pi_2^e), X_2(x_1^e, \pi_2^*), \pi_1^*, \pi_2^*],$$

where x_1^e is defined by function (35). Relative to contingency (a), we should expect

$$W_p^{(c)} < W_p^{(a)} \quad \text{(if the government does not cheat, it is better for the public to believe it),}$$

$$W_G^{(c)} < W_G^{(a)} \quad \text{(if people do not believe it, the government is worse off – Peter and the wolf syndrome).}$$

(d) Not believe, cheat: This is the case of fully anticipated revisions in the plan. The public chooses π_2^e and x_1^e by going through the limited-foresight argument embodied in equations (34) and (35). When period 2 rolls around, the government does cheat, setting $\pi_2 = \pi_2^e$, as expected. The payoffs are

$$W_G^{(d)} = W_G[X_1(\pi_1^*, \pi_2^e), X_2(x_1^e, \pi_2^e), \pi_1^*, \pi_2^e],$$

$$W_p^{(d)} = W_p[X_1(\pi_1^*, \pi_2^e), X_2(x_1^e, \pi_2^e), \pi_1^*, \pi_2^e].$$

Relative to contingency (b), we should expect that

$$W_p^{(d)} > W_p^{(b)} \quad \text{(if the government cheats, people are better off if they have "picked" it),}$$

$$W_G^{(d)} < W_G^{(b)} \quad \text{(if the government cheats, it would prefer people to believe π_2^*).}$$

We can organize the outcomes of the four possible contingencies (a)–(d) in the form of Table 6.1a. The information given in the preceding

Table 6.1b. *Payoff matrix; sample values*

	Government	
Public	Not revise, $(W_p)(W_G)$	Revise (cheat), $(W_p)(W_G)$
Believe	100, 100	70, 120
Not believe	85, 60	90, 80

does not enable a completely unambiguous ordering of the welfare pairs W_p, W_G. In the numerical example of Table 6.1b, we have assumed in addition that $W_G^{(d)} > W_G^{(c)}$ (if the private sector does not believe it, the government is better off cheating). This is the only additional assumption that need be made for the conclusions that follow to be quite general. The numbers in Table 6.1b represent the preceding inequalities measured with respect to a base payoff of $(100, 100)$ for regime (a).

Readers familiar with game theory will notice immediately from Table 6.1b that this is a prisoner's dilemma type of game (see, e.g., Owen, 1982, ch. VII). Two possible equilibrium solutions exist:

1. *The cooperative solution.* The government never revises and the private sector is content to take the government at its word. The difficulty with this solution, as with the prisoner's dilemma, is that there is always an incentive for one party, in this case the government, to cheat.

2. *The noncooperative solution.* The government always cheats and the public is uniformly mistrusting. This is the classic solution of noncooperative game theory. To verify that it is a solution, suppose that the government does cheat. As Table 6.1b shows, it is then in the interests of the private sector not to believe it ($90 > 70$). Thus the proposed solution (P, not believe; G, cheat) is a Nash equilibrium (cf. Sections 6.3 and 6.6). With the payoff element 85 in place as indicated, this solution is also maximin for each player. Thus the government can assure itself of 80 by playing the cheat strategy as against only 60 by not cheating; and the public can assure itself of 85 by not believing as against only 70 by believing. Hence if both players act to maximize their minimum gains, each will play their noncooperative equilibrium strategy.

The preceding setup has constituted a once-and-for-all play of the game. We could imagine a replicated series of such games or, more realistically still, a continuing sequence of two- or even multiperiod horizons, at each stage of which it is open to the government to renege on a previous understanding and to follow instead a kind of feedback control defined in terms of the current state of the system. Such models would then become different formulations of supergames in the jargon of game theory. Although formal solutions to such games are in general very difficult, the simple tit-for-tat solution of Rapoport has achieved wide attention. Each player should play the cooperative strategy so long as the opponent plays a similar strategy. If one player cheats, the strategy is for the other player to immediately "punish" such behavior by playing the noncooperative strategy. The Rapoport rules have dominated all others in empirical trials. The typical result is that such rules rarely win on individual plays of the game or even short blocks of repeated plays but summed out over a long sequence always come out well on top. For an entertaining account of such experiments we refer the reader to the *Economist* article "The importance of being nice, retaliatory, forgiving and clear," November 9, 1985, pp. 99–102, and Axelrod (1984); for more technical surveys see Aumann (1985) and Mertens (1986).

As we have seen, the problem of inconsistency falls naturally into a game-theoretic framework. It is possible to conceive of alternative approaches to the resolution of the problem without reference to the unpleasant indeterminacies of game theory. For example, we could suppose that the private sector, as a result of long experience, forms a subjective probability p that the government will cheat or renege. On the basis of this statistic, it forms a certainty equivalent for the future control value π_2, which although recognized and budgeted for by the government nevertheless remains consistent with the expected policy resulting from the government cheating with the given probability p. Although such a certainty equivalent can indeed be defined as the fixed point of an appropriate expectational equation, its defects as a proposed solution should be readily apparent: If the government knows how the private sector will react, it will promptly take advantage of the fact. The private sector has delivered itself into the government's hands, with damaging consequences for the presumed existence of the probability p. This is simply a reflection of the fact that apart from special cases (e.g., saddle points), deterministic strategies do not usually work for either party in game-theoretic situations.

Argument instability

As we shall later see, rational-expectations equilibria may always be regarded as game-theoretic equilibria, although more usually of the noncooperative kind. At this point it is valuable to examine the implications of the rather simple game just outlined for the way that we model and estimate phenomena involving social interactions. The first point that should be made concerns a rather curious Janus-like property of the rational-expectations hypothesis. In game-theoretic equilibria of the types considered in the preceding, individuals *do* possess perfect foresight so long as the system remains in equilibrium. In the noncooperative equilibrium [regime (d)], both sides correctly perceive the strategy π_2^e to be played by the government. Thus an external observer observing a system in such a noncooperative equilibrium would come to think of the agents as forming rational point predictions π_2^e and acting according to an apparently stable behavioral function of those predictions. Yet the equilibrium has been established *because* agents are not at all behaving in this way! For this particular equilibrium, they are behaving according to a maximin criterion. This entails the formation of point predictions only in the very conditional sense that the equilibrium is assumed to prevail. If we now perturbed that equilibrium, the estimated behavioral function would simply break down, giving no guide either as to disequilibrium behavior or as to equilibrium should an alternative equilibrium (the cooperative equilibrium in this case) be established.

Consider the implications of this for the statistical estimation of behavioral schedules. For brevity we shall confine ourselves to the estimation of the function relating the period 1 decision to its arguments. We may imagine that the relevant sample space is generated by playing the same two-period game repeatedly. Suppose that we are in cooperative equilibrium [regime (a)]. We observe $\pi_1 = \pi_1^*$, $\pi_2 = \pi_2^*$ as set by the government. Given these observations, we may set up and estimate a stochastic model

$$x_1 = X_1(\pi_1^*, \pi_2^*; \epsilon),$$

where the disturbances ϵ would presumably be justified in terms of individual differences, observation errors, imperfectly specified functional forms, and the like. For example, we might specify linearity

$$x_1 = \beta_0 + \beta_1 \pi_1^* + \beta_2 \pi_2^* + \epsilon$$

and hope to estimate the parameters β_i. In a state of cooperative equilibrium we would reasonably hope to carry through such an exercise. We might summarize by saying that in a state of equilibrium, the behavioral function X_1 exhibits argument *stability*.

But suppose that one or other of the disequilibrium possibilities (b) or (c) occurs. Consider regime (b), that is, believe, cheat. The actually observed policies are π_1^*, π_2^c. The behavioral relationship actually holding is

$$x_1 = X_1(\pi_1^*, \pi_2^*; \epsilon),$$

$$\text{observed} \rightarrow (\pi_1^*)(\pi_2^c),$$

(36)

where the observed arguments are entered below in parentheses. Or, consider regime (c), not believe, not cheat. Corresponding to (36), we have

$$x_1 = X_1(\pi_1^*, \pi_2^e; \epsilon),$$

$$\text{observed} \rightarrow (\pi_1^*)(\pi_2^*).$$

(37)

Yet another such equation holds for the noncooperative equilibrium.

Considering an overall time span during which phases of equilibrium and disequilibrium may exist, we may now begin to see the problem. The behavioral function $X_1(\cdot)$ is a perfectly stable function of whatever arguments are currently apposite. The trouble is that the true arguments do not always correspond to the observed arguments. The nonobservability of true arguments seems to indicate a latent-variables problem. But things are not quite as simple as such a relabeling would suggest, for no stable relationship, deterministic or stochastic, exists between the true or latent arguments and those actually observed. We shall call this phenomenon *argument instability.*

It seems inescapable that if true game-theoretic behavior can occur, the resulting behavioral relationships are liable to exhibit argument instability. The applicability of the preceding considerations is not limited to what is in many respects a rather artificial example. In competition among the few – gas stations, supermarkets, airlines, and so on – one typically observes periods of price stability interspersed with fierce price wars of shorter duration. In general terms, the resulting dynamic behavior appears to conform with the tit-for-tat solutions remarked on earlier with respect to supergames. Observed during periods of equilibrium, behavioral schedules describing price increases or volume changes in response to, say, rises in the price of materials or factor inputs would exhibit argument stability. However if price wars are interpreted as a sign of disequilibrium, the incorporation of observations during such periods of instability would entail argument instability. In Chapter 8 we shall return to consider the statistical effects of such a phenomenon.

6.6   Rational expectations and noncooperative equilibria

In its general usage, the term *rational expectations* refers to unbiased expectational states or perhaps even perfect foresight, with no necessary reference to any particular underlying model of interactions or decisions. Thus one could say that the equilibrium state of the dominant-player games of Chapter 4 exhibited rational expectations, as does the cooperative equilibrium considered in the previous section. However, rational expectations has achieved most currency in connection with structural models of multiagent economies, and in this connection the relevant equilibrium is typically that of a Nash solution to a noncooperative game. In the present section we shall review some of the considerations that underpin such an equilibrium.

Let us start by recalling the idea of a Nash equilibrium: Given a set of n players i with strategies a_i, a proposed set of strategies $\{a_i^*\}$ is a Nash equilibrium if given the strategies of the other players, namely, $a_1^*, \ldots, a_{i-1}^*, a_{i+1}^*, \ldots, a_n^*$, it is optimal for player i to play a_i^*. This is true for each player $i = 1, \ldots, n$. In other words, given that everybody also plays their proposed equilibrium strategies, the best thing I can do is to play the strategy designated for me by the proposed equilibrium. In the present section we follow Townsend (1978) and especially Evans (1983, 1985) in exhibiting the classical rational-expectations equilibrium as a Nash game-theoretic equilibrium.

Suppose that agents i form predictions $\pi_i(y_{t-1})$ of the value of a state vector y_t. These need not be one-period-ahead predictions: It is possible to define y_t as an augmented state vector in such a way that the prediction $\hat{y}_t$ encompasses prediction over a future time horizon h of a set of more elementary endogenous variables, in a way that will be familiar to students of systems dynamics. Now suppose that the optimal action (e.g., production decision) of agent i is functionally related to the agent's prediction:

$$a_i = a_i(y_{t-1}) = a_i[y_{t-1}, \pi_i(y_{t-1})].$$

We may think of such an action as arising from an individual optimization problem over the horizon h. If the optimand is quadratic, then the certainty equivalence theory of Simon and Theil (e.g., Theil, 1957) ensures us that optimal decisions are a function of the mathematical expectation of the future state variables conditional upon the available information, in this case at time $t-1$. With actions $\{a_i\}$, $i = 1, \ldots, n$, taken as above, the state vector evolves according to

$$y_t = f(y_{t-1}, \{a_i(y_{t-1})\}, \epsilon_t) = \tilde{f}(y_{t-1}, \{\pi_i(y_{t-1})\}, \epsilon_t), \tag{38}$$

where ϵ_t is assumed to be a white-noise innovation vector. Thus it must certainly be true that if $\pi_i(y_{t-1})$ is to be a good predictor, then it must ultimately depend upon whatever decisions the other agents $(j \neq i)$ are making at the same time. Such a dependence may or may not be explicitly recognized by agent i. Schematically, we must have

$$\pi_i(y_{t-1}) = g_i(y_{t-1}, \{a_j(y_{t-1})\}) = \tilde{g}_i(y_{t-1}, \{\pi_j(y_{t-1})\}) \tag{39}$$

for $i, j = 1, \ldots, n$. Equation (39) represents the essential game-theoretic dependence of any *optimal* forecast upon the forecasts of others.

A rational-expectations equilibrium may be defined either in terms of the a_i or π_i functions (we assume away any possible problems stemming from the lack of a one-to-one relationship between the two sets of functions). Choose the latter. The classic rational-expectations equilibrium relative to a set of individual information sets is then a set of forecast functions $\{\pi_i^*(y_{t-1})\}$ such that the generated dynamics

$$y_t = \bar{f}(y_{t-1}, \{\pi_i^*(y_{t-1})\}, \epsilon_t)$$

is optimally forecasted, given the individual information sets, by the given forecast functions $\pi_i^*(y_{t-1})$. If all information sets are the same, then the rational-expectations predictor is $\pi_i^*(y_{t-1}) = \pi^*(y_{t-1})$.

Notice how close this idea is to the idea of a Nash equilibrium as already described. Suppose that other agents ($j \neq i$) utilize $\pi_j^*(y_{t-1})$ as their forecasting functions. Agent i could try an arbitrary forecasting function $\pi_i(y_{t-1})$. But we know that $\pi_i^*(y_{t-1})$ results in an unbiased forecast by the assumption of the proposed rational-expectations equilibrium. If unbiased forecasts are unique, it is therefore in the best interests of agent i to choose $\pi_i(y_{t-1}) = \pi_i^*(y_{t-1})$. Equivalently, the corresponding actions $a_i = a_i^*$. Thus a rational-expectations equilibrium for this model is a Nash equilibrium, and under suitable regularity conditions, the converse is true (Evans, 1983, p. 76).

The expectations of others

Implicit in the preceding is a role for expectations about the expectations of others. Let

$$\{a_{j(i)}(y_{t-1})\} \tag{40}$$

denote a set of action functions conjectured by agent i to describe the behavior of others ($j \neq i$). Suppose also that the individual effect of agent i is negligible and recognized as such. Substituting the conjectural expectations into (39), the agent will reckon on a prediction function $\bar{\pi}_i(y_{t-1})$. Only in a rational-expectations equilibrium are the conjectural expectations and hence the prediction function $\bar{\pi}_i(y_{t-1})$ not subject to revision-inducing phenomena involving disappointed expectations.

The dependence of rational-expectations equilibria upon assessments by each agent of the opinions of others is a topic worth exploring further. Older or more established forms of the rational-expectations hypothesis bypass this problem, simply assuming that agents are able somehow to form predictions or subject expectations that coincide with objective mathematical expectations without inquiring at all whether they are able, even in principle, to do this. However, if we are forming expectations of a variable such as price that we know depends also upon the expectations of others, our own predictions have to encompass the effects of those expectations. We ought therefore to be cautious in asserting a possibility principle for rational expectations if for no other reason than that human beings are notoriously perverse and unpredictable creatures.

It will be helpful in illustrating the kind of considerations that are involved by means of a static example due to Phelps (1983). Suppose that the aggregate price (i.e., a price index) is measured as a weighted sum

$$p = \sum_i w_i p_i, \quad w_i > 0, \quad \sum_i w_i = 1, \tag{41}$$

of price levels set by individual firms i with fixed weights w_i. In setting prices, individual firms are influenced by (a) their forecasts of the general level of prices as defined by (41) and (b) their forecasts of the money stock m, seen by them as a proxy for the general level of demand they are likely to experience. Denoting their forecasts by F_i, each firm sets its price according to

$$p_i = a_1 F_i p + a_2 F_i m, \tag{42}$$

where the constants a_1 and a_2 are the same for each firm and $0 < a_1 < 1$. An individual zero-mean disturbance could be added to (42) without materially affecting things. We assume that the forecast operators F_i are linear so that $F_i(\lambda x) = \lambda F_i x$ and $F_i(x + y) = F_i x + F_i y$ for all x, y.

Combining (41) and (42), we have

$$p = a_1 \sum_i w_i F_i p + a_2 \sum_i w_i F_i m,$$

or iterating one step further

$$p = a_1 \sum_i w_i F_i \left[a_1 \sum_j w_j F_j p + a_2 \sum_j w_j F_j m \right] + a_2 \sum_i w_i F_i m.$$

We introduce the operator

$$\mathfrak{F} = \sum_i w_i F_i.$$

Then the preceding equations may be written

$$p = a_1 \mathfrak{F} p + a_2 \mathfrak{F} m$$

$$= a_1^2 \mathfrak{F}^2 p + a_1 a_2 \mathfrak{F}^2 m + a_2 \mathfrak{F} m \tag{43}$$

$$\vdots$$

$$= a_1^n \mathfrak{F}^n p + a_2 \sum_{k=1}^{n} a_1^{k-1} \mathfrak{F}^k m, \tag{44}$$

where we have continued the iteration to any level n.

Multiplying equation (43) by $\mathfrak{F}$ and subtracting from the original, we obtain

$$p - \mathfrak{F}p = a_1 \mathfrak{F}(p - \mathfrak{F}p) + a_2(\mathfrak{F}m - \mathfrak{F}^2 m). \tag{45}$$

Now suppose that

$$\mathfrak{F}m = \mathfrak{F}^2 m. \tag{46}$$

This condition says that $\mathfrak{F}(\mathfrak{F}m) = \mathfrak{F}m$: On the average, individual firms are correct in their assessment of the average state of opinion about the stock of money. If the difference $p - \mathfrak{F}p$ is to remain bounded (equivalently, all $\mathfrak{F}^k m$ are bounded), then the only solution to equation (45) under condition (46) is

$$\mathfrak{F}p = p. \tag{47}$$

On the average, people's expectations about the aggregate price level are correct. In this case, it follows from equation (43) that the actual price level is given by

$$p = \frac{a_2}{1 - a_1} \mathfrak{F}m.$$

All of the preceding development has been quite mechanical. However, further discussion of the "expectation-of-expectations" aspect is in order at this point. Underlying and parallel to the formally correct recursion (44) is a process of individual reasoning that runs as follows. In forming its own prediction, each firm realizes that it must necessarily forecast the expectations of others; that these expectations in turn depend upon the expectation of others; and so on ad infinitum. The point was made with characteristic pungency in a much quoted passage of Keynes (1936, p. 158):

Or, to change the metaphor slightly, professional investment may be likened to those newspaper competitions in which the competitors have to pick out the six prettiest faces from a hundred photographs, the prize being awarded to the competitor whose choice most nearly corresponds to the average preferences of the competitors as a whole; so that each competitor has to pick, not those faces which he himself finds prettiest, but those which he thinks likeliest to catch the fancy of the other competitors, all of whom are looking at the problem from the same point of view. It is not a case of choosing those which, to the best of one's judgement, are really the prettiest, nor even those which average opinion genuinely thinks the prettiest. We have reached the third degree where we devote our intelligences to anticipating what average opinion expects the average opinion to be. And there are some, I believe, who practise the fourth, fifth and higher degrees.

Thus in principle each agent must indulge in speculations regressing to an infinite extent about the beliefs or actions of others. In other words, we could imagine each firm following through an implied infinitely recursive reasoning process of the form of equation (44) (with $n \to \infty$). Now the agents may not know the weights w_i and may not even know that the parameters a_1, a_2 are the same for each firm. Each agent forms an expectation $E(p/\Im_i)$ involving a personal information set $\Im_i$, which might incorporate information on the weights w_i and the parameters a_i, a_2. Disparate information sets may produce individually different forecasts and views of market opinion. But if condition (46) is met, that is, individuals are on the average correct in their assessment of average opinion, then price expectations will be correct in the sense of equation (47).

The preceding example raises several general points of importance. First, notice how similar the regress problem is to the "second-guessing" problem inherent in game theory: I have to think about how my opponent is thinking about the way I will be thinking about the way he is thinking.... Thus the problem of rational expectations with many agents, each thinking about the expectations of the others, does indeed have a very strong game-theoretic flavor, regardless of the precise game-theoretic categorization.

A second point concerns the somewhat weaker version of the rational-expectations hypothesis that has emerged. Conditional upon their individual information sets $\Im_i$, individual agents may actually form incorrect expectations: $E_i(p/\Im_i) \neq p$. But on the average, equation (47) tells us individual firms are correct. To an external observer, it might well appear that the rational-expectations hypothesis prevails in the sense that appropriate application of the empirical testing procedures of Chapter 5 would confirm the existence of rational expectations. This would nevertheless be quite consistent with the idea that individual participants may be systematically wrong, an idea that appeals to those of us with stock market experience. All that matters is that on the average they are correct. To ensure this, firms must on the average be correct in their assessment of average opinion.

Such a requirement does not appear to be wildly demanding in its basic informational requirements: One could imagine the existence of some survey of market opinion whose results are made available to participants. Provided that agents reply truthfully to the survey, a suitably unbiased estimate of $\Im m$ would then be available on tap, as it were. The obvious difficulty is that incentives may exist for agents not to respond truthfully, so that we are up against the strategic response problem examined on an empirical level in Chapters 2 and 3. At the moment, it is an open question as to the kind of circumstances in which it is in the private interests of participants to respond truthfully to a survey aimed at assessing market opinion or at least the conditions under which there are no real incentives to dissimulate or lie. Of course, it will be apparent that once we proceed to consider incentives for surveys of opinion – or to respond truthfully to such surveys – then we have in mind elements, at least, of a cooperative, rather than noncooperative, game.

Our discussion of the expectation-of-expectations problems has so far been largely couched in terms of a static, or one-period, model. Similar considerations have been developed in a multiperiod framework by Townsend (1983a). He considers the problem of individual firms facing uncertain demand schedules for their products. "Permanent" changes in demand – represented by Townsend as a Markov process – are overlain by random white-noise elements. In forming their decisions, firms are interested in estimating the permanent realization for the coming period. Townsend calls this a learning problem, but it is in fact a filtering problem in the tradition of the classic signal extraction problem considered by authors such as Wiener and Kolmogorov and especially Kalman (1960), whose methodology is in fact utilized by Townsend. Updating rules are established for aggregate opinion θ_t about the "permanent" signal and also for opinions about the opinions of others in the infinite regression we have already described. If individual agents can be imagined to know these updating rules for aggregate expectations of all degrees, then their own expectations, given the aggregate rules, in turn generate the aggregate rules in a self-fulfilling dynamic or moving equilibrium. Individual firms have disparate expectations generated from different priors (in the Bayesian sense) at the start of the multiperiod process. What results is a classic rational-expectations equilibrium – expectations of all orders are mathematically correct conditional upon individual information sets, including knowledge of the processes governing aggregate opinion. Townsend (1983b) extends this type of system to a multimarket model in which the permanent element represents a signal common to all markets (the general state of demand) and the overlaying disturbances represent market-specific effects, the Phelps–Lucas island paradigm, which is well known to economists. Revealed price information from other markets now constitutes additional information about θ_t. Townsend simulates the multimarket dynamics, again in a classic rational-expectations framework, and comments on the volatility that can result from the transmission across markets of filtering errors in the computation of the permanent "signal."

Disequilibrium considerations

Returning to the Evans model of rational expectations as a noncooperative equilibrium, we observed that it was the task of each agent to form conjectural expectations about the expectations of others, or at least about the aggregate effects of the expectations of others. Only in a rational-expectations equilibrium are these conjectural expectations not subject to revision-inducing phenomena.

The latter idea, which essentially involves disequilibrium adjustment, has tempted some authors (e.g., DeCanio, 1979; Evans, 1983, 1985) to search for conditions under which reasonable revision mechanisms do lead to a rational-expectations equilibrium. The idea here is that individual agents, each insignificant in their effects, will revise their idea of the aggregate expectations function, and the collective expression of these individual revisions becomes the new version of the aggregate forecast function. Thus, let us suppose that all information sets are identical; let $\pi^*(y_{t-1})$ be the rational-expectations forecast function – unknown to the individual agents – and let the dynamics of a moving rational-expectations equilibrium be

$$y_t = \tilde{f}(y_{t-1}, \pi^*(y_{t-1}), \epsilon_t).$$

Let $\pi_0(y_{t-1})$ be some arbitrary forecast function. Given y_{t-1}, the dynamics from there on is described by

$$y_t = \tilde{f}(y_{t-1}, \pi_0(y_{t-1}), \epsilon_t). \tag{48}$$

One might think of revising the forecast on the basis of

$$\pi_1(y_{t-1}) = Ey_{t+1} \quad \text{given the dynamics of (48),}$$

leading potentially to an iterative process in which $\pi_N(y_{t-1})$ is cast in terms of $\pi_{N-1}(y_{t-1})$. One would then seek stability conditions under which the sequence $\pi_N(y_{t-1})$, $N = 0, 1, 2, \ldots$, converges to $\pi^*(y_{t-1})$, the rational-expectations equilibrium forecast function. The argument is that if convergence of such a process does not occur, then one would have little faith in the ability of agents to collectively achieve a rational expectations by any sort of trial-and-error process.

It is unclear as to whether an iterative process of this kind can tell us much, if anything, about disequilibrium convergence. If the iteration index set N is taken to be real time (i.e., coincident with r), the underlying function $\tilde{f}$ describing the system dynamics will not remain stable as time progresses, and it is extremely doubtful that the sequence of functions $\pi_t(y_{t-1})$ would converge to any stable function, let alone $\pi^*(y_{t-1})$, the rational-expectations forecast function. Alternatively, the iteration index N may be regarded as "meta-time" or some similar abstraction; but in this case it is unclear what we are to make of it if the sequence $\pi_N(y_{t-1})$ fails to converge. Moreover the overall limitation of this kind of approach must clearly be understood: It corresponds to an external observer examining the possibility of system equilibrium. In particular, it is difficult to imagine that individual agents think in terms of such an iteration. Indeed, the agents will typically not even know the parameters of the dynamics $\tilde{f}$. In the view of this author, such iteration processes do not provide a sound basis for the study of disequilibrium behavior or properties.

6.7   Evaluation

We started the discussion of this chapter with the idea of a state of rational expectations as the natural representation of the idea of structural invariance in a socioeconomic system, a stochastic representation of perfect foresight conditional upon the information available to each individual. In the classic rational-expectations equilibrium, individuals could have different information sets, some being better than others, but each individual was in his (or her) own rational-expectations equilibrium, in the sense that his subjective expectations coincided with the mathematical expectation given his information set. We saw that the consequence of such a dynamics could be rather devastating for prediction or applications of control theory to social or economic policy. To begin with, one has to correctly identify the structural invariants – the kind of reduced form typically utilized for control purposes can yield very misleading results. A second objection lay in the time inconsistency property. If current decisions depend upon perceptions of future variables, optimal policy settings do not typically obey the Bellman principle of optimality. This leads to a problem of time inconsistency whereby there is always an incentive for the policymaker to revise policy for future periods once the private sector has committed itself. From this point, however, serious problems begin to arise for the rational-expectations hypothesis itself. The only real resolution of the dynamic inconsistency problem is via game theory. A state of rational expectations can exist only in an equilibrium of the resulting game. The interpretation is of rational expectations as an equilibrium state; out of equilibrium, rational expectations is not possible. Thus, in the presence of dynamic inconsistency, the very notion of rational expectations as a guide to action – as providing, as it were, a certainty equivalent upon which decisions may be predicted – will fail.

This led us to consider in detail the relationship of rational-expectations equilibria with various kinds of game-theoretic equilibria. The classic rational-expectations equilibria of multiagent structural models may be interpreted as Nash equilibria to a multiperson noncooperative game. Each agent forms his (or her) decisions by using stable functions of his subjective expectations, which coincide with the current mathematical expectations. In the resulting Nash equilibrium, no clue is given about how agents would form their decisions out of equilibrium – the decisions of other agents are taken to be formed as they are in the proposed rational-expectations equilibrium. An alternative kind of equilibrium was illustrated in the two-person game considered in connection with the consistency problem. In an equilibrium of this game, rational expectations would prevail in the sense that each party would successfully predict the actions of the other. Yet agents cannot act in terms of their expectations, for if they did so, their opponent would immediately take advantage. Instead they have to act according to such criteria as tit for tat or maximin. Such equilibria are not therefore classic rational-expectations equilibria. The difference between the two kinds of equilibrium concepts is related to the number and influence of agents involved. As the number of agents becomes large and their separate effects small, the interactive phenomena disappear. Classic rational-expectations equilibria become a better description of such systems.

We noted also a somewhat weaker notion of a rational-expectations equilibrium, arising where predicted outcomes depended upon expectations of the expectations of others. Provided that people forecasted aggregate opinion correctly, it was possible to have a system in which, although individual forecasts could be wrong ($F_i p \neq p$), the aggregate or average forecast could be correct ($\mathfrak{F}p = p$). This seems to be a rather more attractive way of approaching things. Certainly it is all that we could ever hope to verify empirically.

If rational expectations is an equilibrium concept and corresponds always to a game-theoretic equilibrium "solution," the question arises as to what happens out of equilibrium. We saw the kind of empirical difficulty that could arise: If periods of equilibrium were interspersed with periods of disequilibrium (during which nothing sensible could be said), the result was what we have termed *argument instability*. This appears to pose some problems for the estimation of structural relationships, and we shall return to the phenomenon in Chapter 8. A second problem is whether or under what circumstances a system not initially in a rational-expectations equilibrium can converge to one that is. This in turn involves the kind of game that one has in mind. The Nash equilibrium offers little if any clue as to what happens out of equilibrium. Yet paradoxically it is probably the case that, following the spirit of the Nash rules, a more or less mechanical scheme can be found that will ensure convergence if agents stick to it and resist trying to score off each other. Such schemes are developed in Chapter 7.

A final point is the following. In a state of game-theoretic equilibrium, the assessment of probabilities (if needed to form mathematical expectations) is straightforward in principle. But out of equilibrium, the uncertainty arises from the actions of others. If interactional phenomena are at all important, this raises questions about the conceptual basis of such probabilities. This is not really a problem for agents acting according to maximin or tit-for-tat rules: Probabilities are not used by such individuals, who simply budget for the worst (maximin) or, in the case of tit for tat, adopt a mechanical rule (trust or punish according to what the opponent has done). But if people are to behave on the basis of the kind of certainty equivalences assumed by the rational-expectations theorists, then the agents have to assess probabilities; and as remarked in the preceding, these assessments concern the actions of others. We need to examine the logical basis for such probability assessments. The idea that people act in terms of mathematical expectations underpins a wide variety of normative prescriptions and behavioral hypotheses in economics in particular, but the edifice may be ill-founded if the probability measures concerned are not well defined or are defined only in the limiting and perhaps empirically infrequent contingency of equilibrium.

With respect to rational expectations, one could very well remark the following: no probabilities, no rational expectations. The point has potential application to the theory of policy as well as to the practice of economic statistics. Thus Andersen and Schneider (1986) (see also Kydland, 1976; Blinder, 1982) consider the problem of economic stabilization as powers shared between the government and the central or reserve bank. The question they address with the aid of game theory is whether it is better in terms of the efficacy of stabilization for the two policy agencies to be independent of each other. The game-theoretic element arises because in setting fiscal policy, the government may very well take into account the reaction of the bank in setting its monetary policy and vice versa. If they do not share a common view of desirable policy outcomes, a potential for conflict arises and both cooperative and noncooperative solutions exist. The actual outcome is indeterminate, with even the cooperative solutions lying along a locus rather than a single point. For any given pair of policy settings, outcomes are generated through a model describing the behavior of the private sector, and in this model the expectations of agents play a crucial role. Although Andersen and Schneider follow neoclassical orthodoxy (in one of their models) by assuming that these expectations are rational, it could very well be objected that if the bank and the government are truly independent, then their policy settings, as the solution to their two-person game, are essentially unpredictable. Thus rational expectations on the part of the private sector simply may not exist. One could perhaps claim that this in turn should support the idea of an independent central bank, for as we have seen, rational expectations may lead to an economy that is virtually uncontrollable. However, so far as our present purposes are concerned, the moral is the incompatibility of true gamelike interaction with a regime of rational expectations, in this case those of a third party (the private sector). It might be interesting to speculate about what form the expectational principles or attitudes guiding private sector behavior might in fact take under such circumstances and how one could hope to deduce these expectational schedules – if this is the right expression – empirically.

CHAPTER 7

Disequilibrium and noncooperative expectational games

7.1 Introduction

In the last two chapters we have explored the nature of classic rational-expectations equilibria and the kinds of circumstances in which such equilibria could possibly arise. As we have seen, the idea of an equilibrium characterized by agents acting according to mathematical expectations is at its most convincing in a world of many agents, each with an individually insignificant impact upon the outcome. To date, however, we have not explored a further question that has a bearing on the existence problem: From some initial starting point that may not be an equilibrium state, can the system find its way to a rational-expectations equilibrium? From the game-theoretic point of view this is the problem of solution by real-time (rather than, say, fictitious) play. In the economics literature, it is often referred to as a learning problem. For reasons to be outlined shortly, it is doubtful whether this usage is capable of representing the full complexity of the problem. However, if we agree to adopt a somewhat teleological viewpoint and ascribe learning to the system as a whole rather than to the individuals whose behavior drives the system, the usage refers to the way in which the system as a whole gropes its way toward a full rational-expectations equilibrium, in which every individual participant is in his or her personal state of rational expectations conditional upon the individual information sets. Of course, this assumes that the system is capable of doing this. If it were possible to prove that given a certain underlying structure *no* rules or procedures exist on the part of individual agents under which a disequilibrium system could evolve into a rational-expectations equilibrium, this would clearly vitiate the idea of such an equilibrium as a plausible empirical hypothesis since once the putative equilibrium was perturbed it might be reentered only by chance, if at all.

From the viewpoint of statistical inference, this chapter exhibits the results of an interaction between agents each trying to draw inferences about the world in which they are embedded. In the kind of models that we shall consider, the strategic position of each of the statistician–players is far weaker than the dominant-player mode implied by the observer–subject paradigm of Chapters 2–4. Precisely how the situation relates to the game-theoretic mode of organization or behavior will become clearer as the discussion proceeds. For the moment we note only that unlike earlier disequilibrium modes, this is one of extreme decentralized inference; we suppose many participants, each collecting his or her own information and drawing his or her own conclusions under a greater or lesser degree of ignorance about what other participants are currently up to. In spite of this decentralized aspect, the paradigm does have something in common with the predicaments faced by observer–participants in strategically stronger positions. Outstanding among them is the intangibility of reality. Participants may (in one type of specification) be attempting to estimate something that has no objective reality but that may acquire reality in the very process of being observed, or at least as the outcome of actions predicated upon the observations.

The scheme of the chapter is as follows. Section 7.2 defines the problem of convergence, characterizes it in game-theoretic terms, and discusses also the degree of sophistication or expertise to be assumed of participating agents. A distinction is established between parameter-mediated structures in which all parameters to be learned exist in disequilibrium and structures in which some parameters are defined only in equilibrium. Section 7.3 is an introductory survey of sequential estimation and learning, covering such matters as Bayesian updating, sequential regression, and stochastic approximation. The last of these real-time estimation techniques has a very natural relationship with parameter-mediated learning in the present context, and we give an outline coverage of convergence conditions, referring to Appendix 1 for more detail. Section 7.4 is an extended example involving parameter-mediated convergence to a rational-expectations equilibrium. A nonlinear model of market demand and supply with many parameters can under suitable regularity conditions converge to a rational-expectations equilibrium if agents act as stochastic approximators. As a scenario, this is a favorable case. Section 7.5 raises some doubts as to whether convergence is possible in more general models, especially where structures with heterogeneous information sets are concerned and parameters are defined only in equilibrium.

7.2   Generalities

The reader will recall from Section 6.6 [cf. equation (38)] that we characterized a system in rational-expectations equilibrium as a dynamics of the form

$$y_t = f(y_{t-1}, \{a_i(y_{t-1})\}, \epsilon_t) = \tilde{f}(y_t, \{\pi_i(y_{t-1})\}, \epsilon_t), \tag{1}$$

where y_t is a suitably defined state vector that may incorporate higher order lags. Actions a_i of a set of participants are based on the available y_{t-1} and drive the system together with the stochastic disturbances ϵ_t. The actions are in turn functionally related to the forecasts π_i prepared on the basis of current information y_{t-1}. In rational-expectations equilibrium each forecast function $\pi_t(y_{t-1})$ is conditionally unbiased given individual i's specific information set. In what follows, it will be helpful to distinguish rational-expectations action and forecast functions with an asterisk. Thus a system

$$y_t = f(y_{t-1}, \{a_i^*(y_{t-1})\}, \epsilon_t) = \tilde{f}(y_{t-1}, \pi_i^*(y_{t-1}), \epsilon_t) \qquad (2)$$

would be one in full rational-expectations equilibrium, whereas system (1) represents the dynamics resulting from arbitrary action and forecast functions.

Confining attention to a state of rational-expectations equilibrium, it may well be that the forecast functions $\pi_i(y_{t-1})$ have some parametric content: We write this as $\pi_i(y_{t-1}; \theta)$. An initial complication is that a forecast based upon a coarser information set ($\mathcal{I}_i$ is coarser than $\mathcal{I}_j$ if $\mathcal{I}_i \subset \mathcal{I}_i$) may well entail a different parameter set. We saw something of this kind in Section 5.3, where agents who did not have current information on certain exogenous variables could in effect partly compensate by operating from a different dynamic system with a disturbance process incorporating the unobservable elements of the exogenous variables. Additional lagged terms entered into their optimal forecast. In a rational-expectations equilibrium, any mention of parameters in the forecast functions must therefore be qualified with a reference as to exactly who is looking at the world. In other words we should write each rational-expectations forecast function in the form $\pi_i^*(y_{t-1}, \theta^i)$. If the information sets are homogeneous, that is, all the same, then we may drop the superscript and speak of a common parameter θ.

Finally, there is the question of uniqueness. Given a structure f and the nature of the decision rules a_i, we shall suppose that the set of forecasting functions $\pi_i^*(y_{t-1}, \theta^i)$ is unique. We saw in Section 5.4 that the nonuniqueness of rational-expectations equilibria could be a problem: Each such equilibrium solves an equation such as (2), and each is associated with its own forecasting function. Without the uniqueness assumption it is problematical whether we could expect any kind of convergence to occur.

The problem of convergence to a rational-expectations equilibrium may be stated, not very precisely, as follows. We ask whether there exists a sequence of forecast functions $\pi_t^j(y_{t-1})$ such that given the dynamics based on the structure $(f, \{a_i\}, \epsilon_t)$, namely,

$$y_t = \tilde{f}(y_{t-1}, \{\pi_t^i(y_{t-1})\}, \epsilon_t),\tag{3}$$

the forecast functions become conditionally unbiased given the individuals' specific information sets. Under the preceding uniqueness assumptions we should evidently require the difference between $\pi_t^i(y_{t-1})$ and $\pi^*(y_{t-1}; \theta^i)$ to approach zero, in some suitable norm, as t becomes large. Note that the forecast functions $\pi_t^i(y_{t-1})$ bear a resemblance to the Evans-type trial solutions considered in Section 6.8. However, the crucial point about convergence, or system learning as we have described it, is that it takes place in real time.

The real-time aspect introduces the topic of individual versus system learning. Current forecast rules $\pi_t^i(y_{t-1})$ lead collectively to an outcome y_t such that the forecast rules, however derived, may be far from rational. The "correct" rules $\pi^*(y_{t-1}; \theta^i)$ may have a purely teleological aspect. The parameters θ^i of the individual forecast rules may not exist, in any objective sense, out of a rational-expectations equilibrium. We have exhibited such a system in our discussion in Section 5.3 of structural models with heterogeneous information. If this is the case, individuals may not be trying to learn some unknown but existent parameters θ^i whose objective reality transcends their own personal predicament. But it *may* nevertheless be the case that as time goes on, the revision rules that they do adopt have the property that they ultimately tend to the rational-expectations rules $\pi_i^*(y_{t-1}; \theta^i)$. In this sense one could describe individuals as learning the latter functions. But it is really the case that the system as a whole "learns" the set $\{\pi_i^*(y_{t-1}; \theta^i)\}$ of rational-expectations forecast functions. As in a successful marriage, we seek rules such that individuals can learn to live together and arrive at an equilibrium with desirable properties, in this case that expectations are unbiased and (in view of the Nash equilibrium nature of the equilibrium) that no individual temptation exists to utilize a different set of forecast rules.

Parameter-mediated rules

One possible class of forecast rules is based upon a stable function of estimated parameters. Thus

$$\pi_t^i(y_{t-1}) = \pi^i(y_{t-1}; \hat{\theta}_t^i),$$

where $\hat{\theta}_t^i = \theta_t^i(y_{t-1})$ is a parametric estimate by individual i. One is tempted to view $\hat{\theta}^i$ as an estimate of θ^i, the parametric content of the rational-expectations forecast function $\pi_i^*(y_{t-1}; \theta^i)$. However, we ought to be extremely careful in the advocacy, or even supposition of the existence, of such parameter-mediated disequilibrium forecast rules. As we have earlier remarked, the parameter θ may be defined only in a state of rational-expectations equilibrium. For individuals to attempt to estimate these parameters is tantamount to the supposition that they know the characteristics of the final equilibrium state, never having been there. In general, this is an unpalatable assumption.

In some circumstances, however, the parameters θ may have objective reality even in a state of disequilibrium. The rational-expectations equilibrium will obtain when all individuals in the system are correctly informed about the true value of θ. (It may be noted that such circumstances will usually be characterized by a single common value for such parameters, referring to some physical or exogenous characteristic of the structure in which the agents are embedded: thus we shall in such a context omit the individual superscript i from the θ.) In this case, the rational-expectations equilibrium is the outcome of a more or less straightforward learning process about some features of the world with objective reality whether or not the system is in a state of equilibrium. It is this kind of situation that we shall refer to as parameter-mediated learning. As we have just remarked, there is in such circumstances a coincidence between system and individual learning so that more classical ideas of learning apply. Certainly, this is the easiest case to handle in discussing questions of convergence. It should be stressed, however, that parameter-mediated learning, in the objective sense we have described, is not representative in any sense of the full range of convergence problems.

Reflexivity aspects

Consider, for the sake of simplicity, a parameter-mediated learning process. Given a current set of estimates $\hat{\theta}_t^i$, agents carry out their consequent actions $a_i(y_{t-1}, \hat{\theta}_t^i)$. The system is driven by

$$y_t = f(y_{t-1}, \{a_i(y_{t-1}, \hat{\theta}_t^i)\}, \epsilon_t), \quad \hat{\theta}_t^i = \hat{\theta}^i(y_{t-1}). \tag{4}$$

This should be compared with the rational-expectations equilibrium dynamics

$$y_t = f(y_{t-1}, \{a_i(y_{t-1}, \theta)\}, \epsilon_t), \quad \theta = \text{const.} \tag{5}$$

In a system such as (5), an external observer could reasonably hope to estimate θ by a real-time learning process, confident that the stochastic dynamics generating the observations remains stable over time. Such an assumption is characteristic of learning or sequential estimation in the psychological and engineering sciences. However, the disequilibrium dynamics (4) that we shall study involves a reflexivity element. The function f does in general depend upon the true value θ (assumed to exist objectively in parametrically mediated learning), but it also depends upon the current participant estimation of this parameter. As we shall see, this reflexivity property complicates proofs of disequilibrium convergence.

Game-theoretic aspects

In studying proposed forecasting rules $\pi_t^i(y_{t-1})$ during convergence, similar game-theoretic considerations arise to the study of the equilibrium itself. If, for instance, convergence is parameter mediated, then the estimation procedures $\hat{\theta}_t(y_{t-1})$ must be a matter of public knowledge; this being the case, an incentive might arise for individual agents to "second guess" such rules. In other words, if I know that other agents will be utilizing a sequential least-squares routine to estimate a parameter θ followed by an action of a given functional form predicated upon the resulting estimate, then it might be possible to design an action that yields a better result than following a similar procedure myself. Ideally, perhaps, it might be possible to extend the idea of a Nash equilibrium to disequilibrium behavior: If everybody else adopts the disequilibrium estimation rule $\hat{\theta}$, then it is optimal for me to do so. However, the existence of such a set of estimation and action procedures is problematical. In the example of Section 7.4 we are less ambitious, seeking only to establish conditions under which some rule $\hat{\theta}(y_{t-1})$ exists, whereby if everybody follows such a rule, then convergence to a rational-expectations equilibrium will occur. We do not investigate the stability of such a rule under gamelike behavior during the disequilibrium phase. In this respect the analysis is somewhat similar to disequilibrium models of Cournot behavior in oligopoly theory: Each firm is assumed to take the output of the other as a given datum in spite of the rather obvious knowledge that the other will in fact be reacting. However, the supposition of fixed disequilibrium rules is perhaps rather more palatable in the present context since as remarked in Chapter 6, the notion of a rational-expectations equilibrium is most natural in a system of many individually insignificant agents.

Technique and sophistication

The first task of any study of convergence and system learning is to decide on possibility principles: Is it possible for agents to adopt *some* rule, no matter how complicated, that will guarantee convergence? Assuming that convergence is indeed possible, the question then arises as to just how sophisticated our participants are assumed to be in these rules or, in the case of parameter-mediated convergence, in their estimation procedures. This depends upon our object of study. We may be concerned to show that some real-world system as it currently exists is capable of attaining and sustaining a rational-expectations equilibrium. In other words, we might seek convergence as an underpinning to an empirical statement about a system currently under study. The estimation rule should then reflect the degree of sophistication that participants are assumed to possess, in most cases, probably of mild technicality. Alternatively we could be concerned with a more theoretical study: Given a set of statisticians utilizing state-of-the-art techniques of inference, one asks whether they could collectively attain a state of rational expectations. The distinction between these two problems is hardly absolute and very possibly is time dependent. Thus it could well be argued that with progressive education in numeracy and the development of simply executed but powerful computer routines and packages, the naive statistician is being transformed (statistically speaking) into the expert. Hence any statement about the empirical propensity of a system to converge to rational-expectations equilibrium may very well have a time reference. Disequilibrium systems are therefore indexed by calendar time, and empirically, convergence rules can never be quite invariant over time. In what follows, we shall rather hedge our bets on the two problems just described by assuming an error correction type of convergence rule that is statistically sound yet behaviorally attractive as a description of the behavior of relatively unsophisticated agents.

7.3   Sequential estimation techniques

Before we turn to the substantive problem of convergence under reflexivity, it will be useful to briefly review standard techniques of sequential estimation. The need for a sequential treatment arises from the real-time nature of the learning problem: Knowledge is being continually updated and behavior modified as a result. Whereas the sequential treatment is really only a matter of convenience – computational, representational, or behavioral – for other applications, it becomes quite essential in a reflexive context where the output at each stage depends upon the estimation from the previous stage. However, we shall largely delay the reflexivity aspect until the next section, considering now the estimation of standard invariant or observer-independent models, except where otherwise indicated.

The reader will doubtless have at least a passing familiarity with Bayesian rules for the updating of estimated parameters. Starting from time zero, let us here (and hereafter) adopt n as the time index relative to this origin, reserving the index t for absolute (i.e., calendar) time. The information available at time n is denoted $\mathcal{I}_n$ and obeys the recursion

$$\mathcal{I}_n = \{\mathcal{I}_{n-1}, y_n\}.$$

A system dynamics is given as a structure that specifies y_n in terms of $\mathcal{I}_{n-1}$ and the parameter θ. Thus one can form the density $p(y_n/\mathcal{I}_{n-1}, \theta)$. Given the new information y_n, the Bayesian posterior for θ is then defined as

$$p(\theta/\mathcal{I}_n) = \frac{p(y_n/\mathcal{I}_{n-1}, \theta)\, p(\theta/\mathcal{I}_{n-1})}{p(y_n)}, \tag{6}$$

where

$$p(y_n) = \int_\theta p(y_n/\mathcal{I}_{n-1}, \theta)\, p(\theta/\mathcal{I}_{n-1})\, d\theta.$$

Equation (6) is a recursion in which $p(\theta/\mathcal{I}_n)$ is updated from $p(\theta/\mathcal{I}_{n-1})$, utilizing the system dynamics together with the new observation y_n. The corresponding point estimate is

$$\hat{\theta}_n = E_n(\theta),$$

where the expectation is taken over the posterior density $p(\theta/\mathcal{I}_n)$. If the dynamics is linear with known conditional variances at each step, then a set of computationally tractable updating equations exists for $\hat{\theta}_n$ and the variances $\mathrm{Var}(\hat{\theta}_n/\mathcal{I}_n)$. These may be exhibited in an error correction mode as a special case of the well-known Kalman filter algorithm for sequential filtering.

Good reasons exist for the choice of Bayesian updating rules as a sequential estimation procedure. In general, one learns in order to be able to control or predict. It is a basic result of statistical decision theory that where the criterion function for such problems is quadratic, the minimum-loss procedure replaces the unknown parameters θ by their conditional expectation $E(\theta/\mathcal{I}_n)$ given the available information $\mathcal{I}_n$. A natural estimation procedure therefore exists. As a matter of learning theory, the Bayesian estimator encapsulates the instrumentalist philosophy of learning [see in particular Boland (1982) for a methodological discussion], in which learning and learning procedures are judged as tools for the resolution of practical problems. It is therefore not surprising that in the economics literature, the idea of a maximizing individual updating his or her knowledge of the world in Bayesian fashion has come to be regarded as the incarnation of rational man.

But even rational man is subject to technical limitations, and a major difficulty with Bayesian updating is that only in exceptional cases is the process at all tractable. This does not altogether rule out the possibility that people can nevertheless arrive at Bayesian updating formulas by some unconscious process, the result of some imbedded psychological propensity. An argument thus would presumably be of the billiard table genre:

Players do not have the mathematical training to compute angles and spin momenta, but the Lindrums, Charletons, and other wizards of the table must nevertheless rate as outstanding, if intuitive, applied mathematicians. Nevertheless, the fact that even the most powerful computer in the hands of the most expert and dedicated Bayesian statistician could not compute the updating formulas for even a mildly nonlinear dynamics surely militates against the idea that agents act as though activated by an inboard Bayesian driveshaft. Moreover some experimental evidence exists that people are more conservative in their updating of probabilities than a strict Bayesian analysis would indicate (Edwards, 1968; Fishbein and Ajzen, 1975).

Given the intractability of full Bayesian updating algorithms, alternative models of learning or sequential estimation are clearly worth pursuing. Those based upon sequential or real-time regression have received a fair amount of attention in the literature. Consider the general, possibly nonlinear model

$$Y_n = F_n(\theta) + u_n, \tag{7}$$

generating observations Y_n on a scalar variable Y in terms of a function F_n and a zero-mean disturbance u_n. The function F_n may be of the form $F(X_n; \theta)$ in terms of a stochastic or nonstochastic sequence of exogenous variates X_n, but we shall adopt no special notation for this purpose. Consider now the real-time recursion

$$\theta_n = \theta_{n-1} - a_n[Y_n - F_n(\hat{\theta}_{n-1})]. \tag{8}$$

This is an error correction algorithm with the "prediction error" $Y_n - F_n(\hat{\theta}_{n-1})$ adjusted by a suitably chosen gain sequence a_n, which may depend upon the information set $\mathfrak{I}_n$ as well as on past estimates $\hat{\theta}_{n-1}, \hat{\theta}_{n-2}, \ldots$. Note that if θ is a vector, the gain a_n is also a vector, and among other attributes it directs the consequences of a given prediction error to the revision process in the estimated parameters. More detailed rules for choosing the gain sequence will be given shortly. Under suitable conditions on the functions F_n and the disturbance process u_n and with a suitable choice of the gain sequence a_n, the sequence of estimates θ_n converges – usually in mean square or almost surely – to the true parameter θ.

Experimentally determined observations: stochastic approximation

In the Bayesian or regression algorithms of the type discussed in the preceding, the underlying models generating the observations represent an objective reality; observations Y_n are free of any taint produced by the process of estimation. This is very much a model of estimation by an external observer. A somewhat different class of procedures allows (in fact encourages) the observations Y_n to be actually generated by the experimenter in the sense that Y_n is affected by the current value $\hat{\theta}_{n-1}$ of the estimation process. The problem then essentially becomes one of designing a sequence $\hat{\theta}_n$ to generate measurements on Y_n with the aim of estimating an underlying true value θ, which continues to have objective reality. The basic Robbins–Monro techniques of stochastic approximation may be described as follows. Imagine that it is desired to find a root x^*, assumed unique, of a function $M(x)$, that is, the solution to the equation $M(x) = 0$. Sometimes one sees this as the solution to an equation of the form $M(x) = \alpha$, where α is a known constant, but we shall imagine that α is already absorbed in M, or equivalently that $\alpha = 0$. Common iterative solutions to this problem update an approximation x_n to the required root by a procedure of the form $x_{n+1} = x_n - a(x_n)M(x_n)$ working in terms of an error correction $M(x_n) - 0$ adjusted by some "gain function" $a(x_n)$. The latter may or not depend explicitly upon x_n; a common candidate is $a(x_n) = [M'(x_n)]^{-1}$, that is, the inverse of the derivative evaluated at the current estimate; this is the Newton–Raphson gain. Suppose, however, that the current value of the function $M(x_n)$ cannot be observed directly. The observations are contaminated with noise, so that for a given setting x_n we observe $Y_n = M(x_n) + u_n$, where u_n is a zero-mean random variable that may in some specifications possibly depend upon x_n. The stochastic approximation process utilizes the observed Y_n in place of the unobservable $M(x_n)$, which may indeed be unknown even as to functional form, a point of some potential importance in our particular context. The updating sequence is thus

$$x_{n+1} = x_n - a_n Y_n,$$

and the solution analysis is that of the stochastic difference equation

$$x_{n+1} = x_n - a_n M(x_n) - a_n u_n,$$

where $a_n = a(\dots x_n)$ may depend upon current and previous values of x_n. The problem is to devise conditions on the function $M(x_n)$, the chosen gain a_n, and the error or disturbance process u_n that will ensure convergence to the desired root x^*. The chosen modes of convergence are usually either in mean square $[E(x_n - x^*)^2 \to 0]$ or almost surely $[P(\lim x_n = x^*) = 1]$. Various conditions for the univariate problem have been given; the best known are those of Dvoretsky (1956). We refer the reader to general references such as Fu (1969), who discusses the case of vector parameters and various learning applications (although not of the reflexive kind we shall consider) and especially to Wasan (1969), Nevel'son and Has'minski (1976), and Dupac (1984) for a general survey. Other important references will be given as they arise.

It may be observed that the sequential nonlinear regression routine (8) may be interpreted as a stochastic approximation process. Substituting equation (7) into (8), we find

$$\hat{\theta}_n = \hat{\theta}_{n-1} - a_n M_n(\hat{\theta}_{n-1}) - a_n u_n, \tag{9}$$

where $M_n(\hat{\theta}_{n-1}) = F_n(\theta) - F_n(\hat{\theta}_{n-1})$. A stationary point is characterized by $M_n(\theta) = 0$ for all n. Thus although slightly more complicated in that the function M is now nonstationary, the nonlinear regression may be interpreted as a stochastic approximation process. This fact may be used to facilitate a transference of results and methodology from the one literature to the other. It may also be noted that in either case, the recursion defining $\hat{\theta}_n$ in terms of $\hat{\theta}_{n-1}$ may be "supervised" or "monitored," which means that the sequence $\hat{\theta}_n$ is contained within some preassigned bounds to prevent the recursion running off into regions that are nonsense or produce unstable behavior for the Y_n process.

Returning to the general stochastic approximation process, note that seeking a value $\hat{\theta}$ such that $M(\hat{\theta}) = 0$ is trivially equivalent to seeking a value $\hat{\theta}$ such that $M(\hat{\theta}; \theta) = M(\hat{\theta}) - M(\theta) = 0$, where θ is the true solution. More generally, suppose that we start with a function $M(\theta; \theta_0)$, where θ_0 is unknown but a parameter of some importance. It is known that $M(\theta_0; \theta_0) = 0$ and that $M(\theta; \theta_0) \neq 0$ for $\theta \neq \theta_0$. We can design a stochastic approximation process $\hat{\theta}_n$ that generates successive $M(\hat{\theta}_n; \theta_0)$ and observations Y_n. Now this kind of situation is evidently getting rather close to a reflexive parameter-mediated system learning process of the kind established in the last section. The θ_0 are objective, true parameters, knowledge of which produces a rational-expectations equilibrium. By actions based on their current estimate $\hat{\theta}_n$, agents collectively generate observations Y_n with mathematical expectation $M(\hat{\theta}_n; \theta_0)$. A stochastic approximation recursion based upon Y_n might then result in the identification of θ_0 such that $M(\theta_0; \theta_0) = 0$ and a state of rational-expectations equilibrium would be the outcome. This is the line of attack followed in some detail in the next section. However, it is useful before proceeding further to give a general account of important regularity conditions necessary for such a stochastic approximation process to succeed.

Convergence conditions

Suppose that we can write

$$Y_n = M_n(\hat{\theta}_{n-1}; \theta) + u_n, \tag{10}$$

where $E u_n = 0$. For additional generality we suppose that θ is a vector of parameters (we drop the subscript 0) and $\hat{\theta}_{n-1}$ represents the current estimate prior to the availability of Y_n. Corresponding to (9), we have

$$\hat{\theta}_n = \hat{\theta}_{n-1} - \mathbf{a}_n M_n(\hat{\theta}_{n-1}; \theta) - \mathbf{a}_n u_n.$$

By expanding in exact Taylor series about the true value θ, we obtain

$$\hat{\theta}_n - \theta = (I - \mathbf{a}_n \mathbf{h}_n')(\hat{\theta}_{n-1} - \theta) - \mathbf{a}_n u_n, \tag{11}$$

where the gradient vector $\mathbf{h}_n = (\partial/\partial\hat{\theta}) M_n(\hat{\theta}; \theta)$ at stage n is evaluated at some value along the line joining the current estimate $\hat{\theta}_{n-1}$ and the true value θ.

Iterating backward from equation (11) (see Appendix 1 to this chapter), it is evident that convergence will depend upon the convergence properties of iterated matrices of the form

$$P_n = \sum_{j=1}^{n} (I - \mathbf{a}_j \mathbf{h}_j'), \tag{12}$$

so that we should seek conditions under which some suitable norm $\|P_n\|$ of these matrices approaches zero. This problem has been addressed by Albert and Gardner (1967) in terms of the norm $[\lambda_{\max}(P_n' P_n)]^{1/2}$, where $\lambda_{\max}$ is the maximal eigenvalue of the indicated matrix. Under this norm, $\|I - \mathbf{a}_j \mathbf{h}_j'\| \geq 1$, so that the usual triangle inequality $\|P_n\| \leq \prod_j \|I - \mathbf{a}_j \mathbf{h}_j'\|$ is not likely to be fruitful. Albert and Gardner (AG) establish a set of conditions that do yield $\|P_n\| \to 0$, essentially by breaking up the product (12) into a grouping of successive products. These and related conditions for convergence are surveyed in more detail in Appendix 1 to this chapter. However, we note here two principal requirements of interest.

(i) The two vectors $\mathbf{a}_j$ and $\mathbf{h}_j$ should as far as possible point in the same direction. One of the AG requirements is that the angle between the two must be less than a certain size, uniformly in n, with probability 1. The exact limit in this respect depends upon the conditioning of the sequence of gradient vectors $\mathbf{h}_n$ (see what follows); the poorer this conditioning, the smaller is the allowable angle between the gradient and gain vectors.

(ii) A second set of requirements relates to the sequence of gradient vectors $\mathbf{h}_n$. As in linear and nonlinear regression, we could imagine forming a data matrix with the gradient vector $\mathbf{h}_j'$ as the jth row up to the currently available row $\mathbf{h}_n'$. Normalize this data matrix so that the jth row is in fact $\mathbf{h}_j'/|\mathbf{h}_j|$. Then one must be able to divide the notional data matrix obtained in this way as $n \to \infty$ up into temporal blocks of finite size in such a way that all of the resulting blocks are of full rank. Note that the corresponding requirement for regression purposes would be that the entire matrix whose rows are $\mathbf{h}_j'$ should be of full-column rank so that no multicollinearity should exist. The AG condition is evidently somewhat weaker than this. Nevertheless, it will be convenient to refer to it as a multicollinearity requirement.

Additional conditions relate to the boundedness properties of the gradient and gain vectors. The gain vector must vanish as $n \to \infty$ but not at too fast a rate: Specifically $|\mathbf{a}_n| |\mathbf{h}_n| \to 0$ but $\sum_n |\mathbf{a}_n| |\mathbf{h}_n| \to \infty$. The gains must also satisfy $\sum_n |\mathbf{a}_n|^2 < \infty$, and the gradient vectors must be absolute bounded uniformly in n. The Hessian (matrix of second-order derivatives) of M must also exist.

It should also be noted that the original AG conditions were given where $M(\theta)$ was independent of the action or estimate $\hat{\theta}$ for the nonlinear regression context. However, it is remarked (see Appendix 1) that they extend to the stochastic approximation context, although the proofs that these and other regularity conditions are satisfied in a particular context do become more difficult. It may be noted that the special case where M is linear in $\hat{\theta}$ is quite easy to handle for in this case the gradient vector is independent of the estimates $\hat{\theta}$ and may readily be examined for its conditioning properties. Moreover, in this case the optimal gain vector may be chosen as simply proportional to the now exogenous gradient vector.

This completes our story survey of methods of sequential or real-time estimation. In the next section we apply the ideas of stochastic approximation to the description of a psychologically plausible behavior that can lead to system convergence in the case of a parameter-mediated structure.

7.4   Parameter-mediated learning example

The simple market example that we have chosen to exemplify parameter-mediated learning illustrates quite well the reflexivity aspect referred to in Section 7.2. Producers must decide how much of the commodity to supply based upon their estimation of demand parameters. However, the observational variable that they employ for estimation purposes is market price, and this is in turn based upon supply decisions and hence estimated parameters. Linear models, with a very limited number of parameters, of learning in such market models have been considered by a number of authors (e.g., Frydman, 1982; Fourgeaud, Gourieroux, and Pradel, 1986; Bray and Savin, 1986). In the present section we shall show that such convergence problems can be tackled by stochastic approximation methodology and that in principle, at least, one can handle many parameters and nonlinear functional forms. If agents are interpreted as behaving as stochastic approximators, then under suitable and not very demanding regularity conditions, a system, will converge to a rational-expectations equilibrium in which producers' forecasts of price are unbiased. Moreover the assumption that agents behave as stochastic approximators has some psychological appeal as an error correction mechanism. This is not to say that we should uncritically accept a hypothesis that empirically they do behave in this way or that other problems of information do not arise; we shall delay such considerations until the next section. Our concern is at present to investigate conditions under which convergence *can* occur given apparently reasonable learning behavior on the part of participating individuals.

The basic market model

We suppose a competitive market model for a certain commodity. The market demand function determines price according to

$$P = D(Q, \beta, X_d, \epsilon), \tag{13}$$

where P is price, Q is market (aggregate) supply, β is a parameter vector, X_d is a vector of exogenous variables affecting demand, and ϵ is inserted to indicate that the outcome is random without necessarily implying an additive or separable disturbance. For simplicity one assumes that the current values X_d are known to all the agents; the extension is straightforward. The function D is left as general as possible, although we do assume that the partial derivative D_1 is negative (in economic terms, the good is "normal"; other things being equal, a higher quantity is associated with a lower price). The parameters β may appear in conjunction with the exogenous variables (e.g., in a term of the form $\sum_j \beta_j X_{d_j}$) or may represent other constants such as higher order parameters of the distribution of P.

In this section and the ensuing development we shall be relying heavily on the notion of a representative firm, leaving for later consideration a possible relaxation to cover firms nonidentical in their information sets. We shall assume that aggregate supply Q is related to the supply of the representative firm by an equation of the form $Q = \lambda_0 + \lambda_1 q$. The leading case is where all firms are identical in their cost functions and information endowments, in which case $\lambda_0 = 0$, and $\lambda_1 = \lambda$, say, is simply the number of firms currently operating. Alternatively, we could imagine that this equation represents a theoretical regression (e.g., Cramer, 1961); given output q for a representative firm, the conditional expectation of aggregate output Q is of the form $\lambda_0 + \lambda_1 q$, and the residual error, presumed to be stable in its distribution, can be absorbed into the stochastic component of the demand curve (13). In any event, we shall write

$$P = D(\lambda q, \beta, X_d, \epsilon), \tag{14}$$

absorbing any constant λ_0 or residual aggregation error in the parameter vector β or stochastic innovation ϵ. Equation (14) represents the true or underlying generation of the observed or actual price P.

We turn to the decision processes of the representative firm. We assume that the firm operates on the basis of a perceived demand function

$$P = \hat{D}(\hat{Q}, \hat{\beta}, X_d, \epsilon). \tag{15}$$

The leading – and conceptually the simplest – case is where the firm knows the true form of the process-generating price, so that the functions D and $\hat{D}$ are the same. Unknown are the estimates or assessment $\hat{Q}$ of market supply in the coming period and the parameters in β, which must be estimated as $\hat{\beta}$. However, it is possible to conceive of the functions D and $\hat{D}$ as different; we reserve for later consideration the issues that arise (some of which will be immediately apparent from the existence of corresponding parameters in both D and $\hat{D}$).

The first problem to tackle is the firm's estimate of market supply in the coming period. It seems reasonable that in a variety of markets individual producers will seek and react to information about likely market conditions. The simplest case from the informational point of view is where no public information such as a market forecast exists. Even if individual producers cannot get together and share their private information or expectations, it is assumed that our representative producer assumes that to some extent at least, he (or she) is indeed representative. In other words, he expects that other firms will be affected by the same exogenous variables in the same way so that if he is considering raising his output, he realizes that most probably other firms will be thinking along similar lines. Thus if an agricultural producer has been experiencing favorable weather, he knows that other producers in the area share this experience and revises upward his estimates of aggregate supply in the coming period. We shall refer to this as an extrapolative experience assumption.

With this in mind, the representative firm's optimal output q^* is obtained as follows. A cost function $c(q, X_s)$ exists that may depend upon a vector of exogenous variables X_s (e.g., weather). Sometimes the argument X_s is suppressed for expositional brevity. All parameters of its own cost function are assumed to be known by the firm. The cost function is assumed to be such that $c' > 0$, $c'' > 0$ (e.g., U-shaped average cost curves), where the primes denote derivatives with respect to q. For any assumed value $\hat{Q}$ for aggregate supply, estimated profit is $\pi(P; \hat{Q}) = Pq - c(q)$, and assuming that the firm is risk neutral, the optimal q is obtained as the solution, presumed unique, to the first-order conditions

$$\int [P - c'(q)] \hat{\Phi}(P; \hat{Q}) \, dP = 0. \tag{16}$$

The resulting optimum $q = q(\hat{Q}; X_s)$ may be thought of as a reaction to any assumed level $\hat{Q}$ for aggregate output in the coming market period.

To determine $\hat{Q}$, we draw on the extrapolative experience assumption. Whatever q^* the firm decides on in the current period, it will consider that other firms will be led to similar solutions, so that as a consistency condition, it assumes that $\hat{Q} = \hat{\lambda} q^*$. Substituting in equation (16) the optimal output q^* must therefore solve the equation

$$\int [P - c'(q)] \hat{\Phi}(P; \hat{\lambda} q^*) \, dP = 0, \tag{17}$$

or equivalently,

$$c'(q^*) = \hat{E}\hat{D}(\hat{\lambda} q^*, \hat{\beta}, X_d, \epsilon).$$

Such an equation may be thought of as the outcome of an intraperiod iterative process, in which a number of trial solutions are obtained in some sort of thought experiment as follows. Suppose that the firm thinks tentatively of an output q_{r-1}. If other firms are expected to behave similarly, then $\hat{Q} = \hat{\lambda} q_{r-1}$, where $1/\hat{\lambda}$ is the firm's current estimate of market share, or an equivalent interpretation (see the preceding) in terms of a theoretical regression. The next trial solution q_r is obtained by substituting this value of $\hat{Q}$ into equation (16). Thus q_r is obtained implicitly from

$$\int [P - c'(q_r)] \hat{\Phi}(P; \hat{\lambda} q_{r-1}) \, dP = 0.$$

The process hopefully continues to convergence, at which point $\hat{Q}$ and q are consistent in the sense described in the preceding. Equation (17) is the result. We emphasize that q^* is not viewed as a decision variable where it enters expectations about Q. In other words, the firm does not actually think that by setting q, it can directly influence the behavior of other firms; such a contingency would be more appropriate in an oligopolistic framework. We assume passive competitive behavior but also a recognition that other firms will exhibit similar reactions in response to common external conditions or information sets, what we have called the extrapolative experience assumption.

The upshot of equations (15) and (17) is that in any given period we may write the supply function for the representative firm as

$$q^* = q^*(\hat{\lambda}, \beta, X_d, X_s) \tag{18}$$

and actual market supply as

$$Q = \lambda q^*(\hat{\lambda}, \beta, X_d, X_s). \tag{19}$$

Note that aggregate supply depends upon both the true value λ and the estimated values $\hat{\lambda}$, $\hat{\beta}$ as well as on all the exogenous variables. From equations (15) and (17) we obtain the partial derivative

$$\frac{\partial q^*}{\partial \hat{\lambda}} = \frac{q^* \hat{E} \hat{D}_1}{c'' - \hat{\lambda} \hat{E} \hat{D}_1} < 0, \tag{20}$$

where $\hat{E}$ denotes the expectation with regard to the density $\hat{\Phi}$ as perceived by the firm. As we should expect, if the firm has a higher estimate of the number of competitors, this has a depressant influence on its output decision for a given assessment $\hat{Q}$ of aggregate forthcoming demand. Similarly,

$$\frac{\partial q^*}{\partial \beta_i} \hat{E} \hat{D}_{\hat{\beta}_i} / (c'' - \hat{\lambda} \hat{E} \hat{D}_1), \tag{21}$$

with sign $=$ sign $\hat{D}_{\hat{\beta}_i}$, the derivative of perceived price with respect to the estimates $\hat{\beta}$. These partial derivatives may be of either sign, but it will be necessary to assume that the sign is invariant, that is, does not change over the domain of the parameter estimates. This completes our basic specification of the market model.

The stochastic approximation problem

Given its estimates $\hat{\lambda}$, $\hat{\beta}$, and $\hat{Q} = \hat{\lambda} q^*$, the firm's expected value for price in the coming period is

$$\hat{E}P = \hat{E}\hat{D}(\hat{\lambda}q^*, \hat{\beta}, X_d, \epsilon), \tag{22}$$

where q^* is as defined by equation (18). The expression $\hat{E}P$ is certainly observable by the firm since it is this expectation that is utilized in deriving its optimal output decision q^*. Suppose now that the market has come and gone and that ex post a price P is observed. Then the discrepancy between outcome and ex ante expectations

$$Y = P - \hat{E}P$$

is ex post observable. Its expectation is given by

$$M = EY = ED(\lambda q^*, \beta, X_d, \epsilon) - \hat{E}\hat{D}(\hat{\lambda}q^*, \hat{\beta}, X_d, \epsilon), \tag{23}$$

where $q^* = q^*(\hat{\lambda}, \hat{\beta}, X_d, X_s)$. Let $\theta' = (\lambda, \hat{\beta})$ be the vector of parameters. Then we write $M = M(\hat{\theta}; \theta)$ to indicate that the expectation of the observed discrepancy Y between actual price and ex ante expectations depends upon the true value θ as well as the estimated values $\hat{\theta}$. Note also that M depends upon exogenous X_d and X_s, which we have assumed for simplicity to be ex ante observable. Since these exogenous variables vary over time (n), we shall often indicate this by writing $M = M_n(\hat{\theta}; \theta)$. In the basic model, the function M is affected by the past only via the current parameter estimates $\hat{\theta}$, which are built up by a sequential real-time estimation process to be described shortly. In particular, past values of P are assumed not to enter so that in this sense we are considering a static model. Questions of time dependence are examined in Section 7.5.

Considering the relationship between the estimate $\hat{\theta}$ and the true value θ, suppose that $M_n(\theta; \theta) = 0$. In other words, if $\hat{\theta} = \theta$, then there is no discrepancy between ex ante expectations and the mathematical expectation of the outcome price distribution resulting from collective output decisions predicated upon the ex ante expectations. Such a state of affairs would, given our other assumptions, correspond to a consistent or rational-expectations equilibrium. In turn, this suggests a possible algorithm for the estimation of θ based on stochastic approximation. Write

$$P_n = ED(\lambda q_n^*, \beta, X_{dn}) + u_n,$$

where u_n is a zero-mean residual. Then the observed discrepancy Y is given by

$$Y_n = M_n(\hat{\theta}_{n-1}; \theta) + u_n, \tag{24}$$

which is of the form of equation (10) of Section 7.3. Note that we have introduced a timing convention on the estimates. The meaning is as follows. On the basis of the existing estimate $\hat{\theta}_{n-1}$, agents form ex ante expectations and make decisions predicated upon their expectations that collectively result in a price P_n for the coming period. Once the price P_n is observed, the estimates can be updated as $\hat{\theta}_n$. Given the estimate $\hat{\theta}_{n-1}$, once the current price becomes known, the estimate is updated according to the stochastic approximation scheme

$$\hat{\theta}_n = \hat{\theta}_{n-1} - a_n Y_n \tag{25a}$$

for a suitably chosen gain vector a_n (some examples are given in what follows). Equation (25a) may be interpreted as an error correction process:

$$\theta_n = \theta_{n-1} - a_n(P_n - \hat{E}P_n) \tag{25b}$$

in terms of the observed discrepancy between outcome and the ex ante expectation of price. As such, it could represent a psychological hypothesis about how a firm with only a mild degree of technical sophistication would adjust its parameter estimates. The gain vector a_n directs the consequences of any given surprise or prediction error into revisions of the components of the estimated vector $\hat{\theta}$ of parameters.

Identification and convergence

The underlying stochastic difference equation implied is of a form considered in Section 7.3, namely,

$$\theta_n = \theta_{n-1} - \mathbf{a}_n M_n(\hat{\theta}_{n-1}; \theta) - \mathbf{a}_n u_n, \tag{26}$$

where the gain vector $\mathbf{a}_n$ may also depend upon $\hat{\theta}_{n-1}$ and previous estimates. We turn now to consider conditions under which the sequence of estimates $\hat{\theta}_n$ will approach the true value θ.

As mentioned in the preceding we require $M_n(\theta; \theta) = 0$. This is essentially a consistency condition that requires a certain relationship between the actual and perceived price functions D and $\hat{D}$. The most straightforward case is where at all points in time the representative firm knows the precise form of the probability density function of price; his or her ignorance is confined to its parameters. In this case, D and $\hat{D}$ coincide. It is then obvious that $M_n(\theta; \theta) = 0$; if the agent knows the parameters and the functional form of the density of prices, then ex ante and ex post expectations coincide. A variant is where the functional forms for $\hat{D}$ are parametrically determined members of a class of flexible functional forms. The parameters concerned are among the elements of the vector β. Initially the firm may be operating off a wrong member of the class but comes closer to the true D as learning proceeds and parameters are updated. Thus the firm is learning the functional form parametrically as time proceeds. An alternative interesting possibility is that the firm may never end up knowing the true functional form (D and $\hat{D}$ never coincide) but that some kind of aliasing phenomenon ensures that for some value of $\hat{\theta}$ ($\hat{\theta}^0$, say) $E\hat{D}(\theta^0) = ED$ whatever the latter may be. While noting such possibilities, we do not explore them further. For purposes of exposition we shall henceforth simply assume that the representative firm either knows or is parametrically learning the true functional form D. If this is the case, then $M_n(\hat{\theta}; \theta) = 0$ for all n only if $\hat{\theta} = \theta$. This is a basic requirement: The consistent expectations equilibrium must be unique. It will help in this respect if we can assert that the derivatives of M with respect to $\hat{\theta}$ are invariant as to sign, although this is not a necessary requirement. For this and other reasons, we turn now to a discussion of these derivatives. Considering first the behavior with regard to $\hat{\lambda}$, we have obtained $\partial q^*/\partial \hat{\lambda}$ as equation (20). From expression (23) we obtain

$$\frac{\partial M}{\partial \hat{\lambda}} = \frac{\partial q^*}{\partial \hat{\lambda}} \cdot ED_1 - \left(q^* + \lambda \frac{\partial q^*}{\partial \hat{\lambda}} \right) \hat{E} \hat{D}_1 = (\lambda ED_1 - c'') \frac{\partial q^*}{\partial \hat{\lambda}}. \tag{27}$$

The sign of $\partial M/\partial \hat{\lambda}$ is therefore opposite to that of $\partial q^*/\partial \hat{\lambda}$, which is uniformly positive. With regard to the remaining parameters, we have

$$\frac{\partial M}{\partial \hat{\beta}_i} = (\lambda ED_1 - c'') \frac{\partial q^*}{\partial \hat{\beta}_i}. \tag{28}$$

The sign of these derivatives therefore also depends upon $\partial q^*/\partial \hat{\beta}_i$, which from equation (21) is determined by the sign of $\hat{D}_{\hat{\beta}_i}$, the demand derivative as perceived by the firm. If the latter is invariant, then the same property is true for the corresponding derivatives of M. Under these conditions, we may expect the zeros (in $\hat{\theta}$) of the function $M_n(\hat{\theta}; \theta)$ to be unique.

We turn to a discussion of necessary and sufficient conditions for convergence of the sequence of estimates $\hat{\theta}_n$ to the true value θ following in our specific example the general requirements laid down in Section 7.3. Considering first the multicollinearity requirement [condition (ii) of that section], we start by noting from equations (27) and (28) that the gradient vector $\mathbf{h}_n$ of the function $M_n(\hat{\theta}_n; \theta)$ is given by

$$\mathbf{h}_n = \frac{\partial M_n}{\partial \hat{\theta}_n} = \delta_n \frac{\partial q_n^*}{\partial \hat{\theta}_n}; \tag{29}$$

in other words the gradient vector is proportional at each stage to the derivatives of the optimal decision q^* with respect to the estimated parameters upon which it is predicated. As we shall see, this property can be employed in the design of an appropriate gain vector. For the moment we note that in terms of the multicollinearity requirement, which depends only upon the normalized gain vector $\mathbf{h}_n/|\mathbf{h}_n|$, the proportionality constants δ_n may effectively be ignored. The lack of collinearity must therefore apply to the derivatives $\partial q_n^*/\partial \hat{\theta}_n$ of the action q_n^*. It can be interpreted as a requirement that agents must be aware of a distinct effect of each of the estimated parameters $\hat{\theta}_i$ upon their output decisions q_n^*. Since [cf. equations (20) and (21)]

$$\frac{\partial q_n^*}{\partial \hat{\theta}'} \propto \left[\frac{\partial \hat{E}\hat{D}}{\partial \hat{Q}}, \frac{\partial \hat{E}\hat{D}}{\partial \hat{\beta}'} \right], \tag{30}$$

the multicollinearity requirement can be further translated into collinearity requirements on the estimated expected demand function $\hat{E}\hat{D}$.

A second principal aspect in convergence is the choice of the gain vector $\mathbf{a}_n$. As remarked in Section 7.3, it is desirable for this vector to point in the same direction as the gradient vector $\mathbf{h}_n$. From equation (29), this is evidently the same direction as the vector $\partial q_n^*/\partial \hat{\theta}_n = \mathbf{g}_n$ for brevity. Thus the gain vector should point in the same direction as the derivatives of the action q_n^*, or alternatively [from expression (30)] as the derivatives of the perceived expected demand function $\hat{E}\hat{D}$. The vectors $\mathbf{g}_n$ could be evaluated at some constant value of θ (θ^0, say) to give $\mathbf{g}_n^0 = \mathbf{g}_n(\theta^0)$ or else at the current value $\hat{\theta}_{n-1}$ for given $\mathbf{g}_n = \mathbf{g}_n(\hat{\theta}_{n-1})$. In either case the appropriate gain would be

$$\mathbf{a}_n = \mathbf{g}_n \Big/ \sum_{j=1}^{n} \|\mathbf{g}_j\|^2,$$

where the denominator arises from the boundedness and vanishing considerations discussed in Section 7.3. An alternative possibility is simply $\mathbf{a}_n = (1/n)\mathbf{g}_n^0$.

Such simple gains have some appeal as descriptions of how firms might actually proceed in the absence of any very formalized approach to the estimation process. For any given error or discrepancy between actual and ex ante expected prices, if optimal production (q^* here) is viewed as especially sensitive to a certain parameter, then the estimate of that parameter will receive a greater adjustment as a result of the discrepancy. Moreover, the agent concerned will react less and less to any given discrepancy as time goes on, realizing that the kind of prediction error he or she is observing must eventually settle toward some irreducible mean-square level reflecting the basic noise in the system. The AG sufficient conditions incorporate the vanishing of the gain but not at too fast a rate.

More complicated gains may be devised by exploiting the analogies with sequential regression. For example, we may adapt Plackett's algorithm for sequential linear least-squares regression to the present non-linear context: If G_n denotes the $n \times \dim(\theta)$ matrix whose rows are $\mathbf{g}_n'$, then the least-squares gain is

$$\mathbf{a}_n = P_n \mathbf{g}_n,$$

where P_n is generated recursively as

$$P_n^{-1} = P_{n-1}^{-1} + \mathbf{g}_n \mathbf{g}_n'$$

given some initial value P_0. In this updating process, the vectors $\mathbf{g}_n$ could be evaluated either at a constant θ_0 or continually updated as θ_{n-1}.

If the residuals u_n, the gains $\mathbf{a}_n$, and the gradient vectors $\mathbf{h}_n$ satisfy the AG conditions with probability 1, then the unmonitored stochastic approximation system will converge: $\hat{\theta}_n \to \hat{\theta}$ almost surely. In turn, this will mean that as $n \to \infty$,

$$EP_n = \hat{E}P_n$$

for all n: A rational-expectations equilibrium has resulted.

Heterogeneous agents

Producers may be heterogeneous with respect to either their cost functions or their initial information or priors, in the Bayesian sense, concerning the parameters to be estimated. Thus if we denote estimates by firm i as $\hat{\lambda}^i, \hat{\beta}^i$, the current decision is $q_{in}^* = q_i^*(\hat{\lambda}_{n+1}^i, \beta_{n-1}^i, X_{sn})$ based upon parameter estimates that are now specific to the firm. The true P is given by

$$P_n = D\left(\sum_i q_{in}^*, \beta, X_{dn}, \epsilon\right).$$

However, the assumed distribution of P must be specific to the firm; thus

$$\hat{E}_i P_n = \hat{E}\hat{D}_i(\hat{\lambda}_n^i q_{in}^*, \hat{\beta}_{n-1}^i, X_{dn}, \epsilon).$$

As before, $Y_n^i = P_n - \hat{E}_i P_n$ is observable by the firm, and the expectation $M_{in}(\hat{\theta}_{n-1}^i; \theta)$ exists, where θ combines λ and β. Corresponding to the recursion (25) together with the expression (23), we have

$$\theta_{n+1}^i = \theta_n^i - \mathbf{a}_n^i(P_n - \hat{E}_i P_n), \tag{31}$$

with

$$M_n^i = E(P_n - \hat{E}_i P_n) = ED\left(\sum_i q_i^*(\hat{\lambda}_{n-1}^i, \hat{\beta}_{n-1}^i, X_{sn}), \beta^i, X_{dn}\right)$$
$$- \hat{E}\hat{D}(\hat{\lambda}_n^i q_i^*(\hat{\lambda}_{n-1}^i, \hat{\beta}_{n-1}^i, X_{sn}), \hat{\beta}_{n-1}^i, X_{dn}). \tag{32}$$

This is a stochastic approximation scheme in the supervector $\underline{\theta}_n = \{\theta_n^i\}$ with gain sequence the supervector $\underline{\mathbf{a}}_n = \{\mathbf{a}_{ni}\}$.

It will be recalled that for homogeneous firms the sequence of matrices $(I - \mathbf{a}_n \mathbf{h}_n')$ influenced the limiting behavior of the recursion. In the case of the recursions defined by equations (31) and (32), the corresponding matrix is $(I - \underline{\mathbf{a}}_n H_n')$, where $H_n' = (\underline{\mathbf{h}}_1, \underline{\mathbf{h}}_2, \ldots, \underline{\mathbf{h}}_\lambda)$. Note that the gradient vector $\underline{\mathbf{h}}^i$ with respect to firm i reflects the dependence of M_n^i upon the parameter estimates of other firms as well and is thus a supervector. Two problems are involved in the extension of AG-type conditions to this context: (i) generalization of the multicollinearity and angle conditions to a situation where the product $\underline{\mathbf{a}}_n H_n'$ is of rank λ (the number of firms) rather than unity and (ii) suitable choices of gain vector on the part of individual agents given that these should bear some sensitivity to what other firms are doing. An extrapolative experience assumption may be a possible approach to the design of suitable gain supervectors. At the time of writing we offer only a conjecture that suitable and realistic assumptions can be constructed under which schemes such as (31) and (32) converge. Multivariate schemes have been constructed in the literature on stochastic approximation (see Blum, 1954; Venter, 1967; Wasan, 1969, ch. 5) but do not appear to be directly applicable to the present context.

Conditional and unconditional expectations: serial correlation

As pointed out in the preceding, the models that we are considering are essentially static. Intertemporal dependence can arise only because the current estimate $\hat{\theta}_n$ depends upon previous estimates via a recursive process. Past information affects the current state only by this route. Problems arise when, for example, the supply or demand functions may include as arguments past values (e.g., P_{n-1}) or where disturbance processes (ϵ) may contain moving-average or autoregressive components. As a general matter, convergence properties are very difficult to establish for such a contingency by whatever methodology. Indeed even for linear, nonreflexive models, it is well known that common sequential least squares will converge only in the particular cases where disturbance processes are either white noise or moving average of order 1, and one can expect no better from reflexive models of the type considered in the literature on convergence to rational expectations. In what follows, we review very briefly the kinds of difficulty associated with stochastic approximation processes in this context. The review is not entirely negative in character since it suggests an additional possible notion for an expectationally consistent expectations equilibrium.

Suppose that the aggregate demand function D depends explicitly (rather than just via q^*) upon the past. It may do so because past values $\ldots P_{n-2}, P_{n-1}$ of price are incorporated or else because past innovations $\ldots \epsilon_{n-2}, \epsilon_{n-1}$ also enter into the determination of current price. In either case, the past can be represented schematically by $\mathfrak{B}_{n-1}$, the manifold (technically σ-algebra) of past innovations. Then we may represent the true generation of current price in schematic form as

$$P_n = D(\lambda q^*, \beta, X_{dn}, \mathfrak{B}_{n-1}, \epsilon_n),$$

where we have returned to the assumption of homogeneous firms. Such a firm forms ex ante expectations

$$\hat{E}P_n; \mathfrak{B}_{n-1} = \hat{E}\hat{D}(\hat{\lambda}_{n-1}q^*, \hat{\beta}_{n-1}, \mathfrak{B}_{n-1}, \epsilon_n); \mathfrak{B}_{n-1}.$$

Such expectations are now conditional upon $\mathfrak{B}_{n-1}$, as the notation indicates. Explicit as well as implicit information on the past is now available to assist in the process of expectations formation.

The ex post observable conditional discrepancy is

$$Y_n^c = P_n - \hat{E}P_n; \mathfrak{B}_{n-1},$$

with conditional expectation

$$\begin{aligned} EY_n^c; \mathfrak{B}_{n-1} = {} & ED(\lambda q^*, \beta, X_{dn}, \mathfrak{B}_{n-1}, \epsilon_n); \mathfrak{B}_{n-1} \\ & - \hat{E}\hat{D}(\hat{\lambda}_{n-1}q^*, \hat{\beta}_{n-1}, X_{dn}, \mathfrak{B}_{n-1}, \epsilon_n); \mathfrak{B}_{n-1} \\ = {} & M_n(\hat{\theta}_{n-1}, \theta, \mathfrak{B}_{n-1}), \quad \text{say.} \end{aligned}$$

A natural estimation process is based upon the observed conditional discrepancy Y_n^c as

$$\hat{\theta}_n = \hat{\theta}_{n-1} - \mathbf{a}_n Y_n^c \tag{33}$$

for a suitably chosen gain sequence $\mathbf{a}_n$. The underlying stochastic difference equation is of the form

$$\hat{\theta}_n = \hat{\theta}_{n-1} - \mathbf{a}_n M_n(\hat{\theta}_{n-1}, \theta; \mathfrak{B}_{n-1}) - \mathbf{a}_n u_n. \tag{34}$$

We seek a solution $\hat{\theta}$ such that

$$M_n(\hat{\theta}, \theta; \mathfrak{B}_{n-1}) = 0 \quad \text{almost surely, for all } n. \tag{35}$$

Under suitable identification conditions the only such solution is $\hat{\theta} = \theta$.

As it stands, however, equation (34) is not of the form considered by the stochastic approximation literature. To accomplish the correspondence, we have to replace the conditional expectation $M_n(\hat{\theta}, \theta; \mathfrak{B}_{n-1})$ with the unconditional expectation

$$M_n(\hat{\theta}, \theta) = E_{\mathfrak{B}_{n-1}} M_n(\hat{\theta}, \theta; \mathfrak{B}_{n-1}).$$

With this substitution, equation (34) becomes

$$\hat{\theta}_n = \hat{\theta}_{n-1} - a_n M_n(\hat{\theta}_{n-1}, \theta) - a_n w_n, \tag{36}$$

where w_n is a new, unconditional disturbance.

Several difficulties arise in proving the convergence of the process defined by equations (33) and (34) by reference to standard stochastic approximation arguments based upon equation (36):

(a) The process w_n in (36) is no longer serially independent. This is essentially because the sequence $M_n(\hat{\theta}, \theta, \mathfrak{B}_{n-1}) - M_n(\hat{\theta}, \theta)$ is in general serially correlated. However, processes such as (36) with serial-correlated disturbances have been considered in the literature. Convergence can be proved but requires stronger conditions on the gain sequence $\mathbf{a}_n$. The AG condition is that $\sum_n \sup \|a_n\| < \infty$ where the supremum is taken over the arguments of $\mathbf{a}_n$ (see Appendix 1 to this chapter). Essentially the gain sequence must be of smaller order than $1/n$ as $n \to \infty$. In addition, we have to ensure that the residuals w_n have uniformly bounded variances with probability 1.

(b) A second difficulty concerns the identifiability of the parameter θ on the basis of the unconditional expectation $M_n(\hat{\theta}, \theta)$. The latter may be considered as reduced form in character relative to the conditional expectation $M_n(\hat{\theta}, \theta; \mathfrak{B}_{n-1})$. Suppose that $\hat{\theta}$ is conditionally identified in the sense of equation (35). Thus it may not be unconditionally identified in the sense that the solution to

$$M_n(\hat{\theta}, \theta) = 0 \quad \text{uniformly in } n$$

is only $\hat{\theta} = \theta$. In other words, there may be multiple values or a manifold of values of $\hat{\theta}$ that qualify as possible solutions. For example, β_1 and β may enter separately in the conditional expectation but only as the sum

$\beta_1 + \beta_2$ in the unconditional expectation. This means that in applying the standard arguments based upon the unconditional sequence (36) to prove the convergence of the process (33), all that we could possibly prove is that the sum $\beta_1 + \beta_2$ converges rather than the parameters β_1, β_2 separately. In terms of the conditions given in Section 7.3, multicollinearity difficulties will arise in terms of the notional data matrix constructed from the gradient vectors of the unconditional expectations $M_n(\hat{\theta}, \hat{\theta})$.

Note that these difficulties do not rule out another possible behavioral mode on the part of the representative agent, namely, that he (or she) thinks and acts in terms of unconditional expectations. This may be relevant if the explicit influence of the past is exerted, not by past autoregression terms as such $(\dots P_{n-1})$, but through a serially correlated disturbance. The agent may realize that successive disturbances are correlated but the nature of the correlation is too complex for him to understand. He would like to be right on the average but is prepared to live with the fact that his forecasting errors may be serially correlated. He formulates his sequential estimation procedure in terms of discrepancies of observed prices P_n from his *un*conditional expectations. Equation (36) now applies in terms of his reduced-form parameters, as it were, and no identification problems arise. Assume that the resulting estimates $\hat{\theta}_n \to \theta$, the true value, almost surely. Then his forecasts will be unbiased on the average but no longer unbiased conditional upon $\mathfrak{B}_{n-1}$, the information potentially available to him. We may term such behavior as unconditionally satisficing. As already remarked, an agent exhibiting such behavior realizes that his errors may be correlated over time but is willing to settle for being right on the average over a much longer period of time. His expectations are thus not rational but are long-term unbiased. Of course, the two notions of expectational behavior, rational and unconditionally satisficing, are one and the same if the market demand functions do not depend explicitly upon the realized past.

This concludes our example of parameter-mediated learning. In the course of this rather extended discussion, we have demonstrated a context and a framework in which under reasonably plausible behavioral assumptions, agents *may* by their individual learning procedures collectively achieve a rational-expectations equilibrium. We stress the word *may* since our discussion of the market example remains rather general. If the market demand functions are linear, the information set homogeneous, and the market disturbances serially uncorrelated, no further qualification is necessary. However, a specific demonstration that the angle, multicollinearity, and other AG conditions are actually satisfied remains necessary where one or other of the preceding specifying assumptions are not satisfied.

7.5   Some obstacles

The preceding section has been a rather lengthy discussion aimed at showing that in certain circumstances, a rational-expectations equilibrium can
be attained, the presence of reflexivity notwithstanding. In a sense it can
be regarded as presenting the convergence problem in the most favorable
light. In the present section we redress the balance, as it were, by pointing
out some problematic features of disequilibrium behavior that may in-
hibit or actually prevent a state of rational expectations from ever being
reached.

To begin with, even parametrically mediated schemes have their difficulties. Some of these will be obvious enough: One or other of the identification or angle conditions may not hold or the residuals may be serially
correlated and so forth; in other words one or more of the essential regularity conditions may be violated. Other problems are perhaps less obvious. Note, for instance, the time dependence of the recursions of Section 7.4. As a matter of estimation theory, we should be happy enough to
take as given some origin and to develop the recursion from that point.
In and of itself, this device need not imply that the representative individual starts a recursion wholly unaware of the system. One can incorporate a term into the gains a_n that allow for a contributing influence
from the prior estimate θ_0. Nevertheless, once the origin is decided (recursion time $n = 0$ at some real time point $t = t_0$), the convergence process is set into place in absolute (t) time rather than relative time. In an
ongoing world, one is led to speculate on what determined the chosen
origin, that is, the point at which the current iteration or convergence
process was started up. Perhaps this was the receipt by agents of information that underlying parameter values θ had changed, for instance,
as a result of some policy action. But if this were the case, such changes
could presumably also occur in the future, and this knowledge might be
expected to affect the updating rules used by individuals.

The preceding point has implications for the choice of gain. In general,
the true parameter θ constitutes a signal to be detected against the background noise provided by the disturbance term u_n. The latter (hopefully)
attains a constant variance, but it is never zero or even observable. In
view of our discussion, it seems reasonable to suppose that agents may
suspect that from time to time the signal θ changes. In the recursion analysis of Section 7.4, it was specified as a convergence requirement that the
gain sequence a_n should tend to zero. However, if it is suspected that θ
may change, it would seem worthwhile to "probe" the system from time
to time by arranging for $a_\tau \neq 0$ at some points of time τ. If enough people
make a practice of probing, then because of the reflexivity considerations,

the time path of the observables Y_t (or P_t) is continually being perturbed by such behavior. Post hoc, discrepancies such as $P_t - \hat{E}_{t-1} P_t$ may appear to exhibit patterned behavior, albeit of a rather irregular kind, leading individuals to suspect that their perceptions of θ may not be correct (even if they are) and revise their behavior accordingly. In such circumstances, convergence may never occur.

We remarked in Section 7.2 on the general format of an orderly convergence process: Agents are assumed to follow set rules, and every individual assumes that every other individual will follow similar rules. The presence of the kind of uncertainty described in the preceding militates against such an orderly world. Once any kind of departure from a tacitly agreed on rule is entertained, perhaps for reasons of insecurity, perturbations may arise that make it exceedingly difficult to ever filter out a time-underlying signal and hence for the system to achieve a full rational-expectations equilibrium.

Nonparameter-mediated convergence

Things become even more problematical when the very existence of parameters is predicated upon the existence of a state of rational expectations. Such a contingency was noted in Section 7.2, where we drew upon the structural model of heterogeneous information established in Section 5.3. We recall that this model featured two classes of agents, the informed and the uninformed. If every agent were informed, one structure (i.e, one set of parameters) would prevail. If some were uninformed, the parametric structure facing both sets of agents in their prediction problem is entirely different, being augmented in both cases with new serial correlation parameters. Thus a structure with no parameters of serial correlation is transformed by this limited information specification into: Like a volcanic island, parameters have appeared where there were none before.

At this point, the argument for convergence starts getting teleological. So far as parameter-driven recursion schemes are concerned, agents have the problem of initial specification: If the structure to be estimated *exists* only in a rational-expectations equilibrium, how do individuals who may have no prior knowledge of the characteristics of such an equilibrium know how to specify the structure in the framework of which learning is to take place? We saw (Appendix to Chapter 5) that in the presence of heterogeneous information, the forecasting equation facing even informed agents in a rational-expectations equilibrium was highly specific in form. Thus agents would have to know the details of that specificity. One possibility is that agents begin with an all-embracing forecasting equation, for example, autoregressive terms and lagged exogenous variables of infinite orders. As system convergence proceeds, the terms that do not (in a state of rational-expectations equilibrium) "belong" in that forecasting equation would progressively drop out, ultimately leaving only the correct rational-expectations structure. That a portmanteau approach of this kind might work receives some support from the recursive theory of real-time regression, where in the context of a simple ARMA structure Hannan (1976, 1980) has shown that regression models encompassing the true structure (i.e., the latter is nested within the specified model) can under suitable conditions converge to the true structure, with the otiose terms becoming zero. The natural nesting takes care of the problem of initial-structures specification. Unfortunately, such results cannot be directly applied to the present context; several difficulties arise, of which the most important is the reflexivity aspect. Initial attempts to forecast based upon an ultimately misspecified model, even if one of the encompassing kind, perturb the observations upon which the estimation procedure is to be based. Thus Hannan's results, which presuppose the classical context of invariant structures, do not apply, at least directly. The problem with a reflexive world is that it does not keep still long enough to examine it.

Another possible resolution is to imagine that individuals are endowed with an ability to visualize what the system might look like in a rational-expectations equilibrium. This might be viewed as a version of a principle noted by Winter (1964) that to achieve an optimal information structure, one needs information about that structure. As we noted in Chapter 5, a rational-expectations equilibrium can be viewed as a "neutral" expectational regime; it is as close as we can get to a description of the "fundamentals" of the system. Individuals may be endowed with an appreciation for such fundamentals. In specifying a forecasting procedure based upon these fundamentals, convergence to the very system that they have in their mind's eye, as it were, may very well occur. Again, however, the difficulty arises that expectations can hardly be neutral when basic information sets are incomplete or heterogeneous. It is expecting a great deal of individuals to anticipate such a structure in rational-expectations equilibrium.

Not can they, but do they?

Our stance in all the preceding discussion has been conceptual: We ask whether, given a set of agents of reasonably expert statistical understanding and technique, suitable decision rules exist that if followed would result in a rational-expectations equilibrium. Knowing, however, that such a state has been put forward as an actual empirical hypothesis (Section

5.5 in particular) a rather different question arises as to whether the kind of agents who populate the universe being considered are capable of arriving collectively at a rational-expectations equilibrium. Rutherford (1987) has very ably surveyed such capabilities and psychological propensities in learning and decision making. The general problem is that agents may very well not be very sophisticated statistically. There is experimental evidence that people do not act as good Bayesians in forming their probability judgments and predictions. For one thing they appear to be more conservative in revising their prior probabilities than Bayes's theorem would indicate; and where multivariate parameters or effects are concerned, they appear to be rather poor at judgment of covariation, which would appear to militate against sophistication in assigning a given prediction error to particular parameters. On the covariance aspect the reader is referred to, for example, Kelley (1967), Nisbett and Ross (1980), and Kelley and Michela (1980). Tversky and Kahneman (1974) have argued that people are not Bayesians at all but follow instead some simple heuristic rules in their learning and judgment procedures.

Moreover it is a matter of common knowledge in the stock market or the foreign exchange markets that many participants do not act according to any normal conception of structural models, let alone make any attempt to learn about structure, but employ instead techniques such as chartism to predict future movements. Indeed, many brokers and arbitrage houses employ specialist chartists, much as the Roman Senate contracted on a regular basis the services of diviners from the entrails of geese.

All this seems to militate against the ability or even willingness of participants to learn about the world in which they are embedded. Of course, it may well be that the heuristic decision rules that they adopt do come for some reason to be self-fulfilling. However, it would evidently be a matter for investigation as to the relationship between the heuristic rules and the embedding structure that would allow such rules to become self-fulfilling.

We may conclude that the ability of any system exhibiting reflexivity to converge to a rational-expectations equilibrium remains highly problematical. The best chances appear to obtain for simple systems in which all learning is parameter mediated, where the parameters concerned have a physical or objective meaning independent of the individual or collective action of the participants. For systems with heterogeneous information sets, convergence to a rational-expectations equilibrium may well constitute an impossibility. Yet the observation in Section 5.5 that for many systems we cannot statistically reject the rational-expectations hypothesis appears in that case to constitute a paradox, one to which we shall have to return in the final chapter.

Appendix 1. The Albert–Gardner convergence conditions

Iterating equation (11) back to $n=1$, we obtain

$$\hat{\theta}_{n+1}-\theta = \sum_{j=1}^{n} (I-\mathbf{a}_j\mathbf{h}_j')(\hat{\theta}_1-\theta) + \sum_{j=1}^{n} \sum_{i=j+1}^{n} (I-\mathbf{a}_i\mathbf{h}_i')\mathbf{a}_j\mathbf{u}_j \qquad \text{(i)}$$

where

$$\mathbf{h}_j = \frac{\partial}{\partial\hat{\theta}} M_j(\hat{\theta};\theta)\bigg|_{\hat{\theta}=\bar{\theta}_j},$$

with $\bar{\theta}_j$ some point on the line joining $\hat{\theta}_j$ and θ. It will be seen that the large-sample statistical properties of the estimator $\hat{\theta}_{n+1}$ are critically dependent on the asymptotic behavior of the matrix product

$$P_n = \sum_{j=1}^{n} (I-\mathbf{a}_j\mathbf{h}_j')$$

or at least of a suitably defined norm $\|P_n\|$ thereof. For reasons outlined in Section 7.3, it is necessary to take an indirect route to establish conditions under which $\|P_n\| = \lambda_{\max}^{1/2}(P_n'P_n) \to 0$. Albert and Gardner's (1967) first set of conditions relate to a purely deterministic sequence of arbitrary vectors $\mathbf{a}_j, \mathbf{h}_j$. We shall have $\lim_{n\to\infty}\|P_n\| = 0$ if the following assumptions hold:

A1: $\|\mathbf{a}_n\|\|\mathbf{h}_n\| \to 0$ as $n\to\infty$.

A2: $\sum_{n} \|\mathbf{a}_n\|\|\mathbf{h}_n\| = \infty$.

A3:   There exists a sequence of integers $1=v_1<v_2<v_3\ldots$ such that, with $p_k = v_{k+1}-v_k$, we have

$$p \le p_k \le q < \infty \quad (k=1,2,\ldots)$$

and

$$\liminf_{k} \frac{1}{p_k}\sum_{J_k} \lambda_{\min}\left(\frac{\mathbf{h}_j\mathbf{h}_j'}{\|\mathbf{h}_j\|^2}\right) = r^2 > 0,$$

where J_k is the index set

$$\{v_k, v_k+1, \ldots, v_{k+1}-1\}.$$

A4: $\displaystyle\limsup_{k} \frac{\max_{j\in J_k}\|\mathbf{a}_j\|\|\mathbf{h}_j\|}{\min_{j\in J_k}\|\mathbf{a}_j\|\|\mathbf{h}_j\|} = \rho < \infty.$

A5: $\displaystyle\liminf_{n} \frac{\mathbf{a}_n'\mathbf{h}_n}{\|\mathbf{a}_n\|\|\mathbf{h}_n\|} > \alpha = \sqrt{\frac{1-\tau^2}{1-\tau^2+(\tau/p)^2}}.$

Notice the strength of assumption A5, which is a uniformity assumption in which the allowable limit α depends via τ and ρ on every member of the sequence $\mathbf{a}_n, \mathbf{h}_n$; Albert and Gardner quote an example illustrating that this condition is an essential one, that is, necessary, given the other assumptions.

Once conditions for convergence of the norm $\|P_n\|$ are established, the conditions that the solution path to equation (i) converges almost surely to θ, the true value, virtually reproduce the preceding conditions given also some additional specification on the disturbance process u_n. We shall suppose that the latter is a zero-mean independent process and in particular that this process is independent of the sequence of estimates $\hat{\theta}_n$. The AG sufficient conditions for convergence are as follows (AG theorem 6.3): For every sequence $\hat{\theta}_1, \hat{\theta}_2, \ldots$ and $\mathbf{t}_1, \mathbf{t}_2, \ldots$ (t_i here means a realization of the estimated parameter values sequence), write

$$\mathbf{h}_n = \frac{\partial}{\partial \hat{\theta}} M_n(\hat{\theta}; \theta) \bigg|_{\hat{\theta} = \mathbf{t}_n}$$

and $\mathbf{a}_n = \mathbf{a}_n(\hat{\theta}_1, \hat{\theta}_2, \ldots, \hat{\theta}_n)$. Then

B1: $\lim\limits_n |\mathbf{a}_n| |\mathbf{h}_n| = 0.$

B2: $\sum\limits_n |\mathbf{a}_n| |\mathbf{h}_n| = \infty.$

B3:   There exists a sequence of integers $1 = v_1 < v_2 < v_3 \ldots$ such that with $p_k = v_{k+1} - v_k,$

$$p \le p_k < \infty \quad (k = 1, 2, \ldots)$$

and

$$\liminf\limits_n \frac{1}{p_k} \lambda_{\min} \left(\sum\limits_{j \in J_k} \frac{\mathbf{h}_j \mathbf{h}_j'}{|\mathbf{h}_j|^2} \right) = \tau^2 > 0$$

where $J_k = \{v_k, v_k + 1, \ldots, v_{k+1} - 1\}.$

B4: $\limsup\limits_k \dfrac{\max_{j \in J_k} |\mathbf{a}_j| |\mathbf{h}_j|}{\min_{j \in J_k} |\mathbf{a}_j| |\mathbf{h}_j|} = \rho < \infty.$

B5: $\liminf\limits_n \dfrac{\mathbf{a}_n' \mathbf{h}_n}{|\mathbf{a}_n| |\mathbf{h}_n|} > \infty = \sqrt{\dfrac{1 - \tau^2}{1 - \tau^2 + (\tau/p)^2}}.$

B6: $\{u_n\}$ is a zero-mean independent process and $\sum_n \sup |\mathbf{a}_n|^2 < \infty.$

CHAPTER 8

The view from within

8.1 Introduction

Throughout this study we have stressed the idea that the statistician, whether he (or she) is a dominant player or one insignificant player among many, is part of the system that he is studying; that his is a view from within. In this, the last chapter, we shall review some of the implications of this principle as we have established them in previous chapters and take the opportunity to add a little here and there in the interests of rounding off. Section 8.2 is concerned with the statistical problems arising in the identification of equilibrium structures. The existence of phases of disequilibrium, perhaps during learning or temporary breakdowns of cooperative behavior, will result in argument instability, which implies that the specified disturbances (in, say, a regression context) will not exhibit invariant or stable behavior. The most that one can then hope for is the applicability of conclusions based upon large-sample theory. In such circumstances, the statistical profession's passion for small-sample (or "exact") results may be misplaced. Section 8.3 looks at the problem of structure, reviewing the conclusions that we have arrived at concerning the existence of a stable invariant structure and the pitfalls of a naive positivist methodology in hoping to identify such a structure if it does exist. Section 8.4 turns to the problem of observer-dependent systems, both in the structural aspect (as in rational-expectations models with heterogeneous information) and in the dominant-player mode, the characteristic modus operandi of the professional statistician. In both cases the structure to be identified is in fact observer dependent, as is the use of that structure for predictive purposes. If it is recognized that the statistician is embedded in a game, then the problem of statistical design may be identified with the choice of an optimal strategy for the statistician. Section 8.5 argues for a more activist view of the design process based on this principle. Section 8.6 represents a rather speculative foray into the statistical mechanics of human affairs, drawing on some of the insights from previous chapters. The target for this particular pie-throwing foray is the notion of the stationary stochastic process as it applies to human affairs. We argue that under reflexivity, the existence of inherent nonlinearities combines with the vagaries of change to induce a nonstationary and perhaps even chaotic statistical progression of events. Section 8.7 is a short valedictory section.

8.2 The empirical identification of equilibrium structures

Possibilities for the empirical estimation of socioeconomic structures involving reflexivity begin and in some cases end with the identification of empirical regularities with the operations of the structure in a state of equilibrium. Our understanding of disequilibrium adjustment is limited, to say the least. Nor is the difficulty confined to the imperfections of human understanding. In situations (such as financial markets) where agents constantly monitor their profits or losses, any predictable regularity that emerged in a disequilibrium adjustment may well evoke behavior that will destroy that regularity; so a disequilibrium phase may of necessity be chaotic rather than orderly. It is not surprising, therefore, that where empirical regularities are seen or suspected to exist, recourse is in the first instance to their explanation by means of an equilibrium model.

That the equilibrium structure may well be overlain by disequilibrium elements has an interesting implication for the theory of sampling error and in particular for the distinction between large-sample and small-sample (or exact) theories. As is well known, the sampling theory of various estimators and associated tests of hypotheses is relatively straightforward to work out when the sample size is large ($n \to \infty$) by courtesy of the various versions of the laws of large numbers and the central-limit theorem. The corresponding theory for a finite sample size is usually much more difficult. Whereas one often settles for the asymptotic theory, this is usually seen in the light of faute de mieux – the best we can do – because the exact results cannot be derived, or if they can, the densities turn out to be extremely complicated and not amenable to tabulation.

Now finite-sample theory is typically built on strict invariance and specification assumptions. For instance, in a regression type of framework, the disturbances are assumed to be generated by some stable and invariant law (e.g., white noise or a constant-parameter ARMA mechanism). However, one can argue that this is not likely to be the case in the kind of reflexive contexts we have been studying; and from this we can go on to argue the relative importance of large-sample theory and the limited relevance of small-sample theory.

Suppose, to begin with, that one is (an external observer) studying a linear reflexive system

$$p_t = \gamma_1' \mathbf{w}_t + \gamma_2 \hat{p}_{t/t-1} + \epsilon_t. \tag{1}$$

The notational conventions are those of Chapter 5: $\hat{p}_{t/t-1}$ is an arbitrary predictor of p_t given some information set $\mathcal{I}_{t-1}$, which we shall suppose contains the past exogenous variables $\mathbf{w}_{t-i}$ for $i \geq 1$ and those elements of $\mathbf{w}_t$ known as of time $t-1$ (e.g., seasonals). The structural disturbance ϵ_t is independently and identically distributed (i.i.d.) white noise. Now consider the specific predictor given by

$$p_{t/t-1}^e = \frac{1}{1-\gamma_2} \gamma_1' E(\mathbf{w}_t / \mathcal{I}_{t-1}). \tag{2}$$

This will be recognized as the rational-expectations predictor if equation (1) referred to a system already in a rational-expectations equilibrium. By assumption, our system is *not* in such a state: Individuals may be trying to form the rational-expectations predictor (2) but do not know the parameters (γ) or at least the correct reduced-form parameters $\gamma_1/(1-\gamma_2)$. Following the system-learning discussion of Chapter 7, we shall however suppose that the system is in the process of converging to a rational-expectations equilibrium. This means that the divergence $\hat{p}_{t/t-1} - p_{t/t-1}^e$ is almost surely approaching zero as t becomes large in the process of real-time system learning.

Equation (1) may be written

$$p_t = \gamma_1' \mathbf{w}_t + \gamma_2 p_{t/t-1}^e + u_t, \tag{3}$$

where $u_t \triangleq \gamma_2(\hat{p}_{t/t-1} - p_{t/t-1}^e) + \epsilon_t$ and $p_{t/t-1}^e$ is generated according to equation (2). Suppose that an external observer sets up the model

$$p_t = \gamma_1' \mathbf{w}_t + \gamma_2 p_{t/t-1}^e + \zeta_t, \tag{4}$$

where ζ_t is i.i.d. white noise, and attempts to estimate this model by one or more of the consistent identification methods of the rational-expectations literature (see Section 5.6). The data are actually generated by equation (3). Finite-sample theory would assume that for any given sample ($t = 1, 2, ..., n$) the disturbance sequence ζ_t would be i.i.d. white noise. This is true if the system is already in a rational-expectations equilibrium for then $\zeta_t \equiv \epsilon_t$. For a finite sample starting from the point of learning, however, we will not have $\hat{p}_{t/t-1} = p_{t/t-1}^e$, and a specification error is being committed.

Asymptotically, it does not matter. If system learning is convergent, the true disturbance u_t approaches the i.i.d. sequence ϵ_t almost surely. Thus the limiting behavior of consistent estimation schemes for the parameters γ_1, γ_2 will be those of the rational-expectations scheme (4) with $\zeta_t = \epsilon_t$. Provided that agents are converging in their predictions to a rational-expectations equilibrium, the structural parameters are identifiable by an external observer who sets the problem up as one already in a rational-expectations equilibrium.

It might be remarked that the kind of learning experiment involved is a rather extreme one: At some time $t = 0$ all agents with the same initial information sets are supposed to commence learning. Various alternative possibilities exist. Agents may commence with different prior distributions for the parameters they have to learn (Bray and Savin, 1986); equivalently, they may commence their learning at different times so that at any given point in time they have reached differing estimated probability distribution functions or Bayesian priors for the ensuing time period. A different and potentially more troublesome contingency is that agents may exhibit probing behavior, as described in Chapter 7, with the object of testing for changes in the system in which they are embedded. Even if a system being perturbed in this way is still amenable to the consistent estimation by an external observer of the structural parameters (e.g., γ_1, γ_2), it may be characterized by a permanent quasi-disequilibrium contribution to system "noise" from the probing behavior. Thus the equilibrium innovational variance $\sigma^2 = E\epsilon_t^e$ may not be identifiable even asymptotically.

The question of large- versus small-sample theory also arises, at least implicitly, in the notion of argument stability raised in Section 6.6. There we saw that periods of cooperative equilibrium could be interspersed with disequilibrium periods. In the latter regimes, individuals would not be reacting in terms of announced or observed independent variables but instead to unobserved values of some internally generated inputs. The implied model (at least in the regression context) is of the form

$$y_i = \beta' \mathbf{x}_i^* + \epsilon_i, \quad i = 1, 2, \ldots, n, \tag{5}$$

where the $\mathbf{x}_i^*$ are latent variables. Observed values $\mathbf{x}_i$ are equal to $\mathbf{x}_i^*$, for $i \in E$, equilibrium periods but bear no relationship (in the absence of further theorizing) for i belonging to disequilibrium periods. Note, of course, that only part, instead of the whole, of the vector $\mathbf{x}_i^*$ could be affected by the wedge between observed and actual inputs that is driven by the disequilibrium periods.

At first sight, model (5), with the convention on the relationship between $\mathbf{x}_i^*$ and $\mathbf{x}_i$, looks like the classical missing-observations model [for a review, see Anderson et al. (1983)], and this is indeed true if we have independent information as to which observations i fall in the equilibrium phase and which do not.

However, this is not necessarily the case. Suppose it is not. Let us write

$$x = x^* + \delta, \quad \delta = 0 \text{ if } i \in E.$$

Then model (5) becomes, in terms of the observable $\mathbf{x}_i$,

$$y_i = \beta' \mathbf{x}_i + (\epsilon_i - \beta' \delta_i).$$

The condition for consistency of the resulting estimate of β in least-squares methodology is that

$$\text{plim} \left[\frac{1}{n} \sum_{i=1}^{n} x_i \delta_i' \right] \beta = 0, \tag{6}$$

where we suppose that the structural disturbance ϵ_i is independent of the elements of x_i. The condition (6) is in most circumstances equivalent to

$$\text{plim} \, \frac{1}{n} \sum_i x_i x_i' = \text{plim} \, \frac{1}{n} \sum_i x_i x_i^{*'}.$$

A leading special case is where

$$\text{plim} \, \frac{1}{n} \sum_i \delta_i \delta_i' = 0,$$

meaning effectively that the number and extent of disequilibrium occasions increases at a rate slower than n. Such a circumstance would apply if individuals were gradually learning to live together in the mooted cooperative equilibrium or whatever other equilibrium will emerge as a viable solution to the implied game between agents. Disequilibrium departures occur, but less frequently as time progresses. In this case, the effect of using the observations that would correspond to an equilibrium state (the x_i) in place of the true values (the x_i^*) would in the long run not be crucial for the consistency of the resulting estimators. Note again, however, the inapplicability of small-sample theory to this sort of problem. In both this case and the model with learning, the equilibrium structure is perturbed by sporadic disequilibrium-type departures. The latter are not predictable, lending a chaotic type of behavior to the model disturbances. As a matter of asymptotic theory, however, the consistency of the estimators developed predicated on an equilibrium model will continue to hold. In the long run, empirical regularities will encapsulate the equilibrium structure, and as a model of sampling error, asymptotic theory is more likely to apply than is the finite-sample theory with its extreme assumptions regarding short-run invariance and model stability.

8.3   The problem of structure

So far we have not been very precise about what constitutes a structure, equilibrium or otherwise. Most social scientists would probably share a common mental perception of structure as the framework within which causality operates. It is intimately related to the problem of control (or its alter ego, prediction) since a knowledge of the structure would enable us to predict what happens when one of its inputs is adjusted or when one of the constituent elements of the framework is removed or replaced. The idea of structure as absolute probably represents an unattainable abstract: Behind every proposed structure lurks another of greater comprehensiveness. All that one can hope to identify is the order of structure that enables one to predict, with a reasonable degree of accuracy, the outcomes of the kinds of policy experiment that are of actual or potential concern. This does of course entail the possibility that the kind of structural understanding thought sufficient by one generation of social scientists may be realized as inadequate by the next, much as Newtonian mechanics was eventually replaced by general relativity and quantum field theory and as these in their turn may well turn out to be special cases. Nevertheless one could in principle hope to identify a structure to a desired order by subjecting the system to a series of policy trials, varying this or that input or adopting alternative policy rules, and observing the outcome.

A much more limited view has been espoused in economics in particular, according to which structure – and hence the policy predictions based on it – can be inferred from historically observed regularities in the behavior of a certain variable or of the relationship between two or more variables. For example, on the basis of a claim of an empirical regularity between nominal income and the money supply, a causal relationship is held to exist, leading in turn to the policy prediction that control of the money supply can affect in a predictable way the evolution of nominal income. The empirical claim is based largely upon historical time series data. Associated with this particular claim is a methodological philosophy of naive positivism, which holds that no matter how much a theory might offend the intuition or introspective habits of thought of the observer, it should be judged only upon empirical grounds, the latter to be based on the predictive performance of the theory (in the ordinary course of events) and on its historical coincidence with the observed data in general.

The notion of an empirical regularity, both in its existence and in its deeper predictive significance, does indeed seem to lie at the very heart of any socioeconomic science. Nevertheless, we have seen throughout the present study various aspects of the difficulties (a) in asserting the existence of empirical regularities and (b) in their interpretation or usefulness for policy purposes.

The existence problem came to the fore in discussing the possibility of rational expectations with heterogeneous information sets among the participating agents. We saw that the optimum predictors for informed and uninformed agents will differ but must in each case be of a specific form. In a rational-expectations equilibrium, the parameters that agents need to know for forecasting purposes are themselves functions of underlying structural parameters and are not necessarily known to the informed, certainly not to the uninformed. Thus the parameters that agents must know are constructs and depend upon the particular partition currently holding of the information sets between agents. Should these information sets change, then the parameters of agents' optimal prediction rules will also change. We remarked in Chapter 7 on the difficulty that ensues, namely, that following such a change, parameters have no independent existence and can exist only when the correct new equilibrium is reestablished. This leaves our participating individuals with very little guidance as to how to learn about the new system. Thus in a reflexive system equilibrium and the associated empirical regularities may never come to exist. Or convergence may occur but very slowly and be subject to continued and major disruptions. The empirical detection of even the longest run empirical regularities may in such circumstances be extremely imprecise, if not downright impossible.

Even if empirical regularities do exist, further difficulties may arise in their interpretation for purposes of policy. We reviewed (the Marshak–Lucas critique) the problems that arise when a historical empirical regularity is confused with the "true" structure. The empirical work may have been performed with respect to a period when one type of regulatory policy has been used; it may then constitute a poor or quite misleading guide to the setting of a new policy rule.

This problem comes to a head where the observed empirical regularity results from an underlying structure incorporating the expectations of participating agents. The basic task is now to postulate how expectations are formed (as an additional element of structure) and to estimate those parameters of the augmented structure that do remain invariant to changes in policy rules. We saw in this respect that since informed expectations may involve anticipating the actions of a policymaker, a game-theoretic aspect arises. It may be that the resulting estimation problem has a solution, so to speak, only in the equilibrium of the resulting game. Once again, therefore, we arrive at the necessity of a state of equilibrium to exist in order to be able to infer anything about structure.

Moreover, given the time inconsistency problem and similar game-theoretic phenomena, it may not at all be the case that the true structure can be revealed empirically as a conventional, mechanically estimable regression or Markovian-type law of evolution. For as we remarked in Section 6.5, it may be that in a game-theoretic equilibrium, a perfectly stable "behavioral" function apparently exists, and one can proceed with uplifted hope to estimate its parameters. Yet an empirical regularity inferred in this way will mask the true features of the situation, namely, that individuals and/or the policymaker are playing a game that can potentially degenerate into unstable or disequilibrium behavior. The apparent behavior in the equilibrium state may reflect a kind of aliasing rather than the true structure.

In summary, one should be extremely cautious about accepting a naive positivist methodology. Where reflexivity, expectations, and gamelike elements are involved, a past historical record can be quite misleading in predicting the consequences of an altered policy regime. To identify the structure relevant for such purposes may well require a methodology that is not simply based on the historical data but incorporates also contributions from introspection and explicit theorizing.

Moreover, this contribution may very well extend to the acquisition of data, even in cases where the structure is as simple as a single parameter value. In Chapters 2 and 3, we investigated in detail the implications of a reactive sample space for survey response. A cognate sample space implies that people will be aware of the statistician, his or her purpose, and the possible outcomes of the findings. Although it may be that agents are small in their individual effect, implicit or tacit coalitions emerge whose acts of commission or omission with respect to response can materially affect the veracity of the statistician's view of the world. Selection bias might arise from differential response rates. Or individuals may judge it in their best interests to respond untruthfully.

All this raises the design problem of how to encourage nondifferential and truthful response or the estimation problem of how to correct for nonresponse or veracity bias from the data that has been obtained. This could take the form either of inducements that would render truthful response a dominant strategy or, as an extreme case, of legal threats to penalize nonresponse and untruthful response. A more subtle approach where nonresponse bias is concerned is to make use of the social awareness of the population. Here the idea was to tap the information that exists at large among the population regarding the facts of interest, along with the natural desire of its members to pursue their own self-interest. Publication of preliminary survey results could create homeostatic influences if these results were in apparent conflict with the social apprehensions of the participating population.

One rarely obtains information directly in the social sciences. It has instead to pass through a filter – attitudinal, emotional, financial, and so on. Because agents have an awareness of the measurement processes, the filter may well turn out to be purposive and biasing in its effects. The theory of socioeconomic statistics could be regarded quite as much an exercise in anticipatory ingenuity in bias avoidance as a matter of the traditional analysis of the sampling theory of standard estimation formulas.

8.4   Observer-dependent systems

We have reviewed the problem of detection of a structure that neverthe-less remains invariant throughout the detection process, even if the filter through which it is observed does change in response to the agents' per-ception of the statistician and his or her purpose. However, this is only half the problem. We have suggested that in important instances, the structure that is the object of investigation will itself be affected by the process of measurement, the publication of the results, or both. In this kind of world, no role exists for a passive provider of information or a truly disinterested seeker after the truth. All parties are now players in a game, as it were, acting on the basis of information that they receive, with the dissemination of information as much a player action as is its provision.

We have classified the problems that arise in terms of the implied game being played between those who seek information and those who provide it. The "small-player" paradigm has received much attention in the litera-ture on rational expectations in economics. Players view themselves as powerless to change things: the equilibrium concept is that of the non-cooperative Nash equilibrium, in which each agent takes as given the col-lective decisions of other players and acts accordingly. All parties in this kind of world are statisticians, but there is no special role for the public dissemination of information. Each player has roughly the same sort of information – although some may be better endowed in this respect than others – and agents carry out the same generic estimation procedures. The actions based upon these observations and estimates generate a new state of affairs and hence a new set of observations, estimates, and actions.

Perhaps the most interesting case in this sort of paradigm arises where the players have heterogeneous information sets and parameters necessary for prediction become defined only in the resulting rational-expectations equilibrium. We have labeled the resulting system-learning task (finding the way to the equilibrium) as *nonparameter-mediated* learning and re-viewed the difficulties inherent in convergence under these conditions. It does appear that a degree of a priori knowledge of what the optimal pre-dictors would look like in equilibrium is necessary for the agents to col-lectively find their way to that equilibrium. An uncomfortably teleolog-ical aspect, this evidently constitutes a rather extreme case of Winter's dictum that to be able to deduce anything about structure, one needs to know something of the structure to begin with. In general, the disequi-librium theory – and hence the estimation theory – of the decentralized model remains problematic.

Both more familiar and probably more tractable is the model of the statistician as a dominant player, recognized by the other participants in the implied game as an information gatherer, a public resource, whose findings are usually returned to the public in the form of published results; so that his or her subjects become also the audience. Publication augments the information sets of participating individuals to a greater or lesser degree depending upon the credibility of the statistician and of the findings. So far as the information influences their actions, publication therefore changes the state of the system and the data of interest. We have noted that it is not essential for the information published to be correct, simply that it is believed. One can construct a model, which appears at times to apply to financial markets, in which the "information" published is in reality quite uncorrelated with fundamentals or at least contains extraneous contributions of this character. But provided agents believe that the information does have substance, a self-fulfilling equilibrium results in which the information does acquire genuine predictive power: Pseudoinformation becomes real information – the snake oil actually works. As to credibility and belief, we noted that where an agent realizes that he (or she) is one among many, the credibility of any piece of published information depends upon the agent's perceptions or anticipations on how other agents will react, the expectations-about-expectations problem. Such second-order effects drive a wedge between the individual agent's own skepticism about a published prediction (as a reflection of the current state of play) and appreciation of the possible outcome (once the reactions of others are taken into account). In general, it might be remarked that we are constantly being bombarded with opinions, putative facts, and predictions, only a few of which exert much influence on the evolution of human affairs. The question of which announcements do acquire causal significance (are viewed as credible and evoke a reaction) properly belongs to the real world of social psychology. Nevertheless, it is a question that deserves to be studied further and one that no socioeconomic statistician can afford to ignore in its various implications for a reactive sample space.

Given, however, that the published information is regarded as authoritative and convincing, it may be expected to alter people's behavior in some way. We saw that in the context of a structural model characterized by heterogeneous information sets, publication of the model by an external observer could, by augmenting the information sets of the relatively less informed, drive the system into a disequilibrium from which a new equilibrium may (or may not) emerge. This new equilibrium will not in general be the same as that existing prior to publication. The publication of an estimated structural model may therefore come to constitute a self-defeating exercise in economic history.

Perhaps the most recognizable effect of publication originates in more or less classical prediction contexts, where in recent years we have witnessed some clear indications that publication of a forecast has exerted an independent effect upon the eventual outcome. The noticeability of this sort of effect (the "Los Angeles" effect as it has become known in the travel industry) is doubtless due to the increasing frequency of major sporting and cultural events, all of which are promoted vigorously both at home and abroad. These events carry with them not only the prospect of economic success but also the portent of financial disaster. Mistakes in forecasting can and have been critical in this respect. Their scale and noticeability cast a shadow upon the received theory of prediction in its application to socioeconomic affairs.

Since publication can evidently affect the event being forecast, the statistician acquires the status of the dominant player in a forecasting game. The strategies available include (a) lying, (b) declining to publish a forecast once it is prepared, and (c) choosing to replicate the forecasting exercise one or more times.

We have not treated the first possibility – actually lying – in any detail, although we have remarked on the temptation to lie where it is suspected that reactions are strongly sloping in the vicinity of a breakeven point for success. It is, however, worth noting that purveying an untruth is often not as simple as a direct lie but may include a disregard of evidence that may in time entail unfavorable manifestations. For example, if the forecast is based upon a survey of intentions, it needs no very great sophistication to realize that strategic motives exist for respondents to overstate their probability of attendance (at an event) and that in the absence of any formal discrimination device to detect untruthfulness, the results of such surveys need to be discounted against this kind of enthusiasm. A forecast that is not properly discounted may amount to the suppression of unfavorable indications.

Alternatively, the statistician in the role of dominant player may decide to simply not release a forecast. Perhaps the event is already committed, beyond the planning stage, and those who commission the forecast may feel that its publication would result in unfavorable impressions: For instance, people may not come because of fears of overcrowding, or alternatively, prospective exhibitors may be deterred by forecasts of poor attendance. Now if the forecast is replicated, a second forecast may turn out to be more favorable, if for no other reason than it constitutes a second realization of the normal sampling error. If such a forecast is then released, it will be true that statistically speaking, the *published* forecast acquires a selective character from the implied censoring and is therefore biased as an estimate of true intentions. Apart from those produced as a matter of course or as a legal or contractual requirement, one ought therefore to view with some suspicion the credentials of any published forecast. On the other hand, we should be clear as to the nature of the bias. The published forecast may be biased as a representation of current views or intentions, but if people react favorably to it, the forecast may very well be unbiased or even conservative when viewed in terms of its post hoc predictive success.

A third course of action is to replicate the survey. We have already observed that grounds can exist for treating this as a corrective device in the theory of survey response, inducing a more representative sample. However, the corrective element can apply directly to modify in a desirable fashion the information sets of participating individuals. Thus, if prospective visitors would otherwise be turned away by the prospect of overcrowding, a second survey revealing this discouragement will ameliorate those fears. Beyond this lies a dynamics of estimation, publication, and response. Electoral polls constitute one example, where repeated surveys have come to be regarded as a normal state of affairs. Following publication, the state of the system (attitudes, intentions, etc.) changes. Unless the current state happens to coincide with fixed points of the implied reaction function, the lack of coincidence between forecast and intentions continues no matter how many replications have taken place, although a stationary distribution both of state parameters and of the estimates is, under suitable conditions, eventually arrived at. However, this somewhat indecisive state of affairs can be improved upon. For purposes of forecasting, it turns out in some respects desirable to replace the current review of intentions by a running mean of past and current measurements or more generally a stochastic approximation predictor. Such a forecast converges quickly to the fixed point of the underlying reaction function. The forecast will therefore be at least unbiased.

However, the pursuit of unbiasedness, while doubtlessly good for the statistician's reputation, may have adverse welfare implications. Thus a fixed-point property, if achieved, does not necessarily coincide with the optimization of general community welfare. This sort of consideration forces a realization that where matters of prediction are concerned, there is no such thing as an external observer. Notwithstanding doubts as to who employs the statistician and for what purpose, the conception is often claimed, at least implicitly, of the statistician as a scientific and impartial observer. However, if the decision to publish the survey or forecast is within his or her power of independent action, then there exists the power to influence events. Even such an apparently innocuous matter as whether to replicate a survey carries with it the knowledge that this may affect community welfare or affect the state of the system in a way that is ultimately in conflict with the statistician's own protestations of neutrality.

A further interesting aspect of the dominant-player view of prediction lies in its extremely modest view of structure or at least of the necessity to draw inference about any underlying structure. Thus our treatment of this problem eschewed the approach of trying to identify the form or parameters of any underlying reaction function in favor of a nonparametric approach. The task was instead reformulated as one of devising a predictor that remained invariant to reaction whatever the latter might be. In a sense, this sort of procedure falls within an established line of thought in socioeconomic methodology that regards the identification of the ultimate structure as far too troublesome both in specification and in data requirements. According to this view, the effort may be unnecessary since empirical regularities with a smaller and more innocuous structural content (e.g., the "reduced form" of the econometricians) will suffice for purposes of prediction or policy. We have dwelt at length on the potential traps with this sort of approach. However, the general approach might remain viable if it could be sanitized in some way so that the forecasting (or control) procedure would work whatever the underlying structure, from among a given set of possible structures, could take. A forecast constructed in terms of the running mean of sufficient statistics from survey replications or its stochastic approximation generalization is a potential example of this sort of approach.

8.5   Statistical design and strategic behavior

It is probably fair to say that we have two predominant approaches to experimental design in socioeconomic statistics: that inherited from biometrics as the classical theory of the statistical design of experiments and, on the other hand, no design at all. The latter "approach by default," as it were, is commonly attributed to the cultural, institutional, or moral barriers to effective experimentation in the social sciences. Once we recognize that gamelike behavior is involved in our collection of statistics and in the reactions and outcomes of their publication or application, it should then also be recognized that such a bipartite theory of experimental design is at best incomplete. For if data collection is a game to be played by the statistician against the audience, then statistical design can be interpreted as the problem of finding optimal strategies for the statistician.

We have already referred to one such area of application of this principle in connection with problems of encouraging both nonselective response and truthful revelation. For example, one way of coping with nontruthful revelation is to insert some encouragement that would make truth telling the dominant response strategy on the part of the subjects or at least enable discriminatory testing for residual untruthfulness. Likewise, the feasibility of replicating a survey could assist with the problem of encouraging a more complete nonselective survey response. So far as the established literature on such matters is concerned, the technique of randomized responses could be regarded in this light as a statistician strategy the object of which is to enable truth telling to emerge as a costless strategy on the part of the subjects.

Experimental design extends also to problems of prediction, and we have seen in detail how the replication facility can be used to control for publication effects. If one does wish to pursue a final equilibrium to such dominant-player predictive games, then replication can be used to find the fixed point. The experimental design, in other words, calls for a replicated survey with publication at each step.

A rather more radical prospect was that of the real-time survey, in which subjects have access to progress scores as information conditioning their own responses. We remarked that such a device could not only ensure convergence to an equilibrium without the cost of replication, but might also be used to correct problems of differential self-selection in response. It is still too early to assess whether such a scheme is feasible or will actually perform as anticipated. Yet real-time survey schemes are a good example of a proactive approach to the problem of statistical design in the face of a reactive sample space.

The moral seems to be this, that once we realize that games are involved, our thoughts run naturally to questions of strategy. On this view, statistical design in the social sciences is a matter of the optimal choice of strategy on the part of the statistician with the aim of countering and establishing a working equilibrium with the corresponding strategies on the part of subjects and any other interested party. There is an unfortunate tendency to view any data, however obtained, as measuring what it is purported to measure. In our rush to apply ever more sophisticated inferential and predictive formulas, we appear to have overlooked or suppressed the suspicion that we may already have lost the game or that it may no longer be worth playing. Emphasis on experimental design as strategy may help to introduce a more activist kind of ingenuity into the processes of data collection and dissemination.

8.6   Innovation and the statistical mechanics of human affairs

In the analysis of the statistical dynamics of socioeconomic systems, model builders and statisticians have made heavy use of the theory of stationary stochastic systems inherited from the physical sciences. Where departures from strict stationarity are entertained, they are typically of predictably regular if not ad hoc form – for example, a Markov process with parameters obeying a random walk. Innovations are entertained but are identified statistically with white-noise disturbance or forcing terms and as such are themselves regarded as stationary processes; moreover the system dynamics acts on these forcing terms in a regular, time-invariant way. One wonders, however, whether both innovations and their effects are quite so easily to be modeled in a system of reactive human agents.

The biblical dictum that there is nothing new under the sun has always seemed to this author a gross underestimate of human ingenuity, whether one is discussing the progress of science and technology, the flights of artistic imagination, or the ways of men to inflict suffering upon others. Motivation is the mother of originality, and we should not therefore be surprised that if there is money to be made, new ways will be found to make it. The stock market has always been a fascinating study in the statistical mechanics of innovation and information flows. Analysts have long recognized the importance of new economic information in the determination of stock or bond prices. Perhaps just as important has been a continual flow of a different kind of innovation, namely, claims to the understanding of its dynamics or new methodologies for the prediction of stock market prices. At the time of writing, for instance, stockbrokers and investment companies are investing millions of dollars in what amounts to a continuing act of faith that the movements of stock markets can be successfully predicted. Each such team will ride its mathematical hobbyhorse and may acquire to a greater or lesser extent its band of camp followers. Just as surely the mathematical hobbyhorses will eventually ride off into their computerized sunset, and their followers will quietly fold their stools and scuttle off in pursuit of a new orthodoxy.

What is of interest about such episodes is not so much the insight that they offer into the psychology of fear, hope, and the herd instinct as the realization that the movement of stock prices as the outcome cannot possibly be regarded, under any transformation, as a stationary stochastic process. In part this is a matter of the irregularity and unpredictability of informational innovations. But it is as much a matter of phenomena based upon awareness and reflexivity, the internal information-driven dynamics that follows the innovations. Consider, for instance, a market potentially influenced by any one of several soothsayers, each of whom has developed his (or her) own structural model of forecasting. The credibility attached to any forecaster depends upon his relative success, that is, whether his forecasts have unexpectedly proved close to the mark. Thus the Henry Kaufmans and Robert Prechters of this world acquire credibility predominantly because at at least one point in time they have made a successful forecast when others have not. Now imagine that we are to forecast the market two or more years ahead. At the end of one year we know that one of these forecasters will have been proved right in his one-year projection. He will acquire credibility and under reflexivity the market will correspondingly be influenced as to its actual direction by his forecast. We may begin to perceive the magnitude of our long-term forecasting problem. The market may eventually follow any one of a number of structures, each determined by reflexivity and whatever comes out of the successful forecaster's head (or computer); and the choice of these structures is determined by the contingency that this forecaster rather than the others happened to be correct in the interim, a contingency that in spite of any economic expertise on his part remains a chance event. We therefore have a nonlinear structure heavily influenced by its own sample realizations, a classic recipe for nonstationary processes. Moreover, the dynamic behavior of the resulting system may be chaotic in the technical sense: Small differences in the initial conditions have substantial and unpredictable consequences. Thus the subsequent behavior of the system may be entirely different if forecaster A wins the interim forecasting prize than if forecaster B happens to win.

Financial markets constitute one of the more immediately recognizable applications of reflexive forecasting theory, dependent as they are so heavily on the access of new information and with a volatility borne out of reactions to that information. However, we might expect nonstationarity to apply also to other reflexive forecasting situations of the dominant-player variety – or more correctly here, the oligarchic model with several influential forecasters. Such situations might arise in macroeconomics, where public expectations about inflation or interest rates might be influenced by macroeconomic forecasting firms, academic pundits, or government agencies. As in the financial marketplace, the decisions of producers, investors, and consumers are conditioned by the information available to them, and the relative credibility of the forecasters acquires considerable power; if credibility is determined in terms of a particular realization of the stochastic process, then the same sources of nonstationarity arise.

The rational-expectations hypothesis

In earlier chapters we referred at various points to the apparent empirical success of the rational-expectations hypothesis in "explaining" (if only by default) the movements of stock prices, forex prices, and so forth. What is really meant is that our statistical methodology has been unable to pick up any systematic influence on current prices from the past. On a conceptual level this is hardly surprising; If such systematic influences did exist, market participants would surely come to know it and profit from the knowledge. However, to extend this to the idea that the current prices are identical with the mathematical expectation of the future price given current information is a more debatable proposition. We remarked previously on the highly nonstationary, nonergodic time path that we might expect such a price series to follow. We have also remarked on the game-theoretic nature of such markets. It is a safe enough fact of common observation that large players can and do have a temporary influence on the movement of foreign exchange or bond prices. One could think of this as their profit from the deliberate creation of temporary disequilibria. From the statistical point of view, then, activities add to the chaotic nature of the series they help to create. Given this intrinsically erratic time path, it is a moot point whether market participants can ever form the mathematical or even subjective expectations required of them by the rational-expectations theory. It is even more of a moot point whether the series can be represented as a random walk: $p_t = p_{t-1} + \epsilon_t$, with a stationary or semistationary innovations process ϵ_t. Thus if the rational-expectations hypothesis is interpreted to refer to the inevitability of rejection by current statistical methodology of invariant predictability, then in our view it must be accepted. If, on the other hand, it has more substantive behavioral content in terms of the formation and nature of unbiased expectations, then the verdict must be nonproven. One implication of this distinction is that were a new statistical methodology (or specification) of some kind to be devised, the rational-expectations hypothesis might historically now be rejected. But once this new methodology entered the public domain, the hypothesis could eventually reestablish itself. On the empirical level, therefore, the rational-expectations hypothesis is one that is intrinsically dependent on the development of time series methodology.

8.7   Final cadence

This book has been about statistical inference, the identification of structure and prediction in the social sciences. It has been written at a time of detectable pessimism in the empirical social sciences, in particular in the field of economics. The fervor and optimism that permeates the published work of the fifties and sixties was grounded on the tacit assumption that the mechanics of socioeconomic systems ran true to form: The observable data was generated by a stable underlying model, certainly one that retained its integrity when subjected to the processes of observation and publication, or remained as a basis for prediction in the face of changes in the generation of social or economic policy. If things did not at times seem to work out too well, this could be attributed in a deprecatory paragraph to shortcomings of the available data. The solution was to devote more resources to removing bugs in the data or to achieve a finer temporal or functional disaggregation. We are much less sanguine today, although many of the old school of econometricians and social statisticians still exist, latter-day schoolmen honing ever finer the cutting edge of inapplicable methodology.

We have argued that problems of identification, inference, and forecasting in the social sciences are not to be treated as a more or less mechanical extension of classical statistical or physical systems theory. Our basic problems do not lie with statistical methodology as such but stem from a lack of methodological imagination. It took the rational expectationists, whatever the exaggerations and limitations of their claims, to make us realize that to describe and account for the behavior of a social system, data and statistical techniques are not sufficient: We are dealing with a sample space that is cognitive and anticipative. Socioeconomic statistics is not just an exercise in applied statistics, it is also a study of the political economy of information, anticipation, and prediction, a nexus of interactions that spans the statistician as well as his or her subjects and to which the methodology of game theory in principle also applies. And whereas some of the rational-expectations school proclaim the death of structural econometrics, as the empirical social science closest to their study, we are more sanguine. Things may have gotten harder, but the study of socioeconomic methodology has ceased to be a mechanical and low-caste offshoot of mathematical statistics; it has taken on a life of its own.

References

Albert, A. E., and L. A. Gardner (1967). *Stochastic approximation and nonlinear regression*. Cambridge, Mass.: M.I.T. Press.

Andersen, T. M., and F. Schneider (1986). "Coordination of fiscal and monetary policy under different institutional arrangements." Working paper no. 8602, Department of Economics, University of Linz, Austria.

Anderson, A. B., A. Basilevsky, and D. P. J. Hum (1983). "Measurement: theory and techniques," in P. H. Rossi, J. D. Wright, and A. B. Anderson (eds.), *Handbook of Survey Research*. San Diego: Academic.

Ashenfelter, O., and S. Kelley (1975). "Determinants of participation in presidential elections," *Journal of Law and Economics* 18, 695–733.

Aumann, R. J. (1985). "Repeated games," in G. R. Feiwel (ed.), *Issues in contemporary microeconomics and welfare*. New York: Macmillan.

Axelrod, R. (1984). *The evolution of cooperation*. New York: Basic Books.

Bachelier, L. (1900/64). "Theorie de la speculation," reprinted in English in P. Cootner (ed.) (1964), *The random character of stockmarket prices*. Cambridge, Mass.: M.I.T. Press.

Baillie, R. T., R. E. Lippens, and P. C. McMahon (1983). "Testing rational expectations and efficiency in the foreign exchange market," *Econometrica* 51, 553–64.

Begg, D. K. H. (1982). *The rational expectations revolution in macroeconomics*. Oxford: Phillip Allan.

Bellman, R. (1957). *Dynamic programming*. Princeton, N.J.: Princeton University Press.

Bellman, R., and S. Dreyfus (1962). *Applied dynamic programming*. Princeton, N.J.: Princeton University Press.

Bertsekas, D. P. (1976). *Dynamic programming and stochastic control*. New York: Academic.

Bishop, R. C., and T. A. Heberlein (1979). "Measuring values of extramarket goods: Are indirect measures biased?" *American Journal of Agricultural Economic* 61, 926–30.

Bishop, R. C., T. A. Heberlein, and M. J. Kealy (1983). "Contingent valuation of environmental assets: comparisons with a simulated market," *Natural Resources Journal* 23, 619–33.

Blanchard, O. J., and C. M. Kahn (1980). "The solution of linear difference models under rational expectations," *Econometrica* 48, 1305–15.

Blanchard, O. J., and M. Watson (1982). "Bubbles, rational expectations and financial markets," in P. Wachtel (ed.), *Crisis in the economic and financial structure*. Lexington, Mass.: Lexington.

Blinder, A. S. (1982). "Issues in the coordination of monetary and fiscal policy," in *Monetary Policy Issues in the 1980's*. Symposium sponsored by the Federal Reserve Bank of Kansas City, Kansas.

Blum, J. R. (1954). "Multidimensional stochastic approximation method," *Annals of Mathematical Statistics* 25, 737–44.

Boland, L. A. (1982). *The foundations of economic method*. London: Allen and Unwin.

Bowden, R. J. (1985). "Certainty equivalence for the multiproduct producer under risk." Mimeo, Department of Economics, The University of Western Australia.

(1986). "Self-selection biases in correlational studies based on questionnaires, *Psychometrika* 51, 313–25.

(1987a). "Repeated sampling in the presence of publication effects," *Journal of the American Statistical Association* 82, 476–84 (with discussion).

(1987b). "Volunteered response and real-time survey schemes." Revised mimeo, Department of Economics, The University of Western Australia.

Bowden, R. J., and D. A. Turkington (1984). *Instrumental variables*. New York: Cambridge University Press/Econometric Society.

Bray, M. M., and N. E. Savin (1986). "Rational expectations, learning and model specifications," *Econometrica* 54, 1129–60.

Brooks, C. A., and B. A. Bailar (1978). "An error profile: employment as measured by the current population survey." Statistical working paper no. 3, U.S. Department of Commerce, Washington, D.C.

Brookshire, D. S., M. A. Thayer, W. D. Schulze, and R. C. D'Arge (1982). "Valuing public goods: a comparison of survey and hedonic approaches," *American Economic Review* 72, 165–77.

Bury, K. V. (1975). *Statistical models in applied science*. New York: Wiley.

CABR (1985). "Visitor numbers study, America's Cup defence series 1986/7." Perth: Centre for Applied and Business Research, The University of Western Australia.

(1986). "Follow-up to the visitor numbers study, America's Cup defence series 1986/7: summary report." Perth: Centre for Applied and Business Research, The University of Western Australia.

Carlson, J. A. (1977). "A study of price forecasts," *Annals of Economic and Social Measurement* 6, 27–56.

Chow, G. C. (1975). *Analysis and control of dynamic economic systems*. New York: Wiley.

(1980). "Econometric policy evaluation and optimisation under rational expectations," *Journal of Economic Dynamics and Control* 2, 1–13.

(1981). "Estimation and optimal control of dynamic game models under rational expectations," in R. E. Lucas and T. J. Sargent (eds.), *Rational expectations and econometric practice*. Minneapolis: University of Minnesota Press.

Clarke, E. H. (1971). "Multipart pricing of public goods," *Public Choice* 11, 17–33.

(1972). "Multipart pricing of public goods: an example," in S. Mushkin (ed.), *Public prices for public products.* Washington, D.C.: The Urban Institute.

Cochran, W. G. (1977). *Sampling techniques.* New York: Wiley.

Cox, D. R. (1961). "Tests of separate families of hypotheses," in J. Neyman (ed.), *Proceedings of the Fourth Berkeley Symposium on Mathematical Statistics and Probability,* Vol. 1, Berkeley and Los Angeles, University of California, pp. 105–23.

Cox, D. R., and H. D. Miller (1965). *The theory of stochastic processes.* London: Methuen.

Cramer, H. (1961). *Mathematical methods of statistics.* Princeton, N.J.: Princeton University Press.

Cruz, J. B. (1975). "Survey of Nash and Stackelberg equilibrium strategies in dynamic games," *Annals of Economic and Social Measurement* 4, 339–44.

Csáki, E. (1984). "Empirical distribution function," in P. R. Krishnaiah and P. K. Sen (eds.), *Nonparametric methods: handbook of statistics,* Vol. 4. Amsterdam: North-Holland.

DeCanio, S. J. (1979). "Rational expectations and learning from experience," *Quarterly Journal of Economics* 94, 47–57.

Dohrenwend, B. P. (1966). "Social status and psychiatric disorders: an issue of substance and an issue of method," *American Sociological Review* 31, 14–34.

Doob, J. (1953). *Stochastic processes.* New York: Wiley.

Dupac, V. (1965). "A dynamic stochastic approximation algorithm," *Annals of Mathematical Statistics* 36, 1695–702.

(1984). "Stochastic approximation," in P. R. Krishnaiah and P. K. Sen (eds.), *Nonparametric methods: handbook of statistics,* Vol. 4. Amsterdam: North-Holland.

Dvoretsky, A. (1956). "On stochastic approximation," in J. Neyman (ed.), *Proceedings of the Third Berkeley Symposium on Mathematical Statistics and Probability,* Vol. 1, Berkeley and Los Angeles, University of California Press, pp. 39–55.

Edwards, W. (1968). "Conservatism in human information processing," in B. Kleinmutz (ed.), *Formal representation of human judgement.* New York: Wiley.

Enelow, J., and M. J. Hinich (1984). *The spatial theory of voting: An introduction.* Cambridge: Cambridge University Press.

Engle, R. F. (1982). "Autoregressive conditional heteroscedascity with estimates of the variance of U.K. inflation," *Econometrica* 50, 987–1008.

Engle, R. F., and T. Bollerslev (1986). "Modelling the persistence of conditional variances," *Econometric Reviews* 5, 1–87.

Evans, G. (1983). "The stability of rational expectations in macroeconomic models," in R. Frydman and E. S. Phelps (eds.), *Individual forecasting and aggregate outcomes: "rational expectations" examined.* Cambridge: Cambridge University Press.

(1985). "Expectational stability and the multiple equilibria problem in linear rational expectations models," *Quarterly Journal of Economics* 100, 1217–33.

270   References

(1986). "A test for speculative bubbles in the sterling-dollar exchange rate: 1981–84," *American Economic Review* 76, 621–36.

Fama, E. F. (1965). "The behaviour of stock market prices," *Journal of Business* 38, 34–105.

Ferguson, T. S. (1967). *Mathematical statistics: a decision theoretic approach.* New York: Academic.

Figlewski, S., and P. Wachtel (1981). "The formation of inflationary expectations," *Review of Economics and Statistics* 63, 1–10.

Finney, D. J. (1971). *Probit analysis,* 3rd ed. Cambridge: Cambridge University Press.

Fishbein, M., and I. Ajzen (1975). *Belief, attitude, intention and behaviour.* Reading, Mass.: Addison Wesley.

Flood, R. P., and P. M. Garber (1980). "Market fundamentals versus price level bubbles: the first tests," *Journal of Political Economy* 88, 745–70.

Fourgeaud, C., C. Gourieroux, and J. Pradel (1984). "Rational expectations models and bounded memory," *Econometrica* 53, 977–85.

(1986). "Learning procedure and convergence to rationality," *Econometrica* 54, 845–68.

Freeman, A. M. (1979). "Approaches to measuring public goods demands," *American Journal of Agricultural Economics* 61, 915–20.

Frenkel, J. A. (1981). "Flexible exchange rates, prices and the role of 'news': lessons from the 1970's," *Journal of Political Economy* 89, 665–705.

Friedman, B. M. (1980). "Survey evidence on the 'rationality' of interest rate expectations," *Journal of Monetary Economics* 6, 153–65.

Frydman, R. (1982). "Towards an understanding of market processes: individual expectations, learning and convergence to rational expectations equilibrium," *American Economic Review* 72, 652–68.

Fu, K. S. (1969). "Learning system theory," in L. A. Zadeh and E. Polak (eds.), *System theory.* New York: McGraw-Hill.

Gnedenko, B. V., and V. S. Korolyuk (1951/61). "On the maximum discrepancy between two empirical distribution functions." English translation in *Selected translations in mathematical statistics and probability.* Providence, R.I.: American Mathematical Society, Vol. 1, pp. 13–16.

Gourieroux, C., J. J. Laffont, and A. Monfort (1982). "Rational expectations in dynamic linear models: analysis of the solutions," *Econometrica* 50, 409–25.

Granger, C. W. J. (1969). "Investigating causal relations by econometric models and cross-spectral methods," *Econometrica* 37, 424–38.

Granger, C. W. J., and O. Morgenstern (1963). "Spectral analysis of New York stock market prices," *Kyklos* 16, 1–27.

Granger, C. W. J., and M. J. Morris (1976). "Time series modelling and interpretation," *Journal of the Royal Statistical Society* 139, 246–57.

Greenberg, B., A. L. Abdul-Ela, W. Simmons, and D. Horwitz (1969). "The unrelated question randomised response model, theoretical framework," *Journal of the American Statistical Association* 64, 520–39.

Grossman, J. J., and J. E. Stiglitz (1980). "On the impossibility of informationally efficient markets," *American Economic Review* 70, 393–408.

Groves, J. (1973). "Incentives in teams," *Econometrica* 41, 617–31.

Grunberg, E., and F. Modigliani (1954). "The predictability of social events," *Journal of Political Economy* 62, 465–79.

Gulliksen, H. (1950). *Theory of mental tests.* New York: Wiley.

Hannan, E. J. (1976). "The convergence of some recursions," *Annals of Statistics* 4, 1258–70.

(1980). "Recursive estimation based on ARMA models," *Annals of Statistics* 8, 762–77.

Hansen, L. P., and T. J. Sargent (1981). "Linear rational expectations models for dynamically interrelated variables," in R. E. Lucas and T. J. Sargent (eds.), *Rational expectations and econometric practice.* Minneapolis: University of Minnesota Press.

Hansen, M. H., and W. N. Hurwitz (1946). "The problem of non-response in sample surveys," *Journal of the American Statistical Association* 41, 517–29.

Hausman, J. (1978). "Specification tests in econometrics," *Econometrica* 46, 1251–70.

Hawkins, D. F. (1977). "Nonresponse in Detroit area surveys: a ten-year analysis." Working papers in methodology no. 8, Institute for Research in Social Science, Chapel Hill, N.C.

Heckman, J. (1979). "Sample selection bias as a specification error," *Econometrica* 47, 153–61.

Hoffman, D. L., and P. Schmidt (1981). "Testing the restrictions implied by the rational expectations hypothesis," *Journal of Econometrics* 15, 265–87.

Horwitz, D. G., B. G. Greenberg, and J. R. Abernethy (1975). "Recent developments in randomised response designs," in J. N. Srivastava (eds.), *A survey of statistical design and linear models.* Amsterdam: North-Holland.

Iacocca, L. A. (1984). *Iacocca: an autobiography,* with W. Novak. New York: Bantam Books.

Kalman, R. E. (1960). "A new approach to linear filtering and prediction problems," *Transactions of the American Society of Mechanical Engineers: D* 82, 35–45.

(1980). "Identifiability and problems of model selection in econometrics." Invited lecture, Fourth World Congress of the Econometric Society.

Kelley, H. H. (1967). "Attribution theory in social psychology," *Nebraska Symposium on Motivation* 15, 192–238.

Kelley, H. H., and J. L. Michela (1980). "Attribution theory and research," *Annual Review of Psychology* 31, 457–501.

Keynes, J. M. (1936). *The general theory of employment, interest and money.* London: Macmillan.

Kushner, H. J. (1971). *Introduction to stochastic control.* New York: Holt, Rinehart and Winston.

Kydland, F. E. (1976). "Decentralized stabilization policies: optimization and the assignment problem," *Annals of Economic and Social Measurement* 5, 249–61.

Kydland, F. E., and E. C. Prescott (1977). "Rules rather than discretion: the inconsistency of optimal plans," *Journal of Political Economy* 85, 473-93. Also in R. E. Lucas and T. J. Sargent (eds.) (1981), *Rational expectations and econometric practice.* Minneapolis: University of Minnesota Press.

Lai, R. L., and H. Robbins (1979). "Adaptive design and stochastic approximation," *Annals of Statistics* 7, 1196-221.

Lawley, D. N. (1943). "A note on Karl Pearson's selection formulae," *Proceedings of the Royal Society of Edinburgh: Section A* 62, 28-30.

Lev, B. (1974). *Financial statement analysis: a new approach.* Englewood Cliffs, N.J.: Prentice-Hall.

Loomis, L. H. (1975). *Calculus.* Reading, Mass.: Addison-Wesley.

Louviére, J. J., and D. A. Hensher (1983). "Using discrete choice models with experimental design data to forecast consumer demand for a unique cultural event," *Journal of Consumer Research* 10, 348-61.

Lucas, R. E. (1972a). "Econometric testing of the natural rate hypothesis," in O. Eckstein (ed.), *The econometrics of price determination.* Washington, D.C.: U.S. Federal Reserve/SSRC.

  (1972b). "Expectations and the neutrality of money," *Journal of Economic Theory* 4, 103-24.

  (1976). "Econometric policy evaluation: a critique," *Journal of Monetary Economics* 2 (Suppl): Carnegie-Rochester Conference Series Vol. 1. Also in K. Brunner and A. H. Meltzer (eds.), *The Phillips Curve and Labour Markets.* Amsterdam: North-Holland.

  (1981). *Studies in business cycle theory.* Oxford: Blackwell.

McAleer, M., and M. H. Pesaran (1986). "Statistical inference in non-nested models," *Applied Mathematics and Computation* 20, 271-311.

McCallum, B. J. (1977). "The role of speculation in the Canadian forward exchange market: some estimates assuming rational expectations," *Review of Economics and Statistics* 9, 145-51.

McKelvey, R. D., and P. C. Ordeshook (1984). "Rational expectations in elections," *Public Choice* 44, 61-102.

  (1985a). "Elections with limited information: a fulfilled expectations model using contemporaneous poll and endorsement data as information sources," *Journal of Economic Theory* 36, 55-85.

  (1985b). "Sequential elections with limited information," *American Journal of Political Science* 29, 480-512.

McLeod, P. B., and G. Soutar (1986). "Forecasting visitor numbers for the America's Cup." Paper presented to the Twenty-Seventh Conference, Institute of Management Sciences, Gold Coast Australia.

Mäler, K-G. (1974). *Environmental economics: a theoretical enquiry.* Baltimore: Johns Hopkins.

Mandelbrot, B. (1966). "Forecasts of future prices, unbiased markets, and martingale models," *Journal of Business: Security Prices Supplement* 39, 242-55.

Marshak, J. (1953). "Economic measurements for policy and prediction," in W. C. Hood and T. C. Koopmans (eds.), *Studies in econometric method,* Cowles Commission monograph 14. New York: Wiley.

Martin, E. (1983). "Surveys as social indicators: problems in monitoring trends," in P. H. Rossi, J. D. Wright, and A. B. Anderson (eds.), *Handbook of survey research*. San Diego: Academic.

Meredith, W. (1964). "Notes on factorial invariance," *Psychometrika* 29, 177–81.

Mertens, J-F. (1986). "Repeated games." Lecture given at International Congress of Mathematicians, Berkeley California: mimeo, C.O.R.E. Louvain.

Miller, R. G. (1981). *Survival analysis*. New York: Wiley.

Moore, A. B. (1964). "Some characteristics of changes in common stocks," in P. H. Cootner (ed.), *The random character of stock market prices*. Cambridge, Mass.: M.I.T. Press.

Morgenstern, O. (1963). *On the accuracy of economic observations*. Princeton, N.J.: Princeton University Press.

Mueller, D. C. (1979). *Public choice*. Cambridge: Cambridge University Press.

Muth, J. F. (1961). "Rational expectations and the theory of price movements," *Econometrica* 29, 315–35.

Nevel'son, M. B., and R. Z. Has'minski (1972/76). *Stochastic approximation and recursive estimation,* translation of mathematical monographs. Providence, R.I.: American Mathematical Society.

Nisbett, R. E., and L. Ross (1980). *Human inference: strategies and shortcomings of social judgement*. Englewood Cliffs, N.J.: Prentice-Hall.

Olson, M. (1965). *The logic of collective action*. Cambridge, Mass.: Harvard University Press.

Ordeshook, P. C. (1987). "Public opinion polls and democratic processes: a comment," *Journal of the American Statistical Association* 82, 486–91.

Owen, E. (1982). *Introduction to game theory*. New York: Academic.

Pesando, J. E. (1975). "A note on the rationality of the Livingstone price expectations," *Journal of Political Economy* 83, 849–58.

Pesaran, M. H. (1974). "On the general problem of model selection," *Review of Economic Studies* 41, 153–71.

(1982). "A critique of the proposed tests of the natural rate–rational expectations hypothesis," *Economic Journal* 92, 529–54.

(1987). *Limits to rational expectations*. Oxford: Blackwell.

Phelps, E. S. (1983). "The trouble with 'rational expectations' and the problem of inflation stabilization," in R. Frydman and E. S. Phelps (eds.), *Individual forecasting and aggregate outcomes*. New York: Cambridge University Press.

Phillips, D. L. (1971). *Knowledge from what? Theories and methods in social research*. Chicago: Rand McNally.

(1973). *Abandoning method: sociological studies in methodology*. San Francisco: Jossey-Bass.

Pierce, D. A., and L. D. Haugh (1977). "Causality in temporal systems: characterizations and a survey," *Journal of Econometrics* 5, 265–93.

Pollak, R. A. (1968). "Consistent planning," *Review of Economic Studies* 35, 201–8.

Popper, K. R. (1965). *The logic of scientific discovery*. New York: Harper.

Riker, W. H., and P. C. Ordeshook (1968). "A theory of the calculus of voting," *American Political Science Review* 62, 25–42.

(1973). *Introduction to positive political theory*. Englewood Cliffs, N.J.: Prentice-Hall.

Ritchie, J. R. B. (1984). "Assessing the impact of hallmark events: conceptual and research issues," *Journal of Travel Research* 23, 2–11.

Rossi, P. H., J. D. Wright, and A. B. Anderson (1983). *Handbook of Survey Research*. San Diego: Academic.

Rutherford, M. (1987). "Learning and decision making in economics and psychology: a methodological perspective," in P. Earl (ed.), *Psychological economics: development, tensions, prospects*. Boston: Kluwer Academic.

Samuelson, P. A. (1965). "Proof that properly anticipated prices fluctuate randomly," *Industrial Management Review* 6, 41–9.

Sargent, T. J. (1978). "Estimation of dynamic labour demand schedules under rational expectations," *Journal of Political Economy* 86, 1009–44. Also in R. E. Lucas and T. J. Sargent (eds.) (1981), *Rational expectations and econometric practice*. Minneapolis: University of Minnesota Press.

(1979). "A note on maximum likelihood estimation of the rational expectations model of the term structure," *Journal of Monetary Economics* 5, 133–43.

Sargent, T. J., and N. Wallace (1973). "Rational expectations and the dynamics of hyperinflation," *International Economic Review* 14, 328–50.

(1975). "'Rational' expectations, the optimal monetary instrument, and the optimal money supply rule," *Journal of Political Economy* 83, 241–54.

Shaw, G. K. (1984). *Rational expectations: an elementary exposition*. New York: St. Martins.

Sheffrin, S. M. (1983). *Rational expectations*. Cambridge: Cambridge University Press.

Shiller, R. J. (1978). "Rational expectations and the dynamic structure of macroeconomic models: a critical review," *Journal of Monetary Economics* 4, 1–44.

(1981). "Do stock prices move too much to be justified by subsequent changes in dividends?" *American Economic Review* 71, 421–36.

Simon, H. A. (1954). "Bandwagon and underdog effects and the possibility of election predictions," *Public Opinion Quarterly* 18, 245–53. Also in H. A. Simon (ed.) (1982), *Model of bounded rationality: economic analysis and public policy*. Cambridge, Mass.: M.I.T. Press.

Sims, C. A. (1972). "Money, income and causality," *American Economic Review* 62, 540–52.

Taylor, J. B. (1977). "Conditions for unique solutions in stochastic macroeconomic models with rational expectations," *Econometrica* 45, 1377–85.

(1979). "Estimation and control of a macroeconomic model with rational expectations," *Econometrica* 47, 1267–86.

Theil, H. (1957). "A note on certainty equivalence in dynamic planning," *Econometrica* 25, 346–9.

Thompson, E. A. (1966). "A Pareto optimal group decision making process," in G. Tullock (ed.), *Papers on non-market decision making.* Charlottesville: University of Virginia.

Tinbergen, J. (1952). *On the theory of economic policy.* Amsterdam: North-Holland.

Townsend, R. M. (1978). "Market anticipation, rational expectations, and Bayesian analysis," *International Economic Review* 19, 481–94.

(1983a). "Equilibrium theory with learning and disparate expectations: some issues and methods," in R. Frydman and E. S. Phelps (eds.), *Individual forecasting and aggregate outcomes.* New York: Cambridge University Press.

(1983b). "Forecasting the forecasts of others," *Journal of Political Economy* 91, 546–88.

Turkington, D. A. (1988). "A note on two-stage least squares, three-stage least squares and maximum likelihood estimation in an expectations model," *International Economic Review* 26, 507–10.

Turkington, D. A., and R. J. Bowden (1988). "Identification, information and instruments in linear econometric models with rational expectations," *Journal of Econometrics* 38, 361–73.

Turnovsky, S. J. (1970). "Empirical evidence on the formation of price expectations," *Journal of the American Statistical Association* 65, 1441–54.

Tversky, A., and D. Kahneman (1974). "Judgement under uncertainty: heuristics and biases," *Science* 185, 1124–31.

Uysal, M., and J. L. Crompton (1985). "An overview of approaches to forecast tourist demand," *Journal of Travel Research* 23, 7–15.

Venter, J. H. (1967). "An extension of the Robbins–Monro procedure," *Annals of Mathematical Statistics* 38, 181–90.

Wallis, K. F. (1980). "Econometric implications of the rational expectations hypothesis," *Econometrica* 48, 49–72.

Warner, S. L. (1965). "Randomized response: a survey technique for estimating evasive answer bias," *Journal of the American Statistical Association* 60, 63–9.

Wasan, M. T. (1969). *Stochastic approximation.* Cambridge: Cambridge University Press.

Wegge, L. L., and M. Feldman (1982). "Identifiability criteria for Muth-rational expectations models," *Journal of Econometrics* 21, 245–56.

White, K. T. (1978). "A general computer program for econometric methods – SHAZAM," *Econometrica* 46, 239–40.

Whiteman, C. H. (1983). *Linear rational expectations models: a user's guide.* Minneapolis: University of Minnesota Press.

Whyte, W. F. (1969). "The role of the U.S. professor in developing countries," *American Sociologist* 4, 19–28.

Wickens, M. R. (1982). "The efficient estimation of econometric models with rational expectations," *Review of Economic Studies* 44, 55–67.

Winter, S. G. (1964). "Economic 'natural selection' and the theory of the firm," *Yale Economic Essays* 4, 225–72.

Index